AMERICA'S FOREIGN POLICY 1945-1976:
Its Creators and Critics

Contributors

Robert J. Babbitz
Catharine A. Barnes
James Lewis Baughman
Jason Berger
Miriam D. Bluestone
John D' Emilio
Andrew Eiler
Joshua B. Freidman
Loren R. Goldner
Thomas L. Harrison

Joseph C. Holub
Clark S. Judge
Michael L. Levine
Nelson N. Lichtenstein
Frank H. Milburn
James A. Namron
Eleanora W. Schoenebaum
Glenn Speer
James L. Wunsch

AMERICA'S FOREIGN POLICY 1945-1976:

Its Creators and Critics

by Thomas Parker

Facts On File, Inc.
119 West 57th Street, New York, N.Y. 10019

America's Foreign Policy, 1945-1976:
Its Creators and Critics

Library of Congress Cataloging in Publication Data

Parker, Thomas, 1947-
    America's foreign policy.

    Bibliography: p.
    Includes index.
    1.   Statesmen—United States—Biography.   2.   Legis-
lators—United States—Biography.   3.   Politicians—
United States—Biography.   4.   Diplomats—United States
—Biography.   5.   United States—Foreign relations—
1945-   I.   Title.
E840.6.P37   327.73'0092'2 [B]   80-21192
ISBN 0-87196-456-2

987654321
Printed in the United States of America

Contents

Preface

America's Foreign Policy, 1945-1976: Its Creators and Critics presents profiles of the leading political figures in American foreign policy from 1945 to 1976. Each profile begins with the name of the individual, the date and place of his birth and the date and place of his death. The headnote continues with the title of the most important office or offices he held, or the activity for which he was most noted. In the case of political officeholders, the dates of service are also given; for presidential appointees the date of Senate confirmation is used to denote the beginning of service. The body of the profile then follows, its length roughly commensurate with the significance of the individual. The notation [q.v.] (i.e., quod vide) follows the names of other individuals whose profiles appear in the volume. (To avoid unnecessary repetition this notation does not follow the names of Presidents.) Each profile ends with the initials of its author. Many also include brief suggestions referring the reader to the most relevant books or articles containing additional information on the subject.

Several criteria were used in choosing the political figures in this volume. The most important was presidential influence. The figures chosen were those whose positions the Presidents heeded during the major foreign policy debates within the executive branch. While their advice was not always accepted, it was taken seriously. The majority of these men had direct and frequent access to the Presidents, although an individual like George Kennan made his views known primarily through written analyses. A second form of presidential influence was enjoyed by political figures whose views had to be taken into consideration because they represented the thinking of a major segment of the public. These men were usually congressional critics, like Sen. William Knowland or Sen. William Fulbright, who did not have access to the Presidents and who consistently differed with presidential policies. A leading figure in the anti-Vietnam war movement, William Sloane Coffin, was also included in this category, however, since he spoke for a large minority of Americans. The second criterion for inclusion in this volume was distinguished literary achievement in the field of political analysis. This category consists of authors who expressed the spirit of the times and helped to shape public opinion. It includes Hans Morganthau, who wrote *Power Among Nations*, which introduced university students to the realities of power politics; Arthur Schlesinger, whose book *The Imperial Presidency* highlighted the concentration of power in the post-World War II presidency; and David Halberstam, author of *The Best and the Brightest*, which criticized the policy makers of the Kennedy and Johnson Administrations.

America's Foreign Policy, 1945-1976: Its Creators and Critics includes a brief introduction that describes the most important issues, debates and events of the period and attempts to place them in historical perspective. At the end of the volume, the reader will find a chronology of the period's major events and a detailed bibliography. All of the profiles in this volume were written by trained historians, either advanced graduate students or Ph.Ds.

Introduction

The main goal of United States foreign policy from 1945 to 1976 was the containment of Communism. The nature of the Communist threat, however, was perceived in various ways during this period by policy makers and critics. After an initial period of uncertainty and debate over Soviet intentions and the appropriate U.S. response following World War II, nearly all policy makers and critics came to believe that the USSR constituted a danger to American security and that the expansion of its influence had to be opposed in every instance. Yet they were divided over the question of whether all Communist countries and movements were potential enemies of the United States or whether the threat was limited to the Soviet Union and its satellites. This division of opinion ended in November 1950, when Communist Chinese troops entered the Korean war on the side of North Korea. Thereafter virtually every policy maker and most critics considered Communism a monolithic movement and viewed all Communist nations, including the People's Republic of China, to be enemies of the United States. Following the Sino-Soviet split, however, the idea of a Communist Chinese threat was increasingly questioned during the 1960s, and the assumption was generally discarded following President Nixon's trip to Peking in 1972. Once again U.S. foreign policy focused on containing Soviet expansionism. And by the mid-1970s many policy critics were even rejecting the premise that the Soviets had to be opposed in every instance. Thus, this 30-year period began with a debate over Soviet intentions and the appropriate U.S. response and ended with a similar, though less intense, debate on the same subject.

The principal means available to U.S. policy makers for containing Communist expansion was to increase America's commitments abroad. Such commitments were made initially to Western Europe, but later extended to Asia, the Middle East, Latin America and finally Africa. This trend of growing U.S. involvement in world affairs continued until the late 1960s. Thereafter the nation's foreign commitments, particularly in the military area, tended to decline.

Most of the foreign policy debates between the policy makers in power and their critics out of power centered on the two major issues of the postwar period: the nature of the Communist threat and the proper level of U.S. commitments abroad. From 1945 to the mid-1960s the most influential critics, the congressional conservatives, called for tougher policies towards the Communist world and increased American involvement overseas. Thereafter the liberals in Congress became the more influential critics. They in turn pressured policy makers to adopt a less resolute attitude towards the Communist nations and to reduce America's foreign obligations.

The American public's rejection of the traditional U.S. policy of isolationism made possible the active foreign policy pursued throughout the 30-year postwar period. This crucial break with the past resulted from several factors. Americans began to realize that technology had made the world smaller and more dangerous and that the two huge oceans, which had previously shielded the United States, no longer afforded protection in the age of the aircraft carrier and the longe-range bomber. In addition isolationism was in disrepute; for it was believed that had America remained active in world politics following World War I, Germany and Japan might never have adopted their policies of conquest. Another factor was America's awesome economic and military predominance vis-a-vis its vanquished enemies, Germany and Japan, and its exhausted allies, the Soviet Union and Great Britain, which had borne the brunt of the Allied war effort. The United States easily filled the existing world leadership vacuum. Finally, U.S. foreign policy makers became convinced, shortly after the war ended, that the Soviet Union was not going to withdraw its troops from Eastern Europe; that it meant to impose its political system on the countries which it occupied; that it might try to encourage Communist takeovers in Western Europe and Asia; and that it might have territorial ambitions in Turkey, Iran and elsewhere. America had fought the war in Europe largely to prevent the enormous Eurasian land mass from being dominated by hostile powers and it did not intend to allow the Soviet Union to succeed where Germany and Japan had failed.

The growing perception that the Soviet Union had totalitarian designs on Eastern Europe and perhaps elsewhere came gradually to most U.S. foreign policy makers. During the war Stalin had promised President Roosevelt that he would allow free elections in Eastern Europe. Harry Truman, who became President in April 1945, initially felt that some kind of acceptable compromise could be reached with the Soviets. But throughout 1945 the USSR ruthlessly promoted the establishment of Communist governments in Poland, East Germany, Rumania and Bulgaria, while moving more cautiously in Hungary and Czechoslovakia. Faced with the possibility of totalitarian puppet states in all of Eastern Europe and Soviet troops several hundred miles from the Rhine, Truman's advisers debated Soviet intentions and the appropriate response to them. Secretary of the Navy James Forrestal [q.v.], Deputy Military Governor of Germany Lucius Clay [q.v.] and Assistant Secretary of War John McCloy [q.v.] feared that the Soviet Union might even attack Western Europe and believed that there was little to be gained from negotiations with the Soviets. They argued that the United States should promote the recovery of Germany as quickly as possible as a counter-weight to the Soviet Union. A second group of policy makers, led by Secretary of State James Byrnes [q.v.] and presidential advisers Averell Harriman [q.v.] and Dean Acheson [q.v.], doubted that the USSR would launch an attack on Western Europe but thought that they were deadly serious about bringing the area under their control. Nonetheless they felt that something could be salvaged from negotiations if U.S. economic aid to the Soviet Union were made contingent upon its actions in Eastern Europe. A lone and rather isolated adviser, Secretary of Commerce Henry Wallace [q.v.], felt that U.S.–Soviet relations were suffering from a case of mutual misunderstanding in which each side was overestimating the threat posed by the other. Wallace argued that it was only natural for the Soviets to be suspicious of the United States and Britain since each country had sent a small military force to Russia immediately after World War I in an unsuccessful attempt to crush the young Bolshevik regime. He also contended that Eastern Europe was a natural part of the Soviet sphere of influence and should therefore be of no concern to the United States. According to Wallace a large aid program and a hands-off policy towards Eastern Europe was the best way to dispel the growing tension between America and the Soviet Union.

The debate within the Administration spread to Congress and the public, both of which became increasingly appalled by the Soviets' ruthlessness in crushing non-Communist politicians and political movements throughout Eastern Europe. One of the Senate's leading Republicans, for example, Arthur Vandenberg (R, Mich.) [q.v.], criticized Secretary of State Byrnes's decision to recognize the Soviet-installed governments of Rumania and Bulgaria at the Moscow Foreign Ministers Conference in

December 1945. The country's stiffening attitude towards the Soviet Union corresponded with Truman's own feelings. While leaving open the possibility of negotiations on Germany and Eastern Europe, the President took an increasingly tougher stance. He declined to renew U.S. aid to the Soviet Union, which had ceased automatically at the war's end, and in September 1945 decided to withhold information about the atomic bomb from Stalin. During the spring of 1946 he sent U.S. warships to the eastern Mediterranean to show support for Greece, which was fighting a Communist insurrection, and for Turkey, which was faced with a Soviet demand to relinquish some of its northern territory. In April, Truman obtained the withdrawal of Soviet troops from northern Iran, which they had been occupying despite a previous agreement to leave when the war ended. In September he fired Secretary of Commerce Wallace for giving a speech that criticized the Administration's tougher stand.

A memorandum written in the spring of 1946 by Soviet expert George Kennan [q.v.], a counselor to presidential adviser Harriman, reinforced the Administration's determination to counter the Soviets. Kennan asserted that Soviet policy was based on historic Russian expansionism, Stalin's psychological paranoia and Communist ideology, which assumed that relations with capitalist countries were inevitably hostile. He believed that to avoid being encircled by capitalist powers, Stalin would try to surround the Soviet Union with docile client states. Judging the Soviets too weak to attack the West militarily, he predicted they would try to undermine the capitalist nations politically. Kennan proposed that the United States begin a major economic aid program for Western Europe and Japan to discourage Soviet subversion, and he hoped that when Moscow saw the determination of the West to resist, it might seek to reduce tensions.

Kennan's memorandum, which Truman read personally, had a major impact on the Administration's policy makers. It provided a conceptual framework for the analysis of Soviet policy and reinforced the growing belief that the United States was in for a prolonged period of international tension during which Soviet expansionism would have to be "contained." Truman and his advisers, however, were ready to take Kennan's analysis one step further by emphasizing the need for military as well as economic assistance. Thus, when the British announced they had to withdraw from Greece in February 1947 because of their dire financial situation, the White House asked Congress to extend immediate military and economic aid to Greece and Turkey to prevent Communist takeovers in those countries. While the Administration was united on the necessity for helping Greece and Turkey, it was divided over how the aid plan should be presented to Congress and the American public. The new Secretary of State, George Marshall [q.v.], and Kennan opposed a dramatic appeal that would emphasize the aggressiveness of Soviet policy; for in addition to disliking appeals to the emotions per se, they feared that such an approach would make negotiations with the Soviets more difficult. In contrast Undersecretary of State Acheson, presidential adviser Clark Clifford [q.v.] and Sen. Vandenberg argued that a dramatic appeal would be necessary in order to get a major aid program through Congress. Truman agreed with the Acheson group's analysis. In a speech before a joint session of Congress in March 1947, he accused the Soviets of reckless expansionism and pledged that "it must be the policy of the United States to support free peoples who are resisting attempted subjugation by armed minorities or by outside pressure." This public declaration of America's willingness to extend military as well as economic aid to beleaguered governments, known as the Truman Doctrine, became a cornerstone of U.S. foreign policy.

The aid program for Greece and Turkey was only the prelude to a massive plan of economic assistance for the countries of Western Europe, whose battered economies had hardly begun to recover from the war. Truman's principal advisers, headed by

Acheson and William Clayton, pushed for an enormous aid program directed by the United States, while Kennan, whose analysis of Soviet policy had helped spark the idea in the first place, supported a more modest proposal under European control, for fear that the United States might be overextending itself. Truman supported the more extensive program. The two advisers most instrumental in guiding the proposal through Congress were Marshall, whose prestige as a World War II military leader was enormous, and Acheson, who was one of the most articulate and persuasive foreign policy experts of the 20th century. Even more important, however, was the strong support given the program, dubbed the Marshall Plan, by Sen. Vandenberg. An isolationist before the war, Vandenberg was highly respected by his fellow Republicans, whose ranks still included many quasi-isolationists. His backing discouraged Senate Republicans from treating the Marshall Plan as a partisan issue and convinced a number of them to vote for it. Finally, the Soviets themselves facilitated the Plan's passage; for in destroying the only two democracies in Eastern Europe, Hungary during 1946–48 and Czechoslovakia in February 1948, Stalin strengthened the hand of those who argued that the rest of Europe had to be helped.

Following the destruction of democratic Czechoslovakia, the U.S. public, congressional leaders headed by Vandenberg and all of the Administration's principal members—Marshall, Acheson and Truman himself—believed that negotiations with the Soviet Union and other Communist countries, at least for the immediate future, served little purpose. Another effect of Soviet policy in Hungary and Czechoslovakia was to bolster the position of those advisers, like Forrestal, Clay and McCloy, who had been asserting ever since the end of the war that Germany should be built up as rapidly as possible to offset the Soviet presence. These men were now joined by Marshall, Acheson and Truman, who began to push for the reunification of the three Allied zones of occupation. In response Stalin, who feared a resurgent Germany, began a land blockade of West Berlin in June 1948. Truman immediately instituted an airlift to the isolated city. Soon after, he proposed the establishment of the North Atlantic Treaty Organization (NATO), America's first peacetime alliance.

The proposed alliance faced major opposition in the Senate, where its passage required a two-thirds majority. The Senate opposition was led by Robert Taft (R, Ohio) [q.v.], the leading Republican isolationist. While Taft had reluctantly supported the Truman Doctrine and the Marshall Plan, he rejected America's entry into any permanent peacetime alliance. He argued that such an alliance would give the President the power to enter a war without consulting Congress and characterized it as the culmination of a dangerous trend towards an overly assertive foreign policy: "We have quietly adopted a tendency to interfere in the affairs of other nations, to assume that we are a kind of demigod and Santa Claus. . . . It is easy to slip into an attitude of imperialism where war becomes an instrument of public policy rather than its last resort." But Taft was going against the postwar tide of increasing U.S. commitments; his admonitions would not be heard again until the late 1960s, when ironically they were taken up by liberal Democrats. As was the case with the Marshall Plan, the Senate passed the NATO treaty thanks in part to Sen. Vandenberg.

The Truman Administration also faced major decisions regarding China, where the Communists and Nationalists were waging a bitter civil war. Initially the Administration had hoped that the two sides could be reconciled, and in November 1945 Truman sent Marshall to China to act as a mediator. But by the beginning of 1947, Marshall acknowledged that his efforts had failed, and he told Truman that saving Chiang Kai-shek would require a virtual U.S. takeover of the Nationalist government and an ongoing obligation that would be almost impossible to break. Acheson, who replaced the ailing Marshall as Secretary of State in November 1948, not only agreed with Marshall, but also contended that the Communist Chinese were Chinese first and

Communists second and would therefore remain independent of the Soviet Union. Truman shared the opinions of his advisers and reduced American aid to the Nationalists to a token sum.

Truman's decision not to make a major effort to support Chiang Kai-shek evoked a bitter reaction from a group of Republican congressmen known as the China Lobby, who were to become the most vociferous and influential critics of the late 1940s and early 1950s. Headed by Sen. William Jenner (R, Ind.) [q.v.], Sen. William Knowland (R, Calif.) [q.v.] and Rep. Walter Judd (R, Minn.) [q.v.], the China Lobby argued that the Nationalists were not particularly corrupt; that U.S. aid could help them win; and that the Chinese Communists would most certainly ally themselves with Moscow, thereby forming a powerful bloc with the potential to dominate the world. These critics were so committed to a non-Communist China that they opposed aid to Western Europe on the grounds it was more needed in China. Their position was bolstered by the Communist Chinese victory in October 1949, which precipitated a storm of protest throughout the United States. Because of the intensity of the criticism, Truman did not dare recognize the Communist regime or agree to its admission to the United Nations, as Acheson advised. Furthermore, as a result of the political backlash following the Nationalists' defeat, all U.S. politicians, including a young senator named Lyndon Johnson [q.v.], sought to avoid being associated with the "loss" of another Communist country.

Another major challenge confronted the Truman Administration when North Korea invaded South Korea in June 1950. While the United States had no formal obligation to defend South Korea, nearly every politician, both inside and outside the Administration, supported Truman's decision to send troops under the command of Gen. Douglas MacArthur [q.v.] to defend the embattled country. MacArthur quickly turned the war around by staging a daring landing behind enemy lines at Inchon in September. The maneuver routed the North Koreans and led Truman's advisers to consider crossing the 38th parallel into North Korea in order to reunite the country. Nearly all of the Administration's top echelon, with the exception of Kennan, doubted that the Communist Chinese would intervene, and MacArthur assured the White House that a quick victory was possible. Truman therefore allowed him to advance into North Korea. In November 1950, however, the Communist Chinese did intervene on a massive scale and drove the American troops back into South Korea. Truman and his chief advisers then decided to conduct a limited war with the aim of seeking a redivision of the Korean peninsula. This decision enraged MacArthur and his China Lobby supporters, who demanded the destruction of the Yalu River bridges joining North Korea and China and the supply depots in China. MacArthur and his backers also urged that the Nationalist Chinese be allowed to invade the mainland from their base on Taiwan. After publicly criticizing the Administration's limited war policy and persisting in his calls for action against China in defiance of Truman's orders, MacArthur was fired by the President in April 1951.

The Korean war, which dragged on until mid-1953, had several repercussions. Communist China's intervention in the conflict convinced Truman's advisers that the Communist nations of the world constituted a monolithic bloc which threatened U.S. security; even Acheson mistakenly abandoned his previous view that the USSR and the People's Republic might eventually clash. This belief caused the Administration to send the Seventh Fleet to the Straits of Formosa to defend Taiwan against the possibility of invasion in 1951 and to begin sending military aid to the French for their fight against the Vietnamese Communists, who were now considered an extension of Moscow and Peking. This was the first of a series of decisions that culminated in the massive American military intervention in Vietnam in the mid-1960s.

America's increasingly active role in world affairs was also felt in the Middle East, particularly in Palestine. The departure of the British from Palestine in 1948 and the subsequent possibility of an independent Jewish state presented the Administration with a perplexing issue. Marshall, Acheson and Assistant Secretary of State Robert Lovett [q.v.] feared alienating the Arab states and the possibility of having to send U.S. troops to defend an independent Jewish nation. They therefore recommended a temporary U.N. trusteeship. But because of Truman's sympathy for the survivors of the European holocaust and the importance of the Jewish vote in the upcoming election, which was persuasively pointed out by presidential adviser Clifford, the President decided to recognize the state of Israel when it declared its independence. American diplomatic support was of crucial importance for Israel's subsequent acceptance by most members of the United Nations and indicated how influential the United States had become.

Despite America's increasing strength and influence, the USSR posed an even greater threat to U.S. security following the first Soviet atomic test explosion in 1949. The United States was then faced with the decision of whether to produce the much more powerful hydrogen bomb. Some U.S. scientists, like Robert Oppenheimer [q.v.], opposed the project on both moral and economic grounds, but others, like Edward Teller [q.v.], felt that it was important for America to maintain its lead in nuclear weapons. Truman supported the bomb's development and approved the first experimental explosion in 1952.

America's postwar foreign policy took root during the Truman Administration. U.S. policy makers initially defined their main goal to be the containment of Soviet expansion. In 1950, however, they redefined this goal to include all Communist nations, which were thought to form a unified, hostile bloc, after the entry of the Communist Chinese in the Korean war. Truman also increased U.S. commitments to the point that Washington became the free world's military, economic and political capital. Militarily it protected Western Europe, Turkey and Iran from the Soviet Union and South Korea from North Korea. It also held a monopoly and then a commanding lead in nuclear weapons. Economically it helped to revive the bankrupt nations of Western Europe through the Marshall Plan. Politically it sponsored the creation of the United Nations and the state of Israel. Finally, the Truman years saw the rise of the congressional critics on the right—most notably, the China Lobby—who had a major influence on policy makers in office, particularly with respect to China.

The Eisenhower years were a time of consensus in American foreign policy. Nearly all policy makers and critics shared Eisenhower's intention of continuing the policy of containing Communist expansion and his willingness to expand America's commitments overseas. The only major group opposed to increased involvement, the isolationists of the Republican Party, declined further, particularly following the unsuccessful campaign for the 1952 Republican presidential nomination by their leader Sen. Taft.

U.S.–Soviet relations improved following the death of Josef Stalin in March 1953 and the end of the Korean war two months later. This minor lull in the Cold War lasted until November 1958, when Soviet Premier Nikita Khrushchev began his three-year Berlin offensive, which involved increased harassment of convoys from the West crossing East Germany and demands for the withdrawal of Western troops from Berlin. Relations between the two countries worsened following the downing of a U.S. intelligence-gathering plane over the Soviet Union in 1960 and the subsequent breaking up of the Big Four summit conference in Paris. Nevertheless, during his presidency Eisenhower discarded one of the assumptions of the Truman Administration—that negotiations with the Soviets served little purpose. In doing so he had to overcome the resistance of his more hard-line Secretary of State, John Foster Dulles [q.v.], who was sceptical about the usefulness of negotiations and who feared they might antagonize the powerful Republican right and undercut the unity of the Western alliance. Throughout the 1950s, however, Eisenhower's decision was affirmed by tangible accomplishments: in 1953 U.S.–Soviet negotiations helped to end the Korean war; in 1955 American and Soviet troops were withdrawn from Austria after Eisenhower and Soviet Premier Nikolai Bulganin agreed in Geneva that the country should remain neutral; and in 1958 the United States and the USSR conducted their first sustained arms control talks.

Tensions also eased somewhat between the United States and Communist China, although on two occasions hostilities threatened to break out. In the fall of 1954 the Communist Chinese began shelling the offshore islands of Quemoy and Matsu, which were still held by the Chinese Nationalists. The attack precipitated a major debate within the Administration, the Congress and the military. Dulles favored threatening China with a nuclear attack; Sen. Knowland advocated a naval blockade of the Chinese coast; and the chairman of the Joint Chiefs of Staff, Adm. Arthur Radford [q.v.], recommended bombing the Chinese mainland. But as was often the case during his Administration, Eisenhower rejected calls for military action; he declined to defend the two small islands, whose value he considered insignificant. The shelling of Quemoy and Matsu soon ceased but resumed in August 1958. Dulles publicly threatened to retaliate against China with nuclear weapons but soon realized that the threat carried less credibility than in the past, largely because of the increased Soviet capacity to launch a nuclear strike against the U.S. mainland. With Eisenhower's approval Dulles then made a major policy shift. He stated that the Chinese Nationalists were "rather foolish" in stationing a large garrison on Quemoy and acknowledged that the United States had no obligation to defend the islands. More importantly he agreed to initiate low-level diplomatic contacts with the Chinese Communists at the U.S. embassy in Warsaw. While the meetings yielded no concrete results, they continued on an intermittent basis and held out the possibility of improved relations with mainland China.

One of the most important debates within the Eisenhower Administration took place in March 1954, when the French requested American military intervention to break the Vietnamese Communist seige of the French garrison at Dien Bien Phu. Dulles, Vice President Richard M. Nixon [q.v.] and Joint Chiefs of Staff Chairman Radford all supported the use of American bombers and did not rule out the eventual use of ground troops. But Eisenhower was reluctant to act without congressional and allied support and this was not forthcoming. While the question of immediate U.S. military assistance was subsequently dropped, Eisenhower still hoped that the Vietnamese Communists, who controlled North Vietnam, could be prevented from taking over the newly created state of South Vietnam. He therefore sent about 700 military advisers to help train the South Vietnamese armed forces. In no way, however, did he envision that this initial commitment would grow to more than 500,000 men within 15 years.

Unlike the broad consensus concerning U.S. policy towards the Communist countries, the Eisenhower Administration's policies toward the developing nations encountered a certain amount of criticism from liberal Democrats. Adlai Stevenson [q.v.], the 1952 and 1956 Democratic presidential nominee, and Sen. William Fulbright (D, Ark.) [q.v.] wanted more emphasis given to economic aid and less to military aid. They also called for a more tolerant attitude towards the neutrality that most of the developing countries chose in the rivalry between the United States and the Soviet Union. In a similar vein Sen. John Kennedy (D, Mass.) [q.v.] criticized the Administration's general policy of neutrality towards the conflicts between the Western European nations and their colonies and called for the United States to assume a pro-independence position. Despite these criticisms nearly all politicians supported Eisenhower's policy of actively opposing what were judged to be anti-Western governments in the Third World. This policy was implemented in 1953, when the Central Intelligence Agency (CIA) helped internal Iranian forces to topple their country's prime minister, Mohammad Mossadegh, who was seeking to nationalize the British oil holdings in Iran and to raise the export price of oil. A year later the CIA backed Guatemalan exiles who opposed the left-leaning government of President Jacobo Arbenz. The Agency helped to train and finance the exiles and provided American pilots and planes that were instrumental in the successful invasion of Guatemala from neighboring Honduras. In 1958 Congress gave Eisenhower its almost unanimous support when he sent 14,000 U.S. Marines to Lebanon in a successful operation to protect the country's pro-Western government from leftist forces backed by Egyptian President Gamal Abdel Nassar.

Despite his assertive policies in the developing world, Eisenhower believed in certain limits on Western influence. In 1956, for example, he vigorously opposed the British and French attempt to topple Nassar by military action. Eisenhower supported a U.N. resolution condemning the invasion and forced Britain to halt its intervention by threatening to cut off its oil imports from the Americas. He also compelled Israel to withdraw from the Sinai within one year. Here again Eisenhower had the near unanimous backing of Congress and the public.

The most criticized policies of the Eisenhower Administration were its defense strategy and military spending. Its defense strategy, devised primarily by Radford and expounded by Dulles in 1953, was based on the idea that the best way to respond to Communist aggression, including that by a Soviet ally such as happened in Korea, was to threaten a nuclear attack on the USSR. It was hoped that this policy of "massive retaliation" would avoid indecisive, limited wars like Korea and reduce the costs of maintaining expensive conventional forces around the world. The new strategy drew criticism on several grounds. Acheson felt it implied a unilateralism that precluded consultation with America's allies. Gen. Maxwell Taylor [q.v.] contended that threatening nuclear war against Communist guerrilla fighters lacked credibility. The most persuasive argument, however, was the growing threat of Soviet retaliation against the U.S. mainland, which became increasingly possible following the Soviets' 1957 launching of the first satellite to orbit the earth. By the late 1950s even Dulles was backing away from the emphasis on massive retaliation.

The launching of *Sputnik* also provided additional ammunition to Eisenhower's defense critics. Sen. Kennedy and Sen. Stuart Symington (D, Mo.) [q.v.] charged that the Soviets had demonstrated a technological superiority in rocketry which would soon result in a decisive Soviet lead in intercontinental nuclear missiles. (The "missile gap" controversy became an important issue in the 1960 presidential campaign, although it was later proved to have been nonexistent.) They also assailed him for ignoring the importance of anti-guerrilla warfare. In general, Eisenhower's Democratic critics in the Senate, led by Kennedy and Symington, accused him of not spending enough money on the military.

The major policy trends begun during the Truman Administration progressed during the Eisenhower years. Eisenhower and Dulles pursued an active foreign policy opposed to Communism and they increased U.S. commitments and influence in Indochina and the Islamic world. And similar to the criticism leveled at Truman, Eisenhower's most aggressive opponents accused him of not being tough enough with the Communist world. Instead of focusing on China, however, they pointed to alleged deficiencies in the defense budget.

President Kennedy shared the Truman and Eisenhower Administrations' goal of containing Communism. Yet his Administration differed from its two predecessors in the special air of confidence, energy and dynamism exuded by its members, many of whom regarded the policy makers of the Eisenhower years as rigid, unimaginative and unsophisticated in the area of foreign affairs. The 43-year-old President expressed this new spirit in his 1961 inaugural address, in which he pledged "to pay any price, bear any burden, meet any hardship, support any friend, oppose any foe to assure the survival and success of liberty." A new mood of optimism emerged as a result of several factors. The young President himself was forceful and energetic and his Administration was made up of advisers who were unusually bright and self-confident. This was the generation of Americans who had fought and won World War II, and they reflected the sense of assuredness and mastery that stemmed from their successful wartime experiences. Finally, the United States economy was entering a major period of growth, which provided the financial means to extend even more aid abroad and added to the general feeling of confidence.

True to his campaign promise to pursue a more assertive foreign policy, Kennedy called for a major aid program for Latin America, known as the Alliance for Progress, shortly after taking office. He hoped that the Alliance would duplicate the feat of the Marshall Plan by providing a catalyst for economic growth and would help to contain Castro's Cuba, the first Communist state in Latin America. During his three years in office, Kennedy raised the defense budget by 20 percent and placed 300,000 reservists on active duty. More importantly he increased the number of U.S. military personnel in South Vietnam from the initial 700 advisers sent by Eisenhower to 15,000. His decision to try to prevent a Communist takeover of South Vietnam won almost unanimous support from his aides, Congress and the public, although few people foresaw how difficult the war would become.

Despite the Kennedy Administration's assertiveness and self-confidence, it suffered serious setbacks during its initial year in office. Its first reversal was the abortive CIA-backed invasion of Cuba in April 1961 by anti-Castro Cubans. The planning for the covert operation, which had been initiated by President Eisenhower, was directed by CIA chief Allen Dulles [q.v.], who assured a skeptical Kennedy that a small force of Cuban exiles could ignite internal opposition to Castro, as had been the case with the successful 1954 CIA-backed Guatemalan exile invasion. While few of Kennedy's advisers were enthusiastic about the operation, they felt that it had a reasonable chance for success. The only two advisers to oppose the operation outright were Sen. Fulbright and Arthur Schlesinger [q.v.], who questioned the exiles' political leadership and popular support within Cuba and feared that the United States might be drawn into the fighting. Kennedy rejected their arguments, however, and told the CIA to proceed with the operation, but he ruled out any direct involvement by American military personnel and ordered the exiles not to launch the doomed Bay of Pigs invasion from the U.S. mainland. A second major setback occurred in August, when the Soviets began to erect the "Berlin Wall" in order to prevent East Germans from escaping to the West. With the exception of certain conservative critics, like Sen. Barry Goldwater (R, Ariz.) [q.v.], who called for the destruction of the wall by military action, the consensus within the Administration and Congress was that the United States was powerless given the preponderance of Soviet military might in East Germany.

A year later the fortunes of the Cold War swung in Kennedy's favor. Having been informed in October 1962 that the Soviets were installing nuclear missiles in Cuba, Kennedy organized a series of secret meetings with his top advisers and several members of the Truman Administration. Two major policy options emerged from the meetings, which extended for 10 days. Acheson, Paul Nitze [q.v.], John McCone [q.v.] and the Joint Chiefs of Staff recommended the use of air strikes to destroy the missiles already in place. They argued that any delay would lead to an increase in the number of missiles, thereby necessitating a much larger and more dangerous air attack. Another group of advisers, led by the President's brother Robert Kennedy [q.v.] and Secretary of Defense Robert McNamara [q.v.], favored a naval blockade, arguing that it would be less dangerous than an air strike, which they believed would result in Soviet casualties. After the military stated that it could not be sure of destroying all the missiles already in place (an estimate later judged to be incorrect), Kennedy announced publicly that the U.S. Navy would stop and search all Soviet ships approaching Cuba. Because of America's decisive advantage in intercontinental nuclear missiles and its superiority in conventional forces in the Caribbean, the Soviets agreed to remove the missiles.

The Cuban Missile Crisis proved to be a turning point in U.S.–Soviet relations, as well as the greatest triumph of the Kennedy presidency. Thereafter Soviet rhetoric became less aggressive and its diplomacy somewhat less confrontational. Improved relations led to several important policy initiatives. Under Secretary of Defense McNamara's direction, the United States adopted a new nuclear defense strategy called Mutual Assured Destruction, which ruled out any first strike by the United States against the Soviet Union. A second U.S.–USSR initiative resulted in the signing of a limited nuclear test ban treaty in July 1963, which ended nuclear testing in the atmosphere. Edward Teller, Sen. Goldwater and other critics of the treaty, opposed its ratification because they felt its conditions were unverifiable. But the Senate approved the agreement by a vote of 80 to 19. The treaty's passage indicated that Eisenhower's policy of seeking negotiations with the Soviets had gained strength during the Kennedy Administration, and the decisive margin of victory signaled that the improved tone of U.S.–USSR relations had weakened the influence of right-wing congressional critics.

The Johnson years, which were dominated by the controversy surrounding the Vietnam war, represented the major turning point in the history of U.S. foreign policy from 1945 to 1976. This five-year period saw the rise of congressional liberals who not only opposed the Vietnam war, but also attacked the nation's policy makers for spending too much on defense, resorting too easily to the use of military force and, most importantly, having made too many obligations abroad. Conversely the conservative congressional critics who supported more assertive anti-Communist policies lost additional influence during this period. Another historic development during the Johnson years was the peaking of America's military presence overseas following the 1968 decision to place an unofficial ceiling on the number of U.S. troops in South Vietnam. This decision ended the trend of increasing military commitments that had begun under President Roosevelt and continued during the Truman, Eisenhower, Kennedy and Johnson Administrations.

It is important to note, however, that the number and influence of the liberal critics opposed to additional foreign involvement was not significant in mid-1965, when Johnson ordered 50,000 combat troops to South Vietnam in a bid for military victory. At the time the decision to escalate was made, it was still axiomatic that the expansion of Communism had to be stopped, even at the price of war. The Johnson Administration embraced this proposition for several reasons. Johnson was afraid of the right-wing critics; he confided to the U.S. ambassador to South Vietnam, Henry Cabot Lodge [q.v.]: "I am not going to lose Vietnam. I am not going to be the President who saw Southeast Asia go the way of China." Johnson and most of his advisers also believed in the domino theory, which postulated that successful military expansion fed the appetite of the aggressor and led to further challenges to the status quo. The theory's corollary was that it was best to stop aggression as early as possible in order to prevent the aggressor from building up so much momentum that a full-fledged war became inevitable. Secretary of State Dean Rusk [q.v.] in particular supported the U.S.

commitment to South Vietnam by recalling the consequences of America's initial indifference to Hitler's expansionist policies. Johnson's two other key advisers at the time of the decision to escalate, Secretary of Defense McNamara and presidential assistant McGeorge Bundy [q.v.], also argued that a withdrawal from South Vietnam would shake the confidence of America's allies, particularly those in Asia, to the point that they might seek an accommodation with the Communist nations, most notably Communist China.

The nearly unanimous support for increased U.S. involvement in the war extended to Congress. Following an attack by North Vietnamese patrol boats against two U.S. destroyers in August 1964, President Johnson ordered the first American bombing raid against the North and called for a show of congressional support. Three days later Congress passed the Tonkin Gulf Resolution, which gave the President authority to use military force in Southeast Asia "to prevent further aggression." In the Senate the resolution was sponsored, ironically, by Sen. Fulbright, who was soon to become a leading critic of the war; it passed both houses of Congress with only two dissenting votes. Similarly the decision to seek a military victory was widely supported by the public. Even journalist David Halberstam [q.v.], who later wrote *The Best and the Brightest*, an indictment of the key members in the Kennedy and Johnson Administrations responsible for American policy in Vietnam, initially supported the war effort. It is important to stress, however, that the vast majority of the public and the Congress did not anticipate how difficult the war would be.

The successful use of American combat forces in the Dominican Republic in April 1965 may have facilitated Johnson's decision to send 50,000 troops to South Vietnam two months later. In response to an incipient civil war between left-leaning forces and the military, the President dispatched 30,000 troops to the Caribbean nation to ensure that the Communists would not seize power, as Castro had done in Cuba in 1958. His decision was widely supported, although several liberal Democrats led by Sens. Fulbright, George McGovern (D, S.D.) [q.v.] and Robert Kennedy (D, N.Y.) criticized the move on the grounds that there had been little chance of a Communist takeover. The debate was short-lived, however, for the operation resulted in few casualties and brought the fighting to a halt. Perhaps, it was hoped, the same thing would happen in Vietnam.

But Vietnam was not a small island in the nearby Caribbean; its population, including the North and South, totaled nearly one-quarter of America's population. Furthermore, the North Vietnamese Army, which had defeated a major French force in the 1950s, was skilled in guerrilla warfare. It was thus to little avail that Johnson intensified the bombing of North Vietnam and increased American combat forces to 540,000 men between 1965 and 1968. During this period the public became increasingly disenchanted with what seemed to be an endless war. By November 1967 its disapproval of Johnson's handling of the conflict had grown to 57%, according to a major poll. Even many of Johnson's top aides now shared the public's disillusionment. In 1967 former presidential adviser Bundy warned the President against sending more troops, and Secretary of Defense McNamara resigned after Johnson rejected his advice to halt the bombing of North Vietnam and freeze U.S. troop levels.

During this same time the critics of the war became increasingly vocal, emphasizing different reasons for their opposition. David Halberstam claimed the war was unwinnable because the South Vietnamese government had little support and its army was second-rate. Other opponents, like William Sloane Coffin [q.v.], the chaplain of Yale University, assailed the war on moral grounds, stressing the high numbers of civilian casualties allegedly caused by advanced U.S. military technology (though subsequent research indicated that a higher percentage of civilians suffered in the Korean war and that most civilian casualties were caused by Communist attacks on

South Vietnamese urban centers). Other critics contended that the United States had more important priorities at home. Sen. Symington, who had been one of the leading proponents of higher defense spending during the 1950s, criticized the war because it resulted in inflation and a weakened U.S. dollar abroad. Sen. Robert Kennedy asserted that the money spent on the war was needed to improve the material conditions of America's poor, which were widely blamed as a major cause of the summer race riots during the 1960s. Other liberal critics, like Sens. Fulbright and Eugene McCarthy (D, Minn.) [q.v.], placed the war in a larger conceptual framework and attacked much of America's postwar foreign policy, particularly during the 1960s, on the grounds that too many commitments had been made and that military force had been relied on too often. Their two books—McCarthy's *The Limits of Power* and Fulbright's *The Arrogance of Power*, published in 1967—expressed the spirit of the times and were popular with the public. The most radical opponents of the war were often students. Student leader Tom Hayden, for example, accused the United States of intentionally bombing North Vietnamese civilians in order to intimidate their government and charged that America's foreign policy was in the hands of "the military-industrial complex."

The major turning point in the conduct of the war took place following the Communist Tet offensive in February 1968. The offensive, which penetrated all the major South Vietnamese cities and captured Hue, a major city in the northern part of South Vietnam, convinced most of the American people that the war could not be won without a total military commitment. Six weeks later their feelings were reflected in the New Hampshire presidential primary, in which Sen. McCarthy ran a surprisingly strong second to President Johnson. McCarthy's showing, in turn, led Sen. Robert Kennedy to enter the race for the Democratic Party's presidential nomination on an anti-war platform and contributed to Johnson's decision not to seek reelection. The Tet offensive also caused Gen. William Westmoreland, the commander of U.S. forces in South Vietnam, to ask for over 200,000 more troops. Johnson was reluctant to grant the request and appointed his new Secretary of Defense, Clark Clifford, to head a task force to study the proposal. Although the panel recommended sending an additional 23,000 troops, Clifford counseled the President against further escalation of the war. Soon after Johnson convened an informal advisory group composed of senior statesmen to study the Vietnam situation. After listening to a series of detailed briefings on the war, a solid majority of the group, which included Dean Acheson, George Ball, retired Gen. Mathew Ridgway [q.v.], Arthur J. Goldberg and Henry Cabot Lodge, concluded that there was probably no way to win militarily, short of bombing North Vietnamese civilians or using nuclear weapons. They therefore recommended a halt to the sending of American troops to Vietnam and a cessation to the bombing of North Vietnam. Clifford then played a key role in countering the arguments of Secretary of State Rusk and presidential adviser Walt Rostow [q.v.], who supported further troop increases, and in convincing Johnson to accept the panel's recommendations.

The Administration's involvement in Vietnam was so consuming that it neglected other parts of the world. In 1967, for example, Johnson and his advisers refused to take forceful measures to try to head off the Arab–Israeli war that nearly everyone knew was imminent. Their main goal was to avoid having to help Israel militarily in case it was threatened by defeat and they therefore urged it to avoid war at all costs. Following Israel's overwhelming victory, Johnson and his advisers were too preoccupied with Vietnam to act as mediators between the two sides. The consensus in Congress was also in favor of noninvolvement.

One of the few successful undertakings of the Johnson Administration was an agreement with the Soviets to initiate arms control talks on anti-ballistic missile (ABM) systems. At the July 1967 Glassboro, N.J., meeting between Johnson and Soviet Premier Alexei Kosygin, Secretary of Defense McNamara warned the Soviet leader that such systems, which both countries were on the verge of constructing, would be extremely dangerous since they might tempt one side into believing that it could launch a nuclear attack and then use the ABM to defend itself against a retaliatory strike. While the Soviets were initially skeptical, they agreed to begin negotiations for the banning of such systems the following year.

The liberal critics in Congress continued to gain strength during the 1970s, when they clashed frequently with the Nixon and Ford Administrations. From 1969 to 1973 the White House and its opponents were divided primarily over the pace of the U.S. withdrawal from South Vietnam. Thereafter their differences focused on the nature of the Soviet threat and the proper level of U.S. involvement in foreign affairs. On the one hand Presidents Nixon and Ford, and their principal adviser, Henry Kissinger [q.v.], wanted to continue vigorously the containment of Soviet expansionism and to maintain U.S. commitments at their approximate current levels, with the exception of the Vietnam war. On the other hand congressional liberals, reflecting the growing disenchantment of the public with America's international role, tended to downplay the importance of containing Soviet influence and favored a reduction of the nation's overseas obligations.

The most devisive issue between the two sides was the Vietnam war. While Nixon and Kissinger recognized that a clear military victory by the United States was impossible, they refused to consider an immediate withdrawal, because they felt it would signal allies and adversaries that America was capable of breaking a commitment. They hoped to salvage the situation by turning over the conduct of the war to the South Vietnamese as U.S. forces gradually withdrew; in their view such a course would be an act of policy rather than an act of betrayal. (It is unclear whether they also believed that it might possibly lead to the survival of a non-Communist South Vietnam.) In contrast, congressional liberals, led by Sens. Frank Church (D, Ida.) [q.v.] and Fulbright, felt that South Vietnam was a lost cause and that the war should be brought to an end as quickly as possible. This difference in opinion resulted in a series of political battles between 1969 and 1973 in which the Administration's critics tried to place strictures on Nixon's policies in order to terminate the war more quickly.

The first major clash between the Administration and Congress took place in June 1970, when the Senate passed the Cooper-Church Amendment, which barred any future U.S. military activity in Cambodia. While the House subsequently modified the bill by restricting its application to Laos and Thailand, it still represented the first limitation ever voted on an American President's power as commander-in-chief during a war. In July Senate liberals also supported Sen. McGovern's "end the war" amendment, which mandated the withdrawal of all American combat troops from Southeast Asia by the end of 1971. After a heated debate the Senate rejected the measure by 55 to 39, but the vote indicated that the public and Congress were turning increasingly against the war. Sens. Church, McGovern and Fulbright again led congressional liberals in excoriating the Administration's decision in 1972 to mine the North Vietnamese harbor of Haiphong and to resume the bombing of the North. The liberals finally gained the upper hand following the January 1973 peace agreement, which completed the withdrawal of all U.S. combat troops. When North Vietnam began violating the cease-fire agreement soon after the final American troop withdrawal, Secretary of State Kissinger implored Congress to permit him to use an offer of aid and a threat of bombing in order to persuade the North Vietnamese to abide by the peace accords. But most members of Congress opposed any aid plan for the former enemy and the liberal critics refused to provide funding for a resumption of the bombing. For the first time in the nation's history, Congress ended American involvement in a war.

House and Senate liberals also sought to reduce U.S. commitments elsewhere. In 1971 they supported Senate Majority Leader Mike Mansfield's (D, Mont.) amendment requiring the unilateral withdrawal of half the U.S. troops stationed in Western Europe but lost by a vote of 61 to 36. In 1975 they led the Senate's 54 to 22 vote rejecting Kissinger's request for continued military aid to the pro-Western faction fighting Soviet-backed Cuban troops in the Angolan civil war. The Senate's refusal was extremely significant because it signaled that America's opposition to the expansion of Soviet influence was no longer axiomatic.

Liberal critics accused the Nixon and Ford Administrations of generally spending too much money on defense, and in some cases Congress imposed spending curbs. They also opposed Secretary of Defense James Schlesinger's [q.v.] new defense strategy of limited nuclear warfare. Schlesinger believed that the best way to deter a major act of Soviet aggression, such as an attack on Western Europe, was to be able to threaten the USSR's missile bases with a limited nuclear first strike. He therefore announced in 1975 that the United States was de-emphasizing the targeting of Soviet cities, which had been the policy under Secretary of Defense McNamara's doctrine of Mutual Assured Destruction, and concentrating instead on Soviet missile bases. House and Senate liberals, however, argued that even a restricted attack against missile bases would result in enormous casualties and doubted that a limited nuclear war would stay limited.

The morality of U.S. foreign affairs also became an issue during the Nixon/Ford years. Congressional liberals in particular called for a more idealistic approach to foreign policy. Sens. Church and Edward Kennedy (D, Mass.), for example, criticized America's siding with authoritarian Pakistan against democratic India in the 1971 Indo-Pakistani war. The new stress on idealism was sometimes reinforced by ethnic political pressures. Thus, the 1974 Jackson-Vanik Amendment, which prohibited the granting of most favored nation trade status to the USSR until it liberalized its emigration policies, won congressional support in Congress because of the ideal of free emigration and the support of Jewish-Americans. Similarly, under the leadership of Sen. Church, liberals in Congress passed an ineffectual arms embargo against Turkey, a NATO ally, in 1975 to punish it for its 1974 invasion of Cyprus as well as to placate the Greek-American lobby. The stress on idealism also led to a series of investigations of the Central Intelligence Agency between 1973 and 1975. A congressional investigation committee chaired by Sen. Church charged that the CIA ordered assassination attempts in the early 1960s against Cuban President Fidel Castro and Belgian Congolese leftist leader Patrice Lumumba. They also accused Kissinger of having tried to instigate a coup in 1970 against Chile's democratically elected Marxist leader, President Salvador Allende. These investigations culminated in the passage of the Hughes-Ryan Amendment, which required the CIA to inform approximately 200 members of Congress about any future covert operations.

Another target of House and Senate liberals was the general postwar trend of centralizing foreign policy formulation in the presidency and the consequent exclusion of Congress from policy making. In reaction to this trend Congress passed the 1973 War Powers Act, which limited to 60 days the President's authority to commit U.S. troops in combat situations abroad without congressional approval. The critics of presidential power became even stronger after the 1973–74 Watergate scandal and found their leading exponent in Arthur Schlesinger, who wrote *The Imperial Presidency*, a best-seller that criticized the growing centralization of power in the executive branch.

Despite its frequent attacks on the policies of Nixon and Ford, Congress was generally supportive of the attempts to reach arms control agreements with the USSR and to improve relations with Communist China, the industrialized nations and the developing countries. Kissinger, who generally conducted the detailed negotiations with the Soviets, made two important breakthroughs in the area of arms control: an agreement banning the construction of anti-ballistic missile systems and a temporary freeze on the deployment of additional offensive missile systems. His efforts culminated in President Nixon's signing of SALT I in Moscow during May 1972, the most important arms limitation agreement since the 1963 nuclear test ban treaty. Kissinger subsequently negotiated a tentative agreement, signed by Brezhnev and Ford in November 1974, that placed ceilings on the number of missile launchers permitted to each side, a major area of the arms race. Both arms control agreements were widely applauded in Congress, though some conservatives, led by Sen. Henry Jackson (D, Wash.) [q.v.], charged that they unwisely allowed the Soviets to have larger missiles than the United States.

Nixon and Kissinger also made a major breakthrough with Communist China. Both men believed that the Sino-Soviet split, which dated back to 1959, was irrevocable and that it might encourage China to seek better relations with the United States. They therefore put out diplomatic "feelers" to the Chinese in 1969 via the French, Rumanians and Pakistanis. After the Chinese communicated their interest in a possible summit meeting, Kissinger made a secret trip to Peking in July 1971 and assured the Chinese leaders that the United States considered Taiwan to be part of mainland China and that it would eventually withdraw its defense forces from the offshore island, as tensions in the area eased. This understanding was made official in February 1972, when Nixon visited Peking. The opening to Communist China received wide support in Congress, with the exception of isolated conservatives, like Sen. Goldwater, who feared that Taiwan would eventually be "betrayed."

President Nixon also took a new tack towards America's democratic allies. Previous administrations had tended to encourage the growth of economic power in Western Europe while discouraging the assertion of European political power. The Eisenhower Administration, for example, supported the formation of the Common Market in 1958, and the Kennedy and Johnson Administrations opposed France's development of nuclear weapons in the early 1960s and its withdrawal from NATO in 1966. Nixon and Kissinger reversed this policy outlook. They accepted the assertion of Western European political power, as exemplified by French President Charles de Gaulle, as an inevitable and in some ways positive development. On the other hand Nixon, who tended to direct the Administration's economic policy, was determined to improve the U.S. balance of trade deficit and strengthen the value of the dollar in foreign money markets. Consequently in 1971 he ended the policy of using U.S. gold to redeem dollars held by foreign banks, thereby setting the dollar free to float against foreign currencies. In the subsequent negotiations over the new value of the dollar vis-a-vis the European and Japanese currencies, Nixon rejected Kissinger's more conciliatory approach in favor of Treasury Secretary John Connally's [q.v.] proposal to impose a temporary tax on imports in order to improve America's bargaining position. Despite the abrasive tactics, economic relations improved between the United States and Europe and Japan, and in 1975 the first of a series of annual on-going summit conferences took place in Rambouillet, France.

The Nixon and Ford Administrations also faced political and economic challenges from the developing nations, many of which had become increasingly powerful, unified and assertive by the 1970s. Just how powerful some of these nations had become was not apparent until October 1973, when Egypt and Syria launched a successful invasion of the Israeli-held Sinai peninsula and Golan Heights. In contrast to 1967 the Arabs fought well, and their cause was helped immeasurably by Saudi Arabia's decision to reduce its oil exports and stop oil sales to the United States, which precipitated a major recession in the world economy. In response to the crisis the Nixon Administration's priorities were to ensure Israel's survival; strengthen Arab moderates, like Egyptian President Anwar Sadat; and persuade the Saudis to terminate their oil production cuts and embargo. To these ends Nixon and Kissinger agreed to supply Israel with arms but insisted that Egypt's armies not be crushed. In November 1973 Kissinger then began to act as a mediator among Egypt, Syria and Israel, and over the next two years he orchestrated a two-step Israeli withdrawal in the Sinai and a one-step Israeli withdrawal in the Golan Heights. This diplomatic tour de force won virtually universal support from the American public and the Congress.

The Arab-Israeli war led to a second major challenge for U.S. policy makers. The enormous rise in the price of oil dictated by the Organization of Petroleum Exporting Countries following the war caused other developing nations to wonder if the feat could be duplicated with nonfuel raw material exports. The successful use of the "oil weapon" also galvanized the developing nations into making assertive demands for a "New International Economic Order," consisting of concrete economic reforms and an eventual redistribution of the world's wealth. The Ford Administration was split on how to react to these demands. Treasury Secretary William Simon and other hard-liners showed little willingness to modify a system that had worked well for the West ever since the end of World War II. In contrast, Kissinger favored a more conciliatory approach that included negotiations over the Third World's financial debts to the West and the stabilization of their export earnings, which were based on the often widely fluctuating price of raw material exports. As was usually the case during his Administration, Ford sided with Kissinger, whose political judgment he greatly respected. Subsequent U.S. policy, particularly in international organizations like the International Monetary Fund and the World Bank, reflected the more conciliatory approach of Ford and Kissinger.

Kissinger's final diplomatic initiative took place after he decided that the United States could no longer support the white minority government of Rhodesia in light of the increasing success of the country's native guerrilla forces and the growing presence of Soviet-backed Cuban troops in neighboring Angola and Mozambique. In May 1976 he made an extensive tour of southern Africa during which he called for majority rule in Rhodesia. The trip culminated in successful talks with South African Premier John Vorster and Rhodesian Premier Ian Smith, who reluctantly agreed to hold free elections in the former British colony.

Despite Kissinger's frequent diplomatic successes the Nixon/Ford years were a period of controversy in foreign policy. The frequent clashes between Congress and Presidents Nixon and Ford—over Vietnam, defense spending and strategy, the Mansfield amendment, the CIA investigations, the Turkish arms embargo and Angola—must be seen as part of the general reassertion of congressional power, which for the most part had been dormant since the beginning of World War II. The clashes had a certain partisan element since Congress was controlled by the Democrats and the White House by the Republicans. More importantly, however, Congress felt disappointed and deceived by the executive branch. It blamed the Johnson Administration for the Vietnam war and believed that it had hid some of the truth about the conflict. Furthermore the Watergate illegalities, which culminated in President Nixon's resignation in August 1974, produced a strong resentment against the amount of power that had accumulated in the White House. The reassertion of congressional power was also a reflection of the more general sociological and political attack on authority that took place in the United States during the late 1960s and the first half of the 1970s; during this period many Americans, particularly the young, rejected what they deemed to be traditional American values. Finally, the conflicts between the White House and Congress were a result of differences in opinion about the nature of the

Soviet threat. Congressional liberals felt that the threat had declined and that the United States could therefore pursue a more "idealistic" course, even if it ignored the usual requirements of realpolitik. In contrast, the Republican Administrations felt that the Soviets had to be contained wherever possible.

In reviewing the history of America's foreign policy between 1945 and 1976, two major trends stand out: the changing perception of the Communist threat and the rise and decline of America's engagement in international affairs and its commitments abroad. At the end of World War II, policy makers did not yet consider the USSR to be an enemy and were unsure of how to deal with it. After the Soviet Union's actions in Eastern Europe convinced them of its hostility, they committed America to aid and defend Western Europe and Turkey under the Truman Doctrine, the Marshall Plan and NATO. In addition, by sending U.S. troops to defend South Korea from North Korean invaders, they demonstrated that the United States was willing to oppose the spread of Soviet influence with military force. Following the entry of Communist Chinese troops into the Korean war, the Administration's policy makers joined their conservative critics in considering all Communist nations to be enemies of the United States. This assumption, coupled with the existing opposition to the spread of Soviet influence, led to additional American involvement overseas. Truman ordered the U.S. Navy to defend Taiwan. Eisenhower signed defense treaties with Japan, Taiwan and Thailand; sent military advisers to South Vietnam; backed anti-government Guatemalan exiles; and dispatched 14,000 Marines to counter a perceived left-wing threat in Lebanon. Similarly, Kennedy launched the Alliance for Progress to counter Castro's influence in Latin America and sent military aid to India during its 1962 border war with Communist China. And Johnson ordered military forces to the Dominican Republic and South Vietnam to prevent Communist takeovers. All of these actions, except the later Vietnam troop consignments, had the widespread support of congressional critics and the public. The major reservation among the critics, in fact, was that the United States should have been doing even more to counter the Communists.

Starting around the mid-1960s, however, the tide of opinion began to shift because of the adverse impact of the Vietnam war and the changing perception of the Communist threat. The divisive and inconclusive war in Vietnam soured the public on America's active international role in general and it made the whole idea of containing Communism, particularly by military means, less attractive. Furthermore, the changing perception of the Communist threat made the idea of containment seem less necessary. The widening Sino-Soviet split ended the notion of a unified Communist bloc, and Nixon's 1972 trip to Peking generally laid to rest the assumption that mainland China was hostile to the United States. While policy makers still considered the USSR to be an enemy, it was also seen in a less belligerent light for several reasons. Its more conciliatory diplomacy in Europe following the construction of the Berlin Wall in 1961 and the less abrasive tone of its ideological pronouncements following the Cuban Missile Crisis in 1962 undercut the conviction that it was an inveterate adversary. This notion was further weakened by the somewhat contrived impression of good will surrounding the U.S.-USSR summit conferences in 1967, 1972 and 1974. In addition, the threat posed by the 1973 oil embargo to U.S. economic security caused some observers to wonder whether the developing world might not constitute as great a threat to America as did the Soviet Union. For these reasons the congressional liberals, who had supplanted their conservative colleagues as the most influential critics, and many other Americans no longer viewed the USSR as an uncompromising foe.

The reaction against the unpopular war in Vietnam and the perception of a less dangerous Communist world brought about a reduction of U.S. commitments and a decreased willingness to use military force. In particular the military draft was abolished in 1973 and the United States completely withdrew from Southeast Asia by 1975. These trends were reinforced by the Watergate scandal of 1973–74, which produced a reaction against forceful action by the executive branch and the claims of national security abused by President Nixon in his attempt to hide incriminating evidence. Following the Watergate affair policy critics forced through measures that included an arms embargo against Turkey, restrictions on CIA operations and a cutoff of aid to anti-Communist Angolans fighting Soviet-backed Cuban troops—all of which the Ford Administration had opposed.

The decline of U.S. activism abroad took place in a world that had changed radically since the Truman years. At that time America's power was of colossal dimensions: it produced more than 50% of the world's goods and services, accounted for more than 50% of its defense spending and held more than 50% of all international monetary reserves. By the mid-1970s, however, Europe was outproducing the United States, the USSR was outspending it militarily and Saudi Arabia possessed more monetary reserves. Thus, America's uncertainty about its policy towards the Soviet Union, its weariness with international affairs as a result of the Vietnam war and its declining executive authority following the Watergate scandal left its entire foreign policy in disarray in a world from which it could no longer retreat, as it had before World War II, and which it could no longer dominate by its material strength, as it had briefly after World War II.

Profiles

ACHESON, DEAN G(OODERHAM)

b. April 11, 1893; Middletown, Conn.
d. Oct. 12, 1971; Silver Springs, Md.
Assistant Secretary of State for
Economic Affairs, 1941-44; Assistant
Secretary of State for Congressional
Relations, 1945; Undersecretary of
State, 1945-47; Secretary of State,
1949-53.

The son of an Episcopal bishop of Connecticut, Dean Acheson grew up in comfortable New England surroundings. He attended the Groton School and graduated from Yale in 1915. After serving in the Navy during World War I, he received a law degree from Harvard in 1918. Acheson served as Secretary to Supreme Court Justice Louis Brandeis for the next two years and joined the prestigious law firm of Covington and Burling in 1921. Following the recommendation of Felix Frankfurter, the New Deal's unofficial talent scout, in March 1933 President Roosevelt appointed Acheson undersecretary of the Treasury. Six months later Acheson resigned in protest against what he considered the reckless and unconstitutional action by the President in reducing the gold content of the dollar. Acheson then resumed his legal practice. During 1939-40 he headed a committee to study the operation of the administrative bureaus of the federal government.

Acheson once again became active in public affairs with the outbreak of war in Europe. He worked to promote U.S. aid to Great Britain and collaborated with presidential aide Ben Cohen in drafting the constitutional justification for the 1940 destroyer-bases deal with the British. This brief impressed Roosevelt, who invited Acheson to rejoin the administration as assistant secretary of state for economic affairs.

Acheson served as assistant secretary from 1941 until 1944. Throughout the war he helped coordinate the lend-lease program. He was also liaison with Congress and contributed to the development of such postwar organizations as the United Nations Relief and Rehabilitation Agency (UNRRA), the World Bank, the International Monetary Fund, and the Food and Agriculture Organization. Acheson viewed these agencies as tools to rehabilitate Europe to insure stable pro-American governments and increased markets for surplus American industrial goods. He later lobbied for the U.N. charter in Congress, although he considered the organization impractical and unimportant.

In June 1945 Harry Truman appointed his old political rival, James Byrnes [q.v.], Secretary of State. Byrnes asked Acheson to assume the post of undersecretary. During his year and a half in office, Byrnes was abroad a large portion of the time and therefore Acheson served as acting secretary. He was responsible for the administration of the Department and for continuing the reforms introduced by Edward Stettinius to improve the functioning of the Department's bureaucracy. Acheson introduced a clear, precise chain of command that ended with his office. When Byrnes was out of the country, Acheson briefed Truman daily on foreign affairs and developed a close relationship with the President. Acheson often found himself acting as mediator between Truman, always fearful that Byrnes sought to upstage

1

him, and Byrnes, who was jealous of Truman for winning the vice presidency in 1944.

During the early postwar period Acheson was primarily concerned with the economic reconstruction of Western Europe. He testified before congressional committees in support of extension of aid to UNRRA and for the loan to Great Britain. Acheson even supported a recovery loan to the new government of Poland, already charged by many with being the puppet of the Soviet Union. He considered Poland's recovery crucial for the rehabilitation of Europe.

Acheson was also deeply involved with the development of U.S. policy on atomic weapons. A number of administration officials, led by Byrnes and Secretary of the Navy James V. Forrestal [q.v.], viewed the American nuclear monopoly as an important weapon which the U.S. could use to pressure concessions from the Soviet Union. Acheson disagreed, arguing in a memorandum to Truman in the fall of 1945 for international controls of atomic energy. He supported such nuclear scientists as Leo Szilard who warned that Russia would soon possess the bomb and that unless some control was established, a suicidal arms race would occur. Acheson joined Henry Stimson in advocating that procedures be established between the U.S., Great Britain and the Soviet Union for the exchange of information on nuclear weapons and the eventual international control of atomic material.

In January 1946 Byrnes asked Acheson to chair a committee called to formulate a plan for the international control of atomic energy that would be introduced to the U.N. David Lilienthal, chairman of the Tennessee Valley Authority, and J. Robert Oppenheimer [q.v.], a noted physicist who had led the Manhattan District Project, were among those who joined the Undersecretary on the committee. The panel's report, issued in March, called for the establishment of an international atomic development agency to survey nuclear raw materials and to assume control of dangerous fissionable material and production plants. The agency would make its resources available for peaceful

uses, and control and license all nuclear activities. It would report any attempt to develop atomic weapons to the U.N. members who could take appropriate action. The report stipulated that the U.S. would end manufacture of nuclear devices at some point in the future and transfer atomic energy to the U.N. agency in stages. However, it stressed that there must be no immediate release of atomic knowledge.

Truman and Byrnes then gave Bernard Baruch [q.v.] the responsibility for presenting the plan to the U.N. Baruch, however, refused to accept the proposal as offered. To insure Soviet compliance in disarmament, he demanded that a provision prohibiting Security Council members from using their veto power when discussing atomic energy be included in the American plan. Despite Acheson's objections that this was unnecessary and would lead to the defeat of the proposal, Baruch's recommendations were added. In June the Soviet Union rejected the Baruch Plan.

During the early months of the postwar period, Acheson urged a policy of conciliation with the Soviet Union. However, as a result of Soviet actions in Iran and Turkey and attempts to gain control of the eastern Mediterranean, he changed his position. By the spring of 1946 he had joined George F. Kennan [q.v.] in warning that the Soviet Union was a power bent on world conquest, and he urged the U.S. to develop policies to resist Soviet expansion. He backed Kennan's recommendation for containment of the USSR and, over the remainder of the decade, helped develop programs implementing the plan.

In 1947 Acheson played a major role in the formation of the Truman Doctrine. Following the British announcement of their impending withdrawal from Greece in February 1947, he recommended that the U.S. extend immediate military and economic assistance to the Greek government in its war against Communist insurgents. Acheson formulated the proposal to be submitted to Congress and won congressional backing for the measure. In an emotional plea to congressional leaders, he explained the dire consequences for the U.S. and the West if the Soviet Union achieved control of the eastern Mediterranean. The Undersecretary made it clear that he believed the fate of the West depended on the American response to the crisis.

That spring Acheson also became involved in the formulation of the Marshall Plan of massive aid to war-torn Europe. In March 1947 he recommended a program of aid and coordinated studies on the feasibility of the project. Even before Secretary of State George C. Marshall [q.v.] unveiled the plan in his historic Harvard University address of June 1947, Acheson had already outlined the general philosophy of the proposal in a speech on May 8 in Delta, Miss. He announced that the U.S. must "push ahead with the reconstruction of those two great workshops of Europe and Asia—Germany and Japan." "Free people," he said, "desiring aid to preserve their institutions against totalitarian pressures would receive top priority for American reconstruction aid."

Acheson retired from government service in the summer of 1947. He resumed his legal practice but could not entirely avoid public affairs. He served as vice chairman of the Hoover Commission and lobbied on behalf of the Marshall Plan. In November 1948 President Truman asked Acheson to replace the ailing Marshall as Secretary of State commencing the first of the year.

Acheson's appointment was applauded by many in the U.S. and Europe. *New York Times* correspondent James Reston wrote that the new Secretary combined the best features of his four predecessors. Reston felt Acheson had the experience of Cordell Hull, the handsomeness of Edward Stettinius, the style of James Byrnes and the mental discipline of George C. Marshall. The *Manchester Guardian* called him one of the most creative political minds of the time. Although the elegant, witty, urbane diplomat was distrusted by some members of Congress, most

were impressed by his intellect and his determination to take a strong stand against the Soviet Union.

Despite their differences in backgrounds and personality, Acheson and Truman worked well together. Both men respected each other. Truman admired Acheson's intellect and dedication. Acheson, in turn, respected Truman's determination to make crucial decisions without hesitation. Both shared a desire to defend Western society from what they thought was expansionist Communism. This shared view enabled them to shape American diplomacy in close cooperation.

Acheson viewed Soviet relations in terms of power politics. He opposed a Wilsonian emphasis on internationalism and appeals to abstract principles of right and wrong in the formation of policy. He believed that they were attempts to avoid the responsibility of exercising power. Acheson rejected the possibility of negotiation with the Soviet Union on the grounds that that nation was not ready to bargain. He accepted the inevitability of a bipolar world, at least within the foreseeable future. His major goals, therefore, were to contain Communist expansion and to develop a strong military presence so that America could force the Soviet Union to negotiate on its own terms.

By the time Acheson assumed his post, some of the major aspects of the Administration's containment policy had been developed. The Truman Doctrine had helped prevent a Communist takeover in Greece and the Marshall Plan had helped economically revitalize Europe, thwarting Communist attempts to use economic problems to gain a foothold in that area. Acheson, therefore, concentrated on maintaining a united Atlantic community and building a strong military alliance in Europe. During 1949 he lobbied for the passage of the North Atlantic Treaty (negotiated while he was out of governemnt service) and pushed for increased aid to the alliance.

Germany played a major role in Acheson's strategy of maintaining Western unity because it formed the industrial heartland of Europe. He, therefore, worked for the establishment of the German Federal Republic under the control of internationalists intent on Germany's participation in the Western alliance. Acheson also urged German entrance into the defense alliance and in 1950 took steps leading to the rearmament of that country.

In late 1949, in light of the fall of China to the Communists and the Soviet explosion of an atomic device, Acheson commissioned a study of American foreign policy and defense capabilities. The report, NSC-68, produced by Paul Nitze [q.v.] in the spring of 1950, reflected the evolution of Acheson's thought. Based on the premise that the Soviet Union was expansionist and would refuse to negotiate outstanding issues, it called for a massive military build-up to meet the Russian challenge. However, the report recommended that rather than relying on a multi-national alliance, the U.S., as the world's major nuclear power, assume unilateral defense of the non-Communist world. NSC-68 proposed an increase in defense spending to $35 billion a year or 20% of the gross national product. President Truman was initially reluctant to accept the report's recommendations, but with the outbreak of war in Korea, which the State Department felt might be a prelude to general Soviet expansion, he pushed for increased defense spending.

Acheson was often criticized both at home and abroad for being intransigent in his demands on negotiations and unrealistic in his policies. His opponents pointed out that his willingness to negotiate with the Soviets only the freedom of Eastern Europe and the reunification of Germany made meaningful discussion on outstanding issues impossible. His foes observed that this demand called on the Soviets to capitulate, not negotiate. They pointed out that Acheson's hardline position and emphasis on military superiority forced the Soviet Union to assume a similar stance, thus intensifying the Cold War. Individuals such as Winston Churchill urged the opening of negotiations for fear of future war.

Acheson's diplomacy focused around the North Atlantic community, which he believed represented the peak of mankind's development. Asia was of secondary importance. He had little interest in the area and never felt confident of his understanding of the situation there. However, during his tenure, Acheson was forced to devote a large portion of his attention to the East.

Shortly after assuming his post, Acheson was faced with the problem of policy towards China, where the Nationalists led by Chiang Kai-shek seemed in imminent danger of losing power to the Communists. Critics of the Administration, led by Sen. William Knowland (R, Calif.) [q.v.] and Rep. Walter Judd (R, Minn.) [q.v.] demanded increased aid to Chiang, who they argued was being ignored because of an emphasis on Europe. Acheson unsuccessfully opposed the demand on the grounds that Chiang had lost the support of his people and that no aid short of direct military intervention could maintain him in power. In August 1949 Acheson defended his position in the State Department's White Paper on China. The Secretary believed that the Chinese civil war was the result of indigenous conditions. He thought it imprudent and an illegitimate use of power for the U.S. to become involved. The report characterized the Chiang government as decadent and corrupt and reiterated Acheson's position that it did not have the support of the Chinese people. This factor, he maintained, was one of the most important reasons for the rise of the Communists. "Nothing that this country did or could have done within the reasonable limits of its capabilities," Acheson concluded in his summary of the paper, "would have changed the results. . . ." One month after Chiang fled to Formosa, Acheson, in a speech before the National Press Club stated: "The Communists did not create this condition. They did not create this revolutionary spirit. They did not create a great force which moved out from under Chiang Kai-shek. But they were shrewd and cunning to mount it, and to ride this thing into victory and into power."

For many Americans China's fall to the Communists in December 1949 revealed the bankruptcy of the containment policy. They felt Truman Administration had failed to contain Communism in the largest nation in the world, which had been protected by the U.S. ever since the 19th century. Some conservatives refused to view the event as the result of poor diplomacy. In light of the continuing Cold War and revelations of domestic subversion, they began to charge that there was a Communist conspiracy in the State Department to "sell out" China. The China Lobby, prominent supporters of Chiang, pointed to such China experts as John Carter Vincent as leaders of the pro-Communist contingent in the Far East desk. Little action was taken on the allegations until Sen. Joseph R. McCarthy (R, Wisc.) asserted in 1950 that he had the names of Communists in the State Department. Some, he maintained, were Acheson's most trusted advisers. The Secretary vigorously defended these men in congressional probes and in departmental loyalty hearings. Despite his defense, he was unable to quell the criticism. Acheson gradually assumed the role of villian for the right and became one of the most unpopular secretaries of state in the 20th century.

The conservative backlash prevented Acheson from following his original policy goals in Asia. He had contemplated recognizing the Peking regime but soon abandoned the plan in order not to offend the McCarthy forces. Acheson decided to provide economic help to the Formosa government, but he refused to tie the U.S. to the defense of the island, which the military deemed strategically valueless.

During the early 1950s Acheson extended containment to Asia. He championed military and economic aid to the French colonialists fighting the pro-Communist Viet Minh in Indochina. Although he acknowledged that nationalism was the chief rallying cry for individuals in developing nations, he feared the Communist connection with the movements. Acheson

also wanted the French to participate fully in European military affairs. They could not possibly have done this without U.S. aid in Asia.

In January 1950 Acheson delivered an address to the National Press Club in which he outlined future American responsiblities in Asia following the fall of China. He excluded Korea from America's "defense perimeter," which included Japan, the Ryukus and the Philippines. Six months later North Korea invaded the South. Critics of the Administration, led by Sen. Robert A. Taft (R, Ohio) [q.v.], charged that Acheson's omission of South Korea in his speech had precipitated the invasion. Acheson held Moscow accountable for the Korean war. The Secretary believed that the Soviet Union was continuously probing for weaknesses in Western defense throughout the world and whenever the West failed to stand up to these tests, Moscow achieved another diplomatic victory. He argued that the U.S. must save South Korea not for the Koreans but for the Western European nations still skeptical of the American resolve to defend them. Intervention in Korea, Acheson maintained, would be in the eyes of the NATO allies the final American atonement for its pre-1941 isolationist policy. He, therefore, recommended that the U.S. commit itself to a war in Korea.

Acheson coordinated the policymaking process that led to the Korean intervention, lobbied for support in Congress and at the U.N. and carried on a diplomatic offensive among non-Western nations to justify the war. When it appeared certain that U.N. troops would push the Communists from the South, Acheson advocated the liberation of the North. The Secretary of State and such military planners as Gen. Douglas MacArthur [q.v.] did not take seriously the Communist Chinese threat to intervene in the War if U.N. troops crossed the 38th parallel and moved closer to the Chinese border. He downgraded the military might of Peking as American troops pushed closer to the Yalu River. The Chinese entry into the war in November 1950 caught Acheson and the Administration off guard. After that managing the war became a frustrating experience for the Secretary. He resisted demands by leading Republicans to expand the war to China. Acheson indicated that he would rather settle for a compromise that would set the boundary of Korea at the old 38th parallel.

Acheson failed to secure peace in Korea through diplomatic channels. Although both sides privately acknowledged the inevitability of a divided Korea, they could not reach a compromise. Just as importantly, the Secretary opposed the Communist demands for the forcible repatriation of prisoners of war, many of whom indicated that they did not want to return to their northern homes.

During his years as Secretary, Dean Acheson had difficulty communicating his Cold War strategy to the American people. His intellect, aristocratic appearance and contempt for those of lesser ability prompted many congressional leaders to distrust him. Acheson tried to ignore public opinion, calling his critics "primitives." He once said that he was thankful that there were no opinion polls at Valley Forge.

Acheson left office in a hail of criticism. In 1952 the Republican Party platform promised a new, bold foreign policy that would liberate Eastern Europe. John Foster Dulles [q.v.], the Party's chief foreign policy spokesman, attacked Acheson's diplomacy for being amoral. The right continued to view the Secretary and high Administration officials as traitors. Yet, in spite of attacks on him, his foreign policy accomplished what he intended. Western Europe remained politically and economically strong. It had also been reassured of U.S. military support if attacked. The Secretary refused to dwell on empty promises. He opposed the pledge to liberate Europe because the U.S. lacked the means short of war to accomplish this. In response to the charge that his foreign policy lacked morality, Acheson argued that he had combined morality with power to achieve results. He pointed to NATO, the Marshall Plan and the Korean intervention as examples of noteworthy moral endeavors.

During the Eisenhower Administration Acheson attempted to defend his record against criticism by Secretary of State John Foster Dulles [q.v.] and the right wing of the Republican Party while trying to articulate an alternative foreign policy for the Democratic Party. Acheson charged that the Administration's reliance on "massive retaliation," the use of strategic nuclear weapons as America's prime deterrent, "was a fraud upon words and upon facts." It produced "doubts, fears and loss of confidence in our leadership." To him, massive retaliation implied unilateralism. It was a reversion to isolationism, for Dulles's threat that the U.S. would retaliate "by means and places of our own choosing" precluded any consultation with American allies. This pledge, Acheson argued, showed that the U.S. would recklessly gamble its allies' future to win diplomatic victories.

Acheson maintained that massive retaliation was irrelevant to the past and future skirmishes of the Cold War. Only unified ground action had checked Communist advances in Korea. During the 1956 presidential campaign, he charged that the Republican foreign policy of "bluff and bluster" did not save Dien Bien Phu or prevent Nasser from seizing the Suez Canal. He said that Eisenhower and Dulles could have continued Truman's foreign policy but, instead, had become "the prisoners of the primitive propaganda and slogans of the McCarthy-Taft-Knowland forces." Acheson recommended the return to a proper balance between conventional and nuclear weapons, the end of empty rhetorical threats and the willingness to work with NATO to repair the alleged damage done to American prestige during Eisenhower's first term.

When the Communist Chinese resumed shelling the offshore islands of Quemoy and Matsu in 1958, Acheson denounced Eisenhower's foreign policy once again. He observed that the U.S. seemed to be "drifting, either dazed or indifferent, to war with China." Rejecting Dulles's position that Quemoy was crucial to the defense of Formosa, he maintained that the island traditionally belonged to the mainland. Its population was minimal and it had no strategic value. Acheson warned that Chiang Kai-shek was interested in the island only as a staging area to attack the Communists and would use the crisis to embroil the U.S. in a conflict with the Communist Chinese.

Maintaining his strong mistrust of the Communists into the 1950s, the former Secretary was skeptical of Eisenhower's attempts to relax tensions between the U.S. and the Soviet Union. He counseled the nation to be ever vigilant to meet any Soviet challenge and be cautious of being lured into making premature agreements that could be harmful in the future. He discounted the efficacy of summit conferences with the Soviets, writing in 1958 that the U.S. had nothing to negotiate with the Soviet Union. He opposed George Kennan's [q.v.] call for negotiations on American and Soviet withdrawal from Eastern and Western Europe and the reunification and neutralization of Germany. Acheson thought neutralization would eventually push Germany into the Soviet camp, while withdrawal of American troops would leave NATO countries vulnerable to Communist infiltration. As late as 1959 he opposed summit meetings, where he thought the Soviet Union would possess all the advantages. Soviet Premier Nikita Khrushchev, he believed, would endeavor to obtain concessions from the West on Berlin and try to obtain American endorsement of the status quo in Eastern Europe. To make such an agreement, Acheson wrote, would be tantamount to "Munich."

Although formally out of government, Acheson served as a foreign policy adviser during the Kennedy Administration. In March 1961 Kennedy invited him to undertake a special study of German problems, including those posed by the Russian threat to sign a peace treaty with East Germany and make Berlin a "free city" theoretically independent of Eastern or Western control. Acheson's analysis and his recommendations reflected his view of Communism and the pivotal role Germany should play in American strategy. He saw the confrontation over Berlin as a Russian pretext for testing the general American resolve to resist a Soviet challenge. Because the U.S. was engaged in a conflict of wills over a strategically important area, America had no choice but to show the Soviet Union that it would risk nuclear war rather than abandon the status quo in Germany. In Acheson's view negotiations would only be a sign of weakness. Consequently, he recommended that America build up both its conventional and nuclear forces in preparation for an "inevitable" armed confrontation with the Soviet Union. However Kennedy, seeking a more flexible approach to the conduct of the Cold War, rejected Acheson's advice and in July 1961 announced a policy of negotiation combined with continued military buildup.

Acheson was again called to advise the President in October 1962 after Kennedy learned of the presence of Soviet missiles in Cuba. Believing that the missiles not only threatened America's security but also its position as leader of the Western world, Acheson advocated bombing of the missile sites to show U.S. resolve against this new Soviet challenge. He opposed Attorney General Robert Kennedy's [q.v.] suggested blockade, believing that any delay in attacking would increase Soviet missile strength and eventually necessitate a larger American counter-strike, thus increasing the chances of nuclear war. Again rejecting Acheson's advice, Kennedy announced a "quarantine" of the island and demanded the removal of the missiles on Oct. 22.

In March 1968, following the request of high military officials for over 200,000 additional ground troops for Vietnam, President Johnson asked Acheson to assess the Administration's war policy. Not trusting the briefings given by the Joint Chiefs of Staff, Acheson conducted his own investigation of the situation. Despite his earlier support of the war, Acheson concluded that he could no longer back the policy of seeking military victory. He believed that such a goal was impossible without the application of the nation's total resources and was not consistent with American interests. Acheson recommended that America get out of Vietnam as soon as possible because the public no longer supported the war. He reiterated his position at a meeting of the Senior Advisory Group on Vietnam on March 25 and 26. Acheson's recommendation was one of the factors contributing to Johnson's announcement of de-escalation on March 31, 1968.

Acheson died of a heart attack on Oct. 12, 1971.

[EWS]

For further information:
Dean Acheson, *Present at the Creation*, (New York, 1969).

BALL, GEORGE W(ILDMAN)
b. Dec. 21, 1909; Des Moines, Iowa.
Undersecretary of State for Economic Affairs, January 1961-November 1961; Undersecretary of State, November 1961-September 1966.

Following his graduation from Northwestern University Law School in 1933, Ball worked for the Farm Credit Administration and Treasury Department. In 1935 he returned to Illinois and joined a Chicago law firm where Adlai Stevenson [*q.v.*] was one of his colleagues. Ball reentered government service in 1942 in the Office of Lend-Lease Administration and in 1944 was appointed director of the U.S. Strategic Bombing Survey.

After the war he resumed private law practice and became a specialist on international trade. Ball worked closely with Jean Monnet on plans for the new European Coal and Steel Community. He later represented it and several other Common Market agencies in the U.S. In 1952 and 1956 Ball played an important role in Stevenson's presidential campaign and in 1960 served as Stevenson's manager at the Los Angeles convention. Despite Ball's support of Stevenson, President Kennedy, impressed with a report on economic and commercial policy that the lawyer had written, designated Ball as undersecretary of state for economic affairs in January 1961.

During the early months of the Kennedy Administration, Ball was primarily involved in the formation of U.S. trade policy. Concerned with America's continued adverse balance of payments and anticipating increased problems after Britain's expected entrance into the Common Market, Ball advocated a complete revision of U.S. trade policy to bring down tariff levels and give the President flexibility to meet new conditions. These proposals were embodied in the Trade Expansion Act of 1962, which Ball helped draft. This measure cut tariffs by 50% to 100% on many foreign goods and gave the President wide discriminatory powers to retaliate against foreign import restrictions.

In addition to his activities as economic adviser, Ball was concerned with U.S. policy toward the Congo, where the secession of mineral-rich Katanga province shortly after Belgium had granted independence in June 1960 threatened the viability of the central government. Despite his close connection with Western Europe and sympathy for the plight of the Belgians, Ball supported the policy of the State Department's "New Africa" group, led by men such as Harlan Cleveland, which advocated the use of force against Katanga if necessary to achieve reunification. Ball lobbied behind the scenes at the U.N. and within the Administration for the adoption of this policy. Reunification was achieved in January 1963 through the use of U.N. troops backed by American military support.

In November 1961 Ball replaced Chester Bowles as undersecretary of state, the second-ranking position in the State Department. The change was made because of Kennedy's desire to place trusted aides in the State Department, which he felt had not performed effectively, and because of continual clashes between Bowles and Kennedy advisers, particularly Attorney General Robert Kennedy [*q.v.*].

During the Cuban missile crisis of October 1962, Ball served as a member of Excom, the committee of high-ranking advisers formed to counsel the President after the discovery of Soviet offensive missiles in Cuba. After Kennedy proclaimed a "quarantine" of Cuba on Oct. 22, Ball directed the arrangement of a program to inform the allies of the U.S. decision and to write a legal justification of the action.

During the early 1960s Ball became increasingly involved with the growing war in Vietnam. In 1961 when the Administration was discussing policy options in Vietnam, Ball opposed the recommendation of Maxwell Taylor [q.v.] and W. W. Rostow [q.v.] to introduce combat forces into that country because he felt it would lead to an ever-increasing involvement. The recommendation was not approved.

Ball strongly opposed the regime of South Vietnamese President Ngo Dinh Diem and his brother Ngo Dinh Nhu. In August 1963 he urged that American support of the government be withdrawn to force either a change of policy or a coup. Following the August 1963 attack of Nhu's secret police on Buddhist dissidents, Ball, in conjunction with Michael Forrestal, Averell Harriman [q.v.] and Roger Hilsman, drafted the "August 24 Cable" sent to Henry Cabot Lodge [q.v.], the new U.S. ambassador to Vietnam. The message stated that the U.S. could not accept Nhu's crackdown. It also informed Lodge that "Diem must be given [a] chance to rid himself of Nhu" but cautioned that if Diem did not take that step the U.S. "must face the possibility that Diem himself cannot be preserved." Lodge was also instructed to privately inform South Vietnamese generals contemplating a coup that if Nhu remained, the U.S. would "give them direct support in any interim period of breakdown [of the] central government mechanism." The coup failed to take place immediately because of the generals' inability to achieve a favorable balance of forces in the Saigon area and because of doubts about the firmness of U.S. commitments to Diem's overthrow. However, a coup, staged by different military leaders, was eventually carried out in November 1963.

Ball's opposition to American involvement in the war continued during the Johnson Administration. Following the spring 1965 decision to increase troop commitments and launch regular bombing attacks upon North Vietnam, Ball wrote a memorandum in July entitled "Cutting our Losses in South Vietnam," which argued for de-escalation and political compromise. Ball viewed South Vietnam as a "lost cause" because of the lack of popular support for the Saigon regime and the deep commitment of the Communists. He cautioned that continued troop increases would not assure victory.

Ball recommended that the Administration hold forces at current levels while arranging a conference to negotiate a withdrawal. He recognized that America would lose face before its Asian allies, but he felt that the loss would be of short duration and that the U.S. would emerge as a "wiser and more mature nation." If this step were not taken, "humiliation would be more likely than the achievement of our objectives— even after we paid terrible costs."

In January 1966 Ball again wrote a memorandum to Johnson opposing the bombing of North Vietnam because that policy contained "a life and dynamism of its own" and could result in retaliation by Hanoi or involve the U.S. in a war with China. Drawing on his wartime experience he also argued that massive air strikes would strengthen, not weaken, North Vietnamese resolve.

Convinced that he could not change American policy, Ball left office in September 1966 to return to his law firm and to investment banking. In March 1968 Ball served as a member of the Senior Advisory Group on Vietnam. This gathering of "elder statesmen" had been called by President Johnson to advise him on the military's request for over 200,000 additional troops. In their high level meetings Ball continued to press for de-escalation. A majority of Johnson's advisers, fearing the domestic social and political consequences of still another troop increase, now supported the point of view advanced for so long by Ball. On March 31 Johnson announced a policy of gradual de-escalation and a curtailment of the bombing.

A quiet man who remained personally loyal to Johnson and Secretary of State Dean Rusk [q.v.], Ball's determined opposition to the war only became widely known after the publication of the *Pentagon Papers* in 1971.

Ball was one of the leading Democratic critics of the Nixon Administration's Vietnam policy. In a 1969 *Foreign Affairs* article he wrote that the lesson of the Vietnam War was that "there are regions in the world where modern arms cannot be effectively used and thus should never have been committed." "We must never again be beguiled by the false assumption," Ball continued, "that whenever the Western presence is withdrawn . . . a power vacuum is created." Ball recommended in the *New York Times Magazine* that the U.S. "de-escalate the importance of Vietnam." Nixon's Vietnamization policy disturbed Ball. He suggested that the phased withdrawal of American troops would be responsible for the U.S. losing its bargaining strength in possible negotiations and would be interpreted by Hanoi as a signal that Washington could not win the war. Nevertheless, Ball believed that the withdrawal could be a positive step if Washington made it clear that it was now Saigon's responsibility to win the war. If the South Vietnamese failed, the U.S. would thus be absolved from complicity in its defeat.

Ball was equally critical of Nixon's China policy. He supported the Administration overture to Communist China but questioned the need for Nixon's trip in 1972. Arguing that summit conferences tended to accomplish very little, Ball suggested that it would have been better if Secretary of State Henry Kissinger [*q.v.*] negotiated the normalization of relations with China. He was also angered by the Administration's failure to consult Japan. By refusing to involve Tokyo, Ball warned, the U.S. had insulted the proud, fiercely nationalistic Japanese. This blunder could encourage Japan to embark on its own China policy which could be detrimental to American interests.

In his book, *In Diplomacy For A Crowded World* (1976), Ball expressed displeasure with Kissinger for his personal style of diplomacy. He accused the Secretary of State of reducing the importance of the State Department, Congress, and, most important, the European alliance. Ball also criticized detente. He feared that the overselling of detente would lull the West into minimizing the Soviet threat. This would substantially weaken the North Atlantic Treaty Organization. Nevertheless, Ball did endorse the efforts to reach a strategic arms limitation agreement.

In the 1976 presidential campaign, Ball advised a number of presidential aspirants including Jimmy Carter. In 1979 he headed a presidential advisory panel which recommended that the U.S. should withdraw its support from the Shah of Iran.

[JB]

For further information:
David Halberstam, *The Best and the Brightest* (New York, 1972).
U.S. Department of Defense, *The Pentagon Papers*, Senator Gravel Edition (Boston, 1971), Vols. II and IV.

BERLE, ADOLF A(UGUSTUS), JR.

b. Jan. 29, 1895; Boston, Mass.
d. March 17, 1971; New York, N.Y.
Chairman, Interdepartmental Task Force on Latin America, January-July 1961.

The descendant of German liberals who fled to America in the 1850s, Berle received a rigorous education at home and entered Harvard College at the age of 14. After taking a law degree in 1916, he served in Army intelligence during the war and attended the Paris Peace Conference. Moving to New York City, Berle began a long teaching career, mainly at Columbia University, and became involved in a number of liberal causes, particularly in defense of American Indians. In 1932 he and Gardiner C. Means published *The Modern Corporation and Private Property*, an influential work which argued that ownership and control of capitalist enterprise had become divorced, hence concentrating excessive power in the hands of top management. He was one of Franklin D. Roosevelt's original "brain trusters," advising FDR in the 1932 campaign and preparing much of the early New Deal legislation. Until 1938 Berle also was involved in New York City government, where he helped Mayor Fiorello H. La Guardia reorganize the city's finances. He was assistant secretary of state for Latin American affairs through 1944 and then served as ambassador to Brazil, where he supported military insurgents who overthrew the dictatorship of Getulio Vargas in 1945. Since he was both an architect and an instrument of Roosevelt's Good Neighbor Policy, Berle earned a popularity in Latin America unusual for a North American.

During the 1950s Berle confined himself to his law practice, to his activity with the New York State Liberal Party and to participation in some of the studies sponsored by the Rockefeller Brothers Fund. Following the November 1960 elections, John F. Kennedy asked Berle to head a six-man task force designed to make recommendations on both immediate Latin American problems and long-range policy.

The recommendations, made in January 1961, found their most significant expression in the new Administration's Alliance for Progress, which marked a change from the Latin American policy pursued in the Eisenhower-Dulles years. The task force report, reflecting Berle's fear of Castro's Cuba, stated that the Communists intended to "convert the Latin American social revolution into a Marxist attack on the United States itself." Believing that the social revolution was inevitable, Berle advised the U.S. to decrease its support of right-wing dictatorships and openly support democratic-progressive political movements. To Berle, Latin America in 1960 resembled Europe in 1947. The situation called for a new Marshall Plan to defeat the Communist effort to bring the Cold War to this hemisphere. Although Berle wanted a massive economic and military aid program for Latin America, he emphasized the need for a dynamic ideology and philosophy to guide

U.S. policy and counter the Communists. The Alliance was intended to be a more vigorous version of the Good Neighbor Policy.

In his autobiography Berle wrote that Richard N. Goodwin, Kennedy's special assistant, had talked to him about becoming assistant secretary of state for Latin American affairs in December 1960, but Berle felt that he was too old for a "third-string office." His task force, in fact, advised that a State Department undersecretaryship for the Western Hemisphere be set up, "thus ending stepchild status of this area in U.S. policy." Berle, however, decided to serve as head of an interdepartmental task force on Latin America with authority at least equal to that of an assistant secretary of state. The task force was to be directly responsible to the President and the Secretary of State.

Berle served in his new post from January through July of 1961. He played no role in planning the Bay of Pigs invasion, although his advice was occasionally solicited. He wrote that he "did not dissent," although he disliked the covert nature of the Central Intelligence Agency's (CIA) plan and the Agency's indifference to the politics of the Cuban exiles whom they trained. Berle preferred that the U.S. government and the CIA aid only those Cuban exiles who had been part of the 26th of July Movement, which he thought Castro had betrayed. He devoted much of the first three months explaining U.S. policy on Cuba to Latin American heads of state and to the Cuban exile groups.

When Berle left his post in July, he was on good terms with Kennedy but was disturbed that the State Department was so slow in implementing new policies. He had also warned the U.S. to take more forceful action against Castro with the cooperation of the other American nations, but he found that the Inter-American machinery, particularly the Organization of American States, was ineffective. Berle remained active until his death, writing on Latin America and economics, offering his advice to the government and participating in New York City politics.

[JCH]

For further information:
Adolf A. Berle, Jr., *Latin America: Diplomacy and Reality* (New York, 1962).
Beatrice Bishop Berle and Travis Beal Jacobs, eds., *Navigating the Rapids, 1919-1971: From the Papers of Adolf A. Berle* (New York, 1973).

BRICKER, JOHN W(ILLIAM)
b. Sept. 6, 1893; Madison Co., Ohio.
Republican Senator, Ohio, 1947-59;
Chairman, Senate Commerce Committee, 1953-55.

John W. Bricker grew up in rural Madison Co., Ohio, and received his B.A. from Ohio State University in 1916. During World War I he served as an Army chaplain. After the war he entered local politics and in 1938 he was elected governor of Ohio. In 1946 Bricker was elected to the Senate, where he became a major supporter of Senator Robert Taft (R, Ohio).

In 1953 Bricker challenged the Eisenhower Administration when he sponsored an amendment to restrict the federal government's treaty-making powers. He had advocated such a proposal since the Truman Administration. As reported by the Judiciary Committee in June 1953, the Bricker amendment first voided any provision of treaties which conflicted with the Constitution. Second, it stipulated that treaties, executive agreements and international organizations could not determine domestic policy (i.e., a body such as the U.N. could not make social policy) without accompanying federal or state legislation. Known as the "which clause," this section raised the possibility that a single state could nullify an international compact. More importantly, the amendment delimited Congress's powers. Because of a 1920 Supreme Court ruling, Congress appeared empowered to extend its authority over states in enacting social legislation whenever it was carrying out the obligations of a treaty. Bricker's article would have prevented Congress from passing laws—as argued, for example, by some civil rights advocates—on the basis of that court precedent. Finally, the amendment made all executive understandings with foreign powers subject to Senate ratification. Bricker and other Republican nationalists had condemned Franklin D. Roosevelt's secret World War II agreements with the Soviet Union. They identified undisclosed, undebated understandings with Russian expansion into Eastern Europe immediately after the War. The Ohioan had long been a foe of those he called "One Worlders," generally liberal easterners like Eleanor Roosevelt, who promoted international agreements in social and economic policy. Repeatedly, Bricker worked against American funding of the U.N.'s International Labor Organization or its International Atomic Energy Commission. The U.N.'s Covenant on Human Rights particularly incensed Bricker. This covenant, under negotiation between 1948 and 1954, included provisions that suspended such rights as freedom of speech during times of national emergency.

The fight for the Bricker amendment quickly evolved into a mass crusade. Many associations had long advocated a clarification of the statuatory effect of treaties and world organizations upon domestic law. The 1952 Republican platform had endorsed Bricker's article, as had Taft, the American Bar Association (ABA) and especially its past president, Frank E. Holman. Besides the ABA, pro-amendment associations included the American Farm Bureau, American Legion and the Daughters of the American Revolution. Special committees like the Vigilant Women for the Bricker Amendment organized spontaneously. Viewing it as a defense of states rights, Southerners opposed to federal civil rights legislation overwhelmingly backed the proposal.

The most pronounced critics of the measure tended to be liberal, long-standing internationalists. Championing a strong chief executive, they deemed the Bricker amendment a hazardous weakening of presidential powers. Amendment foes also viewed the mass movement for the article as "new isolationism," a variation of that stand more widely held in the 1920s and 1930s.

Mindful of a growing public debate that

threatened party unity, Eisenhower initially refused to take a stand on the issue. His biographer Emmet J. Hughes claimed that the Bricker matter upset the President more than any other single crisis of his presidency. The amendment, Eisenhower complained one day, "is a damn thorn in our side." Secretary of State John Foster Dulles [q.v.], who had called for "some" sort of treaty-making amendment in 1952, urged Eisenhower to oppose Bricker's proposal.

In January 1954 the Administration declared itself opposed to the Bricker amendment. Eisenhower stated publicly in January that ratification would signal America's intention "to withdraw from its leadership in world affairs." His chief aide, Sherman Adams, recalled that the President had become "thoroughly disgusted with what he now considered a direct attempt to undermine the constitutional structure of the executive branch." The Administration assigned at least one lobbyist for each Republican senator.

The Administration beat Bricker but barely. On Feb. 26, 1954, a milder version, sponsored by Sen. Walter F. George (D, Ga.) and also opposed by the White House, fell one vote short of the required two-thirds majority. One day earlier, Bricker's original amendment had lost 42-50. Bricker inexplicably abandoned his crusade thereafter; though he reintroduced the article in 1955, he never again labored strenuously for it.

In 1958 Bricker unexpectedly lost his Senate seat. He had originally planned to retire from politics, but Eisenhower, despite the amendment quarrel, urged him to seek a third term. Bricker agreed to run but lost because of a "right-to-work" referendum on the ballot. After his election defeat, Bricker practiced law in Columbus, Ohio.

[JLB]

BUNDY, McGEORGE
b. March 30, 1919; Boston, Mass.
Special Assistant to the President for National Security Affairs, January 1961-February 1966.

Born into a distinguished New England family, Bundy grew up in a household where discussion of domestic policy and foreign affairs was a daily routine. His father, Harvey Bundy, had worked closely with Henry L. Stimson during several tours of high government service. Stimson proved a great influence on the younger Bundy, instilling in him a consciousness of the power of his class and the importance of disinterested public service.

A brilliant scholar, Bundy graduated first in his class from the Groton School and first from Yale in 1940. In 1941 he became a junior fellow at Harvard University. Bundy served in the Army during World War II and participated in the planning of the invasions of Sicily and France. Following his discharge in 1946, he helped Stimson research and write his autobiography. In April 1948 Bundy went to Washington to work for the agency responsible for implementing the Marshall Plan. He left government in September to join Thomas Dewey's presidential campaign as a foreign policy adviser. Following Dewey's defeat Bundy became a political analyst for the prestigious Council on Foreign Relations.

In 1949 Bundy was appointed a lecturer in government at Harvard, teaching a course in modern foreign policy that reflected many of Stimson's ideas. A teacher whose force of mind impressed those he met, Bundy rose rapidly within the department, becoming a full professor in 1954 without the usual academic credentials necessary for the position. The year before, Bundy had been appointed dean of arts and sciences, the second-ranking position at Harvard. There, as in other fields, he proved his ability through the adroit handling of the University's complicated bureaucracy and a faculty noted for its independent spirit.

A nominal Republican, Bundy backed Eisenhower in 1952 and 1956. However, he withdrew his support of the Republican Party after its 1960 nomination of Richard M. Nixon [q.v.]. Instead, Bundy helped organize a scientific and professional committee in support of Sen. John F. Kennedy. Following his election, Kennedy, impressed with Bundy's intellectual brilliance, organizational ability and philosophical pragmatism, offered him several positions in the State and Defense Departments and on the U.S. disarmament team. Bundy was not interested in these appointments but accepted one as the President's special assistant for national security affairs.

Bundy's position suited his philosophical background and prior experience. He was, in the words of Joseph Kraft, an "organizer of process," more interested in the process of informed decision-making than in advocating particular policies. It was Bundy's job to gather information from the Defense and State Departments and the intelligence agencies and present them to the President in a concise fashion. More importantly, he also controlled access to the President. These functions gave him great power in determining what issues received priority and the policy options from which Kennedy could choose. Bundy was also responsible for organizing the meetings of the National Security Council and helped assemble the task forces that Kennedy often used in place of State Department officials to deal with special diplomatic problems. Because of Bundy's background he generally drew men from the ranks of the academic and business establishments for these assignments and thus indirectly determined how many situations would be approached.

Bundy's influence became even greater following the April 1961 Bay of Pigs invasion. Angered by what he considered the State Department's poor advice during the months prior to the attack, Kennedy began relying more and more upon Bundy for foreign policy information and counsel. At Kennedy's urging Bundy reorganized and streamlined his staff and gathered at the White House a group of scholars and intellectuals such as Carl Kaysen and Ralph Dungan who later became important forces in formulating Administration foreign policy. Bundy also set up a communications system that equaled those of the State and Defense Departments and permitted him to have the information available to these bureaucracies. By the end of 1961 he had come close to achieving what Arthur Schlesinger, Jr. [q.v.], described as Kennedy's desire to have a small

semi-secret office to run foreign affairs "while maintaining the State Department as a facade . . . ." Bundy became, in Kennedy's words, one of his "inner circle," the very small group of advisers who the President consulted daily and whose counsel he trusted in times of crisis.

The role Bundy played in the Kennedy Administration was most evident during the Cuban missile crisis of 1962. Late in the afternoon of Oct. 15 Bundy was informed of the presence of Soviet missiles in Cuba. He delayed telling the President about this until the next morning, ostensibly to give the intelligence agencies time to compile all necessary data and to permit Kennedy to rest before dealing with a potential nuclear confrontation. Bundy was then instructed to set up the meetings of the Excom, a special panel to advise the President and gain bipartisan support for Administration action. This group included many men with long experience in foreign affairs, among them Dean Acheson [q.v.], Robert Lovett [q.v.] and John J. McCloy [q.v.].

At the meetings Bundy was anxious to keep the process of decision-making open until all policy ramifications had been explored. At the Oct. 17 meeting when majority sentiment seemed to favor an air strike to remove the missiles, Bundy advocated using a diplomatic approach. Two days later when sentiment favored a blockade, Bundy advocated an armed strike. Because a blockade was technically an act of war, Kennedy instituted a "quarantine" of Cuba on Oct. 23.

In the early 1960s Bundy began an involvement in Vietnam affairs that would grow during the remainder of his government service. Following the August 1963 attack on Buddhist dissidents by the regime of Ngo Dinh Diem, the Kennedy Administration began a reevaluation of American policy toward the South Vietnamese government. During the two-month debate on the subject, some advisers, such as Roger Hilsman advocated U.S. withdrawal of support in hope of precipitating a coup. Others, such as Secretary of Defense Robert McNamara [q.v.], insisted that the U.S. continue to support Diem but demand governmental reform. Bundy believed that the U.S. should not thwart any coup that seemed potentially successful but should have the "option of judging and warning on any plan with poor prospects of success." On Nov. 1 South Vietnamese generals staged a successful coup. The U.S. had given no direct aid to the rebels but made no move to stop the change in government.

Unlike many of Kennedy's close associates, Bundy did not leave government following the assassination. Instead, asserting that he served the presidency, not the president, he remained at the White House as an adviser to Johnson. Despite initially cool relations between the two men, Bundy eventually became one of Johnson's closest foreign policy consultants. Bundy considered himself a pragmatist and was, therefore, anxious to base American policy on reactions to specific situations rather than on what he believed were long-term commitments prompted by ideological abstractions. Consequently, much of his counsel was directed at advising the President of all possible policy options and in keeping choices open until a major decision was unavoidable.

Bundy frequently served as Johnson's personal representative on important fact-finding and troubleshooting missions. In May 1965 Johnson sent him to the Dominican Republic to find a solution to the crisis precipitated by a civil war between leftists and a rightist military junta. After the April landing of American troops to prevent what the President thought would be a Communist takeover, the U.S. ambassador and the military had supported the junta. This policy threatened to continue the conflict and increase American involvement. Bundy forced the American military into genuine neutrality and initiated negotiations on the formation of a coalition government. At the last minute his plan collapsed because the junta refused to participate. However, Ellsworth Bunker successfully worked out similar arrangements in August.

As the Johnson Administration became increasingly absorbed by Vietnam, Bundy became an important force in policy formation. During early 1964 he was on the periphery of decision-making, helping to direct the targeting of South Vietnamese torpedo-boat raids against the North. These missions, known as 34A operations, were theoretically independent efforts by the South Vietnamese, but they were in fact planned and initiated by the U.S. military command and high-level officials in Washington.

Bundy's role in the Administration's reappraisal of U.S. policy during late 1964 is a matter of historical controversy. The reassessment was carried out in November by the National Security Council Working Group under the leadership of Bundy's brother William [q.v.]. The Group recommended an extensive air campaign against the North, with the intensity of raids varying with the rate of Communist troop infiltration and military action in the South. Journalists such as David Halberstam have suggested that McGeorge Bundy did not take a stand on bombing during the debate. However, Ralph Stavins has maintained the McGeorge Bundy was an early proponent of increased bombing but was told to mute his advocacy until after the presidential election.

By January 1965 Bundy had become convinced that the President would have to make a decision on further U.S. action within the near future. In his opinion both the military effort and the political situation in Saigon had deteriorated to such an extent that a major American commitment was necessary if South Vietnam were to remain a viable nation. The decision was, to Bundy, a litmus test of America's readiness to save the rest of Southeast Asia. He believed a formidable effort was important to maintain the world's trust in American willingness to prevent the spread of world Communism.

Following a trip to Vietnam in early February, Bundy recommended that the U.S. adopt the plan suggested by the Working Group. According to Lyndon Johnson, Bundy opposed any attempt to negotiate a withdrawal on the grounds that it would mean "surrender on the installment plan." President Johnson approved the plan in February, and the bombing raids, called Operation Rolling Thunder, began in March. During the remainder of his stay at the White House, Bundy reviewed targets for the raids and became a leading spokesman for the Administration's policy in Vietnam.

Bundy was unable to accommodate himself to Lyndon Johnson's style of dealing with advisers and therefore resigned in December 1965. Over the next two years he did not dissociate himself from American Vietnam policy, but in early 1967 he wrote a private letter to Johnson opposing further escalation of the war as counterproductive. During a symposium held at DePauw University in October 1968, Bundy, whose counsel had contributed to large-scale involvement in Vietnam, called for lowering the cost of the conflict and systematic reduction of the number of American troops there.

Following his resignation from the White House staff, Bundy became president of the Ford Foundation. He left his position in 1979 to teach at New York University.

[EWS]

For further information:
Leslie Gelb, *The Irony of Vietnam* (Washington, 1979).

BUNDY, WILLIAM P(UTNAM)
b. Sept. 24, 1917; Washington, D.C.
Deputy Assistant Secretary of Defense for International Security Affairs, January 1961-October 1963; Assistant Secretary of Defense for International Security Affairs, October 1963-February 1964; Assistant Secretary of State for Far Eastern Affairs, February 1964-March 1969.

William Bundy, one of the prime architects of the Johnson Administration's policy in Southeast Asia, was born into a socially and politically prominent New England family. A brilliant student, he was educated at Groton and Yale, graduating from the latter in 1939. After serving in the

Army during the war, Bundy received his law degree from Harvard in 1947 and entered the prestigious Washington law firm of Covington and Burling. Three years later he joined the Central Intelligence Agency, where he was put in charge of overall evaluation of international intelligence.

In 1960 Bundy became staff director of the President's Commission on National Goals, which had been founded to formulate broad, long-term objectives and programs.

President Kennedy appointed Bundy deputy assistant secretary of defense in charge of international security affairs in January 1961. In this post he was responsible for coordinating military aid programs throughout the world. In the fall of 1962, when Communist China invaded disputed areas on its border with India, Bundy organized the shipment of American arms to India and attempted to get other U.S. allies to supply that country.

Although his role in Vietnam policymaking was less well-known than that of his brother McGeorge, William Bundy was an important figure in America's growing involvement in the war. In the fall of 1961 he was one of the officials who analyzed South Vietnam's request for a bilateral defense treaty and increased American military aid. Bundy recommended "an early, hard-hitting operation" to arrest Communist expansion. However, President Kennedy decided to send only support troops and equipment in November 1961.

Bundy carried his hawkish views to the State Department when he became assistant secretary of state for Far Eastern affairs in February 1964. As the political and military situation in Vietnam deteriorated in the fall of 1964, President Johnson ordered the National Security Council Working Group, led by Bundy and John McNaughton, to review operations and make recommendations on the future course of the war. The panel was asked to determine the pace of future bombing in North Vietnam, which until then had been carried out only in retaliation for specific attacks on American bases. The committee was also told to investigate the need for increased American ground forces and to analyze the relationship between U.S. military strategy and its overall political goals.

In its report, completed at the end of November, the Group recommended aerial attacks on the North, their intensity to vary with the level of Communist infiltration and the pace of the war in the South. The panel based its recommendation on the belief that an American defeat in Vietnam would make the defense of the rest of Southeast Asia extremely difficult. Bundy did not support the domino theory, which held that if Vietnam fell the rest of Southeast Asia would shortly become Communist. However, he calculated that a Communist takeover would be probable by the end of a decade.

The panel did not believe that the use of air power would settle the war but rather saw the bombing strikes as a means of upholding and improving South Vietnamese morale. In Bundy's estimation the prospect was "for a prolonged period without major strikes or escalation, but without any give by Hanoi." He rejected a negotiated settlement at this time because he believed it would neither lead to a stable peace nor help South Vietnamese morale.

Johnson adopted the committee's proposals in February 1965. These recommendations determined the course of the war until July 1965, when the Administration committed extensive ground forces to the conflict. In the months that followed the decision to launch what was known as Operation Rolling Thunder, Bundy was one of the officials responsible for choosing targets for the bombing campaign.

Despite his support of bombing Bundy was reluctant to back the large-scale introduction of American troops, fearing that the U.S. would have the same experience as the French in Indochina. However, once the decision was made he supported the position and eventually became a leading defender of the Administration's policy.

During the years that followed the introduction of systematic bombing raids, Bundy helped formulate the conditions under which the U.S. would halt the attacks and begin peace negotiations. In May 1966 he submitted a memorandum to Secretary of State Dean Rusk [q.v.] that served as a guideline for U.S. policy until 1969. In this paper bombing was seen as a means of driving North Vietnam to the negotiating table. The U.S. would stop bombing only if North Vietnam agreed to limit infiltration and end Communist action in the South. A halt in return for an agreement to negotiate was considered unacceptable.

In the spring of 1967 Bundy opposed the continued escalation of the conflict, and particularly the proposed mining of Haiphong harbor, on the grounds that such action would not change Hanoi's position but would have an adverse effect on relations with U.S. allies. Further buildups, he believed, would also convince the South Vietnamese that the U.S. could win the war without their all out support. Despite the lack of progress in the war, he argued against negotiations as useless and, instead, favored "sticking it out if necessary."

Bundy left the government in March 1969 to become a visiting professor at the Massachusetts Institute of Technology's Center for International Studies. In 1972 he became editor of *Foreign Affairs*.

[EWS]

For further information:
U.S. Department of Defense, *The Pentagon Papers*, Senator Gravel edition (Boston, 1971), Vols. III and IV.

BYRNES, JAMES F(RANCIS)
b. May 2, 1879; Charleston, S.C.
d. April 9, 1972: Columbia, S.C.
Secretary of State, July 1945-January 1947; Governor, S.C., 1951-55
1951-55.

Byrnes, the son of Irish immigrants, was apprenticed as a law clerk at 14 and worked as a court stenographer at 21. In 1903 he was admitted to South Carolina bar and purchased the *Aiken* (S.C.) *Journal and Review*, which he edited for four years. Byrnes ran successfully for solicitor of the second judicial court in 1908.

Two years later he won a seat in the U.S. House, where he served until 1925. He was elected to the U.S. Senate in 1930. During the early New Deal Byrnes emerged as one of Franklin D. Roosevelt's chief legislative tacticians. An innately optimistic man with the talent for finding compromises, he helped gain Southern support for key New Deal measures, despite his reservation about increasing the power of the federal government. As Roosevelt's recovery program became more radical, Byrnes joined the Democratic opposition to the New Deal. However, he continued to support Roosevelt's foreign policy, vigorously pushing for repeal of the Neutrality Act and the passage of lend-lease. In 1941 Roosevelt named Byrnes to the Supreme Court.

Sixteen months later Byrnes resigned to head the Office of Economic Stabilization, the wartime agency charged with keeping a lid on inflation. In 1943 Byrnes became director of the Office of War Mobilization. Known as the "assistant President on the home front," he supervised the production of war and consumer goods, thus releasing Roosevelt to devote his attention to fighting the war and planning for peace. Government officials, the press and the public all praised Byrnes for his administrative ability. His reputation as a compromiser enabled him to work closely with Congress and the confused bureaucracy Roosevelt had established to run the war effort. As the election of 1944 drew closer, it seemed certain that Roosevelt would not choose Vice President Henry Wallace [q.v.] to run again, and Byrnes became one of the front runners for the second spot. When Roosevelt chose Harry Truman, Byrnes felt cheated.

Byrnes accompanied Roosevelt to the Yalta Conference in April 1944 and played a major role in getting Congress to accept the agreements reached there. Before the Conference ended Byrnes returned to the U.S. and, in a series of conferences with congressional leaders, explained and justified the "Declaration of Liberated Europe" which reaffirmed the principles of the Atlantic Charter and called for the formation of provisional governments in Eastern Europe representing all parties. The Declaration also pledged the establishment of free elections. Reaction from the press and Congress was initially favorable.

Following the retirement of Edward Stettinius [q.v.] in July 1945, Truman appointed Byrnes Secretary of State. Truman realized that because of the presidential succession law, Byrnes would be next in line for the presidency. Since Byrnes had had extensive administrative experience and knew Congress well, he was a wise choice for that position. Truman also later acknowledged that he had chosen Byrnes out of guilt over receiving the vice presidential nomination in 1944.

From the beginning of his tenure, Byrnes had difficulty working with Truman. Intent on being a strong Secretary of State and used to having virtual autonomy from the President, Byrnes often acted as an independent agent. He refused to keep Truman informed of events on a regular basis. Byrnes also failed to establish a close working relationship with the State Department. His reluctance to consult subordinates, frequent absences at international conferences and poor administrative ability undermined morale in the Department.

Byrnes and Truman initially approached foreign policy with two objectives in mind—to maintain the wartime alliance and restrain the Soviet Union in Eastern Europe. They both saw Soviet leaders not as ideologues anxious to assert a philosophy but as fellow politicans willing to compromise. Unable to understand the Soviet Union's desire for security on its Eastern border, they pushed for a postwar settlement that would result in the revitalization of Germany, the withdrawal of Soviet troops from occupied lands and the establishment of representive government in Eastern Europe.

Byrnes accompanied Truman to the Potsdam Conference called, among other reasons, to establish a reparation policy for Germany and to discuss a settlement of the Eastern European question. Determined not to permit German restoration to become a burden on the U.S., Byrnes negotiated a reparation settlement that permitted the taking of reparations only after imports essential to maintain the German economy had been paid for. The final agreement permitted the occupying powers to take what they wanted only from their own sections. Great Britain and the U.S. granted the Soviet Union from their zones 10% of "such industrial capital equipment as is unnecessary for the German peace economy." The Soviet Union was also given an additional 15% in return for food and other commodities from its zone. In return for this agreement, however, Truman and Brynes had to transfer part of Eastern Germany to Poland. Efforts to secure Stalin's stronger commitment to the Declaration of Liberated Europe also failed.

The reparations agreement helped solidify a divided Germany. Many leading Americans at the Conference came away ambivalent about future cooperation with the Soviet Union. Byrnes, however, maintained that the agreement reflected the realities of the situation in Eastern Europe and felt confident about future negotiations. This assurance was reinforced by America's successful use of the atomic bomb against Japan. America's monopoly on the weapon would, Byrnes asserted, "make Russia more manageable in Europe." The Secretary did not intend to use the bomb as a threat. But he did hope to hinge an agreement on nuclear disarmament on Soviet concessions in Eastern Europe.

The London Conference of foreign ministers, held in September, surprised and disappointed Byrnes. The Russians demanded U.S. recognition of Soviet imposed governments in Rumania and Bulgaria. Byrnes, in turn, reiterated U.S. willingness to see governments friendly to Moscow in the area, but maintained that they must be democratically elected. The two parties remained deadlocked. U.S. atomic power, upon which Byrnes had placed so much reliance, proved an ineffective weapon. The Soviets seemed to almost go out of their way to ignore it. In addition, Truman undermined Byrnes's position when, on Oct. 3, he implied that the U.S. was committed to international control. Upon his return to the U.S. Byrnes warned, "we are facing a new Russia, totally different than the Russia we dealt with a year ago. . . . Now that the war was over they [are] taking an aggressive attitude and stand on political and territorial questions that [is] indefensible." Publicly however, the Secretary maintained a conciliatory posture.

During the fall Byrnes was unwillingly drawn into the growing debate on international control of atomic energy. Believing that the U.S. monopoly on the atomic bomb would make Russia easier to deal with, he opposed discussing this subject until the European peace treaties had been signed. After Truman committed himself to eventual international control in October, Byrnes managed to delay discussion for a time. Nevertheless, by November he had been pushed into beginning discussions in preparation for impending talks with the British and Canadians. The U.S. proposal, drawn up over a weekend by Vannevar Bush, called for the establishment of a U.N. Commission that would work for the control of atomic energy to ensure its peaceful uses, the elimination of nuclear weapons, and the establishment of effective safeguards to protect complying nations against violations. The accord was approved in November.

That month Byrnes pressed for another meeting with the Soviets to solve the Rumanian and Bulgarian questions. Having put aside his reservations about the Soviet Union, he hoped that he could reach a compromise with the Russians on the issue. In Moscow Byrnes won Soviet acceptance of the American atomic energy plan. He also worked out an agreement with Stalin to broaden the Rumanian and Bulgarian governments. This made it possible for Byrnes to justify extending diplomatic relations to the two states and permitted the negotiations on peace treaties with the Eastern European nations to continue. In return, the U.S. made token concessions on Japan, permitting the Russians to play a role in the occupation without jeopardizing American authority.

Although the press initially reacted favorably to the agreements, Byrnes's compromises met with a storm of protests. Powerful congressional Republicans who had long resented Byrnes's failure to consult them on foreign policy and had feared his tendency to compromise, lashed out at the accord. Sen. Arthur Vandenberg (R, Mich.) [q.v.] termed it "one more typical American 'give away'." The President, too, was angered by the agreement and the manner in which it was concluded. Byrnes, he said, had "lost his nerve at Moscow." His anger was fanned by the Secretary's refusal to keep him informed during the Conference and by Byrnes's public presentation of the results before reporting to the President.

In response to congressional pressure, changing public opinion and the recommendations of such Soviet experts as George Kennan [q.v.], the Administration moved toward a policy of confrontation with the Soviet Union. Rather than compromise, Byrnes proposed "patience with firmness." The Secretary first formally expressed this hardened policy in February 1946 during a speech to the Overseas Press Club. He denounced the Soviets for stationing troops in Eastern Europe, refusing to negotiate peace treaties and seizing enemy property before reparation agreements were made. Byrnes concluded, "If we are to be a great power we must act as a great power, not only in order to ensure our own security but in order to preserve the peace of the world."

The manner in which Byrnes handled the Iranian crisis the following month confirmed the Administration's new policy. When the deadlock for Soviet withdrawal of troops from Iran passed, Byrnes demanded an immediate withdrawal. Throughout March the U.S. kept pressure on the USSR through diplomatic channels and at the U.N. When the Soviet Union asked that the question be withdrawn from Security Council debate in return

for a promise to withdraw troops within five or six weeks, Byrnes refused. The issue was resolved only after the Soviets and Iranians announced a formal agreement.

The Secretary continued his hardline policy throughout the summer. While at the Paris Peace Conference Byrnes, according to one observer, "gave the impression of a clever politician determined not to give an inch." During the Conference Byrnes attempted to push for a four-power accord guaranteeing the disarmament of Germany as a means of testing the Soviet objectives in the area. The Soviets rejected the proposal. Byrnes, convinced that Russia would not live up to the Potsdam agreements on the eventual unification of that nation, moved toward the establishment of a divided Germany as an alternative to a Russian dominated state. In an important reversal of the American position which had stressed unification, Byrnes announced in September 1946, "If complete unification cannot be secured, we shall do everything in our power to secure maximum possible unification." He warned, "We do not want Germany to become a satellite of any power. Therefore, as long as there is an occupation army in Germany, American armed forces will be part of that occupation army."

Discouraged by continued criticism that he was an appeaser, Byrnes left the State Department in January 1947. The year and a half he served proved to be a difficult period in his life. The response to the Moscow compromise hurt him, and his constant traveling isolated him from policy formulation. In addition, Byrnes, a segregationist and an economic conservative, did not want to continue to be associated with an Administration he considered pro-civil rights and too liberal. Byrnes remained in Washington practicing law and occasionally delivering speeches condemning the Administration's domestic policies.

In 1950 Byrnes, then 70 years old, won the governorship of South Carolina on a states' rights platform. During his four years in office, Byrnes attempted to preserve segregation in the state. Unable to succeed himself, he retired in 1955. Byrnes died in 1972 at the age of 92.

[JB]

For further information:
James F. Byrnes, *Speaking Freely* (New York, 1947).
————, *All In A Lifetime* (New York, 1958).
George F. Curry, *James F. Byrnes* (New York, 1965).

CHURCH, FRANK (FORRESTER)
b. July 25, 1924; Boise, Ida.
Democratic Senator, Ida. 1957-

Frank Church, a 1950 graduate of the Stanford University Law School, practiced law in his native city of Boise until elected to the Senate in 1956. As a member of the Foreign Relations Committee, Church advocated reduced foreign aid expenditures. He called for a phasing out of aid to prosperous Western European nations and Japan. He also urged an end to military assistance to nations like India, Pakistan, Greece and Turkey that seemed likely to engage in future hostilities.

Church was critical of U.S. military involvement in South Vietnam and in 1963 opposed aiding the regime of Ngo Dinh Diem. In June 1965 he called for direct negotiations with the National Liberation Front, free elections in South Vietnam and a scaling down of the U.S. war effort. Nevertheless, during 1965 and 1966 he voted for the supplemental arms appropriations bills necessary for sustaining the war effort. In May 1967 Church drafted a letter signed by 16 anti-war senators warning the North Vietnamese that "our objective is the settlement of the war at the conference table, not the repudiation of American commitments already made to South Vietnam or the unilateral withdrawal of American forces from that embattled country." In 1969 Church coauthored a bill to prohibit the use of U.S. ground combat troops in Laos and Thailand.

During the Nixon Administration, Church, fearing an expansion of the war, began to campaign to get Congress to use its funding power to force the President to seek peace in Asia. In the spring of 1970, Church and Sen. John Sherman Cooper (R, Ky.) introduced an amendment to a foreign military sales bill barring funds for future military operations in Cambodia. Capitalizing on the outrage many in the nation expressed toward the escalation of the war into Cambodia, Church and his supporters got the amendment passed by the Foreign Relations Committee. After a seven week filibuster, the Senate passed it in late June by the vote of 58 to 37. The House, however, rejected the measure. A watered down version was passed in December as part of a defense appropriation bill. The rider prevented the introduction of ground troops into Laos or Thailand. The adoption of the Cooper-Church amendment represented the first limitation ever voted on the President's power as commander-in-chief during a war situation.

In April 1972 Church, this time joined by Sen. Clifford Case (R. N.J.) introduced an amendment to a State Department appropriations bill authorizing a cutoff of funds for all U.S. combat operations in Indochina after Dec. 31 subject to an agreement for the release of American prisoners of war. The Foreign Relations Committee and the Democratic Party Caucus approved the Church-Case Amendment, but the Senate reduced its effectiveness by attaching a rider which made it effective only if an internationally supervised ceasefire was negotiated.

Church also questioned other Administration defense and foreign policies. He called for a reduction of American troops in Western Europe. Church voted against the deployment of the anti-ballistic missile system, backed ending the construction of the C5A plane, and opposed arms aid to repressive regimes.

In January 1975 the Senate created a bipartisan, select committee to investigate alleged abuses by the Central Intelligence Agency, the Federal Bureau of Investigation and other government intelligence and law enforcement agencies. Church was selected chairman. Over the next year and a half the Church committee heard testimony from cabinet heads, top military officials, the leadership of the CIA and the FBI, retired intelligence operatives and those Americans who felt victimized by the unconstitutional activities of both organizations. Among other things, the probe revealed CIA involvement in plots to assassinate world leaders and in the coup against Chile's Marxist president Salvador Allende. It also uncovered a series of covert operations by the FBI against organizations J. Edgar Hoover had considered radical.

In a November 1975 letter to Church, President Ford requested that the panel not make its assassination report public because it would "do grievous damage to our country," and be "exploited by foreign nations and groups hostile to the United States." Church responded that the Committee's intention to make the report public had "long been clear." Moreover, he felt the national interest would be "better served by letting the American people know the true and complete story" behind the death plots. The committee's report charged the U.S. government had ordered the assassination of two foreign leaders—Fidel Castro and Patrice Lumumba—and had been involved in assassination plots against three other foreign officials—Raphaelo Trujillo, Ngo Dinh Diem and Rene Schneider. Although four of the five leaders were assassinated, none of them died as the direct results of the plans initiated by U.S. officials.

In 1976 Church made an unsuccessful bid for the Democratic presidential nomination. Following his defeat, he continued to be one of the leading liberal spokesmen in the Senate.

[JB]

CLAY, LUCIUS D(uBIGNON)
b. April 23, 1897; Marietta, Ga.
d. April 16, 1978; Chatham, Mass.
Deputy Military Governor of Germany (U.S. Zone), March 1946-March 1947; Military Governor of Germany (U.S. Zone), March 1947-May 1949.

Great grandnephew of Henry Clay and son of a U.S. senator, Clay followed a military career. He graduated from West Point in 1918 and during the next two decades was an Army engineer. During World War II he coordinated the production and procurement of Army supplies as director of materiel. In 1944 he became deputy director for war programs and general administrator in the Office of War Mobilization and Reconversion.

In March 1945 Clay was appointed deputy to Gen. Dwight D. Eisenhower [q.v.], supreme commander of Allied forces, with the understanding that upon Germany's surrender he would be placed in charge of the American occupation.

As the war drew to a close, Clay emerged as a leading advocate of a lenient policy toward the vanquished enemy. Along with Secretary of War Henry L. Stimson and Assistant Secretary John J. McCloy [q.v.], he became increasingly concerned about the danger that the Soviet Union presented to postwar Europe. They therefore favored the establishment of an economically and politically strong Germany as soon as possible as a citadel against Soviet expansion. In May 1945 Clay protested Joint Chiefs of Staff order 1067/6 which reflected the harsh position advocated by Secretary of the Treasury Henry Morgenthau. The directive precluded the occupation from becoming involved in the rehabilitation and maintenance of the German economy except to maximize agriculture. Only the production of light consumer goods was to be encouraged. Clay asserted that the directive had failed to deal with the economic realities of the situation. Germany, he maintained, would have to revive its industrial production immediately for it would starve unless it could produce for export. As the Cold War developed through the balance of 1945 and into 1946, Clay gained allies for his position. By the time he assumed full responsibility of the occupation, the Administration supported a resurgent Germany as a barrier to the Soviet Union.

The American military commander saw the creation of the German state as occurring in two stages: the development of local government and the economic reunification of the British, French and American zones. He moved quickly to meet his first goal. Elections were held during the first half of 1946. By December each of the states in the American Zone had ratified constitutions and elected state parliaments. During the spring of 1946 Clay pushed for the unification of the French, British and American zones. The French demurred, fearing an industrialized, strong Germany, but during the next year and a half extensive administrative and economic unification was achieved in the British and American zones. The most important step toward economic unification was the introduction of a common currency in 1948. This action had been planned for several years. The French at first resisted but acquiesced when Clay, after extensive negotiations and some compromise, threatened to go forward without them. The new currency was introduced to the Western zones on June 20 and to the Western zones of Berlin three days later. It was this last action and the clear indication it gave that the Western powers intended to go forward with the creation of a West German state with the inclusion of West Berlin that prompted the Soviets to blockade Berlin on June 24.

The Soviets had made clear for some time that they would cut off Berlin should the new currency be introduced there. As soon as they acted, Clay called for the city to be supplied by air. Over the next year he became a leading advocate of waiting out the Soviets. He resisted suggestions from Washington that he slow the pace of currency reform or negotiate the issue, believing that U.S. prestige was at stake. He did not think that the Soviets wanted war over Berlin, and he tended to discount the strength of their threat. In July he suggested sending out an armed convoy from the city to challenge the Soviets. While Washington turned down this suggestion,

it backed Clay's plan for an airlift to the beleaguered city. At the height of the airlift, planes ferried 13,000 tons of supplies to the city a day. The blockade was lifted on May 12, 1949 as a consequence of negotiations at the United Nations, talks which were kept secret from Clay. Clay declined to meet the first train to arrive in Berlin.

While the blockade was in force, Clay was involved in the negotiations to establish a German constitution. The Allies differed on the type of government to be granted Germany. The French proposed a weak central government, the British a strong one. In January 1949 Clay succeeded in getting the two nations to accept the American plan for a moderately strong federal government with limited taxing power. Clay also convinced both major German parties to accept the plan. The military governors approved the final draft of the constitution in Berlin on the day the blockade was lifted.

The approval of the new constitution ended the military's phase of the occupation. On May 15, 1949 Clay left Germany and was replaced by John McCloy, the civilian high commissioner for Germany. Clay retired on returning home. A year later he became chairman and chief executive officer of the Continental Can Co. He played an active role in the effort to persuade Eisenhower to seek the presidency in 1952 and served as a liaison between the General and the professional politicians campaigning for him throughout the U.S. Clay was a close adviser to the President for the next eight years, becoming, among other things, one of the principal architects of the interstate highway program.

Clay also served as a foreign policy advisor to John Kennedy. In August 1961, when the Kremlin and East Germany threatened to cut off Western access to East Berlin and make Berlin a "free city," theoretically independent of both Eastern and Western control, Clay was sent as President Kennedy's personal representative to West Berlin. To assure Berlin of U.S. support and assert Western access rights into the Soviet sector, Clay, on a number of occasions, ordered American diplomats to drive into the Eastern zone. When East German authorities stopped American officials on Oct. 27, Clay ordered armed convoys to accompany the diplomats to ensure entry. In the ensuing crisis American and Soviet tanks faced each other across the border for the first time in the postwar era. American armored forces were withdrawn after the Soviet Union pulled back its tanks.

During the winter of 1962 U.S. newspapers reported that Clay was dissatisfied with the President's order that all major U.S. responses to Soviet measures be cleared in advance with Washington because the requirement prevented quick reaction to border incidents. According to these reports Clay believed the Communists would have torn down the Berlin wall in August 1961 if American officials had threatened its destruction. Clay subsequently denied the report. In May 1962, after the crisis subsided, he returned to the U.S. and resumed his business activities.

In November 1965 Clay, along with 104 other well-known Americans, signed a statement supporting the Johnson Administration's policy on Vietnam. The statement declared that U.S. domestic critics "have a right to be heard but they impose on the rest of us the obligation to make unmistakably clear the nation's firm commitment in Vietnam."

In 1970 Clay retired as chairman of the board of the Continental Can Company.

[EWS]

For further information:
Lucius D. Clay, *Decision in Germany* (New York, 1950).

CLIFFORD, CLARK (McADAMS)
b. Dec. 25, 1906; Fort Scott, Kan.
Special Counsel to the President, June 1946-February 1950; Secretary of Defense, January 1968-January 1969.

Clifford, the son of a railroad official, was raised in St Louis, Mo. He received a law degree from Washington University in 1928 and entered practice with the firm of Holland, Lashly and Donnell. Initially handling the defense of indigent persons, Clifford gained a reputation as a successful trial attorney specializing in corporation and labor law. He was commissioned a lieutenant in the naval reserve in 1944, and he became assistant to President Truman's naval aide, James K. Vardaman, the following year. In 1946 Clifford replaced Vardaman. Aside from his military responsibilities, he assisted Truman's leading speech writer and special counsel, Samuel Rosenman. The young man impressed Rosenman and Truman with his speech, writing ability and, more importantly, with his shrewd political common sense. After Rosenman retired in February 1946, Clifford undertook some of the President's legal work. He prepared an important study on universal military training and helped establish the National Intelligence Agency, the forerunner of the Central Intelligence Agency. In June Clifford succeeded Rosenman as special counsel.

Although possessing little political experience Clifford became one of Truman's most trusted advisers, playing critical roles in the development of the Administration's foreign and domestic programs. Known as the "Golden Boy" of the Administration, Clifford attempted to avoid publicity. He rarely gave interviews and never delivered speeches, preferring, instead, to lobby within the White House for his positions. His influence was such that he was considered one of the most powerful men in Washington.

Clifford's power was based primarily on his strong personal friendship with Truman. The President was comfortable with him. Truman admired his charm and self-assurance and appreciated the encouragement, reassurance and counsel the young man could give him. Just as importantly, Clifford spoke Truman's political language. He was a political pragmatist whose outwardly cordial manner concealed a tough inner resolve. He reinforced Truman's penchant for action, urging the President to stand fast and fight rather than go slow and compromise.

Clifford was a major force in molding what came to be known as the containment policy against the Soviet Union. At Truman's request the aide worked during the summer of 1946 on a memorandum evaluating Soviet policy and suggesting the U.S. response. The report, entitled "American Relations with the Soviet Union," was submitted in September. Clifford based his memo on his belief that "the key to an understanding of current Soviet foreign policy . . . is the realization that Soviet leaders adhere to the Marxian theory of ultimate destruction of capitalist states by Communist states." Although he did not think that the Russian leaders were planning for war in the near future, he predicted that they would tighten their grip on areas under their control in preparation for a future conflict. He advised the U.S. and Great Britain to build up a strong military alliance to resist Soviet aggression and confine Moscow to its present territories. "The language of military power," he said, "is the only language which disciples of power politics understand. The United States must use that language in order that Soviet leaders will realize that our government is determined to uphold the interests of its citizens and the rights of small nations. . . ." Clifford maintained that the U.S. must be prepared to wage atomic and biological warfare to contain the Soviet Union. Confronted with such strength, he assumed that Moscow might seek accommodation with the West. Until such time, "the United States should enter no proposal for disarmament or limitation of armament."

In 1947 Clifford reiterated and elaborated on these ideas in his draft of Truman's speech requesting aid to Greece and Turkey. He found the State Department's version of the address too bogged down in economics. Believing that the speech should be "the opening gun in a campaign to bring people up to [the] realization [that] war was not over by any means," he redrafted it. Clifford played on the emotions of Congress and the people by stressing the danger to the Western world if Greece and Turkey fell to the Communists and promising U.S. aid against Communist aggression. The President's address proved a success, and the Truman Doctrine, as it became known, proved one of the foundations of the Administration's foreign policy.

Clifford was also credited with playing a major role in reversing the Administration's policy on Palestine. The President had originally supported partition of the area into Arab and Jewish states. However, Secretary of State George Marshall [q.v.] and Assistant Secretary Robert Lovett [q.v.] had convinced him to recommend a temporary U.N. trusteeship for fear that American troops might have to defend the fledgling Zionist state. During the spring of 1948 Clifford managed to convince Truman that he would need Jewish votes in the upcoming presidential election and should therefore recognize the state of Israel as soon as independence was declared.

While Clifford returned to private law practice during the Eisenhower Administration, he again became a presidential adviser to Presidents Kennedy and Johnson. In the fall of 1965 Clifford visited Southeast Asia as chairman of the Foreign Intelligence Advisory Board. During the trip, he later recalled, "the optimism of our military and Vietnamese officials on the conduct of the war . . . confirmed my belief in the correctness of our policy." Clifford opposed the 37-day halt in the bombing of North Vietnam beginning at Christmas 1965 because he felt that it "could be construed by Hanoi as a sign of weakness on our part." In Washington Clifford's position on the bombing question earned him a reputation as a "hawk." As an adviser to President Johnson at the 1966 Manila Conference, he remained convinced that the U.S. was winning the war and that its Vietnam policy was sound.

In a July 1969 article for Foreign Affairs, Clifford suggested that his doubts about Vietnam began to take shape during the late summer of 1967, when he and Gen. Maxwell Taylor [q.v.] toured Southeast Asia at the request of the President. The purpose of this trip was to determine why America's Asian allies, New Zealand, Australia and the Philippines, had sent only token detachments to assist U.S. troops in Vietnam. Clifford discovered that these nations were less troubled by Communist aggression in Vietnam than the U.S. was, despite the fact that they were seemingly more vulnerable. "I returned home," wrote Clifford, "puzzled, troubled, concerned. Was it possible that our assessment of the danger to the stability of Southeast Asia and the Western Pacific was exaggerated? Was it possible that those nations which were neighbors of Vietnam had a clearer perception of the tides of world events in 1967 than we?"

Clifford's doubts were not widely publicized, and when he was named Secretary of Defense in January 1968 it was generally believed, even by the President, that Clifford would advocate an even more aggressive U.S. military posture in Vietnam than his predecessor, Robert S. McNamara [q.v.].

Clifford was confirmed by the Senate Jan. 30, 1968 and sworn in March 1. He assumed office during a critical moment in the war. On Jan. 31, 1968 Communist guerrillas and their North Vietnamese allies launched the Tet offensive, a massive attack on South Vietnam's cities and military installations. Before being driven back the Communists had overrun the ancient city of Hue, the cultural capital of South Vietnam, and had even penetrated the American Embassy at Saigon. Some military experts thought the Tet offensive the last desperate effort of a beaten enemy; to many others, however, Tet suggested that the U.S. and their South Vietnamese allies had made little progress in limiting the ability of the Communists to wage war.

On Feb. 28, 1968, two days before Clifford assumed office, he was named chairman of the President's Ad Hoc Task Force on Vietnam. The ostensible purpose of the group was to determine how best to raise the over 200,000 additional troops for Vietnam that had been requested by the Joint Chiefs of Staff and Gen. William C. Westmoreland. In fact, at Clifford's request, the Task Force debated the need for these troops and the nature of the entire U.S. role in Vietnam. Among other members of the Task Force, Gen. Earle Wheeler, chairman of the

Joint Chiefs of Staff; Walt Rostow [q.v.], special presidential assistant; and Gen. Maxwell Taylor favored the troop request. Deputy Undersecretary of Defense Paul Nitze [q.v.], Undersecretary of State Nicholas Katzenbach and Paul Warnke of the Defense Department stood opposed. Clifford remained neutral, attempting to use the debate to develop his own position. "After days of analysis," he later wrote, "I could not find out when the war was going to end; I could not find out whether the new requests for men and equipment were going to be enough, or whether it would take more and, if more, when and how much; I could not find out how soon the South Vietnamese forces would be ready to take over. All I had was the statement, given with too little self-assurance to be comforting, that if we persisted for an indeterminate length of time, the enemy would not choose to go on."

The Task Force eventually recommended immediate deployment of 23,000 additional troops in Vietnam, approval of reserve call-ups, larger draft calls and lengthened tours of duty to provide additional men. In transmitting these recommendations to the President, Clifford made known his serious reservations about the entire U.S. Vietnam policy.

According to Undersecretary of the Air Force Townsend Hoopes in his study *The Limits of Intervention*, the President was troubled by Clifford's new skepticism and "the warm, long-standing friendship between the two men suddenly grew formal and cool." Clifford held to his position and at a March 13 cabinet meeting presented a pessimistic picture of the American military situation in Vietnam.

On March 28 Clifford met with Secretary of State Dean Rusk [q.v.], Walt Rostow, Assistant Secretary of State William Bundy [q.v.] and Harry McPherson, a White House speech writer, to discuss a draft of a scheduled presidential address on Vietnam. McPherson presented a speech that called for a modest 15,000-man troop increase and made a proforma appeal to the North Vietnamese to negotiate. The draft made no mention of a bombing halt, which the North Vietnamese had declared a prerequisite for peace talks.

Townsend Hoopes called the speech "defiant, bellicose. . . . "

After reading the draft Clifford declared: "The President cannot give that speech! What seems not to be understood is that major elements of the national constituency—the business community, the press, the churches, professional groups, college presidents, students and most of the intellectual community have turned against this war. What the President needs is not a war speech, but a peace speech." Clifford spoke for several hours and proposed that an alternative draft be presented to the President that would include the suggestion that the U.S. stop all bombing north of the 20th parallel, with a promise of total cessation of the bombing if Hanoi refrained from attacking the South Vietnamese cities. McPherson thought Clifford "brilliant" in convincing Rusk and Rostow to reverse their long-standing positions on the war.

President Johnson accepted the peace draft and delivered it over nationwide television on March 31, 1968. His address included the stunning announcement that he would not seek another term as president. However, the speech did not end debate on Vietnam within the Administration. Clifford aligned himself with W. Averell Harriman [q.v.] and Cyrus T. Vance, U.S. representatives to the Paris peace talks, who urged the President to order a total bombing halt to speed the negotiations with North Vietnam. Rusk, Gen. Westmoreland and Gen. Taylor argued that the bombing remained a military necessity. In October President Johnson yielded to the Clifford position and ordered a complete end to the bombing of the North.

Clifford left office in January 1969 and returned to his legal practice. In July of that year he urged unilateral withdrawal of American troops from South Vietnam.

During the Carter Administration, he sometimes served as a foreign policy adviser.

[JLW]

For further information:
Townsend Hoopes, *The Limits of Intervention* (New York, 1969).

COFFIN, WILLIAM SLOANE, JR.
b. June 1, 1924; New York, N.Y.
Chaplain, Yale University, 1958-76.

Coffin came from an upper class family. His father was vice-president of the family furniture business, W. & J. Sloane, Inc., and his uncle, the Rev. Henry Sloane Coffin, was president of the Union Theological Seminary and a fellow of the Yale Corporation. After attending Phillips Exeter Academy Coffin entered Yale, but his studies were interrupted by four years of service as an officer in the Army. He returned to Yale in 1947 and later spent a year at the Union Theological Seminary. There Coffin became a follower of the theologian Reinhold Neibuhr, whose doctrine of "Christian realism" justified and encouraged political activism. From 1950 to 1953 he worked overseas for the Central Intelligence Agency, specializing in Russian affairs. After completing theological studies at Yale, Coffin was ordained a Presbyterian minister in 1956. He served as chaplain at Phillips Andover Academy and Williams College before being appointed Yale University chaplain in 1958.

Beginning in 1965 Coffin was strongly critical of American conduct in Vietnam. He argued that "the war is being waged with unbelievable cruelty and in a fashion so out of character with American instincts of decency that it is seriously undermining them. The strains of war have cut the funds that might otherwise be applied to antipoverty efforts at home and abroad—which is the intelligent way to fight Communism." After first restricting his protests to letters and petitions, Coffin became acting executive secretary of the National Emergency Committee of Clergy Concerned about Vietnam in January 1966.

By the fall of 1967 Coffin was counseling active resistance to the war and was one of the original signers of the September 1967 statement, "A Call to Resist Illegitimate Authority," which supported draft resistance and the refusal of servicemen to obey orders to participate in the war. On Oct. 16 Coffin was the main speaker at ceremonies at the Arlington Street Church in Boston, sponsored by New England Resistance, during which draft-eligible men burned or handed in draft cards. Four days later Coffin was part of a delegation that turned over these and other draft cards to Justice Department officials in Washington. On the steps of the Justice Department he stated: "In our view it is not wild-eyed idealism but clear-eyed revulsion which brings us here," and concluded, "we hereby publicly counsel . . . refusal to serve in the armed services as long as the war in Vietnam continues. . . ."

For these and other acts Coffin, Benjamin Spock, Marcus Raskin, codirector of the Institute of Policy Studies, writer Mitchell Goodman and Harvard graduate student Michael Ferber were indicted on Jan. 5, 1968 for conspiring to "counsel, aid and abet" young men to "refuse and evade service in the armed services. . . ." After a widely publicized trial all but Raskin were convicted on one conspiracy count, and on July 11, 1968 they were sentenced to fines and two-year prison terms. The convictions were overturned a year later, when the First U.S. District Court of Appeals ruled that the trial judge, Francis J. W. Ford, had made prejudicial errors in his charge to the jury. Coffin and Goodman were ordered retried, while charges against Spock and Ferber were dismissed. On April 22, 1970 the charges against the two remaining defendants were dismissed at the request of the Justice Department. Coffin announced his resignation as Yale University Chaplain in February 1975, effective the next year. He subsequently became head minister of Riverside Church in New York City.

[JBF]

For further information:
Jessica Mitford, *The Trial of Dr. Spock* (New York, 1969).

COLLINS, J(OSEPH) LAWTON
b. May 1, 1896; New Orleans, La.
U.S. Special Representative in Vietnam, November 1954-May 1955.

J. Lawton Collins, the son of Irish-Catholic parents, was born in New Orleans.

After graduating from the United States Military Academy in 1917, Collins commanded a battalion of the occupation forces in Germany during 1919. Collins served in various military capacities in the 1920s and 1930s, and by the outbreak of World War II, he had achieved the rank of brigadier general. During World War II he saw active duty in the Pacific, where he helped reorganize American defenses on Hawaii, and in France, where he spearheaded a series of crucial Allied combat victories in 1944. After the War Collins was assigned to the Pentagon and from 1948 to 1953 served as Army Chief of Staff. In 1953 President Eisenhower appointed him U.S. representative to the North Atlantic Treaty Organization.

Following the partition of Vietnam in 1954, Collins became prominently involved in the policy debate over U.S. support of South Vietnam Premier Ngo Dinh Diem, appointed as a result of pressure from the U.S. Collins spoke out forcefully against continuing to back Diem, whom he thought totally incapable of leading South Vietnam. However, leading American officials, spurred by Col. Edward Lansdale, the principal American intelligence agent in Vietnam, prevailed upon Eisenhower to pledge his support to Diem. To reinforce the Administration's position, Eisenhower dispatched Collins to Vietnam in November 1954 as his personal representative bearing the rank of ambassador.

Arriving in Saigon convinced that a strong pro-Western government in South Vietnam was important to prevent Communist expansion throughout Southeast Asia, Collins began a systematic program of aiding Diem in establishing security, in starting a military training program for the South Vietnamese Army and in paving the way for agrarian reforms. Shortly after his arrival Collins helped the Vietnamese leader exile his major rival, Gen. Nguyen Van Hinh, who commanded the loyalty of the well-equipped South Vietnamese Army and of the Saigon police. However, Collins proved unable to establish a close relationship with Diem. The Vietnamese leader repeatedly refused to listen to what Collins considered to be sound military and political advice. For his part, Diem found Collins insufferably arrogant and condescending.

By March 1955 Collins and other U.S. officials in both Saigon and Washington, distressed by Diem's refusal to institute suggested reforms, began to reconsider U.S. support for the Premier. The issue stirring up the most hostility was the Premier's refusal to reorganize the government to include representatives from South Vietnam's powerful political-religious sects. When Diem turned down the sects' demands for a coalition government in late March 1955, fighting broke out in the streets of Saigon between government forces and the sects, principally the Binh Xuyen. Recalled to Washington in early April, Collins implored Eisenhower to withdraw U.S. support from Diem. Impressed by Collins's arguments and by reports he was receiving from the State Department, the President agreed to approve whatever Collins recommended. The State Department recommended a compromise that would retain Diem as a national symbol while real political power passed to Dr. Phan Huy Quat of the Dai Viet party. Collins accepted the suggestion, but before it could be implemented, Diem's forces crushed the sects. Eisenhower and Secretary of State John Foster Dulles [q.v.] then reversed American policy to full support of Diem.

Collins, who symbolized American opposition to Diem, was soon replaced. The General returned to Washington in May 1955 and shortly thereafter resumed his duties as U.S. representative to NATO.

Retiring in 1957, he served until 1969 as a director of Charles Pfizer and Co., Inc., and as vice president of Pfizer International Subsidiaries until 1972. Throughout these years Collins remained skeptical about U.S. policy in Vietnam and, as one of a small group of "dovish generals," opposed the continual escalation of American involvement in Southeast Asia.

[RJB]

CONNALLY, JOHN B(OWDEN), JR.
b. Feb. 27, 1917; Floresville, Tex.
Secretary of the Treasury, February 1971–May 1972.

The son of a tenant farmer, Connally attended the University of Texas at Austin, where he earned his law degree in 1941. His introduction to state and national politics, however, took place in 1938 when Lyndon B. Johnson, a freshman Democrat in Congress, invited him to Washington to serve as Johnson's aide. Connally joined the U.S. Naval Reserve in 1941 and worked in the office of the chief of naval operations and on the planning staff of Gen. Dwight D. Eisenhower. Later as a fighter plane director aboard the aircraft carrier USS *Essex* in the Pacific, he was awarded the Bronze Star. Connally returned to civilian life in 1946 and two years later managed Johnson's successful bid for the U.S. Senate. Connally worked as Johnson's administrative assistant in 1949. Thereafter he remained active in Texas Democratic Party politics and helped Johnson take over the Party machine in 1956. In 1960 Connally managed Johnson's unsuccessful campaign for the Democratic Party's presidential nomination. Connally also worked as an attorney representing the oil interests of his state.

In early 1961 President John F. Kennedy appointed Connally secretary of the Navy on the recommendation of Johnson and Secretary of Defense Robert S. McNamara [q.v.]. Connally resigned his post in December 1961 to enter the Texas gubernatorial race, in which he defeated his Republican opponent the following year.

On Nov. 22, 1963, Connally was riding in the presidential limousine in Dallas at the time of the assassination of John F. Kennedy and was himself seriously wounded. Connally's near-martyrdom made him a nationally known political figure and facilitated his re-election as governor of Texas in 1964 and 1966.

In December 1970 President Nixon appointed Connally to succeed David Kennedy as Secretary of the Treasury.

In addition to numerous appearances before congressional committees to promote the Administration's domestic economic policies, Connally played a key role in U.S. foreign economic policy in 1971-72, a time of the worst monetary crisis since World War II.

In May 1971 Connally entered the arena that was to occupy his attention for the rest of his tenure at the Treasury. President Nixon sent him as the ranking representative to the International Banking Conference of the American Bankers Association in Munich, where Connally spoke on the international monetary crisis that had just forced the European countries into a joint currency float earlier that month. In his speech Connally articulated the archnationalist tone that characterized his stance with Europe and Japan over the following year. Connally attributed the exchange crisis to a shift of economic power from the U.S. to Europe and Japan. He complained about restrictions on U.S. industrial and agricultural exports to foreign nations and underlined the failure of other countries to share the defense burdens of the West. The "unalterable position" of the U.S. concerning the dollar, as expounded by Connally, was: "We are not going to devalue. We are not going to change the price of gold."

The position of the U.S. dollar and the U.S. economy continued to deteriorate throughout the summer of 1971, however, and by early August, it was obvious that drastic action was necessary. On August 13-15, Connally, Nixon, Office of Management and Budget Director George Shultz, Federal Reserve Board Chairman Arthur Burns, Council of Economic Advisers Chairman Paul McCracken and New York Federal Reserve Bank President Paul Volcker conferred on the situation at Camp David, Md. Connally throughout the conference was an advocate of aggressive action, including the "closing of the gold window," or an end to the U.S. legal obligation to exchange its gold reserves for dollars held by foreign central banks.

When Arthur Burns, Connally's major opponent on the gold question, argued that such a move would severely tax the good will of the major U.S. trading partners, Connally replied, "We'll go broke getting their good will." Connally's views prevailed, and on the night of Aug. 15, in a nationwide television broadcast, Nixon announced his "New Economic Policy" (NEP), which included a closing of the gold window, a 10% surcharge on foreign imports and an 8% devaluation of the dollar.

Throughout the fall and winter of 1971, Connally was chief U.S. representative in all economic negotiations over the realignment of exchange rates. His first foreign appearance after his May 1971 speech in Munich was at the Group of Ten meeting of Sept. 15-16 in London, which Connally chaired. He reiterated the Administration's general policy, announcing the U.S. intention to promote a $13 billion swing in its balance-of-payments deficit over the next year, a figure whose dimension frightened the European representatives because they saw a shift for the worse in their own trade positions as a result. Connally also repeated his demands that U.S. trading partners reduce their tariff barriers to U.S. goods and share defense expenses more equally.

On Sept. 26, at a second Group of Ten meeting, Connally said that appropriate currency revaluations by foreign countries would make it easier for the U.S. to drop the 10% import surcharge. At the annual meeting of the International Monetary Fund in Washington on Sept. 27-30, Connally again defended the U.S. position and, in a closed session, attacked Latin American countries who encouraged U.S. investment and then expropriated U.S. companies. In October, Connally said that the surcharge "is going to stay on for awhile because it is frankly to our advantage to keep it on for awhile." Shortly thereafter he went to Japan for top-level talks about a revaluation of the yen. He was widely referred to as "Typhoon Connally" in the Japanese press because of the hard bargaining position he took.

Connally's actions in the international economic sphere created serious tension in the high echelons of the Nixon Administration. Both Arthur Burns and Henry Kissinger [q.v.], National Security Council adviser, were appalled by Connally's apparent lack of concern for the sensibilities of America's allies. Rep. Henry Reuss (D, Wis.) had publicly called on Nixon to replace Connally with Arthur Burns as the top U.S. negotiator abroad. Kissinger, who had only a limited interest in economic matters, was equally worried about Connally's impact on U.S. foreign relations in general, a concern complicated by a certain rivalry growing out of Connally's intrusion into what Kissinger considered his domain.

Burns and Kissinger allied to convince Nixon of the dangers posed by Connally's behavior, and Burns urged Nixon to allow Dr. J. Zijlstra, president of the Bank of International Settlements, to draw up a currency realignment plan without Connally and to present the plan to the November 1971 meeting of the Group of Ten in Rome. Connally became incensed at Burns's intrusion into his activities and refused to have anything to do with Zijlstra's plan. At the time of his departure for Rome, Connally also refused to include any State Department officials in his delegation, a direct slap at Secretary of State William Rogers [q.v.], who was a passive ally of Burns and Kissinger in the struggle for Nixon's allegiance. Finally, on Nov. 24, Burns and Connally met with Nixon to discuss the situation, and at that meeting, in one observer's comment, Connally "got the message."

At the December 1971 Smithsonian monetary meeting Connally, confronted by a uniformly hostile group of foreign finance ministers alienated by six months of his unilateral actions and pressure tactics, pulled perhaps the most dramatic coup of his period in office. Tensions were mounting in the negotiations after long hours during which Connally had coaxed the European and Japanese representatives for greater revaluations of their own currencies against the dollar, without the slightest hint that the U.S. would reverse its refusal to readjust the dollar against the price of gold. After a French negotiator had snapped at Connally, "If that is your position, we can all go home," French Finance Minister Giscard d'Estaing asked the Secretary what the U.S. contribution to realignment would be. Connally answered laconically: "Well, we leave that up to you. What change in the gold price do you want, eight, nine, ten percent?"

After the stunned Europeans and Japanese had digested this first hint that the U.S. would raise the gold price, a British representative remarked that Connally's negotiating tactics were "not economics, but jujitsu." After the conclusion of the Smithsonian conference, at which the U.S. obtained much greater revaluations, particularly from Japan, than anyone thought possible, British Chancellor of the Exchequer Anthony Barber remarked that "a lesser man, a man less tough than Connally, could not have done it."

Connally also periodically advised President Nixon on foreign policy and strongly supported his decision to mine Haiphong harbor in May 1972. Later in the same month, however, Connally resigned his post.

In 1980 he unsuccessfully sought the Republican presidential nomination after having joined the Party in 1973.

[LRG]

DULLES, ALLEN W(ELSH)
b. April 7, 1893; Watertown, N.Y.
d. January 29, 1969; Washington, D.C.
Director of Central Intelligence, 1953-61.

Dulles's family had a background in diplomatic service. His grandfather, John W. Foster, served as Benjamin Harrison's Secretary of State. His uncle, Robert Lansing, held the same post in the Wilson Administration; another uncle, John Walsh, had been minister to England. Dulles's father, however, was a Presbyterian minister who imbued his sons with a strong belief in the conflict of good and evil. Dulles attended private schools in upstate New York and Paris and then earned his B.A. and M.A. degrees at Princeton University.

Beginning in 1916 Dulles served in a number of posts in the diplomatic service, including an assignment with the U.S. delegation to the Versailles Peace Conference of 1918-19. From 1922 to 1926 he was the chief of the State Department's division of Near Eastern affairs. After receiving his LL.B. from George Washington University in 1926, he resigned from government work and joined a Wall Street law firm with his brother, John Foster [q.v.].

With the outbreak of World War II, Dulles returned to government service as director of the Office of Strategic Services. He supervised espionage activities against Germany and played an important role in the surrender of German troops in Italy in 1945. After the War he helped draft the National Security Act of 1947, which established the Central Intelligence Agency (CIA), and in 1948 he headed a three-man committee that studied the intelligence functions of the organization. In 1951 Dulles left his law practice to become the deputy director of the CIA, in charge of covert operations.

In 1953 President Dwight D. Eisenhower appointed Dulles Director of Central Intelligence, a position that gave him power not only to run the CIA but also to oversee all U.S. intelligence activities. Dulles's personal style quickly became the public's image of the CIA and its formal standard of behavior. Pipe-smoking, urbane and educated in the Ivy League like many early CIA officials, Dulles was able to impress upon his listeners in public and government circles the need for absolute secrecy in CIA operations. During his tenure there was little outside oversight of his agency, largely because of his close relationship with Eisenhower and powerful congressional leaders who shared his views on secrecy.

During the Eisenhower Administration the CIA and State Department worked harmoniously because of the closeness of Allen Dulles and his brother, Secretary of State John Foster Dulles. The two men shared the view that the Cold War was a moral crusade against Communism. Foster utilized diplomacy as his weapon, while Allen employed subversion and manipulation. Both used their belief in the need and right of democracy to triumph over totalitarianism to justify their policies.

Under Dulles the CIA helped overthrow several left-wing governments and establish regimes supporting U.S. policy. The CIA's first major success occurred in Iran in 1953, when operatives, directed by Kermit Roosevelt, helped topple the leftist government of Prime Minister Mohammed Mossadegh. When questioned about CIA involvement in the coup, Dulles demonstrated his characteristically evasive style. He replied, "I can say that the statement that we spent many dollars doing that [inciting street riots] is utterly false."

Two years later Dulles helped plot the overthrow of Guatemalan President Jacobo Arbenz, whose leftist government had initiated land reform programs that threatened the interests of the powerful American-owned United Fruit Co. In June a small army of exiled Guatemalans, trained and financed by the CIA, crossed the Honduras-Guatemala border to overthrow Arbenz. A secret CIA-organized air force, piloted by Americans, provided the army with necessary air cover. When the invasion faltered Dulles convinced Eisenhower to send additional American planes to the small, crippled air force. As a result of the attack, Guatemalan army officials deserted Arbenz, and he was forced to capitulate. With CIA guidance, negotiations brought the rightist Col. Carlos Castillo-Armas into power. In 1957 Castillo-Armas was assassinated after he closed down a gambling casino dominated by American financial interests. The CIA also backed anti-Communist regimes with little popular support. In South Vietnam, for example, the Agency helped President Ngo Dinh Diem solidify his hold on the central government despite opposition from military and sect leaders.

During Dulles's tenure intelligence-gathering operations were expanded and new technological means of surveillance, such as the U-2 and SR-71 spy planes, were developed. Emphasis was put on the use of technology rather than traditional operatives in collecting data.

On March 17, 1960 President Eisenhower ordered the CIA to help unify opposition to the Cuban government and to recruit and train a force of Cuban exiles capable of guerrilla action against it. Richard M. Bissell, CIA deputy director for plans, was placed in charge of the project. According to a 1975 Senate Select Committee report, that summer Bissell also initiated attempts to kill Cuban leaders Raul and Fidel Castro. Bissell claimed that Dulles was fully informed of these activities. The Senate Select Committee also reported that in August 1960 Dulles authorized a CIA effort to assassinate Congolese Premier Patrice Lumumba. (Lumumba was killed by Congolese rivals before the CIA plans were carried out.) It was unclear whether or not Eisenhower directly authorized these activities, or was fully aware of them.

President-elect Kennedy announced that he would retain Dulles as Director of Central Intelligence on Nov. 10, 1960. Eight days later Dulles and Bissell briefed Kennedy on the training of the Cuban exile force, which was already well underway at a CIA camp in Guatemala, and on initial plans for landing them in Cuba. On Nov. 29, after a second more detailed briefing, Kennedy approved continuation of the training. It was unclear after the 1975 investigation whether Kennedy had been informed in this or in any other briefing of the parallel plans to assassinate Castro. After a series of top-level meetings, at which Dulles and Bissell presented and defended the CIA invastion plan, Kennedy gave his approval in early April 1961.

On the day of the invasion at the Bay of Pigs, Dulles was in Puerto Rico delivering a long-planned speech, which he apparently declined to cancel to avoid any suspicion that a major CIA operation was underway. Dulles was therefore not in Washington when Kennedy decided to cancel one of the two planned CIA air strikes. In Dulles's absence, Bissell was in charge of the Cuban operation, which ended in complete defeat for the invasion forces.

On April 22 Kennedy established a panel headed by retired Gen. Maxwell D. Taylor [q.v.] to investigate the CIA role in the Cuban invasion. Also serving on the panel were Dulles, Attorney General Robert F. Kennedy [q.v.] and Chief of Naval Operations Adm. Arleigh A. Burke . Members of the Taylor panel disagreed as to whether or not the invasion plans had had any chance of success. Dulles took a middle position, arguing that in spite of certain important problems, if the original plans had been followed, including both air strikes, the invasion might have succeeded. The panel recommended that the CIA be permitted to continue to conduct clandestine operations but not to undertake major paramilitary operations unless they could be plausibly denied.

During the early months of the Kennedy Administration, Dulles was also involved in efforts to bolster the deteriorating position of U.S.-supported forces in Laos, where the CIA had long been involved. During this period Dulles opposed the proposed establishment of the Defense Intelligence Agency (DIA), a plan supported by Secretary of Defense Robert S. McNamara [q.v.]. Dulles urged the continuation of individual military service intelligence agencies, each separately represented on the U.S. Intelligence Board, which he headed. Over Dulles's objections, McNamara proceeded in October 1961 with the creation of the DIA.

According to David Wise and Thomas B. Ross in The Invisible Government, Kennedy had been planning major changes in the CIA even before the Cuban invasion. After the failure of that project, the CIA leadership was quietly replaced. On July 31, 1961, Administration spokesman Pierre Salinger confirmed that Dulles would soon retire, and on Sept. 27 Kennedy accepted his resignation. (Bissell and CIA Deputy Director Gen. Charles P. Cabell also left the CIA in the following months.) On Nov. 28 Kennedy presented a National Security

Medal to Dulles at the recently opened $46-million CIA headquarters in Langley, Va., which had been planned and constructed during Dulles's tenure.

Following his resignation Dulles returned to his former law firm, Sullivan and Cromwell. In November 1963 President Johnson [q.v.] appointed Dulles to the Warren Commission charged with investigating the assassination of President Kennedy. In June 1964, following the disappearance of three civil rights workers in Philadelphia, Miss., Dulles went to Mississippi as Johnson's special emissary to evaluate "law observance problems." Dulles died in Washington, D.C. on Jan. 30, 1969.

[JBF]

For further information:
Allen W. Dulles, *The Craft of Intelligence* (New York, 1963).
David Wise and Thomas B. Ross, *The Invisible Government* (New York, 1964).
U.S. Senate, Select Committee to Study Intelligence Activities, *Alleged Assassination Plots Involving Foreign Leaders* (Washington, 1975).

DULLES, JOHN FOSTER

b. Feb. 25, 1888; Washington, D.C.
d. May 24, 1959; Washington, D.C.
Secretary of State, January 1953-April 1959.

Dulles was descended from a family of diplomats and clergymen. His maternal grandfather, John W. Foster, served as ambassador to Russia, Spain and Mexico and was Secretary of State under Benjamin Harrison. Dulles's paternal grandfather, John Welch Dulles, was a Presbyterian missionary in China. His father, Allen Dulles, taught philosophy at Auburn Theological Seminary and was a Presbyterian minister in Watertown, N.Y., where Foster grew up.

Dulles graduated from Princeton University in 1908 and spent a year studying at the Sorbonne. Although he had expressed an interest in entering the ministry, he decided to become a lawyer. He received his degree from George Washington University in 1911 and began a long association with the prestigious New York law firm of Sullivan & Cromwell. Dulles served as a special agent for the State Department in Central America in 1917. During World War I he worked with the Army intelligence service and was an assistant to the chairman of the War Trade Board.

At the request of his uncle, Robert Lansing, Dulles served as President Woodrow Wilson's staff at the Versailles Peace Conference of 1919. He was head of the U.S. delegation to the Reparations Committee and earned high praise for convincing the British and French to lower reparation demands. Dulles returned from Paris to become a partner in his law firm. An austere man and compulsive worker, during the next 30 years he earned a distinguished record as a specialist in international law.

Throughout the 1930s Dulles lectured and wrote on foreign affairs. His reactions to the growth of fascism and the impending war in Europe were presented in *War, Peace and Change*, published in 1939. Devoid of the moral tone that would later typify his work, the book was a systematic, legalistic inquiry into the reasons men go to war. Dulles ascribed the troubled situation in Europe to the failure of the Treaty of Versailles. By insisting on the maintenance of the status quo, the victorious Allies had forced Germany to take violent action to achieve needed change. Dulles saw the threat to peace coming from the system of nation-states advancing their self-interest. He suggested that war could be avoided through the creation of "international mechanisms" (which he did not clearly define) to manage change.

Dulles was deeply disturbed by the war in Europe and believed the United States could avoid entering the struggle by developing a moral solution to the crisis. In 1940 he assumed the chairmanship of the Federal Council of Churchs' Commission on a Just and Durable Peace. Dulles's major goal was to create a successor to the League of Nations without its weaknesses. In May 1943 he set down an abstract plan for preventing war in a report entitled "The Six Pillars of Peace." In contrast to his early works, it contained a strong moral theme. Dulles believed that peace could be achieved only when nations were acting in conjunction with moral law. The U.S. had a particular moral obligation in guiding the postwar world and in forming the international organization that would maintain peace.

During the 1944 presidential campaign Dulles served as a foreign policy adviser to Republican candidate New York Gov. Thomas Dewey. A supporter of a bipartisan foreign policy, Dulles also undertook several diplomatic assignments for the Roosevelt and Truman Administrations. In 1945 he was a member of the U.S. delegation to the U.N. Conference in San Francisco. From 1946 to 1950 he was a delegate to the U.N. General Assembly and an adviser to the State Department. Dulles served as Dewey's adviser during the 1948 presidential campaign and backed the candidate's decision not to attack strongly Truman's foreign policy. During the immediate postwar period Dulles endorsed the Truman Doctrine, the Marshall Plan and the North Atlantic Treaty, as well as the President's conduct of the Korean war.

In the last half of the decade Dulles's assessment of the world situation changed. No longer did he see peace threatened by the system of nation-states and the selfishness of all countries. Instead, it was jeopardized by the evil intentions and ideologies of specific states, particularly the Soviet Union. In a 1946 *Life* article he warned that the Soviet Union would continue its expansionist policy. Dulles called for military measures to meet the threat, but more importantly, he preached a need for a spiritual rebirth and a recommitment to American institutions to counter the threat. Despite his hatred of Communism, he urged a more conciliatory attitude toward the USSR, believing it might lift the Iron Curtain and permit the entrance of beneficent Western influence.

In 1949 Dewey appointed Dulles to fill an unexpired Senate term. He was defeated when he ran as a Republican for a full term in 1950. Dulles became a consultant for State Department and in 1950-51 negotiated the U.S.-Japanese peace treaty. This agreement restored Japan's sovereignty and allowed U.S. bases to remain in that nation.

During the early 1950s Dulles, by then the Republican Party's most prominent foreign policy figure, became increasingly conservative. Historians such as Walter LeFeber have attributed this movement to the rise of McCarthyism and Dulles's hope that a Republican victory in the 1952 presidential election would result in his selection as Secretary of State.

Dulles outlined his new stand in a *Life* article in 1952. He contended that Truman's policy of containment had been only partly successful in preventing Communist expansion and had, in fact, failed to roll back the Communist sphere of influence in Eastern Europe and China. Containment offered the American people only the status quo. Instead, Dulles suggested a policy of liberation for nations of the Eastern bloc. Dulles opposed Truman's reliance on convential weapons, maintaining it would bankrupt the nation. He recommended that the U.S. use nuclear weapons when necessary. In his words, the primary way of countering Communist aggression was "for the free world to develop the will and organize the means to retaliate instantly against open aggression by Red Armies, so that, if it occurred anywhere we could and would strike back, where it hurt, by means of our own choosing."

Dulles's ideas impressed both moderate and conservative Republicans. In 1952 he was asked to draft the foreign policy plank in the Republican platform. There he condemned containment as "negative, futile and immoral" because it abandoned "countless human beings to despotic and godless terror." The Party promised the liberation of Eastern Europe. Dulles campaigned vigorously for the Eisenhower ticket but was rarely seen with the General or asked for his advice. The reasons for the candidate's coldness remain uncertain, but historian Townsend Hoopes suggested it was the result of Eisenhower's reluctance to associate himself with Dulles's policy of liberation.

The press widely assumed that Dulles would be chosen Eisenhower's Secretary of State. However, several of his close aides maintained that the President-elect had ambivalent feelings about the man. According to C. D. Jackson, Eisenhower contemplated naming John J. McCloy, a man interested in managing a bureaucracy as well as formulating foreign policy, to head the Department. Dulles, who showed no interest in management, was to have been chief foreign policy adviser. Eisenhower contacted McCloy with the suggestion, but he rejected it. Dulles was named Secretary of State in late November.

Relations between the men were initially extremely formal. The aloof Dulles had difficulty dealing with the President. Eisenhower, in turn, found his Secretary of State dull, verbose and legalistic in his discussions. Yet the two men gradually developed a close relationship. Eisenhower spoke to Dulles daily. The Secretary was the one member of the Cabinet who did not have to go through presidential assistant Sherman Adams to see the President.

Over the decade the two men molded a foreign policy that reflected a moralistic view of the Cold War. Eisenhower often gave Dulles a free hand in shaping and carrying out policy. He consequently became one of the most powerful Secretaries of State in U.S. history. Yet the President was not Dulles's cypher as critics claimed. Dulles initiated and gave shape to policy, but Eisenhower continually modified it, often softening his Secretary's hard-line attitudes.

Dulles considered himself primarily the President's personal foreign policy adviser, and he jealously guarded his position within the White House. He objected to independent foreign policy initiatives by such advisers as Harold Stassen in the field of disarmament and Nelson Rockefeller in the field of Latin American relations. Each of these men resigned, in part, because the Secretary frustrated their plans.

Because he thought of himself as an adviser, Dulles was not concerned with the administration of the State Department. His many trips were, in part, a result of the desire to escape the problems of department management. Dulles rarely consulted his staff on policy. His contacts were most often for facts with which to support his stand. According to George Kennan [q.v.], this policy weakened morale within the Department and destroyed creativity into the 1960s.

Dulles entered office well aware of the need for good relations with Congress. During his early life he had seen Woodrow Wilson's dream of American participation in the League of Nations destroyed by his inability to deal with Congress. After World War II he saw Dean Acheson [q.v.] hampered by the same failure. Dulles was particularly concerned with maintaining good relations with the powerful Republican Right, led by such senators as William Jenner, (R, Ind.) [q.v.], Styles Bridges (R, N.H.) and Joseph McCarthy (R, Wisc.).

Very early in his career he became involved in attempts to placate the Wisconsin Republican, who had charged that the State Department harbored subversives. Dulles instituted strict security reviews under the direction of Scott McLeod, a McCarthy supporter. Over the next few years investigations resulted in the dismissal or forced resignation of several hundred State Department employes as security risks or because of drunkenness, homosexuality, incompetence or "incompatibility." The last reason was used for those whose policy judgments displeased the Republican Right. Among those removed were John P. Davies and John Carter Vincent, China experts under attack as pro-Communist because they opposed all-out aid to Chiang Kai-shek during the 1940s. Dulles, reviewing their files, found no security violations. Nevertheless, he refused to support these men and asked for their resignations on the grounds of lack of judgment, discretion and reliability.

Dulles did, however, support the nomination of Charles E. Bohlen to be ambassador to the USSR. The diplomat was accused of being a security risk and was attacked because of his role in the formation of the Yalta agreements. The appointment was confirmed, but while the Senate debate was in progress, Dulles insisted that he not be seen too frequently in Bohlen's company. Bohlen left Washington with the impression that Dulles was a man with "one obsession: to remain Secretary of State."

Dulles entered his office with the desire to implement a policy of boldness and action. No longer would the U.S. simply react to Communist challenge; it would take the offensive against the adversary. Although he had no long-range plans to implement this idea, his policy initially dealt with four considerations: ending the Korean war without changing the status quo in the rest of Asia; developing anti-Communist alliances in the Middle East; unifying Western Europe; and, maintaining the Cold War against the Soviets.

Shortly after the inauguration Dulles and Eisenhower took steps to end the Korean war. They intensified the pressure on China to accept a compromise agreement. In his State of the Union message, Eisenhower announced he would remove the Seventh Fleet from the Formosa Straits, thus "unleashing" Chiang Kai-shek for a possible attack on the mainland. The Administration also revealed plans to increase U.S. air power in Korea, enlarge the South Korean Army and place nuclear weapons on Okinawa. At the same time Dulles firmly pushed South Korea into accepting an armistice by refusing to give in to President Syngman Rhee's demands for resumption of the war if Korean unification was not achieved within three months of an armistice. The agreement was signed on July 27, 1953.

In the Mideast Dulles attempted to forestall Communist expansion through the establishment of pro-Western governments and the formation of a military alliance similar to the North Atlantic Treaty Organization (NATO). The leftist government of Iranian Premier Mohammed Mossadegh was overthrown in August 1953 with the help of the Central Intelligence Agency (CIA). A pro-Western regime loyal to the Shah took its place. In attempting to form alliances, the Secretary was frustrated by growing nationalism in Arab nations, particularly Egypt. Reacting to years of British colonial rule, Egyptian leader Gamal Abdel Nasser refused to accept membership in any

mutual defense organization giving Britain or any other colonial power the right to return to Egypt if strategic interests were threatened. Nasser did not perceive the Communist threat as serious and attempted to maintain a policy of neutrality to prevent domination by either the Western or Soviet bloc. In 1954 the British succeeded in forming the Bagdad Pact, a military alliance with Turkey, Iran, Iraq and Pakistan. Dulles, however, was reluctant to recognize the alliance, not wanting to be associated with colonial powers. Fearing that American membership would antagonize Arab leaders, he sent an "observer" rather than an ambassador to the new organization.

As Secretary of State, Dulles was particularly concerned with American policy in Western Europe, which he thought would be the major battlefield of the Cold War. Throughout his tenure he attempted to promote European unification, maintaining that Europe, "the world's worst fire hazard," could not be rebuilt on the old system of nation-states. The Secretary supported such moves toward economic unification as the formation of the European Iron and Steel Community, and he wanted them complemented by steps toward military unification. By the time Dulles came to office, an agreement on the formation of the European Defense Community (EDC), establishing an inter-European army, had already been initialed by the governments concerned: France, Germany and Benelux. However, popular opposition to the plan, particularly in France, which feared German rearmament, endangered ratification. During the early months of 1953, Dulles flew to various European capitals in an attempt to increase support for the EDC. Intent upon gaining acceptance, he suggested that a defeat of the proposal would result in "an agonizing reappraisal" of American commitments in Europe. However, his efforts failed. The proposal died in August 1954, when the French Assembly refused to consider the plan.

Dulles was particularly upset by the defeat because he felt it necessary to integrate West Germany into the mainstream of European politics as quickly as possible lest the nation make an accommodation with the Soviet bloc. However, the U.S. allies were angered at Dulles's strident stand during the debate over the EDC, and the Secretary was forced to leave the negotiation of the German issue to the British. Over the next few months Foreign Minister Anthony Eden laid the groundwork for the introduction of Germany into NATO while placing constraints on German rearmament to please the French. Dulles supported the plan, approved at a foreign minister's conference convened in London in September.

A strident cold warrior, Dulles opposed any attempt at conciliation with the Soviet Union. When the Soviet leadership made a series of peace overtures following the death of Stalin in March 1953, he recommended no public acknowledgement. He dismissed them as a "tactical retreat" and suggested that the U.S. take advantage of the confused situation in the Kremlin to begin a diplomatic and propaganda offensive against the Communists. When Eisenhower determined to respond publicly to the gesture, Dulles recommended that the speech contain a list of "deeds," including political self-determination for Eastern Europe, to test the sincerity of the Russian proposals. These were included in the President's statement, which despite Dulles's advice, suggested the possibility of accommodation.

Dulles also opposed a summit conference in 1955. He believed that the meeting would accomplish nothing substantial and would antagonize the powerful Republican Right. The Secretary insisted that the U.S. require the USSR to begin withdrawal from Eastern Europe before serious talks began. Eisenhower, however, ignored his Secretary's advice and accepted an invitation to meet with the Soviet leaders in July. Although Dulles had advised him to wear an "austere countenance" when photographed with Premier Nikolai Bulganin, the President conducted himself in a warm, friendly manner. The conference resolved none of the issues dividing the nations—Germany and disarmament—but the fact that the leaders of the two super-powers had discussed differences gave hope of improved chances for peace and led to the "Spirit of Geneva," a thaw in the Cold War.

Dulles, however, had a pessimistic assessment of the meeting. He remained convinced that the Soviet Union had called the summit to gain strategic respite. The Secretary believed that the Soviets had overextended themselves in the arms race and were hence forced toward conciliation with the West. He conceded that the new Soviet policy "might assume the force of an irreversible trend" which should be encouraged. However, he refused to accept the current situation in Europe and warned that Russian actions did not justify "the free world relaxing its vigilance or substantially altering its programs for collective security."

Although Dulles and his defenders hailed his policies as a departure from those of the Truman Administration, they were in essence continuations of containment. The major innovation was the introduction of the "New Look" defense policy with its reliance on strategic deterrence or "massive retaliation" as it became known. Fashioned chiefly by Adm. Arthur Radford [q.v.], chairman of the Joint Chiefs of Staff, the New Look was based on a desire to hold down defense costs and prevent debilitating ground wars such as those in Korea. It called for the movement away from the use of both conventional forces and nuclear weapons toward the acceptance of nuclear weapons delivered by bombers or missiles as a primary deterrent against aggression. Although its origins could be traced to Dulles's 1952 *Life* article, "The Policy of Boldness," the Secretary had very little to do with the actual formulation. In military matters he was content to rely on the Pentagon. Yet the Secretary was given the task of explaining the New Look to the American people. In a speech before the Council on Foreign Relations during January, Dulles told the audience that the use of conventional forces had traditionally given the enemy the initiative. He recommended that local defenses be strengthened with the further deterrent of massive retaliatory power. The Secretary promised that the U.S. could "depend upon a great capacity to retaliate instantly by means and at places of our own choosing."

Foreign policy observers had difficulty trying to understand what Dulles meant by this ambiguous statement. Many thought the Secretary promised nuclear war for any Soviet infraction of the status quo. Dulles attempted to clarify the use of the term, but his several attempts at explanation confused the issue further. Walter Lippmann [q.v.] wrote that "official explanations of the New Look have become so voluminous that it is almost a career to keep up with them." That concept with its ambiguity played an important role in the development of Dulles's foreign policy. The Secretary saw the threat of deterrence as a potent diplomatic weapon to brandish before the Communists.

Dulles's use of his new weapon was tested twice during 1954: in Vietnam and in the Formosa Straits. During the spring of 1954 the French asked for direct American intervention in Vietnam to relieve their garrison at Dien Bien Phu, then under attack by the Communist Vietminh. The French confided in Dulles their desire to reach a settlement in the Indochina war and told him they would restrict military operations to achieve that goal. The Secretary opposed the French decision, believing it would further the expansion of Communism in Southeast Asia. He also rejected Radford's call for bombing raids to relieve the fort, because the proposal was too narrow in scope. Instead, he proposed using the deterrence doctrine to achieve not a compromise settlement but the defeat of Communism in Southeast Asia. On March 29, in a major policy address at the Overseas Press Club, Dulles articulated his policy: "The United States feels that the possibility of Communist control should not be passively accepted, but should be met with united action."

Over the next month Dulles attempted to generate congressional and allied support for his plan. Congress, however, turned down his request for a resolution allowing American intervention because the allies had not been consulted. The British and

French, too, refused his overture. They were angered at Dulles's presumption that he could speak for Europe and were wary of a military commitment in light of the implications of his "massive retaliation" speech. In addition, both nations felt that, though the Secretary had emphasized deterrence, Dulles intended to commit the allies to a ground war in Asia to prevent a French withdrawal. His proposal, therefore, would have prevented a peaceful compromise settlement.

Dulles entered the Geneva Conference on Indochina in April 1954 opposed to a negotiated settlement. Reacting to pressure from the Republican Right and to his own anti-Communism, he refused to acknowledge the Communist Chinese delegation. The Secretary remained at the Conference for only one week while he tried to convince the British and French to join the U.S. in an alliance that would influence the outcome of the meeting. When this failed, he returned to Washington. During the substantive sessions, Undersecretary of State Walter Bedell Smith represented the U.S. but on Dulles's order took virtually no part in the discussion.

On July 21 the Geneva Conference reached an agreement on Vietnam. Under the Accords, as the agreement was known, Vietnam was temporarily divided along the 17th parallel with the Communists, led by Ho Chi Minh, controling the north and a pro-Western government, headed by Ngo Dinh Diem, in the south. The nation was to be reunified through free elections scheduled for 1956. On Dulles's order the U.S. refused to sign the treaty but "took note" of it. In a statement after the agreement had been reached, Smith announced that the U.S. "would view any renewal of the aggression in violation of the aforesaid agreements with grave concern and as seriously threatening international peace and security." Thus Dulles committed the U.S. to support a pro-Western government in Southeast Asia.

Over the next few months Dulles worked to prevent Communist expansion in Vietnam. In September eight nations (the U.S., Great Britain, France, Australia, New Zealand, Pakistan, Thailand and the Philippines) formed the Southeast Asia Treaty Organization, pledged to resist Communist aggression in the area. That fall Dulles announced that the U.S. would give both economic and military aid to the Diem government. American military advisers such as Edward Lansdale [q.v.] were sent to Vietnam to help Diem solidify his position. In a shift from his massive retaliation philosophy, the Secretary began backing reliance on "local defense" to counter Communist aggression. At Dulles's behest, Diem resisted British and French pleas to meet with representatives of the Vietminh to set up consultations on the proposed all-Vietnam elections. The elections were never held.

During the fall of 1954 Communist Chinese artillery began shelling the Nationalist held islands of Quemoy and Matsu off the mainland coast. Members of the Administration differed on how to interpret the action. Dulles believed it was a possible prelude for an invasion of Formosa; but several military leaders questioned the Communists' military capacity to stage such an action. The Secretary joined Radford and most of the Joint Chiefs of Staff (except Gen. Matthew Ridgway [q.v.]) in proposing that Eisenhower permit Chiang to bomb the mainland. If Peking retaliated, they suggested the U.S. send bombers to help the Nationalists. Eisenhower, however, rejected the proposal, preferring to work out a diplomatic solution to the crisis. To prevent military action by the Nationalist Chinese, he sent Dulles to negotiate a mutual security treaty between the two countries. This agreement, signed in December 1954, reflected both Eisenhower's desire that the U.S. commitment be limited to the defense of Taiwan and Dulles's and the congressional right wing's desire to defend the offshore islands. The treaty focused on Taiwan, but accompanying documents extended the commitment to "such other territories as may be determined by a mutual agreement."

The bombing continued into the spring of 1955. Eisenhower still held firm, arguing that the islands were not worth fighting for, but he permitted Dulles to publicly threaten Peking with nuclear reprisals. Vice President Richard Nixon [q.v.] joined Dulles in this stand, and Eisenhower, himself, refused to rule out the possibility of bombing military targets. In April the crisis died down as the Chinese tapered off shelling. Dulles was quick to credit the threat of nuclear attack for the change.

As the 1956 presidential campaign approached, Dulles began defending his controversial policies. In a *Life* interview, he suggested that his successes resulted from the art of what came to be called "brinksmanship." "We were brought to the brink of war," he said, "the ability to get to the verge without getting into the war is the necessary art. If you can't master it you inevitably get into war . . . . we walked to the brink, and we looked it in the face. We took strong action." Yet Adlai Stevenson, [q.v.] the Democratic presidential candidate, and other liberals pointed out that Dulles's threats were useless because nations knew that the U.S. would not be the first to use nuclear weapons.

Dulles's tendency to think in terms of Communism versus anti-Communism limited his response to the growing nationalism in the Middle East. In 1955, Nasser turned to the U.S. for arms. Dulles, however, denied him the help, believing that the U.S. should not become involved in an arms race in the area. Instead, the U.S. offered Egypt assistance in building the Aswan High Dam. Nasser reluctantly turned to the Soviet bloc for military aid. Although Nasser did not wish to become closely allied with the USSR, Dulles viewed the arms deal as a dangerous drift to the left. Egyptian recognition of Communist China strengthened his belief. Angered at Nasser's conduct (which he thought was an attempt to play one side against the other in the Cold War) and prompted by domestic opposition to the dam, on July 19 Dulles terminated negotiations on the project.

In retaliation Nasser seized the Suez Canal one week later, promising to use the toll money to build the dam. The seizure threatened British and French interests in the Middle East. Both nations began drawing up military plans to regain control of the waterway, but Dulles advocated a negotiated settlement of the issue. At the London Conference, called at his behest in September, he proposed that the U.N. supervise canal operations. Several weeks later he suggested forming an association of canal users to collect tolls and direct piloting. The organization would then give Egypt what it considered a fair share of canal revenues. Dulles's proposals angered both Egypt and the European nations. The British and French resented the fact that they had not been consulted before the proposals were presented. Egypt disliked the plans because they would take control of the Canal out of its hands.

As the negotiations dragged on, the allies became impatient with U.S. leadership. In the fall French and British troops seized the Canal, while the Israeli Army invaded the Sinai. Dulles turned on the British and French for what he considered to be an immoral breach of the peace. With Eisenhower's approval, he joined the Soviet Union at the U.N. to pass a resolution calling for the withdrawal of the invading forces from Egypt. Faced with unanimous world opinion and the prospect of Russian involvement, Britain, France and Israel withdrew. Dulles's refusal to back the military action strained U.S. relations with the allies for months, and in the case of France, years.

Following the Suez crisis the Soviet Union's prestige grew in the Middle East. To prevent the further erosion of the American position there, Dulles and Eisenhower asked Congress to provide them with a joint resolution granting the President authority to send troops to the area if a pro-Western government required assistance against Communist subversion. Congress approved this request, known as the Eisenhower Doctrine, in January 1957. In 1958 the pro-Western Lebanese government, fearing a pro-Nasser revolt which it believed was infiltrated by Communists, asked for American assistance, Eisenhower sent troops to quell the insurrection.

Dulles's activities during the second Eisenhower Administration were curtailed by his bout with cancer. Nevertheless, he continued to expound his hard-line policies despite a changing world situation. The Secretary still opposed accommodation with the Soviet Union. He also continued to oppose neutralism in the Third World, while young diplomats saw it as a means of preserving peace and depolarizing the world situation.

Dulles, however, did oversee a change in American policy on Quemoy and Matsu. In August 1958 the Communist Chinese resumed heavy shelling of the islands. The Secretary again threatened nuclear reprisal but soon found he had no support for this policy at home or abroad. In September Premier Nikita Khrushchev reminded Eisenhower that the Soviet Union could also employ nuclear weapons in a crisis. Dulles then made a major shift in policy. He stated that Chiang was "rather foolish" in stationing a large garrison on Quemoy and acknowledged that the U.S. had made no guarantees to defend the islands. He visited Taipei to persuade Chiang to thin out his Quemoy garrison. In addition, the U.S. initiated contacts with Communists. Using the American embassy in Warsaw, headed by Ambassador Jacob Beam, the two nations discussed the problem, preventing an open rupture in the Formosa Straits.

Dulles faced his last crisis in November 1958, when Khrushchev demanded the West withdraw its troops from West Berlin and make it an autonomous city. If this did not occur within six weeks, he warned, he would then turn the access routes over to the East Germans and force the West to negotiate with them. Dulles approached the crisis as he had in the past. He viewed the Soviet action as reckless and urged the West not to negotiate under duress. Although he confided that the crisis could be surmounted without going to war, he urged the West to be ready to use nuclear warfare if necessary to protect Berlin. Western strategy had not been agreed upon at the time of Dulles's resignation on April 15. On May 24 Dulles died in his sleep.

[JB]

For further information:
John Robinson Beal. *John Foster Dulles: A Biog-*

raphy (New York. 1957).

Richard Goold-Adams. *The Time of Power: A Reappraisal of John Foster Dulles* (Boston. 1962).

Michael Guhin. *John Foster Dulles: A Statesman and His Times* (New York. 1972).

Townsend Hoopes. *The Devil and John Foster Dulles* (Boston. 1973).

Hans Morgenthau. "John Foster Dulles." in Norman Graebner. ed.. *An Uncertain Tradition: American Secretaries of State in the Twentieth Century* (New York, 1961).

EISENHOWER, DWIGHT D(AVID)

b. Oct. 14, 1890; Denison, Texas
d. March 28, 1969; Washington, D.C.
President of the United States, 1953-61.

Born into a family of Swiss descent, David Eisenhower was raised in Abilene, Kan., where his father worked at a local creamery. While a child he earned the nickname "Ike," which remained with him throughout his life. Despite his mother's pacificism and his father's lack of political influence, Eisenhower won appointment to West Point in 1911. He enrolled under the name Dwight D., which he used thereafter. He graduated in 1915 near the bottom of his class.

Eisenhower served as a tank instructor during World War I and remained in the Army after the armistice. He graduated from the Command and General Staff School in 1926, the Army War College in 1929 and the Army Industrial College in 1932. During the 1930s he worked under Gen. Douglas A. MacArthur, both as his personal assistant and as assistant military adviser to the Philippine Commonwealth.

After the American entry into World War II Eisenhower served as Gen. George C. Marshall's chief of operations. In 1942 he assumed command of the U.S. forces in Europe and oversaw the Allied invasion of North Africa in 1942 and Sicily and Italy in 1943. The following year, as supreme commander of all Allied forces, he took charge of planning the Normandy invasion.

Eisenhower's strength as a commander lay in his political ability to unite and utilize Allied leaders, maintain good public relations and administer a vast bureaucracy. He was also a noted strategist.

In 1945 President Harry S. Truman appointed Eisenhower Army Chief of Staff. He remained at that post until 1948, when he accepted the presidency of Columbia University. Uncomfortable in the academic world, he resigned his appointment in 1951 to assume command of forces being organized under the North Atlantic Treaty Organization (NATO).

During the late-1940s and early-1950s representatives of the liberal Eastern wing of the Republican Party—politicians such as Sen. Henry Cabot Lodge (R, Mass.) [*q.v.*] and financiers like Paul Hoffman [*q.v.*] attempted to persuade Eisenhower to run for President. These men, anxious to win control of the Party from Midwestern nationalists led by Sen. Robert Taft (R, Ohio) [*q.v.*], felt the General would be their ideal candidate. He supported their stand for a strong American economy unencumbered by government. More importantly he was anxious to continue a bipartisan foreign policy with full U.S. participation in European affairs. They thought that Eisenhower, with his lack of political background and high moral purpose, could lead a crusade that would return the U.S. to its traditional values. "The people want another George Washington," wrote Harry A. Bullis to Eisenhower, "to them you are the man who can best help them keep their liberty and their freedom." However, Eisenhower, anxious to develop a collective security system in Europe and opposed to military men in politics, refused.

By 1951 he had begun to change his mind. Private discussions with Taft left him convinced that a Taft presidency would jeopardize American interests in Europe. Lodge had also convinced Eisenhower that he was the only man to unite the Republican Party and prevent it from becoming a splinter group outside the mainstream of American politics. The following year, Eisenhower defeated Taft for the nomination and won an easy victory in the November election.

As President, Eisenhower was primarily interested in foreign and defense policy. During his eight years in office, he worked closely with Secretary of State Dulles to mold a policy that reflected his conception of a bipolarized world engaged in a struggle between freedom and Communism. Dulles was the conceptualizer and prime mover of foreign policy. Nevertheless, Eisenhower knew his own mind on foreign affairs, and in many crises, he exercised restraint on his more headstrong Secretary. Although often resorting to bellicose language, Eisenhower dismissed war as an option. His primary goal was to remain at peace while containing Communism and extending American influence throughout the world.

Shortly after he was elected President, Eisenhower began steps to end the Korean war. Fulfilling his campaign pledge to go to Korea, he staged a brief visit in November to inspect troops and to talk to South Korean President Syngman Rhee. The journey did not aid peace efforts, but it reassured the American people that the new President, with his vast military experience, was focusing his attention on the problem. After his inauguration Eisenhower began pressuring both Communist China and South Korea into accepting an armistice. He removed the Seventh Fleet from the Formosa Straits, thus "unleashing" Chiang Kai-shek for a possible attack on the mainland. He also increased U.S. air forces in Korea and announced that nuclear weapons were being moved to Okinawa. While developing a hard-line attitude toward Communist China, he firmly opposed South Korean demands for an agreement to resume fighting if Korea was not unified within 90 days of an armistice. The peace agreement was signed on July 27.

Eisenhower's primary focus was on Europe, which he considered the major front of the Cold War. There he continued Truman's containment policy of redeveloping and eventually unifying Western Europe economically and militarily to prevent further Communist expansion. The President quickly stopped his attacks on the Yalta and Potsdam agreements, which conservatives contended led to the division of Europe. He feared that repudiation might deny Western access rights to Berlin, affirmed at Yalta, and he disliked the prospect of renouncing agreements he had carried out while Army Chief of Staff. In a resolution to Congress during the early months of 1953, Eisenhower pointed to a Soviet perversion of the agreements rather than a Roosevelt betrayal as responsible for Communist expansion in Eastern Europe. He also dropped calls for the "liberation" of Eastern Europe, which the Republican Party had pledged during the 1952 campaign and which had become hollow in light of U.S. impotence during the 1953 East German uprising. The President's attempt to unify Western Europe met with only modest success. Despite his and Dulles's vigorous support, the French voted down the European Defense Community for fear of German rearmament. He did, however, succeed in integrating West Germany into NATO.

Despite his continuation of Cold War policies and often strident rhetoric, Eisenhower believed that a reduction in tensions between the two superpowers was possible. However, the conditions he imposed made accomodation unlikely. Over the objections of his Secretary of State, he responded to the Soviet peace overtures made shortly after the death of Stalin. In a speech before the American Association of Newspaper Editors in April, Eisenhower deplored the price of the continued arms race. "This is not a way of life at all," he said, "in any true sense. Under the cloud of threatening war, it is humanity hanging from a cross of iron." He expressed American hope of cooperation and announced that he would regard even a "few clear and specific acts of reciprocation," such as the beginning of Soviet withdrawal from Eastern Europe, as "impressive signs" that the Russians shared his desires. Because of domestic pressures on both sides, the peace overtures produced no results. Two years later Eisenhower, again over the objections of Dulles, attended a summit conference between Soviet leaders and those of the Western bloc. No agreement was reached on the issues dividing them—Germany and disarmament—but the fact that leaders had actually confronted problems led to a brief period of relaxed tensions.

Eisenhower faced two major threats to peace during 1954: in Vietnam and in the Formosa Straits. In the spring of 1954 the French requested American military aid to relieve their beleagured garrison at Dien Bien Phu in northern Vietnam. Eisenhower refused the Joint Chiefs of Staff's plans for using American air strikes and atomic weapons if necessary against the Communist Vietminh.

Several months later the President resisted further suggestions that the U.S. permit Nationalist China to bomb the mainland in retaliation for Communist shelling of the Nationalist held islands of Quemoy and Matsu. Instead, he sent Dulles to negotiate a mutual defense treaty to prevent China from undertaking offensive operations without American consent. Meanwhile, Eisenhower put pressure on the Communists. In January 1955 he asked Congress to pass the Formosa Resolution, giving the President full authority to take whatever action he deemed necessary to defend Formosa. Shortly after passage Eisenhower conceded that the U.S. would use atomic weapons in a general Asian war. The Chinese diminished shelling, and in 1955 they indicated they were ready to negotiate the issue.

Eisenhower's defense policy was determined by several factors but principally his belief that a large defense budget would weaken the U.S. economy. "This country could choke itself to death piling up military expenditures," he said, "just as surely as it can defeat itself by not spending for protection." He, therefore, worked to reduce and hold down the size and coast of the military establishment. Eisenhower also assumed that the U.S. would never start a war and should therefore focus its resources on deterrence rather than attack. Refusing to become involved in ground wars that drained the military and sapped the economy and believing that future wars would quickly turn into nuclear combat,

Eisenhower relied on the delivery of nuclear weapons by strategic aircraft as America's major deterrent. This program was designed to provide an alternative to the costly Truman policy of funding both conventional and nuclear forces.

Eisenhower began implementing the new plans in fiscal 1955. In a policy paper approved in October 1954, the Administration called for a 25% reduction in the size of the American military in 1956. This was to be achieved primarily through cutbacks in Army and Navy manpower and budgets. On the other hand, the Air Force was slightly enlarged and its funding increased. Despite opposition from the Army and some Navy personnel, Eisenhower, playing on the belief that as a military man he understood the situation, pushed the budget through Congress.

During his first term, Eisenhower was forced to devote a large amount of his time to assuaging the Republican Right. Throughout his presidency he was challenged by the China bloc, a group of conservative members of Congress led by such men as William Knowland (R, Calif.) [q.v.], who opposed any accommodation with Communist China. It was partly in response to this attitude that Eisenhower remained stridently opposed to the admission of Communist China to the U.N. and rejected suggestions of negotiating differences with the mainland.

Eisenhower's handling of two diplomatic crises during the 1956 campaign strengthened his electoral position. In the fall the British, French and Israelis attacked Egypt in an effort to regain control of the Suez Canal, nationalized after American refusal to finance the Aswan Dam. Eisenhower refused to join the invasion and instead brought the matter before the U.N. There the U.S. joined the USSR in calling for a ceasefire and withdrawal. In late October, Hungarians rebelled against Russian occupation. Eisenhower personally appealed to Soviet leaders to let Hungary alone, but did nothing to aid the rebels.

Eisenhower's greatest domestic problems in his second term came in the fall of 1957 following the Soviet Union's launching of the *Sputnik*, the first artificial earth satellite. The announcement, coming just after the USSR had successfully fired an intercontinental ballistic missile, destroyed the U.S. sense of security and opened debate on American defense policy. Eisenhower faced open criticism from the military, which objected to his limiting defense expenditures and to continuing reliance on the policy of massive retaliation in light of growing nuclear parity. Members of the Army and Navy, led by such men as Gen. Maxwell Taylor [*q.v.*] and Adm. Arleigh Burke, maintained that future conflicts would be primarily limited wars and insisted that increased funds be given to conventional forces. The Air Force, in turn, stressed the need for an accelerated program of missile development to maintain U.S. superiority. It was joined by a number of influential individuals, including Sens. Stuart Symington (D, Mo.) [*q.v.*] and John F. Kennedy (D, Mass.) [*q.v.*], who suggested that Eisenhower had permitted a potentially fatal "missile gap" to grow between the U.S. and the USSR. Eisenhower, who had given up the concept of nuclear superiority in favor of one of sufficiency, vainly attempted to convince his critics that despite USSR superiority in missiles, American nuclear delivery capacity still far outweighed that of the Soviet Union.

In 1958, Eisenhower became increasingly preoccupied with the growing strength of radical forces in the Middle East that threatened to take over in Jordan, Iraq and Lebanon. He asked and received Congressional authority to use U.S. forces in the area; and in response to a request from Lebanese President Camille Chamoun, Eisenhower sent American troops in July to prevent a possible coup by Pan-Arab elements which the Lebanese leader thought might have Communist ties.

Just as Lebanon settled down the Communist Chinese resumed shelling Quemoy and Matsu. Eisenhower again attempted to use a hard-line posture to force the Chinese to back down. In September he announced that the U.S. was prepared to defend the islands. However, his stand won support neither in the nation nor among the U.S. allies, and he was forced to retreat. Dulles acknowledged that the U.S. was under no

obligation to defend the islands and termed Chaing Kai-shek's stationing of large garrisons on Quemoy "rather foolish." Responding to Eisenhower's signal, Peking gradually reduced its shelling.

The last two years of his Administration marked an Eisenhower resurgence. America's position in foreign affairs also improved. The USSR retreated from its stand on Berlin, announcing that the West would be given an 18-month extension to consider its proposals. Khrushchev's visit to the U.S. in September 1959 produced a thaw in U.S.—USSR relations. The two superpowers took their first step toward nuclear weapons limitation in December 1959, when both countries joined 10 others in signing the Antarctic Treaty, establishing a nuclear free zone in the area.

After the death of Dulles in May 1959, Eisenhower concentrated foreign policy in his own hands. Increasingly he felt that his historic mission was to encourage a "just and lasting peace." He told the nation: "There is no place on this earth to which I would not travel, there is no chore I would not undertake, if I had any faintest hope that, by so doing, I would promote the general cause of world peace." Eisenhower undertook a series of goodwill visits to Latin America, Asia and Africa which, while doing little to settle outstanding issues, increased his personal standing.

Eisenhower gradually began reorienting U.S. policy towards Latin American. Still intent on preventing Communist expansion in the area, he initiated steps to bring down the government of Fidel Castro, the left-wing Cuban leader who had come to power in 1959. In response to the confiscation of American property in July, Eisenhower cut Cuba's sugar quota by 700,000 tons. Later that year he took steps to prohibit Cuban sugar from the U.S. market for the early part of 1961. In March 1960 he approved a Central Intelligence Agency plan to train Cuban exiles for an invasion of the island.

In other areas of Latin America, however, the President began efforts to prevent Communist expansion through the use of massive long-term economic aid. He warned that the choice was "social evolution or revolution." In September 1960 the

Administration proposed a program, known as the Act of Bogata, to assist health services, expand housing and educational facilities and aid agriculture. It was supported by all Latin American nations with the exception of Cuba. Eisenhower's policies formed the basis for President Kennedy's Alliance for Progress.

Two events marred Eisenhower's last months in office. In May his summit meeting with Khrushchev was canceled following the Soviet downing of a U.S. spy plane over Russian territory. The President took personal responsibility for the incident. For the first time in history a head of state openly admitted that his nation engaged in espionage against another country. In June his trip to Japan was canceled because of anti-American riots generated by the Japanese Parliament's ratification of an unpopular military treaty with the U.S.

In his January farewell address to the nation, Eisenhower delivered one of his most famous speeches. He warned of the pervasiveness of a growing "military-industrial complex." He regretted the "conjunction of an immense military establishment and a large arms industry. . . . The total influence—economic, political, even spiritual —is felt in every city, every state house, every office of the federal government." He warned of the need to guard against its unwarranted influence and its potential "for the disastrous rise of misplaced power." The weight of this combination, he suggested, could "endanger our liberties or our democratic processes."

Eisenhower retired to his farm near Gettysburg, Pa. The General, as he wished to be called, consistently opposed increases in defense spending during the Kennedy Administration. He also called for reduced troop commitments to NATO. Eisenhower remained the most popular leader of the Republican Party, but his refusal to join in party infighting limited his political influence during the remainder of his life. He supported President Lyndon B. Johnson's Vietnam policies and frequently advised the President. Eisenhower endorsed Nixon for President in 1968 and denied that he had "never really liked or supported or really believed in Nixon." Three weeks before the election he suffered a severe heart attack from which he never recovered. Eisenhower died on March 28, 1969.

During the decades after Eisenhower left office, historians and political scientists' assessments at his presidency changed. In the late-1950s and early-1960s, Eisenhower was criticized for his formalist view of the presidency, his lack of an activist domestic program and his cold war rhetoric. William Shannon viewed the Administration as a "time of great postponement" while others described it as "the bland leading the bland." Richard Rovere termed Eisenhower's leadership "mastery in the service of drift." In polls asking scholars to evaluate the presidency in terms of previous ones, Eisenhower was ranked near the bottom with James Buchanan and Chester Arthur.

By the end of the 1960s historians' assessment of the Eisenhower Administration had changed. Disillusioned with the "Imperial Presidency" and reacting to the domestic tensions of the period, scholars viewed Eisenhower as a man of peace. He had united a deeply divided society, prevented the development of political extremism and furthered the acceptance of the welfare state. More importantly, Eisenhower held down the arms race and gave the nation almost eight years without war.

[EWS]

For further information:
Sherman Adams, *Firsthand Report: The Story of the Eisenhower Administration* (New York, 1961).
Charles Alexander, *Holding the Line: The Eisenhower Era, 1952-1961* (Bloomington, 1975).
Dwight D. Eisenhower, *The White House Years*, 2 vols. (Garden City, 1963-65).
Emmet John Hughes, *The Ordeal of Power: A Political Memoir of the Eisenhower Years* (New York, 1963)
Arthur Larson, *Eisenhower: The President Nobody Knew* (New York, 1968).
Herbert S. Parmet, *Eisenhower and the American Crusade* (New York, 1972).

FAIRBANK, JOHN K(ING)
b. May 24, 1907; Huron, S.D.
State Department adviser.

Fairbank received his bachelor's degree from Harvard University, summa cum laude, in 1929. A Rhodes scholar, he went to China in 1932, studying and lecturing for three years at Tsinghua University in Peking, where his major interest was the impact of Western imperialism on Chinese society. He received his Ph.D. from Oxford in 1936 and joined the Harvard faculty that same year.

In 1941 Fairbank was granted a leave of absence from Harvard to serve in the Washington office of the Coordinator of Information and with the Office of Strategic Services. He went to China in 1942 as a special assistant to the U.S. ambassador. During 1944 Fairbank worked with the Office of War Information, where he also acted occasionally as the deputy director in charge of Far Eastern operations. The following year he returned to China as the director of the United States Information Service. In 1946 he resumed his position at Harvard.

In *The United States and China,* published in 1948, Fairbank attempted to analyze China in terms of its cultural and historical background. He emphasized China as a society different from the West, one of authoritarian traditions that did not easily lend itself to the development of liberal capitalism. His book was praised as a scholarly work, although some critics disagreed with Fairbank's criticism of Chiang Kai-shek's government. Fairbank accused Chiang of presiding over a corrupt regime of "carpet-bagging generals and politicians" with as "shameful a record of official looting as modern history has displayed." He also criticized Chiang's government for its use of force against intellectuals and demonstrating students, its ineffective administration and for the Generalissimo's failure to develop any sort of rural reconstruction program.

The following year Fairbank argued, in *The Next Step in Asia,* that the United States had to accept the fact that the Communists had defeated the Nationalists in China. He urged the United States to take a more practical approach and support the inevitable changes with American aid and technology. In a *Harvard Crimson* article in 1950, Fairbank called for the recognition of Communist China, which in his view was not an act of moral approval but only a realistic step in which the United States could "deal with the Communists but be under no compulsion to accept their terms."

After Communist China's entry into the Korean war, Fairbank spoke out against extending the conflict to China. He pointed out that there was a lack of installations in China worth bombing, and he maintained that an attack would only serve to spur the Chinese war effort. Fairbank said it would be a "fallacy" to think that the application of force would result in defeating the Communists.

In 1951 and 1952 the Senate Permanent Investigations Subcommittee probed charges that Fairbank was a Communist. Fairbank testified before the panel in March 1952, repeating under oath his previous denials that he had ever been a member of the Party. He criticized what he termed the "totalitarian" methods used by the group. He did admit that he had once supported an effort to bring about an amalgamation of Communists and Nationalists in the Chinese government, but he pointed out that this policy had been advocated by George C. Marshall [q.v.] and other Chinese experts.

Although Fairbank was ultimately cleared of the charges, he was for a time refused a passport. During the 1950s and 1960s he continued his academic career. In the mid-1960s he emerged from obscurity with the renewal of public discussion of America's China policy. He presented the view that there was continuity in Chinese leadership and opposed the vision of a distinct Communist dictatorship.

[GS]

For further information:
John K. Fairbank, *The United States and China* (Cambridge, Mass., 1958).

FORD, GERALD R(UDOLPH)
b. July 14, 1913; Omaha, Neb.
President of the United States, August 1974-January 1977.

Raised in Grand Rapids, Mich., Ford attended the University of Michigan, where he was a college all-star football player, and Yale Law School, where he earned his law degree in 1941. After serving in the Navy during World War II, he practiced law in Grand Rapids. In 1948, at the urging of Arthur H. Vandenberg, Ford successfully challenged an isolationist incumbent U.S. representative in the Republican primary. Ford then easily defeated his Democratic opponent and, in 12 subsequent elections, always captured over 60% of the vote. During the 1950s he aligned himself with the Eisenhower internationalist wing of the Republican Party and became a staunch proponent of large defense budgets and military alliances to prevent Communist expansion. Fiercely partisan, Ford compiled a conservative voting record in domestic affairs.

During Nixon's first term in office, Ford proved himself a staunch Administration loyalist and maintained his conservative voting record. Ford supported Nixon's decision in March 1969 to seek appropriations for deployment of the Safeguard anti-ballistic missile system (ABM) and accused its opponents of proposing unilateral disarmament "in the face of a serious threat from the Soviet Union."

Ford consistently supported Nixon's Vietnam policy. In September 1969 he denounced the proposals of anti-war activists for immediate troop withdrawal as "tantamount to surrender." He voted against all efforts to curb military spending in Southeast Asia and to place a time limit on American troop involvement in the war. In 1971 he voted to extend the draft and in 1973 voted against the War Powers Act. In the spring of 1972 he defended the intensified bombing of North Vietnam as "the right course." In May, when Nixon announced the mining of North Vietnamese harbors, Ford praised the President as "generous in his bid for peace but firm in his determination that we will not surrender."

On Oct. 12, 1973, two days after the resignation of vice president Spiro T. Agnew, President Nixon named Gerald Ford to replace Agnew. The choice was widely viewed as an effort to win congressional support for the Administration in light of the growing Watergate scandal. The initial reaction in Congress was overwhelmingly favorable since Ford, though extremely partisan, was also well-liked and admired for his extreme honesty and candor.

On Aug. 9, 1974, Nixon resigned from the presidency after admitting that he had ordered a halt to the FBI probe of the Watergate break-in, and Ford was sworn in as the nation's 38th President. In addressing the country he said, "Our long national nightmare is over. Our Constitution works. Our great republic is a government of laws and not of men." He pledged an Administration of "openness and candor" and moved quickly to meet with cabinet members, congressional leaders, national security officials and economic policy advisers. Ford took office with a great reservoir of good will.

As President, Ford pursued a policy of detente with the Soviet Union and sought to defuse tensions in the Middle East. The legacy of Vietnam, moreover, affected his conduct of foreign affairs. Congress was unwilling to let the President have a free hand in the making of foreign policy and public pressure against further entanglements abroad forced a generally low profile for the United States.

Ford voiced strong support for Henry Kissinger [q.v.] and kept him on as both Secretary of State and head of the National Security Council. Kissinger was viewed as the chief architect of East-West detente and in October 1974 he visited the Soviet Union in pursuit of a new arms limitation agreement. Upon Kissinger's return, Ford announced that he would travel to the Soviet port city of Vladivostok in November to meet Soviet leader

Leonid Brezhnev. There, the two heads of state announced an agreement to limit the numbers of all strategic offensive nuclear weaponry including the controversial MIRV delivery system. In contrast to the 1972 Strategic Arms Limitation Agreement (SALT), the new pact set the principle of equivalency in offensive weaponry for the two nations. Ford also revealed that SALT II talks would resume in Geneva in January and described the pursuit of a further agreement as in "the best interest" of the United States. Little further progress was made, however, and a year later in November 1975 Ford was forced to concede that the "timetable doesn't look encouraging" for a new SALT pact in the near future.

Ford also encouraged Kissinger's efforts at "shuttle diplomacy" to achieve a peace settlement in the Middle East. In March 1975, after Kissinger failed to win agreement for a second Egyptian-Israeli troop withdrawal from the Sinai, Ford angrily announced that his Administration was totally reassessing Middle East policy, and pointedly said that if Israel "had been a bit more flexible" the chances for peace would have been better. In June Ford held separate meetings with Egyptian President Anwar Sadat and Israeli Premier Yitzhak Rabin which led to a revival of Kissinger's peace-making efforts in August. On Sept. 4 Ford was able to announce that a new Sinai pact had been reached that called for a further Israeli troop withdrawal from the Sinai and the stationing of U.S. civilians there to monitor the pact. The agreement received widespread approval.

In other areas of foreign policy, Ford found his freedom to maneuver hampered by increasing congressional assertiveness. Revelations by the press of massive illegal intelligence operations by the Central Intelligence Agency (CIA) led Ford, in January 1975, to appoint a commission headed by vice president Nelson Rockefeller to investigate the charges. The report, issued in June, acknowledged violations of law, but disputed claims that the violations were serious or widespread.

Both the Senate and the House, disturbed by reports that the CIA had plotted assassinations of foreign leaders, conducted their own investigations which caused Ford to warn against "sweeping attacks" on foreign intelligence operations. In September 1975 he refused to grant the House Select Committee on Intelligence access to classified material until it yielded any right to make the information public, a concession which the House granted. Concern about CIA activities, however, remained widespread and in December 1975 Congress, over the strong objections of Ford and Kissinger, voted to cut off funds for covert CIA operations in the Angolan civil war. Ford called the decision "a deep tragedy" but was powerless to do anything about it.

Congressional wariness about military involvement abroad was also apparent in its response to the final stages of the Vietnam war. Concerned about the upsurge in fighting there, Ford asked Congress in January 1975 for an additional $522 million in military aid for South Vietnam and Cambodia. As the Communist offensive in both countries intensified and it became obvious that victory was imminent, Ford pleaded for action, but Congress remained adamant and merely approved funds for an emergency evacuation of American personnel from South Vietnam. After the capture of the capitals of Pnompenh and Saigon in April, Ford blamed Congress for the collapse but admitted that the end of hostilities "closes a chapter in the American experience."

Shortly thereafter, on May 12, 1975, Cambodian forces seized an American merchant vessel, the Mayaguez, and its American crew, in the Gulf of Siam. Ford called the action "an act of piracy" and two days later ordered a dramatic rescue operation involving air, sea and ground forces. Although the action was successful and received praise from leaders of both parties, some analysts saw it as an excessive display of force intended to symbolize the willingness of the United States to take firm action in world affairs.

During his final year in office, Africa

became another major preoccupation for Ford and he successfully pushed for a commitment from Rhodesian Prime Minsiter Ian Smith for black majority rule.

Ford was defeated, however, in the 1976 election by Governor Jimmy Carter. After leaving office, he continued to speak out on public affairs but declined to run again for the Presidency in 1980.

As with President Nixon, opinions about Gerald Ford's foreign policy were mixed. Liberal critics argued that his support of the South Vietnamese and Cambodian governments only prolonged the military struggle needlessly. Most critics, however, agreed that Ford made important breakthroughs in the areas of Egyptian-Israeli relations, arms control and majority rule in Zimbabwe-Rhodesia.

[JD]

For further information:
Gerald Ford, *A Time to Heal* (New York, 1979).
Richard H. Reeves, *A Ford Not a Lincoln* (New York, 1975).
Jerald F. terHorst, *Gerald Ford* (New York, 1974).

FORRESTAL, JAMES V(INCENT)
b. Feb. 15, 1892; Beacon, N. Y.
d. May 22, 1949; Bethesda, Md.
Secretary of the Navy, May 1944-July 1947; Secretary of Defense, July 1947-March 1949.

James Forrestal was the son of an Irish building contractor who was active in New York state politics. In 1912 he entered Dartmouth College and a year later transferred to Princeton, where he was active in student affairs and became editor of the *Daily Princetonian.* Voted most likely to succeed, he was forced to leave school six weeks before graduation because of a lack of funds. Forrestal held a number of jobs in New York City before becoming a bond salesman. He joined the Roosevelt Administration in June 1940 and later in the same year became undersecretary of the Navy.

A vigorous anti-Communist, Forrestal was one of the first of the presidential advisers to urge the abandonment of cooperation with the Soviet Union. He warned both Roosevelt and Truman that the Russians would not live up to their wartime agreements granting representative government in Eastern Europe. Forrestal was convinced that the Kremlin would exploit the postwar anarchy and expand into Europe, Asia and the Middle East. For this reason, he argued that the U.S. should not demobilize but rather remain ready to resist agression. "Peace without power to enforce it must remain an empty dream," he said.

During the early postwar period Truman resisted Forrestal's advice. He hoped to reach some agreement with the Soviet Union over Eastern Europe and wanted to accomodate domestic desires for a quick reconversion to peace. Nevertheless, Forrestal continued to do everything within his power to maintain military readiness and show an American military presence abroad. In 1946 he sent a naval ship to Greece and Turkey, then under threat of Communist attack, to show the U.S. presence in the area. On the home front he opened a drive to recruit officers and urged pay increases for the armed forces. He also advocated the development of a permanent core of civil servants modeled after the British system.

Forrestal supported a revived, rehabilitated Germany and Japan to serve as checks on the Soviet Union. The Secretary questioned the Administration's efforts to negotiate a truce in China between the Communists and Nationalists, maintaining that Gen. George C. Marshall [q.v.], who headed the mission, did not understand the Communist menace. Forrestal recommended that the U.S. increase its aid to the pro-Chiang forces to win the civil war and thus remove the Soviet Union from Asia.

During the spring of 1946, as negotiations with the Soviets broke down and public opinion became more anti-Communist, the Administration took a firmer stand toward the Soviet Union. Forrestal applauded the move and supported George Kennan's [*q.v.*] recommendation for a policy of containment of Communist expansion. When the British withdrew military and economic aid from Greece and Turkey in 1947, the Secretary urged the U.S. to take over assistance. He recommended a complete mobilization of the American people to defeat the Communists and urged a program of massive economic aid to rebuild the shattered economies of Europe. Forrestal supported the Marshall Plan and early attempts to form a defense alliance in Western Europe.

Beginning in 1948, however, Forrestal began showing signs of a potential nervous breakdown. At times during meetings Forrestal was easily distracted from the topic. He suffered from forgetfulness, memory slips, and mistakes in identity. Forrestal also began believing he was being followed by Zionists and Communists. Reluctantly he resigned as of March 28, 1949. On that day Truman presented him with the Distinguished Service Medal. Forrestal then went to Florida for a rest but suffered a nervous breakdown on April 2. He was admitted for psychiatric observation at the Bethesda Naval Hospital in Maryland. His recovery impressed the doctors, but on May 22, Forrestal leaped to his death from his window on the 13th floor. Commenting on the suicide, President Truman stated, "This able and devoted public servant was as truly a casualty of the war as if he had died on the firing line."

[JB]

For further information:
Arnold A. Rogow, *James Forrestal: A Study of Personality, Politics and Policy* (New York, 1963).

FOSTER, WILLIAM C(HAPMAN)
b. April 27, 1897; Westfield, N.J.
Chief Delegate, Geneva Conference on the Prevention of Suprise Attacks, November 1958-December 1958; Director, Arms Control and Disarmament Agency, September 1961-January 1969.

Prior to his appointment as director of the U.S. Arms Control and Disarmament Agency in September 1961, Foster had a varied career in government, serving as undersecretary of commerce, administrator of the Economic Cooperation Administration and deputy secretary of defense during the Truman Administration. He left government for private industry after Dwight D. Eisenhower's 1953 election, and from 1953 to 1961 he served as an executive for a number of large chemical corporations. In 1958 Foster headed the U.S. delegation to the abortive disarmament conference with the Soviet Union.

Despite the conference's failure, it did have long-range benefits. The technical papers the U.S. prepared for the meeting provided valuable data on weapons and inspection technology for future negotiations. More importantly, it marked the first time the U.S. had developed concrete proposals rather than vague principles for weapons control. It also was a major turning point in U.S. thought on the issue of disarmament and arms control. Instead of focusing on control of fissionable materials, the U.S. stressed the elimination of nuclear warfare through the control of the means of delivery of nuclear arms. Foster, testifying before the Senate Subcommittee on Disarmament in January 1959, said the conference had shown him the need to define the issues involved in control and disarmament more clearly. It had also given him valuable experience in dealing with the Soviets and in understanding the importance they placed on defending their security.

In September 1961 Foster was appointed director of the U.S. Arms Control and Disarmament Agency. As head of the Arms Control and Disarmament Agency, Foster was responsible for running an autonomous department formed to coordinate government policy on disarmament and nuclear testing free from the influence of other federal agencies. Foster counseled the President on all major decisions involving nuclear policy. When the Soviet Union resumed atmospheric nuclear testing in September 1961, he advised the President to resume American atmospheric tests for two reasons: first, if America performed no new tests the Soviets might gain an important nuclear advantage from its testing series; second, if the USSR gained superiority it might be difficult to sustain U.S. support for a test ban treaty, particularly in the Senate, which would have to ratify the document. Although Kennedy resumed underground testing in September 1961, he held off the final decision to resume atmospheric tests until March 1962. In September 1961, Foster, along with Arthur Dean, helped Kennedy prepare his U.N. address that included a proposal for "General and Complete Disarmament in a Peaceful World."

During the re-evaluation of American test ban policy made in the summer of 1962, Foster served as a member of the ad hoc committee formed to study U.S. options. At the group's meetings Foster backed two of the suggestions advanced: to present a simplified treaty involving an unsupervised ban on atmospheric, outer space and sea bed tests, and to propose a modified comprehensive treaty that provided for on-site inspection inside the Soviet Union but relied on internally coordinated and standardized national control posts.

Despite the fact that a partial test ban would not stop nuclear proliferation, Foster felt that the treaty would prevent tests that produced radioactive fallout and, therefore, caused the greatest concern. In addition, it would permit the U.S. to continue testing and thus maintain U.S. nuclear superiority. He also supported the second plan, which he believed would maintain pressure on the Soviets to accept inspection. Foster assured the committee that this measure was scientifically feasible and that the needed detection system could be put into operation immediately. These two proposals were tabled simultaneously in Geneva in August 1962 and were rejected by the Soviet Union.

Throughout the winter of 1962-63 Foster attempted unsuccessfully to break the deadlock, both in meetings with Russian officials in New York and in Geneva, where he replaced Arthur Dean as head of the U.S. delegation to the 18 Nation Disarmament Conference in February. However, the issue remained stalemated until June 1963

when Premier Nikita Khrushchev accepted Kennedy's personal suggestion that negotiations be carried on by private emissaries in Moscow. Because Kennedy had given repeated assurances to Congress that the Disarmament Agency would not appropriate the treaty-making functions of the State Department, Foster was not one of the men sent to Moscow. The delegation, led by W. Averell Harriman [q.v.], was able to conclude a limited test ban treaty by July 25.

Foster played an important role in the Administration's fight for treaty ratification. Under the direction of the President, an ad hoc committee composed of Foster, his deputy Adrian Fisher and several other top Administration officials was responsible for contacting individual senators and soliciting their support. At the treaty hearings held in August 1963, Foster was the only non-scientific expert to testify. He stressed that while there were real dangers in the test ban the risk of not signing the document were greater. He argued that it would constitute a significant step in achieving control over the spread of nuclear weapons, would eliminate radioactive fallout and would be the first step in bringing the arms race under control. To ensure continued support for the proposal, Foster or his deputy stayed in the gallery during the ratification debates to direct Administration forces when necessary. The test ban treaty was ratified in September 1963.

Foster retained his post as director of the Arms Control and Disarmament Agency throughout the Johnson Administration. In conjunction with Fisher, he served as chief delegate to the 18 Nation Disarmament Conference in Geneva and helped negotiate the nuclear nonproliferation treaty of 1968. Foster left government service in January 1969. He became president of Porter International Company in 1970.

[EWS]

For further information:
E(edson) L(ouis) M(illard) Burns, *A Seat at the Table* (Toronto, 1972).
Arthur Dean, *Test Ban and Disarmament: The Path of Negotiation* (New York, 1966).

Harold D. Jacobson, *Diplomats, Scientists and Politicians* (Ann Arbor, 1966).

Mary Milling Lepper, *Foreign Policy Formulation: A Case Study of the Nuclear Test Ban Treaty of 1963* (Columbus, 1971).

FULBRIGHT, J(AMES) WILLIAM
b. April 9, 1905; Sumner, Mo.
Democratic Senator, Ark., 1945-75.

Fulbright, the son of a banker and successful businessman, graduated from the University of Arkansas in 1925. He then attended Oxford University on a Rhodes Scholarship, receiving a B.S. in history and political science with honors in 1928 and an M.A. in 1931. Three years later Fulbright earned an LL.B. from George Washington University. In 1934 he joined the Antitrust Division of the Justice Department, where he helped prosecute the Schechter chicken case. He left the Justice Department the following year to become an instructor of law at George Washington. In 1936 he returned to Arkansas to teach law at the University and to manage the family business. Three years later Fulbright, then 34, was appointed president of the University. He was the youngest university president in the United States. Fulbright's efforts to raise the standards of the university gained him national attention. However, his outspoken opposition to isolationism won him some local emnity, including that of Homer Adkins, who, after his election as governor in 1940, forced Fulbright from his post.

In 1943 Fulbright won a seat in the U.S. House, where he was appointed to the Foreign Affairs Committee. As a representative, he supported the war policies and postwar plans of Franklin D. Roosevelt and, several months after beginning his term, defended them in floor debate against the attack of Rep. Claire Booth Luce (R, Conn.) . In June 1943 Fulbright introduced a resolution giving House support to U.S. participation after the war in an international organization dedicated to the preservation of peace. The resolution, which passed both Houses by overwhelming margins, was an important step toward the creation of the United Nations. The next year Fulbright served as an American representative to an international conference on education held in London. There he presented a four-point program for reconstructing essential education facilities. The conference accepted his proposal and urged that an organization be established to implement it. These recommendations became the foundations for the U.N. Economic and Social Council.

In 1944 Fulbright, in a campaign that emphasized his conservative record on domestic issues, defeated his old adversary, Homer Adkins, for a seat in the Senate. During his first term Fulbright continued to vote conservatively on domestic affairs, opposing civil rights legislation and supporting such anti-labor measures as the Case labor disputes bill and the Taft-Hartley Act. Despite being assigned initially to the Banking and Currency Committee and not the foreign relations panel, Fulbright's primary interest was in foreign policy. (He won a seat on the Foreign Affairs Committee in 1949.)

Fulbright became distressed by the diplomacy of the postwar world. He was particularly unhappy with the United Nation Charter. He had hoped for a tempering of the concept of sovereignty which the agreement failed to consider. In a November 1945 radio address he proposed that the U.N. be empowered to limit armaments and the atomic bomb. He recommended abolition of the veto in the Security Council because he saw it as a barrier to the effective working of the United Nations. He wanted to see a stronger World Court empowered to make binding decisions and an ascendance of law and legal forms rather then power in international affairs. "Our government," he said, "does not seem to appreciate the function of law in the makings of peace." Fulbright voted for the Charter because of the lack of an alternative course, but the speech marked his break with the Administration. Prior to it Fulbright had been mentioned as a possible vice presidential or even presidential candidate for 1948. His speech, because of its harsh criticism of Truman, ended all such talk.

During this period Fulbright became increasingly critical of the Truman Administration's policy toward the Soviet Union. He had supported Roosevelt's attempts to mollify the Russians and assure the Soviet Union of the United States' peaceful intentions. He found the Truman Administration's policies increasingly belligerent. In his November 1945 radio address, Fulbright charged that the Truman Administration's policy was drifting. The U.S. was demanding strategic concession from the Soviets without offering any of its own. Increasingly an atmosphere of confrontation was developing, he said. In April 1946 Fulbright criticized the Administration for antagonizing the Soviet Union with continued atomic tests. The planned test on Bikini Island, he charged, had no military or other value, but was simply a device for displaying American strength.

Fulbright's views changed when the Soviet Union rejected an American plan for the internationalization of atomic weaponry. The USSR became, in Fulbright's eyes, a confirmed adversary. In a May 1946 speech discussing this change of view, Fulbright said, "there are doubts in the minds of many of us that Russia will ever submit to rules of conduct in any field." Fulbright endorsed the Truman Doctrine in March 1947 and voted for aid to Greece and Turkey. He supported full funding of the Marshall Plan in 1948 while lamenting that it would act to restore the separate countries of Europe rather than promote European unity of which he was an advocate. Fulbright voted for the North Atlantic Treaty in 1949.

Fulbright won reelection without opposition in 1950. His support of Truman's foreign policy continued into his second term. Although he had made no public statement about the Korean conflict in 1950, when the Administration came under fierce public attack for the recall of Gen. Douglas MacArthur [*q.v.*] in 1951, Fulbright became a vocal Administration supporter. He denounced both MacArthur's insubordination and the military strategy the General espoused. Fulbright proved an effective inquisitor of MacArthur when he appeared before a joint meeting of Senate Armed Services and Foreign Relations Committee.

During the 1950s Fulbright frequently clashed with President Eisenhower and Secretary of State John Foster Dulles [*q.v.*] over U.S. foreign affairs. He urged a reorientation of U.S. policy from one based on an ideological confrontation with the Soviet Union to one resting on big power interests. He stressed the need to supply economic and technical rather than military aid to U.S. allies and questioned the Administration's dependence on nuclear weapons for defense.

Fulbright also opposed the President's emphasis on the formation of defense pacts with underdeveloped nations. He disapproved of the Southeast Asian Treaty of 1954, which established the Southeast Asia Treaty Organization (SEATO), and the formosa Resolution of 1955, giving the President the right to use force to defend Formosa and the Pescadores. In 1957 the Senator opposed the Eisenhower Doctrine, which authorized the President to use the Armed Forces to aid a Middle Eastern nation resisting "armed attack from any country controled by international Communism." Fulbright used the hearings on the resolution to denounce Eisenhower's foreign policy, which he claimed would weaken Western influence in the Middle East, was disastrous to the North Atlantic Treaty Organization and damaging to U.S. friendship with Great Britain and France. The resolution passed the Senate in March 1957. Fulbright was one of 19 senators who voted against it.

Fulbright was widely mentioned as a possible choice for Secretary of State following John F. Kennedy's 1960 election. The President-elect admired his scholar's mind and supported Fulbright's demand for a reassessment of American foreign policy goals. Just as importantly, Fulbright could enhance the Administration's influence on Capitol Hill. However, the Senator was rejected for the post because his civil rights record would have made it difficult for him to deal with African nations and because his refusal to support an anti-Nasser foreign policy had alienated many in the Jewish community. In addition, Kennedy felt that Fulbright did not have the administrative experience necessary to lead a large bureaucracy.

During the Kennedy Administration Fulbright used his position as chairman of the Senate Foreign Relations Committee to advocate a reappraisal of the basic tenets upon which Soviet-American diplomacy had been conducted. In a series of speeches and articles and in two books, *Prospects for the West* (1963) and *Old Myths and New Realities* (1964), Fulbright urged the U.S. to abandon the postwar assumption that Russia and the U.S. were locked in uncompromising ideological combat. He thought this premise had produced continual confrontations between the two nuclear powers. Instead, the Senator recommended that the U.S. view relations with the Soviet Union in terms of traditional great power rivalry and use quiet diplomacy to settle differences.

Fulbright said America's goal should not be to change the Soviet Union's internal social, economic and political structure or destroy Communism but to block Russian imperialism. He maintained that although contemporary Soviet leaders were opportunists anxious to expand Soviet power, they were also rational individuals who would seek to fulfill this goal through the extension of their influence rather than through territorial conquest. Asserting that the West was the "ultimate determinant of the fortunes of Communism," Fulbright believed that America and her allies could prevent this expansion through a unified foreign policy that clearly defined Western interests and potential reactions to Soviet challenges. More importantly, the West could forestall Communist growth by strengthening its "internal free societies" through international cooperation "to make

them impregnable to external ideological assault and at the same time magnetic examples of social justice and material well-being for the entire world."

The Senator played down the influence of Communism in the emerging nations, terming it "a scavenger" rather than an initiator of revolutions. He believed that upheavals in the Third World were the result of virulent nationalism and consequently that the Communists would find little future in the developing areas. The West could ensure Soviet failure through the use of foreign aid, not to bolster specific regimes, but to provide the basis for economic growth vital for the development of a "free society," according to Fulbright.

Fulbright's philosophy shaped his response to many of the foreign policy issues of the Kennedy Administration, particularly those involving Cuba. During the opening months of 1961 when the Administration debated whether to carry out a planned invasion of that island by U.S.-trained Cuban exiles, Fulbright opposed the action. In a March 30 meeting with the President, the Senator questioned the exiles' political leadership and popular support and reminded Kennedy that, regardless of the outcome, the U.S. would be condemned as imperalist. He also cautioned that if the invasion succeeded the nation would find itself responsible for a bankrupt country in a grave state of disorder.

Fulbright maintained that the U.S. did not have to fear "competition from an unshaven megalomaniac" because Cuba would be unable to compete within the inter-American system. Instead of an invasion he recommended that the U.S. isolate the island from the rest of the hemisphere. The Senator again presented his objections to an attack in an April 4 meeting with the President and his highest military and civilian advisers. His recommendations went unheeded, and the invasion was launched on April 17. Two days later Castro crushed it.

Fulbright took a dramatically different stand during the Cuban missile crisis of 1962. At the Oct. 22 meeting with congressional leaders in which the President advised them of his decision to blockade the island to force removal of the missiles, Fulbright argued against the move. He agreed with Kennedy that decisive action was imperative to show the Soviet Union that the U.S. would not tolerate missiles so close to its territory. Yet, because of his belief that the U.S. should avoid direct military confrontation with Russia, he counseled an actual invasion as the most prudent step. The Senator maintained that since a blockade could lead to a clash with Russian ships, the President's measure would be more likely to provoke a nuclear war than an invasion in which Americans would presumably be fighting only Cubans. Kennedy did not accept this advice and on Oct. 24 instituted the naval "quarantine."

During the Kennedy Administration Fulbright began an involvement in Vietnam affairs which would become his major preoccupation for the remainder of his Senate career. In June 1961 he delivered a major address to the Senate which outlined his thoughts on the U.S. role in the nationalistic struggles of the developing nations. Citing the example of Vietnam, Fulbright argued that American aid to that country was only a "qualified success" because stress had been put on military rather than long-term economic assistance. As long as this emphasis continued, he thought, the effort was doomed to failure.

Nonetheless, Fulbright was an enthusiastic supporter of Lyndon Johnson after Kennedy's assassination and in early 1964 backed his actions in Vietnam. While calling for a reassessment of Vietnam policy, Fulbright said that given the unstable political and military situation the U.S. had no choice but to support the South Vietnam government and its army "by the most effective means available." The Senator ruled out a negotiated settlement as impractical because South Vietnam's military setbacks had left it in a weak bargaining position.

At the request of President Johnson, Fulbright introduced the Tonkin Gulf Resolution in the Senate on Aug. 6, 1964. The Resolution, prompted by a reported North Vietnamese attack on American warships patrolling the Gulf of Tonkin, gave the President almost blanket authority to conduct the war as he wished. In debates on the proposal Fulbright defended the measure against critics, such as Sen. Gaylord Nelson (D, Wisc.) and Sen. Wayne Morse (D, Ore.) who feared that it would lead to a large-scale military involvement without congressional control. He refused to accept a Nelson amendment that stated, "Except when provoked to a greater response, we should continue to attempt to avoid a direct military involvement in the Southeast Asian conflict." However, Fulbright assured the Senate that the amendment was an accurate reflection of Johnson's policy. The upper house passed the Resolution with only two dissenting votes on Aug. 7.

In later years Fulbright termed his support of the Tonkin Gulf resolution the most humiliating experience of his public career. The Senator attributed his unquestioning support of the President's request to his belief that his old friend would not deceive him and to his desire to see Johnson elected president in 1964. Believing that the election of conservative Sen. Barry Goldwater (R, Ariz.) [q.v.] would lead to a dangerous escalation of the Cold War, Fulbright later said he had not wished to jeopardize Johnson's victory by engaging in a divisive policy debate.

During February 1968 Fulbright held closed hearings to determine if the U.S. had provoked the Tonkin Gulf incident, if North Vietnam had actually attacked U.S. ships and if the Administration had misled Congress into passing the Tonkin Gulf Resolution. The probe uncovered evidence that the commander of the U.S. operation had warned his superiors that North Vietnam considered his ships enemies. It further revealed that, because of poor weather conditions and technical problems, there had been uncertainty over whether the attack had actually occurred. Appearing on national television, Fulbright charged that the resolution was introduced under "a completely false idea of what had happened" and that his own support was "based upon information which was not true." Although he denounced the Resolution Fulbright did not attempt to have it repealed at that time because he believed that some senators who opposed the war would feel compelled to support the President on this issue. The Resolution was eventually repealed in 1970.

After Johnson had ordered systematic bombing of North Vietnam in the spring of 1965, Fulbright publicly voiced his doubts about U.S. policy in Vietnam. In a speech in March and a memorandum sent to the President in April, he questioned the Administration's belief that a defeat in Vietnam would lead to Communist Chinese expansion throughout Southeast Asia. Fulbright suggested that the conflict in Vietnam was a nationalistic movement rather than the result of Chinese aggression. Despite this critique Fulbright still expressed general approval of Johnson's Vietnam policy.

Fulbright's first major dissent from Administration foreign policy occurred in a debate over U.S. intervention in the Dominican Republic, where a civil war had broken out between leftists and a rightist military junta. Alleging the danger of a Communist takeover, the President had sent American troops to the island in April 1965. Johnson said that the move was necessary to protect American property and lives and to prevent another Cuba in the Caribbean. In a speech delivered on the Senate floor in September, Fulbright warned that Johnson's action was a throwback to the Cold War period of the 1950s. He questioned the President's credibility and warned that the indiscriminate use of force in civil wars and against national movements might actually push developing nations toward Communism. Fulbright's speech resulted in an open break between the President and the Senator. Thereafter Fulbright was pointedly denied the usual courtesies extended to important committee chairmen by the White House.

Fulbright's criticisms of the Administration's Vietnam policy grew increasingly caustic during the Foreign Relations Committee hearings in February 1966. He used the televised probe to suggest alternatives to Johnson's policies and to make the public aware of the larger issues involved in the Vietnam dispute. During the opening days of the hearings, the nation heard testimony from such respected military and diplomatic figures as James Gavin and George Kennan [q.v.]. These men questioned the strategic need for U.S. involvement in Southeast Asia and cautioned that continued escalation could involve the U.S. in a war with Communist China. The following week Maxwell Taylor [q.v.] and Dean Rusk [q.v.] defended the Administration. They insisted that the U.S. was fighting a limited war that was necessary to prevent Chinese expansion into Southeast Asia. Throughout the investigation Fulbright tried to introduce larger issues into the discussion, asking witnesses about the propriety of drawing a peaceful people into a struggle about which they cared little. The debate was inconclusive, but it served the educational function Fulbright had intended.

In a series of lectures given at Johns Hopkins University in April 1966, Fulbright delivered his most critical examination of American foreign policy. The Senator stated that America was in danger of succumbing to the "arrogance of power which has afflicted, weakened and in some cases destroyed, great nations in the past." He denounced the Administration's rhetoric, which portrayed the war in terms of a moral crusade, and questioned whether the continued American presence in Vietnam was not a result of prideful reluctance to accept a solution short of victory. He warned that the war was destroying plans for social reform, endangering relations with old allies and having a corrosive effect on the American spirit. The lectures were published in 1967 as *The Arrogance of Power*, which became a best-seller.

In his book Fulbright outlined the steps he would take to achieve peace. He suggested that the U.S. cease bombing North Vietnam and reduce military activity in the South to facilitate truce negotiations. The belligerents could then draw up plans for self-determination in South Vietnam and for an eventual referendum on the reunification of the North and South. If the proposed conferences failed to produce agreements, the Senator believed that the U.S.

should consolidate its military forces in defensible areas in South Vietnam and maintain them there indefinitely.

After Nixon took office in 1969, Fulbright initially muted his criticism of the Vietnam War. He praised the eight point peace plan which Nixon offered in May, and applauded the President's announced intention gradually to withdraw all U.S. troops. By the autumn, however, Fulbright had resumed his criticism of the war. In October 1969, after nationwide protests against the war captured the attention of the public, he deplored Nixon's call for a moratorium on dissent and instead urged a "moratorium on killing." The next month Fulbright declared that Nixon had taken "fully as his own the Johnson war" by acting on the assumption that the war was a fight against an international Communist conspiracy.

In a major speech in St. Louis in December, he attacked "Vietnamization" as another form of waging "a continuing war of stalemate and attrition" and warned that "every day this war goes on the sickness of American society worsens." In February and March 1970, Fulbright held extensive public hearings on the effectiveness of Nixon's Vietnamization policy. He expressed skepticism that the prospects for peace had improved, and a report by his Committee's staff cast serious doubt on the chances of Vietnamization succeeding.

Fulbright attacked the President's decision to invade Cambodia and, in June 1970, supported the Cooper-Church amendment to cut off funds for combat operations in Cambodia. In 1971, after the United States provided support for a South Vietnamese invasion of Laos, Fulbright announced that he would hold "end-the-war" hearings in order to propose legislation to curb the President's war making powers. He supported legislation aimed at that purpose which Sen. Jacob Javits (R, N.Y.) introduced. As finally passed by Congress, the 1973 War Powers Act limited to 60 days the President's ability to commit U.S. troops to combat abroad without Congressional approval.

Fulbright presented his most extreme attack on American foreign policy in his 1972 book, *The Crippled Giant.* Surveying U.S. policy abroad since World War II, he charged that the nation's policymakers seemed "driven by a sense of imperial destiny." The exercise of power had become an end in itself, he charged, "purposeless and undisciplined" in its use. "History did not prepare the American people for the kind of role we are now playing in the world," he said. Fulbright warned that the unbridled resort to force in foreign affairs would cripple the United States, leaving a "moral wasteland." Already it was destroying the constitutional balance of power between Congress and the President and unless it was stopped, the "ultimate casualty" would be democracy itself.

After Henry Kissinger [q.v.] became Secretary of State in 1973, Fulbright's criticism of the Nixon Administration's foreign policy lessened. Fulbright respected Kissinger's abilities and approved of his willingness to abandon Cold War myths in the conduct of foreign affairs. He supported Kissinger's pursuit of detente with the Soviet Union and approved of the friendly initiatives toward mainland China. Kissinger's reassertion of a strong role for the Department of State in making foreign policy and his obvious preference for negotiation and diplomatic initiatives over the use of force was more in line with Fulbright's own thinking. The Senator also praised Kissinger's evenhanded approach to a Middle East peace settlement.

Fulbright's preoccupation with foreign affairs put him increasingly out of touch with the voters of his state. In 1974, in his bid for a sixth term in the Senate, he lost the Democratic primary to Gov. Dale Bumpers. When Fulbright retired from the Senate, he had amassed the longest tenure as chairman of the Foreign Relations Committee of any previous senator.

[JD]

For further information:
Haynes Johnson and Bernard M. Gwertzman, *Fulbright: The Dissenter* (New York, 1968).

GOLDWATER, BARRY M(ORRIS)
b. Jan. 1, 1909; Phoenix, Ariz.
Republican Senator, Ariz., 1953-65; 1969- .

Heir to a Phoenix department store, Barry M. Goldwater left the University of Arizona after one year to run his family's business. After a tour of duty with the Army Transport Command during World War II, he won election to the Phoenix City Council in 1949. Three years later he upset Senate Majority Leader Ernest W. McFarland (D, Ariz.) despite the state's previously strong Democratic traditions. As one of the most conservative and anti-Communist Republicans, Goldwater defended Sen. Joseph R. McCarthy (R, Wisc.) and voted against his censure in December 1954. A member of the Senate Labor and Public Welfare Committee, Goldwater frequently criticized leaders of organized labor.

Goldwater repeatedly demonstrated his strident anti-Communism on foreign policy issues. He joined three Republican colleagues in January 1961 in voting against the confirmation of Chester Bowles as undersecretary of state because of Bowles's positions on disarmament and the recognition of mainland China. During the 1962 congressional elections Goldwater attempted to make the Administration's Cuban policy an issue, and on Nov. 5 he claimed in a joint statement with Rep. Robert C. Wilson (R, Calif.) that Kennedy had pledged not to invade Cuba and had thus "locked Castro and Communism into Latin America and thrown away the key to their removal." After the naval blockade of Cuba, Goldwater frequently challenged Administration claims that its action had forced the Soviet Union to remove its offensive missiles and troops from the island.

During the debate on the nuclear test ban treaty in September 1963, Goldwater offered an amendment that would have made ratification contingent upon the removal of all Soviet troops and weapons from Cuba. The Senate rejected the Goldwater provision 75 to 17. Announcing that the test ban agreement would "erode our military strength," Goldwater took the side of those generals who publicly or privately opposed the Treaty of Moscow. He joined 18 other senators in voting against ratification of the agreement on Sept. 24, 1963. The following year Goldwater suffered an overwhelming defeat in the 1964 presidential election.

Goldwater was one of the Senate's strongest advocates of America's Vietnam involvement. In 1972, for example, he attacked critics of the renewed bombing offensive against North Vietnam begun by Nixon after the Communists had started an offensive in the South. When raids against the port of Haiphong raised fears about Soviet involvement if Russian ships were hit, Goldwater said the raids were better than the "dilly-dally" bombing of supply lines that had gone on before.

Goldwater opposed all congressional efforts to legislate an end to the war. These included the 1970 Cooper-Church Amendment to limit the President's authority to conduct military operations in Cambodia and the 1973 amendment by Sen. Thomas F. Eagleton (D, Mo.) to halt American combat operations in Laos and Cambodia. At the same time Goldwater supported the Nixon Administration's attempts to end the war through negotiations. When a peace treaty was concluded in 1973, Goldwater warned the Saigon government not to be an obstacle to the peace agreement the U.S. had signed. Goldwater was one of the strongest congressional supporters of the Saigon government. He continued to support military aid for South Vietnam after the peace treaty was signed. When the Senate Armed Services Committee debated the Ford Administration's request for additional military aid in April 1975, two weeks before the Communists captured Saigon, Goldwater favored sending at least an additional $101 million. The

Committee rejected both this proposal and a $70 million proposal, which Goldwater opposed as inadequate.

While an advocate of a strong defense posture, Goldwater was one of the leading congressional opponents of the military draft. In 1970 he was one of 12 Senators who introduced legislation to implement the recommendations of a presidential commission that studied the creation of an all-volunteer force. The commission, headed by former Secretary of Defense Thomas S. Gates, called for ending the draft when the draft law expired on June 30, 1971. As requested by the Nixon Administration, Congress extended the draft until 1973, when an all-volunteer force was established.

[AE]

HALBERSTAM, DAVID
b. April 10, 1934; New York, N.Y.
Foreign Correspondent, *New York Times*, 1961-66.

The son of an Army surgeon, David Halberstam spent his childhood on various military posts but went to high school in Yonkers, N.Y. He attended Harvard, served as managing editor of the *Crimson* and graduated in 1955. Believing that civil rights would be the major issue of the late 1950s, Halberstam joined the staff of the West Point, Miss., *Daily Times Leader*. Shortly thereafter he began four years as a reporter with the Nashville *Tennessean*.

In the fall of 1960 he joined the *New York Times*. After six months in Washington and a year in the Congo, the 28-year-old Halberstam succeeded veteran *Times* foreign correspondent Homer Bigart in Vietnam. Halberstam arrived in Saigon in September 1962 at a particularly difficult time for journalists covering the war. Although American troop strength had increased to 16,000 and economic aid had risen to over $500 million, the war was not going well for the South Vietnamese government. American correspondents who accurately reported this state of affairs were coming under increasing suspicion by the regime of Ngo Dinh Diem. *Newsweek* reporter Francois Sully, for example, had just been expelled from the country for writing an unflattering article about the powerful Madame Ngo Dinh Nhu, Diem's sister-in-law.

With colleagues Malcolm Browne of the Associated Press and Neil Sheehan of United Press International, Halberstam began to investigate and report the deteriorating military situation in strategic areas such as the Mekong Delta. This small corps of American reporters also reported that Diem's regime was aloof, autocratic and indifferent to the needs of most of the population. They gave opposition groups in the large Buddhist community better press coverage than either Diem or American mission officials would have liked.

The incident which finally drew national attention to what columnist Joseph Alsop derisively called a group of "young crusaders" was the first major battle of the Vietnam war at Ap Bac in January 1963, during which a South Vietnamese division was routed by a small force of insurgents. Halberstam reported the battle in detail, including the deaths of three American military advisers killed while trying to induce reluctant Vietnamese soldiers to fight. Halberstam, Browne and Sheehan wrote stories quoting one of the U.S. advisers, Lt. Col. John Vann, on the enemy's combat skill and the cowardice of the South Vietnamese troops.

After writing the Ap Bac story Halberstam was subject to personal attacks. During the summer of 1963 the Pentagon began to monitor Halberstam's sources and record his whereabouts, contacts and telephone conversations. Meanwhile, White House Press Secretary Pierre Salinger declared that press reports from Vietnam were "emotional and inaccurate." When in late October 1963 *New York Times* publisher Arthur Ochs Sulzberger paid a courtesy call on John F. Kennedy, the President asked Sulzberger to reassign Halberstam because he was, in the Chief Executive's words, "too close to the story, too involved." Sulzberger refused to shift Halberstam, although the reporter left Vietnam in early 1964 to spend a year at the *Times's* New York bureau.

For his reporting in Vietnam Halberstam shared a 1964 Pulitzer Prize with Browne. In 1965 he published *The Making of a Quagmire*, a personal account of his fifteen months in Vietnam. The book was an immediate success. As Bert Cochran later wrote in *The Nation*, ". . .it had an electrifying effect on a new generation of dissenters. It opened the eyes of a wider public to the sordid activities concealed by official [bombast]." Although critical of U.S. failures in Vietnam, Halberstam defended the essential thrust of American policy: "A strategic country in a key area, it [Vietnam] is perhaps one of only five or six nations in the world that is truly vital to U.S. interests."

Halberstam was assigned in January 1965 to the Warsaw bureau of the *Times*. Expelled in December because of reports distressing to the Polish government, he returned to the New York bureau of his newspaper but soon resigned to become a contributing editor of *Harper's* magazine. After writing profiles of McGeorge Bundy [*q.v.*] and Robert McNamara [*q.v.*] for *Harper's*, Halberstam wrote *The Best and the Brightest*, a best-selling indictment of American Vietnam policy published in 1972.

[FHM]

For further information:
David Halberstam, *The Making of a Quagmire* (New York, 1965).
———, *The Best and the Brightest* (New York, 1972).

HARRIMAN, W(ILLIAM) AVERELL
b. Nov. 15, 1891; New York, N.Y.
Ambassador to the Soviet Union, 1943-46; Secretary of Commerce, 1946-48; Special Assistant to the President, 1950-51; Director, Mutual Security Agency, 1951-53; Ambassador at Large, January 1961-November 1961; Assistant Secretary of State for Far Eastern Affairs, November 1961- March 1963; Undersecretary of State for Political Affairs, March 1963–February 1965. Ambassador at Large, February 1965-March 1968; Chief U.S. Representative to the Paris Talks, March 1968-January 1969.

The son of railroad industrialist Edward Henry Harriman, Averell graduated from Yale in 1913. Two years later he became a vice president in his father's railroad company, the Union Pacific. In 1917 Harriman founded the Merchant Shipping Corp. and, in 1920, W. A. Harriman Co., a private bank. Harriman became chairman of the board of the Union Pacific in 1932 and astonished the nation by modernizing the company during the Depression.

In 1928 Harriman, initially a Republican, joined the Democratic Party. He entered government service the following year when, upon the advice of Harry Hopkins , President Franklin D. Roosevelt appointed him an administrator of the National Recovery Administration. Harriman was chairman of the Business Advisory Council of the Department of Commerce from 1937 to 1940. In 1941 he coordinated lend-lease aid with Great Britain and the Soviet Union. During his numerous trips to Moscow, he won the trust of Josef Stalin. In 1943 Harriman became ambassador to the Soviet Union, where he worked to continue aid to that nation. He attended the Tehran and Yalta conferences of allied leaders called to plan the postwar world.

Harriman was an early advocate of a firm policy toward the Soviet Union. Just before Roosevelt's death in 1945, he cabled the President analyzing Soviet policy in the postwar world. Ideology, he maintained, had replaced security as the chief determinant of Soviet policy. The Soviet Union wanted cooperation with the U.S. at the U.N. However, he warned, Stalin would attempt to create a security ring of friendly nations on Russia's western border to prevent a third major invasion during the century. The USSR would control not only foreign policy in these nations but also regulate their internal affairs. Democratic government would not be permitted. The Ambassador predicted that the Soviets would attempt to penetrate other nations and through Communists parties in those countries try to establish governments friendly to Russia. Harriman advised Roosevelt that Stalin viewed American acquiescence to the Soviet occupation of Eastern Europe as a sign of weakness. He recommended that the U.S. take a firmer stand, tying economic aid to Soviet political concessions in that area. The Soviets, he predicted, would not react violently because they needed assistance.

Harry Truman, who assumed the presidency a few days after Harriman's cable had been received, was deeply impressed with the analysis. The Ambassador briefed Truman before the President's meeting with Soviet Foreign Minister V. N. Molotov in April. On Harriman's advice Truman took a tough position during the talks. Using "words of one syllable" he berated the Foreign Minister for Soviet failure to live up to Yalta Accords. His directness horrified Molotov, who protested being lectured by the President. Although Truman's conduct gratified Harriman, it upset many in the Administration who desperately sought to avoid confrontation with the Russians.

In keeping with his desire to use economic aid as a weapon to gain cooperation with the Soviets, in May 1945 Harriman suggested the U.S. curtail lend-lease shipments to Russia since the war in Germany had ended. The stoppage, he warned, should be done firmly "while avoiding any implication of a threat or any indication of political bargaining." Truman approved Harriman's recommendation. However, the Foreign Economic Administration dramatically recalled ships already at sea. Truman ordered them to proceed once again to the Soviet Union but Moscow interpreted the abrupt cessation of lend-lease as an unfriendly act.

Truman's conduct with Molotov and the cutback of lend-lease signaled a departure from the policy of conciliation maintained under Roosevelt. Many who did not want a dramatic break with Stalin held Harriman responsible for the anti-Soviet tone of the Administration. In his memoirs, *Special Envoy* (1975), Harriman claimed that Roosevelt had already decided a confrontation would be inevitable. He assumed that Roosevelt was more astute politically than Truman and could have postponed the inevitable longer.

Following the end of the war in Japan, Harriman requested permission to resign. Truman persuaded him to remain in Moscow at least until the end of the year. On Jan. 23 Stalin had his last meeting with Harriman. The Ambassador requested help in trying to effect a truce between the Nationalists and Communists in China. Stalin cooly replied that his government recognized the Nationalists and had little contact with the Communists.

Truman appointed Harriman ambassador to Great Britain in March 1946. He served there seven months before Truman made him Secretary of Commerce. While at the Commerce Department foreign affairs continued to take up most of his time. Following Secretary of State George C. Marshall's [q.v.] call for a massive economic recovery program in Europe in June 1947, Truman appointed Harriman chairman of President's Committee on Foreign Aid to translate Marshall's proposal into a program and lobby for its passage in Congress. The Committee report on "European Recovery and American Aid," released in November, claimed that if Congress refused to provide aid, all Europe, the Middle East and North Africa would fall to the Communists. The panel stressed the importance of Germany in the success of the aid program and recommended special emphasis be put on assistance to that nation to redevelop its purchasing and producing power and prevent it from falling into the hands of the Soviet Union. The Committee report also contended that the Marshall Plan was needed to support the continuation of American trade with Europe. It predicted serious problems if Europe's 1948 projected seven billion dollar deficit with the U.S. was not corrected. In 1948 Harriman left the Commerce Department to head the European Cooperation Administration's (ECA) Office of the Special Representative in Europe, where he supervised distribution of Marshall Plan funds. He also continued to push for economic unity among European nations.

In 1950 Harriman became special assistant to the President and acted as troubleshooter for Truman. He played a role in the decision leading to U.S. entry in to the Korean war and served as liaison between Truman and Gen. Douglas MacArthur [q.v.]. In 1951 Harriman took part in talks over allied contributions to the North Atlantic Treaty Organization and unsuccessfully attempted to mediate the dispute between Iran and Great Britain over the nationalization of the Anglo-Iranian Oil Co. During the last two years of the Truman Administration, Harriman served as director of the Mutual Security Agency, responsible for the distribution of foreign aid.

Harriman ran unsuccessfully for Democratic presidential nomination in 1952 and 1956. From 1954 to 1958 he was governor of New York.

In large part because of Harriman's age, 69, John F. Kennedy passed him over for a high diplomatic post in the new Administration. Instead Kennedy offered him a roving ambassadorship. Still vital, hard-working and ambitious, Harriman accepted, ready, in his own words, "to start at the bottom and work your way up." The President first assigned Harriman to help resolve the lingering political-military crisis in Laos. By 1960 American support of a rightwing strongman, Gen. Phoumi Nosavan, had pushed neutralist Premier Souvanna Phouma into a working relationship with the Soviets and had inadvertently driven neutralist army elements into an accommodation with the Communist-led Pathet Lao insurgency. Gen. Phoumi's troops were in retreat, and the Pathet Lao had overrun the strategic Plain of Jars by February 1961, threatening the Laotian administrative and royal capitals at Vientiane and Luang Prabang. In early 1961 Harriman was among those in the new Administration who urged the neutralization of Laos as a solution to the crisis there. He met with Soviet Premier Nikita Khrushchev in February and reported to Washington that the Russian leader had made it plain that he did not want a war over Laos. After Harriman met with Souvanna Phouma in New Delhi in March, he recommended that the Administration support Souvanna's efforts to form a new neutralist government. At the same time Harriman urged a limited commitment of troops to Thailand to underline American opposition to a total Communist takeover in Laos. His proposal was offered in opposition to suggestions from the Joint Chiefs of Staff that up to 60,000 troops be deployed in Laos. Kennedy publicly adopted Harriman's perspective on March 23, 1961 when he called for "a truly neutral government, not a Cold War pawn" in Laos.

In May 1961 Kennedy appointed Harriman as the American representative to the reconvened Geneva conference on Laos, where he spent the rest of the year attempting to negotiate a coalition neutralist government among the three Laotian factions. Despite Soviet support for the idea of a neutral Laos, the Geneva negotiations proceeded slowly. Gen. Phoumi, backed by American military aid and encouraged by some American representatives in Laos, created obstacles, demanding control of key defense and interior posts in the new government. Kennedy's promotion of Harriman from ambassador at large to assistant secretary of state for Far Eastern affairs in November 1961 helped Harriman apply increasing pressure on Phoumi. He first persuaded Kennedy to cut off the money used to pay the Laotian general's troops in February 1962 and then insisted that all United States agencies in Laos replace every American who was a personal friend of Phoumi's. During this period Harriman earned the nickname "the Crocodile" from his colleagues who had their "heads snapped off" when he regarded their ideas as stupid or irrevelant.

The Pathet Lao captured the town of Nam Tha in May 1962, decisively defeating 3,000 of Phoumi's best troops. During this offensive Harriman again supported an American show of force in Indochina, which this time included transfer of the Seventh Fleet into the Gulf of Siam and an airlift of another 1,800 troops to Thailand. The new Pathet Lao offensive, combined with Harriman's year-long pressure, finally forced Phoumi to yield in June 1962 to a neutralist-dominated government headed by Souvanna Phouma. The next month the United States and thirteen other nations signed the Geneva accords neutralizing Laos. Although these agreements were violated by North Vietnam and China (and eventually, as later revealed, by the United States), Harriman defended the accords with the Kennedy Administration because the settlement won the Laotian neutralists away from an alliance with the Pathet Lao and prevented a great power confrontation in the small Asian nation.

Following the conclusion of the Laotian negotiations, Harriman handled several important diplomatic assignments for the Kennedy Administration. When China invaded the mountainous regions along India's northern frontier in October 1962, Prime Minister Jawaharlal Nehru asked for Western support. Harriman led an American delegation to the subcontinent to survey Indian military requirements. Along with United States Ambassador John Kenneth Galbraith, Harriman pressed for a resolution of India's dispute with Pakistan over Kashmir to ensure that military aid to the subcontinent would not pit one American-supplied army against another. Before American pressure could win results, the Chinese declared a unilateral ceasefire, and the incentive for resolving the India-Pakistan dispute evaporated.

Kennedy promoted Harriman to undersecretary of state for political affairs in March 1963 and two months later put him in charge of negotiating the nuclear test ban treaty with the Soviets in Moscow. Reportedly, Khrushchev recognized that Kennedy's appointment of the former ambassador to the Soviet Union to head the American delegation signaled the President's serious intention to reach an agreement. Harriman carried out his assignment in Moscow with characteristic restraint and toughness; a member of the British delegation called him "the great man of the meeting." By July 23 Harriman had persuaded the Soviets to drop their demand that a NATO-Warsaw Pact nonaggression treaty be signed simultaneously with the test ban agreement. (The United States and Britain objected to the nonaggression pact idea because it would have implied Western recognition of East Germany and a permanent division of Europe.) Harriman also assured the Russians that the signatures of China and France were not vital to a successful test ban treaty. On July 25 Harriman initialed the treaty for the United States in Moscow, and it was ratified by the Senate and signed by President Kennedy on Oct. 7, 1963.

As the American role in Vietnam expanded, Harriman maintained a skeptical attitude toward a purely military solution to the civil war there. Along with Roger Hilsman, the new assistant secretary of state for Far Eastern affairs, and Michael Forrestal, a White House aide assigned to work on Vietnam, Harriman repeatedly questioned the military's optimistic reports on the progress of the counter-insurgency program in Southeast Asia. During the spring and summer of 1963, this "Harriman group" urged that the Administration separate the American effort in Vietnam from the fortunes of the increasingly repressive Ngo Dinh Diem regime. The turning point in American policy came in August 1963 after Diem's secret police, led by his brother, Ngo Dinh Nhu, began a crackdown on opposition Buddhists in Saigon and Hue. With Undersecretary of State George Ball [q.v.], Harriman, Hilsman and Forrestal drafted a cable to Saigon Aug. 24 instructing Ambassador Henry Cabot Lodge [q.v.] on U.S. policy. The message stated that Diem must be "given [a] chance to rid himself of Nhu," but if he refused the U.S. had to "face the possibility that Diem himself cannot be preserved." Lodge was also instructed to inform leading South Vietnamese generals that the U.S. would not support the government unless reforms were made. In addition, he was given permission to tell the generals that U.S. would give them "direct support" in case of a "breakdown" in the central government. Because of dissention among the President's advisers, these instructions were canceled on Aug. 20 and Lodge was ordered to work for reform of the regime. A coup toppled the Diem government on Nov. 1.

In 1965 President Lyndon Johnson appointed Harriman ambassador-at-large with the principal duty of handling Southeast Asian affairs. During 1965 and 1966 he traveled around the world seeking support for U.S. Vietnam policy while sounding out the possibilities of a negotiated settlement of the war. When Johnson's announcement of American de-escalation in March 1968 led to the opening of preliminary peace talks two months later, Harriman went to Paris as chief U.S. negotiator.

During the opening months of the conference, talks revolved around two main issues: Hanoi's insistence on a total American bombing halt as a precondition for serious discussions and Saigon's refusal to enter negotiations in which the National Liberation Front (NLF) was represented. The U.S. refused to halt bombing completely without assurances that North Vietnam would respect the demilitarized zone, cease shelling major South Vietnamese population centers and promise a withdrawal of its troops from South Vietnam. Hanoi rejected these demands and continued to insist on a total U.S. bombing halt. However, major attacks did diminish in June and July. Harriman then recommended that the lull be regarded as a signal that North Vietnam had accepted the U.S. preconditions. He advised the U.S. to institute a full bombing halt. Despite the Ambassador's continual pleas, Johnson vetoed the proposal. After four months without progress, in September the President finally gave his approval of a halt upon the "unilateral understanding" that if America stopped bombing, North Vietnam would respect the demilitarized zone. In November the U.S. ended the bombing of North Vietnam. Johnson announced that in exchange for a bombing halt, Hanoi had agreed to the participation of the South Vietnamese government at the Paris talks, while the U.S. had approved a role for the NLF.

When discussions between the U.S. and North Vietnam on procedures for holding the enlarged conference of U.S., North Vietnamese, South Vietnamese and NLF representatives finally started in December, they bogged down in an argument over seating arrangements. South Vietnam refused to participate in any negotiations at which the NLF had equal status; thus they rejected the rectangular seating arrangement demanded by Hanoi. North Vietnam insisted on such NLF representation and would not permit the use of a round table suggested by the U.S. This arrangement would have permitted each party to interpret the status of the other representatives as it wished. The impasse continued through the end of the year and was not solved until the beginning of 1969, when all parties agreed to a round table with two rectangular tables placed at opposite ends. In January 1969 Henry Cabot Lodge [q.v.] succeeded Harriman as chief U.S. negotiator.

During the Nixon Administration Harriman continued to press for a complete withdrawal of Americans from Vietnam on a fixed schedule and in 1970 scored the Cambodian invasion as an unwarranted expansion of the war. In 1971 he urged Congress to use its power of the purse to end the conflict.

[EWS]

For further information see:
Averell Harriman, *Special Envoy to Churchill and Stalin* (New York, 1975).

HELMS, RICHARD M(cGARRAH)
b. March 30, 1913; St. David's, Pa.
Deputy to the Director for Plans, Central Intelligence Agency, 1952-62; Deputy Director for Plans, 1962–65; Director of Central Intelligence, June 1966-December 1972; Ambassador to Iran, February 1973-May 1977.

Richard Helms grew up in an upper middle class family, which lived first in

New Jersey and then Europe, where Helms received his secondary education. On his return to the U.S., Helms entered Williams College and graduated in 1935. He then worked as a correspondent for the United Press and later as advertising director of the Indianapolis *Times*.

Commissioned a lieutenant in the Navy in 1942, Helms was transferred to the Office of Strategic Services one year later. After his discharge in 1946 he remained in intelligence work, joining the Strategic Services Unit of the Department of War. The following year he helped organize the Central Intelligence Agency and during the 1950s became one of its key staff officers. During those early years he reportedly worked on covert operations or "plans" and helped recruit and train top agents.

In 1952 Helms was appointed deputy to the chief of the plans division. Although his exact functions were never made public, he was said to have supervised U.S. espionage in the Soviet Union, including the U-2 reconnaissance flights. Sometime during the 1950s, Helms also became involved in the CIA's program of domestic surveillance, which included the opening of mail and the compiling of files on 10,000 private American citizens in violation of the CIA's 1947 charter. Helms reportedly opposed the establishment of a CIA Domestic Operations Division in 1962.

According to a 1975 Senate report, between 1960 and 1965 Helms helped to plan the assassinations of Congolese Premier Patrice Lumumba and Cuban Premier Fidel Castro. The first of the plots against Castro employed underworld crime figure John Roselli to carry out the assignment. Other plots involved the use of explosives, high-powered rifles and poisoned ball-point pens and cigars to assassinate the Cuban leader. In January 1963 a skin-diving suit contaminated with a poisonous fungus was prepared as a gift to be given to Castro by James Donovan, who was then negotiating for the release of Cuban prisoners taken during the Bay of Pigs invasion. The plan failed because Donovan decided to give Castro an uncontaminated suit.

Although Helms, Richard Bissell and CIA Director Allen Dulles [*q.v.*] were implicated in these plots, the 1975 Senate Select Intelligence Committee investigating the assassination plans could not determine whether Presidents Dwight D. Eisenhower [*q.v.*], John Kennedy or Lyndon B. Johnson [*q.v.*] were aware of them. Helms testified that the presidents under whom he served had never asked him to consider assassination. The investigation revealed that Helms had withheld information from Johnson and Attorney General Robert Kennedy [*q.v.*] and did not tell John McCone [*q.v.*] of the CIA's use of underworld figures to kill Castro when McCone became CIA director in 1961.

According to ex-CIA employee Victor Marchetti, Helms was involved in the planning of the April 1961 Bay of Pigs invasion, but his participation was not documented. Helms was promoted to deputy director for plans in February 1962 upon the resignation of Richard Bissell, who had planned the ill-fated invasion. From April 1965 until June 1966, Helms served as deputy director of the CIA under Adm. William Raborn. Because Raborn had little experience in intelligence operations or foreign affairs, he relied heavily on his subordinate. During Raborn's term in office relations with other departments deteriorated and morale within the CIA declined. Reacting to criticism of the Agency, President Johnson appointed Helms director in June 1966. The President hoped that the appointment of an experienced CIA executive would improve morale and would result in needed organizational and management reforms.

While Helms was director of the CIA, the Agency was involved in numerous projects designed to ensure the establishment and preservation of friendly foreign governments. A congressional investigation in 1975 and 1976 revealed that the CIA had become deeply involved in Chilean domestic politics. During that country's 1964 presidential race, the CIA underwrote slightly more than half of the cost of the Christian Democratic Party campaign and mounted a massive anti-Communist propaganda drive designed to forestall the election of the Marxist candidate, Salvador Allende. The intervention enabled the moderate Christian Democrat, Eduardo Frei, who was unaware of the CIA's action, to win a clear majority in the election instead of the expected plurality. In the five years following that election, the CIA conducted a variety of covert activities designed to strengthen Chile's moderate parties. These actions included monetary support of political and intellectual groups, establishment of leftist splinter parties to draw support away from Allende, continued propaganda and liaison activities with Chile's internal security, and intelligence services to meet any threat posed by leftists. The total cost of CIA involvement in Chile during those years was $2 million. CIA activity in Chile culminated in 1970, when President Nixon instructed Helms to attempt to prevent Allende from taking power. The Agency, therefore, supported a group of military plotters planning a coup. The plot collapsed in the fall of 1970.

At the end of 1972 Helms was replaced as DCI and was appointed ambassador to Iran several months later. He was often called back from his post, however, to defend his activities as DCI during the congressional probes of the CIA from 1973 to 1976. Initially Helms denied any CIA involvement in Chile. After additional evidence came out, however, he did admit to some covert activity and narrowly escaped indictment for perjury because of his initial cover-up.

Following his retirement as ambassador in 1977, Helms opened up a consulting firm in Washington D.C.

[JB]

For further information:
Judith F. Buncher, *The C.I.A. & the Security Debate: 1971-1975* (New York, 1976).
————, *The CIA and the Security Debate: 1975-1976* (New York, 1977).
Victor Marchetti and John D. Marks, *The C.I.A. and the Cult of Intelligence* (New York, 1974).

HERTER, CHRISTIAN A(RCHIBALD)
b. March 28, 1895; Paris, France.
d. Dec. 30, 1966; Washington, D.C.
Governor, Mass., 1953-57; Undersecretary of State, February, 1957-April 1959; Secretary of State, April 1959-January 1961.

The son of expatriate American artists, Adele and Albert Herter, Christian Herter was born in Paris. After receiving his primary education there, he went to the Browning School in New York and in 1915 graduated from Harvard. Herter entered Columbia University's School of Architecture but left in 1916 to join the Foreign Service. He was assigned to the American embassy in Berlin. In 1918 Herter was a member of the U.S. delegation to Versailles and served on the special commission that negotiated a prisoner of war agreement with the Germans. The following year he helped Herbert Hoover supervise the American Relief Administration. When Hoover became Secretary of Commerce in 1921, he asked Herter to be his assistant. Herter held this post until 1924, when he left government service to become editor of *The Independent* and *The Sportsman*. He also lectured on international relations at Harvard.

A Republican, Herter sat in the Massachusetts House of Representatives from 1930 to 1942; for the last four of those years, he was Speaker of the House. In 1942 he won a U.S. House seat, which he held for 10 years. A member of the internationalist wing of the Republican Party, he supported the creation of the United Nations and the development of the Marshall Plan.

From 1953 to 1957, Herter served as governor of Massachusetts. In 1957 he was chosen to be Undersecretary of State, and he soon developed a close relationship with Dulles. Dulles, in fact, personally designated Herter as his successor.

Herter assumed the office of Secretary of State in April 1959. Characterized as an impeccable patrician, Herter was known for his gentleness and inner toughness. Cruelly bent by arthritis, he was frequently seen stooped over crutches. Although initial relations between Eisenhower and Herter were cool and some suggested Herter's appointment had been made only to please Dulles, the Secretary soon gained Eisenhower's confidence. However, he never wielded the power Dulles had used. During his first year in office, many of his duties were of a ceremonial nature, accompanying the President on trips and standing by to advise.

Herter's first major problem as Secretary was to coordinate the Allied response to Soviet Premier Nikita S. Khrushchev's November 1958 demand that the Western Allies withdraw their troops from West Berlin in six months and make it a "free city." In April 1959 Herter attended a Paris conference at which he mediated conflicting policies on the issue. At the end of the meeting the Western foreign ministers announced they were in complete agreement on strategy to be presented at a May conference with the Soviet Union in Geneva. The plan called for a four-stage "permanent settlement in Europe": stage 1—the unification of East and West Berlin through free elections; stage 2—the establishment of a "mixed" German committee to expand technical contacts between the two Germanys; stage 3—the election of an all-German assembly to establish a "liberal, democratic and federative system" in Germany; stage 4—the recognition of a unified Germany. The conference, held in May and again in August, resulted in a deadlock on the issue.

Herter was also rebuffed in Administration attempts to negotiate a disarmament treaty with the Soviet Union. In a speech before the National Press Club in Washington in March 1960, he outlined the U.S. disarmament program. The plan called for disarmament under the supervision of an international controls panel and for the establishment of talks beginning on the technical level and leading to the eventual reduction of military forces. However, throughout the remainder of the Eisenhower Administration, the Soviet Union refused to accept the proposal because of its provision for on-site inspection of missile stations and atomic installations.

On May 5, 1960, just before the scheduled East-West Summit Conference, Khrushchev announced that the Soviet Union had downed an American U-2 plane on a reconnaisance mission over the USSR. The Administration initially denied the charge. However, Herter argued that Washington should accept responsibility for the flights with an explanation of why they were needed. On May 7 the State Department admitted that a flight over Soviet territory had been made by an "unarmed civilian U-2." Two days later Herter defended the missions and indicated that they would continue to prevent possible Communist aggression. With the U-2 incident still in the headlines. Herter left on May 12 for Geneva to prepare for the meeting between Eisenhower, Khrushchev and British Prime Minister Harold Macmillan. The Summit collapsed five days later, when Khrushchev demanded that Eisenhower apologize for the U-2 flight.

Worsening relations with Cuba plagued Herter during his last year in office. In response to Cuban Premier Fidel Castro's virulent attacks against the U.S. and his decision to confiscate American property, Herter urged a policy of restraint. Eisenhower accepted the recommendation, promising in January 1960 that there would be no reprisals for Castro's actions. However, in August, after Castro began to accept Soviet weapons, Herter obtained a resolution from the Organization of American States censuring the dictator.

With the coming of the Kennedy Administration, Herter resigned his post and retired from public life. In November 1962 President John F. Kennedy named Herter chief planner and negotiator on foreign trade. His main duty was to head talks with the European Economic Community as a special representative of the President. He remained in this post until his death in December 1966.

[JB]

For further information:
Bernard Noble. *Christian A. Herter* (New York. 1970).

JACKSON, HENRY M(ARTIN)
b. May 31, 1912; Everett, Wash.
Democratic Senator, Wash., 1953- ;
Chairman, Interior and Insular Affairs
Committee, 1963- .

After two years in private legal practice "Scoop" Jackson won his first elective office in 1935. Five years later he was elected to the House of Representatives where he compiled a generally liberal voting record. He advanced to the Senate in 1952. As a member of the Armed Services Committee, he evolved into a prototype "Cold War liberal," advocating large defense expenditures in order to counter growing Soviet military power. He forged close ties with organized labor.

Jackson's influence in defense matters declined under a Democratic administration. He was skeptical about Kennedy's efforts to control the arms race and even opposed the 1961 bill creating the Arms Control and Disarmament Agency. He refused to vote for the 1963 nuclear test ban treaty until his "safeguards" were added to the treaty term.

The Senator was a staunch supporter of the Johnson Administration's Vietnam policy, although he tended to favor the Pentagon's military solutions over the Defense Department's. In December 1968 President-elect Nixon approached Jackson with an offer to head the Defense Department. Jackson declined, apparently wishing to leave open more options for his political future.

During the 1970s Jackson was one of Congress's most powerful figures. He increasingly used his power to attack the Nixon Administration's policy of *detente* and detente's chief architect, Secretary of State Henry Kissinger [*q.v.*]. He criticized the May 1972 Strategic Arms Limitation Talks (SALT) accords on defensive nuclear weapons with the Soviets by arguing that the "agreements are likely to lead to an accelerated technological arms race with greater uncertainties, profound instabilities and considerable costs." At the same time, he claimed that they gave strategic advantages to the Soviets. Jackson's price for ratification of the treaty was an amendment which contained hard-line instructions for SALT negotiators. It requested that any future permanent treaty on offensive nuclear arms "not limit the United States to levels of intercontinental strategic forces inferior to" those of the Soviet Union. Any treaty was to be based on "the principle of equality."

Jackson's suspicions of the Soviets and his concern for Soviet Jews were made clear again in October when he and 75 Senate cosponsors introduced an amendment to the East-West Trade Relations Act aimed at denying the USSR most-favored nation status as long as it barred emigration or imposed "more than a nominal tax . . . on any citizen as a consequence of emigration." The Soviet leadership responded violently to the action, calling it unjustified interference in internal matters. Both the Soviets and the Administration were embarrassed, but in June 1974 Kissinger reportedly got a pledge from the Soviets to allow the emigration of 45,000 Jews a year. Jackson found the figure inadequate. Kissinger later carried more Soviet assurances to Jackson and in December 1974 the comprehensive trade bill with the Jackson amendment was passed by Congress. The USSR canceled the treaty the next month because of the emigration clause. Jackson claimed that Kissinger and President Ford were seeking to blame Congress, and him specifically, for their failure.

In the midst of the Watergate investigations in February 1973 the Government Operations Committee's Permanent Subcommittee on Investigations, which he chaired, initiated research on the circumstances surrounding the sale of grain to the USSR in the summer of 1972. Jackson charged the Department of Agriculture with mismanagement which led to excessive profits for the grain exporters and bargain prices for the Soviets at the expense of farmers and consumers. In the subcommittee's final report of August 1974 Jackson said that the "great grain robbery" resulted in depleted U.S. grain reserves, higher food prices and a crisis in the livestock industry. His pressure led to a temporary halt of grain shipments in October.

In 1976 he made an unsuccessful bid for the Democratic presidential nomination. Following his defeat, he continued to be a leading Senate spokesman.

[JCH]

For further information:
Peter J. Ognibene, *Scoop: The Life and Politics of Henry M. Jackson* (New York, 1975).

JENNER, WILLIAM E(ZRA)
b. July 21, 1908; Marengo, Ind.
Republican Senator, Ind., 1944-45, 1947-59.

A 1930 graduate of Indiana University, Jenner earned his law degree from George Washington University Law School in 1932. In 1934 he won a seat in the Indiana State Senate. He became minority leader in 1937 and served as president pro-tempore and majority leader from 1939 to 1941. Jenner than left politics to join the Army Air Corps during World War II. Upon discharge he became the first veteran to enter the U.S. Senate, when he was appointed to fill the unexpired term of the late Sen. Frederick Van Nuys (D, Ind.). Jenner served for seven weeks from 1944 to 1945 and then returned to his state to become chairman of the Republican State Committee. He won a full Senate term in 1946.

Jenner immediately joined the "Class of 1946," a group of new Republican legislators whose conservatism and pro-Nationalist Chinese, anti-European foreign policy spelled problems for the Truman Administration. He voted against most of the President's Fair Deal social legislation and supported anti-labor and anti-Communist measures.

The Indiana Republican was a prominent member of the "China Lobby," a group of Americans and Nationalist Chinese who pressed for increased aid to Chiang Kai-shek. It charged that the Truman Administration's focus on Europe was part of a left-wing plot to bankrupt the U.S. while China, the nation's most valuable ally, fell under Communist rule. Jenner, therefore, labored to cripple Truman's containment program because it did not do enough for China. He led attempts to reduce American funds to the Marshall Plan in 1948. From his back row seat in the Senate, Jenner claimed that spending in Europe was no longer necessary. The policy "leaves the Republicans and the taxpayer holding the bag," he maintained. He expressed outrage that aid went to socialist Britain. Jenner vehemently opposed the ratification of the North Atlantic Treaty in 1949. Aid to the North Atlantic Treaty Organization (NATO), he prophesed, would bankrupt the nation. After a world tour in 1949, he noted that the Russians were winning the Cold War. The Europeans used American aid not for international peace, he stated, "but to fan the fires of nationalist rivalries." In 1952 Jenner voted against peace treaties granting Germany increased freedom and linking it with NATO because the agreements might "be expiated by holy young American blood."

The Senator was an ardent foe of Gen. George C. Marshall [*q.v.*], whom he blamed for Communist expansion and the loss of China. During the fall of 1950, when the Senate was asked to modify the National Security Act of 1947 to permit Marshall to become Secretary of Defense, Jenner voted against it. Marshall became the target for one of Jenner's most hostile speeches. During the debate over the nomination, Jenner called the General a "living lie" who was an eager "front man for traitors." Marshall, he maintained, had helped set the stage for the Soviet victory that is now "sweeping the earth." Jenner charged that Marshall had contributed to the betrayal of Eastern Europe at the wartime conferences and was the inaugurator of the "sell-China-down-the-river line." The General's advocacy of withholding aid from Nationalist China, he charged, had paralyzed the Chiang government. Jenner angrily proclaimed, "our boys are dying in Korea" as a result of Marshall's policies.

Jenner joined the vocal group of conservative Republican senators who supported Gen. Douglas MacArthur [q.v.] in his policy dispute with Truman. When the President fired the popular General in April 1951, Jenner proclaimed on the Senate floor, "I charge this country today is in the hands of a secret inner coterie which is directed by agents of the Soviet Union. Our only choice is to impeach President Truman and find out who is the secret invisible government." The Senator also called for the ouster of Secretary of State Dean Acheson [q.v.].

During the Eisenhower Administration Jenner continued to be one of the leading members of the China bloc in the Senate. In May 1954 he called on the U.S. to arm 20 million Nationalist Chinese, Korean, Japanese and other anti-Communists in Asia to support Taiwan's attacks on the mainland and divert Communist forces from Indochina. Jenner expressed outrage that the U.S. prevented Chiang Kai-shek from raiding the mainland and opposed any further attempts by the U.S. government to resume normal relations with Communist China. He also asked the President to issue a "final statement" that the U.S. would not recognize Communist China or sanction its admission to the U.N. During the Quemoy-Matsu dispute of late 1954, Jenner supported a blockade of the mainland. On April 28, 1955, Jenner introduced a resolution that would have repudiated in advance any concessions that the U.S. might make to Peking.

In December 1957 Jenner announced he would not run for reelection. He resumed his law practice in his home state.

[JB]

JOHNSON, LYNDON B(AINES)
b. Aug. 27, 1908; Stonewall, Tex.
d. Jan. 22, 1973; Stonewall, Tex.

President of the United States,
November 1963-January 1969.

Lyndon Johnson, the grandson of a populist member of the Texas state legislature and the son of a cattle speculator, was born on a farm in the rugged hill country of south-central Texas, near Austin. He attended local public schools, graduated from Southwest Texas State Teachers College in 1930 and the next year became secretary to a Texas congressman. While in Washington Johnson was urged to pursue a political career by Rep. Sam Rayburn, a close political confidant and later speaker of the House of Representatives. In 1934 he married Claudia Alta Taylor, known as Lady Bird, who was credited with being a steadying influence on him.

In 1935 President Roosevelt appointed Johnson as Texas state administrator of the National Youth Administration. The job also provided Johnson with a wide political base for a successful congressional campaign in 1937. He ran on a strong New Deal platform rooted in a personal relationship with Roosevelt, who Johnson later declared "was like a Daddy to me." But after 1938 Johnson, like many other Southern congressmen, became more conservative. His political career was interrupted by service with the Navy in World War II. In 1948 he won a bitterly fought Democratic senatorial primary runoff election by 87 votes out of one million cast. In 1977 a former Texas voting official, Luis Salas, said that he had certified enough fictitious ballots to enable Johnson to win the election.

Befriended by powerful Sen. Richard Russell (D, Ga.), a member of the Senate "establishment," Johnson rose quickly through the Senate hierarchy, winning the post of Senate minority leader in 1953 and majority leader two years later. In 1955 he made a rapid recovery from a massive heart attack.

As majority leader, Johnson established a near-legendary reputation for his command of the legislative process and his assessment of the needs, ambitions and weaknesses of individual senators. As his own national ambitions increased, Johnson's political stance moved from conservative to moderate. He guided through Congress a number of programs that were opposed by the Republican Administration and helped gain passage for the Civil Rights Acts of 1957 and 1960, despite considerable Southern resistance.

In 1960 Johnson made an unsuccessful bid for the Democratic presidential nomination but accepted his party's vice-presidential candidacy. After the successful November election, Johnson served as Vice-President, but had little actual power. Johnson was catapulted into the Presidency, however, after the assassination of President Kennedy in 1963.

Johnson's first foreign policy challenge involved the Panama Canal riots which broke out in January 1964. The Panamanian government suspended diplomatic relations with the U.S. and demanded a revision of the 1903 Canal Zone treaty. Johnson, who had little experience in foreign affairs, took an unexpectedly hard line in the crisis, insisting that law and order be restored before negotiations could begin. In April 1965 Johnson faced another Latin American crisis when the Dominican Republic's ruling military junta was threatened by rebel forces. On April 27 the President announced that he had ordered the evacuation of U.S. citizens from Santo Domingo; the next day he revealed that 400 U.S. Marines had been dispatched to the city. As the number of troops there rose to 30,000, the President asserted that Communist influence in the rebellion justified U.S. military intervention. Johnson came under vigorous criticism for his policy in the Dominican Republic, and Sen. J. William Fulbright's (D, Ark.) [q.v.] Foreign Relations Committee conducted nine days of closed-door hearings on the crisis. Many liberals who supported the President's escalation of the war in Vietnam were nevertheless sharply critical of what they regarded as a new, hard-line foreign policy in Latin America.

In the first several months of his presidency, Johnson's chief concern in Vietnam was to continue the policy he had inherited from President Kennedy. He retained Kennedy's top foreign policy advisers—Dean Rusk [q.v.], Robert McNamara [q.v.], W. W. Rostow [q.v.] and McGeorge Bundy [q.v.]—and relied heavily upon their ad-

vice in the conduct of the war. Johnson believed firmly in the "domino theory." Shortly after the assassination he told Ambassador to South Vietnam Henry Cabot Lodge, "I am not going to lose Vietnam. I am not going to be the President who saw Southeast Asia go the way of China." Plans for an escalation of the war began in early 1964, when it became apparent to the White House that the South Vietnamese government could not hold its own against the National Liberation Front (NLF). In February 1964 the U.S. initiated a secret "Operation Plan 34A" by which the U.S. provided tactical air support for South Vietnamese air strikes against the North. In April Johnson named Gen. William Westmoreland commander of the 20,000-man U.S. force in South Vietnam, and in June he appointed Gen. Maxwell Taylor [q.v.] as ambassador to South Vietnam to replace Lodge. Both Westmoreland and Taylor favored greater use of U.S. troops in the South.

On Aug. 4, 1964 two U.S. destroyers patrolling the Gulf of Tonkin off the coast of North Vietnam reported that they were under enemy attack. Although Johnson soon received information suggesting that the reported attack might not have occurred or, if it had, had been grossly exaggerated, he withheld this information from the public and ordered retaliatory bombing of North Vietnamese coastal bases and oil depots. At Johnson's request Congress three days later passed the Tonkin Gulf Resolution, which gave the President broad authority to use military force throughout Southeast Asia "to prevent further aggression." The resolution passed both houses of Congress with only two dissenting votes.

Throughout the autumn of 1964 Johnson received reports that the NLF was tightening its hold on the South Vietnamese countryside. Taylor and Westmoreland urged the President to authorize systematic bombing of North Vietnam as a means of bolstering morale in the South and cutting infiltration from the North. Campaigning as a peace candidate in the fall, Johnson postponed action on their requests. Nevertheless, the Pentagon Papers later disclosed that the actual decision to undertake the bombing of the North had been made as early as October 1964. "I suddenly realized that doing nothing was more dangerous than doing something," Johnson told Doris Kearns.

In February 1965 Communist guerrillas attacked the U.S. military compounds at Pleiku and at Qui Nhon. Johnson immediately ordered retaliatory air raids on North Vietnamese military and industrial sites. By the end of the month, the bombing of the North had become continuous, though limited to targets outside the Hanoi area. Johnson also authorized the landing of two combat-ready Marine battalions to defend the large airbase at Da Nang. On April 1 Johnson agreed to Westmoreland's request that he be authorized to use the troops for offensive actions anywhere in South Vietnam. By early June there were 50,000 American ground troops in Vietnam. Over the next three years Johnson agreed to almost all of Westmoreland's troop increase requests. In 1968 there were over 500,000 American soldiers in Vietnam.

Backed by Bundy and McNamara, Johnson's escalation of the war took place in a gradual, step-by-step fashion. He chose this course for three reasons. First, Johnson and most of his civilian advisers feared that a major escalation would precipitate active Chinese or Russian intervention in the war. Second, they hoped that the relatively slow increase in the pressure on the North might force Hanoi to negotiate in order to prevent the terrible damage that large-scale bombing would inflict. Third, Johnson feared the domestic consequences of a rapid expansion of the war. In 1965 he worried that congressional conservatives would use the war as an excuse to reduce funding for Great Society programs. Later, after Johnson himself had begun to cut back on domestic social legislation, he feared that a dramatic escalation of the war would add to the growing list of liberal war critics.

During the years from 1965 to 1967, Johnson announced repeatedly that he favored negotiations with the North Vietnamese, and several bombing halts were called, ostensibly to facilitate the start of talks. Hanoi leaders did not respond to the President's numerous "peace feelers," in part because the Communists insisted upon an American commitment to an unconditional halt to the bombing of the North but also because they were convinced they were winning the war in the South. Meanwhile, the Joint Chiefs of Staff continually pressed Johnson for an expansion and intensification of the bombing, but Secretary of Defense McNamara grew increasingly skeptical over the diplomatic or military efficacy of continued air attacks. In a September 1967 speech delivered at San Antonio, Johnson promised to halt the air war indefinitely if North Vietnam agreed promptly to begin peace negotiations and not to "take advantage" of the bombing cessation to send men and material to the South. Since over 100,000 North Vietnamese troops had to be supplied in the South, Hanoi soon rejected the "San Antonio Formula."

As the Vietnam war dragged on and its domestic consequences began to make themselves felt, Johnson encountered ever growing anti-war sentiment. The students and intellectuals who protested the war as early as 1964 were joined by an increasingly large number of congressional liberals in 1966 and 1967. Even Vietnam war "hawks" grew dissatisfied with Johnson's conduct of the war because of the restraints he imposed upon the military. By 1967 the hostility of the protest movement had virtually barred Johnson from most public appearances except those held on military bases. He denounced his critics as "nervous nellies . . . blind to experience and deaf to hope," but Johnson was personally shaken when close associates like Moyers, McNamara and Bundy shifted to a more "dovish" position. Meanwhile, the Republicans made large gains in the 1966 off-year elections. Johnson's personal approval ratio, as measured by the Gallup Poll, dropped more than 30 points during the course of the war. By November 1967, 57% of the public disapproved of his handling of the conflict.

Johnson reached the decision to begin de-escalation of the war only after the enemy's dramatic Tet offensive of February 1968 forced a reassessment of strategic thinking in the White House. Following the NLF's invasion of the South Vietnamese cities, Gen. Westmoreland asked for over 200,000 more troops, but Johnson hesitated to fulfill this request. Instead, the President appointed his new Secretary of Defense, Clark Clifford [q.v.], as head of a task force to study the proposal and examine its impact on the budget, public opinion and future prospects for negotiations. Although a "hawk" until then, Clifford came to the conclusion that the war had to be wound down. By repeatedly reminding Johnson that the cost of victory had risen sharply and by rigorously challenging the optimistic reports from Saigon, Clifford helped check the momentum for increasing the war effort.

Johnson simultaneously was receiving further evidence of public disenchantment with the war. In the New Hampshire primary Sen. Eugene McCarthy (D, Minn.) [q.v.], a vigorous critic of the war, ran a surprisingly strong race against the President in the March 13 balloting. Three days later Robert Kennedy announced he would enter the race for the Democratic Party's nomination on an anti-war platform.

Johnson relieved Westmoreland of his command on March 22. Shortly thereafter he convened at the White House an extraordinary informal advisory group, composed of such Establishment figures as Dean Acheson [q.v.], George Ball [q.v.], Douglas Dillon, Arthur Goldberg, Matthew Ridgway [q.v.] and Henry Cabot Lodge. After listening to detailed briefings, a solid majority of the group concluded on March 26 that Johnson had to de-escalate the war and begin negotiations with the North Vietnamese.

Johnson went before a nationwide television audience on the night of March 31 to announce a unilateral halt to air and naval bombardment of North Vietnam except in the area immediately north of the demilitarized zone. He called on North Vietnam "to respond positively and favorably to this new step toward peace." At the close of his speech Johnson stunned the nation by declaring, "I shall not seek and will not accept the nomination of my Party for another term as your President." Three

days later North Vietnam agreed to open negotiations in Paris, and the long-sought talks finally began in May.

Although Johnson had pledged to remain aloof from domestic politics in 1968, his influence on the campaign was considerable. He threw his still substantial influence behind the candidacy of Hubert Humphrey, thus helping the Vice President to win the Democratic presidential nomination despite a series of primary victories by his two anti-war opponents. At the Democratic National Convention Johnson vetoed a compromise Vietnam plank, which favored an immediate halt in all bombing of North Vietnam. In the fall Johnson maintained a continued pressure on Humphrey to adhere to the Administration's hard-line policy until late October, when Johnson himself announced a complete end to American bombing of North Vietnam. Many historians have speculated that if Johnson had softened his position on the war somewhat earlier, Humphrey might have won the presidential election in November.

After 37 years in Washington, Johnson retired to his Texas ranch following Richard Nixon's inauguration. In May 1971 he dedicated the $18.6 million Lyndon Baines Johnson Library complex on the Austin campus of the University of Texas. In November of that year his memoir, *The Vantage Point: Perspectives on the Presidency, 1963-1969*, was published to reviews that were generally critical of the book's blandness. During the next two years Johnson's health declined, and on Jan. 22, 1973 he died of a heart attack at his ranch.

Although most historians have applauded Lyndon Johnson's extraordinary skill in pushing through Congress the landmark civil rights and Great Society legislation of the mid-1960s, his reputation as President remained tarnished by his immense failure in Vietnam. Eric Goldman saw Johnson as a "tragic figure" whose preoccupation with Vietnam destroyed the potential of his latter-day New Deal liberalism. Arthur Schlesinger, Jr. [q.v.] offered a darker interpretation from the vantage point of the mid-1970s. He argued that Johnson's decision to escalate the Vietnam war without fully informing either Congress or the American people of his real intentions was a decisive step in the growth of an "imperial presidency" that Richard Nixon then sought to strengthen and institutionalize.

[FHM, NNL]

For further information:

Rowland Evans and Robert Novak, *Lyndon B. Johnson: The Exercise of Power* (New York, 1966).

Eric F. Goldman, *The Tragedy of Lyndon Johnson* (New York, 1969).

Lyndon B. Johnson, *The Vantage Point: Perspectives on the Presidency, 1963-1969* (New York, 1971.)

Doris Kearns, *Lyndon Johnson and the American Dream* (New York, 1976).

Tom Wicker, *JFK and LBJ* (New York, 1969).

JUDD, WALTER H(ENRY)
b. Sept. 25, 1898; Rising City, Neb.
Republican Representative, Minn., 1943-63.

Judd graduated from the University of Nebraska Medical School in 1923 and two years later became a medical missionary in China. He contracted malaria and was forced to return to the U.S. in 1931. Judd accepted a teaching position at the University of Minnesota Hospital. In 1934 he returned to China to run a hospital in Shansi Province. When the Japanese conquered the area in 1938, Judd fled to the U.S. The doctor then embarked on an extensive speaking tour, informing the nation of the brutality of the Japanese occupation and pleading for more American aid to the Nationalists. Discouraged by the isolationism of the period, he settled down to practice medicine in Minnesota. In August 1942 Judd announced his candidacy for a seat in the House of Representatives. Endorsed by liberals and labor impressed with his humanitarian concern for the Chinese and his demands for U.S. involvement in the war, Judd defeated his isolationist opponent, Oscar Youngdahl.

Judd quickly emerged as a major spokesman for the Chinese interests. His maiden speech deplored the discriminatory exclusion acts and demanded their repeal. He also pleaded for keeping both Russia and China in the war and denounced American diplomacy during the 1920s and the 1930s as based on attempts to impose American ideas on people to whom they were alien. Judd labored to build up the Nationalists as a significant power in Asia so that they would first defeat the Japanese and then the growing Communist movement, led by Mao Tse-tung. One of the most vigorous anti-Communists in Congress, Judd disagreed with many China experts who assumed that Mao's movement was based more on nationalism than doctrinaire Communism. He said in 1945, "I am increasingly convinced that the Chinese Communists are Communist first and Chinese second." He defended Chiang Kai-shek's government from charges that it was hopelessly corrupt and reactionary by requesting Americans to understand the difficulties of unifying and governing a large nation.

After the war Judd emerged as a leading spokesman for the "China Lobby," a powerful pressure group composed of officials from the Nationalist embassy in Washington, propagandists, and leading conservative American businessmen, journalists, union leaders and policy groups. The Lobby was formed to pressure the Administration to increase aid to Chiang in the face of growing criticism of his regime and Nationalist defeats on the battlefield. Judd considered it hypocritical on the Administration's part to provide arms and economic assistance to Europe and not to Asia, where actual battles were being fought.

The former missionary joined the growing number in the Lobby who began to believe that only a pro-Communist conspiracy in Washington during and after the war had stymied attempts to aid the Nationalists. These conspirators had portrayed the Chiang government as corrupt while lauding the democratic agrarian roots of Mao's movement. Judd charged that this conspiracy existed in the Far East desk of the State Department, which he called the "Red Cell." But in his opinion the conspiracy also took place in the high offices of the Roosevelt Administration. In 1946 Judd joined 65 other prominent Americans in signing the "Manchurian Manifesto." This document charged that at the Yalta Conference the U.S., behind China's back, had promised to turn over Manchuria and Mongolia to the Russians following their entry into the war. Later Judd made John S. Service the focus of his attacks on Chinese experts in the State Department.

Judd continued to criticize Truman's China policy into 1947. He denounced the Marshall Mission, formed to mediate the Chinese civil war, complaining of Gen. George C. Marshall's [q.v.] lack of understanding of the Chinese problem. When the mission failed, Judd pressured the Administration into sending Gen. Alfred C. Wedemeyer to China to reassess the situation. Truman also lifted the arms embargo to China and replaced the controversial John Carter Vincent as director of the Office of Far Eastern Affairs. The President requested a moderate increase in aid to Chiang, but the bill was held up by economy-minded Republicans in the House Appropriations Committee.

Following the fall of China to the Communists in 1949, Judd became one of the most vocal supporters of the new Formosa regime. He joined many conservatives in denouncing the White Paper on China which placed the blame for the fall on corruption in the Nationalist regime. Judd praised the Nationalist government for understanding the gravity of the threat of international Communism in Asia. He claimed that the White Paper should be read by Americans as "a confession that the leaders of our government possessed no such understanding." Judd further charged that evidence favorable to Chiang was omitted from the document. "We have not tried to win the war in China," Judd proclaimed. "We have tried to

end it. But the only way to end the war with Communism—anywhere—is to win the war."

In 1950 Judd backed Sen. Joseph R. McCarthy's (R, Wisc.) charges of conspiracy in the State Department. He repeated his earlier accusation that the responsibility for China's fall lay with "the Communists and their stooges both inside our government and among writers, lecturers, commentators, and so forth." He also agreed with the Wisconsin Senator that the Korean war could have been averted if the Americans had stood up to the Communists earlier. During the war Judd began a campaign, with which he was associated far into the Johnson Administration, to pressure Truman not to recognize Communist China and to oppose China's entry into the United Nations.

During the Eisenhower Administration the Congressman continued to press for a hard-line policy on Communist China. In the summer of 1953 Judd, who was chairman of the Foreign Relations Committee's Subcommittee on Far Eastern Affairs, introduced a resolution opposing the admission of Communist China to the United Nations. The Congressman believed that it would be "plain hypocrisy" to admit a regime "which brazenly went to war with the U.N. itself." More importantly, he argued, admission would have increased the prestige of the enemies of the U.S. and the U.N. The House unanimously adopted the resolution in July.

In the fall of 1953 Judd and other leaders of the China Lobby formed the Committee for One Million Against the Admission of Communist China to the U.N. With the blessings of Eisenhower and the backing of the American Legion, the American Federation of Labor and the General Federation of Women's Clubs, the Committee collected the million signatures in just nine months.

Judd reacted vigorously to the Communist Chinese capture of two American flyers in 1954 and the resumption of hostilities between Nationalist and Communists in 1955. He objected to Eisenhower's call for a cease-fire between the two belligerents. In his opinion such a move would have neutralized the Nationalist Chinese instead of permitting them to remain a threat to the mainland's flank and prevent Communist expansion into Southeast Asia. He also urged Eisenhower not to permit relatives to visit the downed flyers and thus draw attention away from the conflict.

Shortly thereafter Judd helped reconstitute the Committee for One Million as the Committee of One Million Against the Admission of Communist China to the U.N. The organization then launched a broad campaign to rally public opinion against not only admission of China to the U.N. but also diplomatic recognition or trade relations with the Communist Chinese. In 1957 the Committee organized a nationwide postcard mailing that helped kill proposed Senate hearings on trade with mainland China. In 1959 it issued a rebuttal to the Colon Report, a widely publicized private study urging closer U.S.-China relations.

Judd delivered the keynote address at the Republican National Convention in 1960. During the campaign The Committee of One Million supported the Congressman for Secretary of State, but the effort died with John F. Kennedy's election.

During the Kennedy Administration Judd supported the President on several important foreign policy measures, including the Trade Expansion Act of 1962, but he opposed such programs as medicare. Although he described himself as a "progressive conservative," Judd became associated with the burgeoning Far Right during the early-1960s. He participated in the Christian Anti-Communist Crusade but was critical of the John Birch Society. In 1962 Judd lost reelection by a small margin.

[TLH]

For further information:
Stanley D. Bachrack, *The Committee of One Million* (New York, 1976).
Foster Rhea Dulles, *American Policy Toward Communist China 1949-1969* (New York, 1972).

KENNAN, GEORGE F(ROST)
b. Feb. 16, 1904; Milwaukee, Wisc.
Chairman, Policy Planning Staff, State Department 1947-49;
Counselor, State Department, 1949-50; Ambassador to the Soviet Union, 1951-52; Ambassador to Yugoslavia, 1961-63.

Kennan graduated from Princeton in 1925 and entered the Foreign Service the following year. After duty in Central Europe, he was transferred to Eastern Europe. In anticipation of the eventual recognition of the Soviet Union, the State Department sent Kennan to the University of Berlin, where he studied Russian language and culture from 1931 to 1933. He served with the first embassy to Moscow from 1933 to 1936. In this position Kennan soon emerged as a hardened anti-Communist who was particularly troubled by Stalin's repression of religion and civil liberties. The young diplomat was stationed in Prague and Berlin during the opening years of World War II. Kennan was interned by the Nazis from December 1941 to May 1942. During the early years of the war, he served at the American embassy in Portugal. In 1943 he joined the European Advisory Commission in London, where he worked on plans for a postwar Germany. The following year he became counselor to Averell Harriman [q.v.], ambassador to the Soviet Union.

Throughout the war Kennan warned against a close alliance with the Soviet Union. Just after the German invasion of Russia, he wrote, "It seems to me that to welcome Russia as an associate in the defense of democracy would invite misunderstanding." In 1944, after the Soviets had repulsed the Germans, Kennan pleaded for a "full-fledged and realistic political showdown with the Soviet leaders" and advocated ending land-lease aid. He thought that Soviet-American collaboration would be unnecessary after the war. Although he opposed the Communist occupation of Eastern Europe and recommended that economic aid to the Soviet

Union be cut off to encourage Soviet withdrawal from that area, he felt that there was little the U.S. could do about the situation. He believed that the Soviets could not maintain their hegemony in Eastern Europe and recommended that, for the time being, the two nations recognize each other's spheres of influence. The State Department ignored his advice.

In February 1946, in light of the collapse of wartime alliance and growing domestic anti-Communism, the State Department asked Kennan to draft a report analyzing American policy toward the Soviet Union. He replied in the "Long Telegram," clearly, carefully pressing the views long ignored. Kennan's analysis created a sensation. Truman read it, and Secretary of the Navy James V. Forrestal [q.v.] made it required reading for high military officers. It provided the Administration with an intellectual framework upon which to base Soviet-American policy for the remainder of Truman's presidency.

Soviet policy, Kennan asserted, was based on the ideological conviction of the inevitability of socialist-capitalist conflict. To avoid being encircled by capitalist powers, Stalin would strengthen his control at home and surround himself with friendly client states. Kennan assumed that Russia was too weak to attack the West militarily and would attempt to subvert the capitalist nations politically, thereby isolating the United States.

Kennan was called back to Washington in April 1946 to lecture on foreign affairs at the National War College. During the early months of 1947, he took part in discussions over the framing of the Greek-Turkish aid proposal. Kennan opposed recommendations by Sen. Arthur Vandenberg (R, Mich.) [q.v.] and Dean Acheson [q.v.] to couch the plan in terms of a moral crusade against Communism. He argued that the Soviet Union was not a military threat in Turkey. However, his reservations were ignored.

In April 1947 Secretary of State George C. Marshall [q.v.] invited Kennan to head the Department's newly created Policy Planning Staff and charged him with the responsibility for long range planning of U.S. actions in foreign policy. His first task was to formulate a proposal for the massive reconstruction of Europe. Given only two days in which to draft suggestions, Kennan outlined in general terms a two stage proposal of rehabilitation; short-term action to eliminate immediate needs and a long-term program to rebuild the European economy. While the short-term project could be primarily the responsibility of the U.S., the long-term program must, according to Kennan, be evolved by Europeans with minimum American influence. He urged studies in Europe and the United States to delineate needs, conditions and terms of assistance. Kennan emphasized that the rehabilitation of Germany must be a primary consideration while avoiding the specter of a rearmed Germany. He recommended that the program be offered to all nations including the Soviet Union. However, by making conditions for inclusion stringent, he promised Moscow would never accept the offer. Kennan's memorandum and follow-up reports provided the material for the Secretary's Harvard University address in June 1947 during which he proposed the Marshall Plan.

Kennan wrote a justification for the Plan in a July issue of *Foreign Affairs* in an article entitled, "The Sources of Soviet Conduct." Preferring to remain anonymous, he signed the article "Mr. X," but his identity quickly became known. As he had in the "Long Telegram," Kennan outlined the basis for Soviet foreign policy and discussed probable Russian action. He foresaw the Soviet Union probing for weak links in the Western alliance. To meet this threat Kennan recommended "a long-term patient but firm and vigilant containment of Russian expansive tendencies through . . . the adroit and vigilant application of counterforce at a series of constantly shifting geographical and political points, corresponding to the shifts and maneuvers of Soviet policies." For the near future, he thought containment did not promise victory over the

USSR but the preservation of the status quo. Kennan hoped that when Moscow saw the determination of the West to stand up to future aggression, tensions could eventually be reduced. When this occurred the Kremlin leaders would lose their justification for a police state and liberalize their regime.

Kennan's ambiguous use of the term "counterforce" prompted many in Washington to think the diplomat recommended military measures to contain Soviet expansion. In subsequent articles and speeches Kennan argued that he had never viewed containment in this manner. Reiterating that he did not see the USSR as a military threat, he maintained that he had attempted to justify the economic redevelopment of Western Europe and Japan to serve as buffer states against Russia. Despite his protestations, policymakers began viewing the struggle in terms of military force.

When Dean Acheson became Secretary of State in 1949, Kennan assumed the post of counselor of the department. His brief tenure was marked by constant clashes with the Secretary over containment. Kennan questioned the need for the formation of the North Atlantic Treaty Organization, reiterating his belief that the Soviet threat was primarily political. He maintained that a military alliance based on conventional weapons "obsolete in the nuclear age" would be not only useless but also an additional source of aggravation in the Cold War. Kennan also clashed with Acheson over the role of Germany. Although he had initially considered the redevelopment and integration of Germany into Europe necessary to contain Communism, by 1949 Kennan had concluded that tensions in the area could be reduced by joint U.S.-USSR troop withdrawal and the development of a neutralized, demilitarized state. Kennan proposed this at a time when the Administration believed that Germany should play a strong role in NATO. The two men also disagreed over policy in Korea. Kennan had originally supported U.S. intervention in the area. However, he opposed Acheson's decision to order the troops to cross the 38th Parallel on the grounds that this would invite the Communist Chinese entry into the war.

Kennan resigned his post in 1951 to become a member of the Institute of Advanced Studies at Princeton. The following year Kennan became ambassador to the Soviet Union. He found service in Moscow frustrating. Washington failed to ask his advice, and he thought living in the Soviet Union under Stalin's rule to be stifling. When Kennan left Moscow in September 1952 to attend a Conference in London, the Soviets declared him *persona non grata*. This apparently resulted from Kennan's comment made comparing life in the American Embassy to that in a Nazi internment camp during the war. Kennan returned to the U.S. to await a new assignment from the incoming Eisenhower Administration. However Secretary of State John Foster Dulles [*q.v.*] refused to appoint him to a new post, thus forcing the diplomat into early retirement.

During the 1950s Kennan was one of the Eisenhower Administration's foremost critics. Arguing that Communist expansion was ideological and economic, not military, he opposed reliance on military alliances such as the North Atlantic Treaty Organization. He also objected to Dulles's defining the struggle against the USSR in terms of a moral crusade.

At the end of 1957 Kennan delivered a series of lectures over the British Broadcasting Corp. that called for a reassessment of American policy toward the USSR. He suggested that since Stalin's death in 1953 a liberalizing trend had appeared in Russia which made the Kremlin leaders more inclined to diplomatic negotiation than military conquest. Kennan dismissed the Administration's idea of giving Germany nuclear arms to prevent Russian expansion. Instead, he recommended that the U.S. use the threat of that possibility to negotiate with the Russians on the neutralization of Central and Eastern Europe. The Soviet Union and the U.S. could then withdraw or "disengage" their forces from the area.

Kennan's disengagement policy generated a debate among foreign policy officials. Dean Acheson [q.v.] and Henry Kissinger [q.v.] were among his most forceful critics. Acheson wrote that Kennan "has never in my judgment grasped the realities of power relationships, but takes a rather mystical attitude toward them." Disengagement, the former Secretary of State claimed, would be the "new isolationism." Professor Kissinger argued that the Russians should still be considered a military threat to Western Europe and American troops should remain there as a major deterrant. Sen. John Kennedy (D, Mass.) [q.v.], on the other hand, wrote Kennan complimenting his lectures for their "brilliance and stimulation." Walter Lippmann [q.v.], who had advocated disengagement in the late-1940s, praised Kennan's change of position.

In 1959 Kennan questioned the Eisenhower Administration's reliance on nuclear weapons of indiscriminate mass destruction for America's defense. He proposed, instead, that the U.S. and Russia abolish them and that this country rely on conventional forces to defend itself.

Kennan was a leading expert on Russian history as well as a foreign policy commentator. His book, *Russia Leaves the War* (1956), won the Pulitzer Prize of 1957. Its sequel, *The Decision to Intervene* (1957), was equally well received. Kennan's short book, *American Diplomacy: 1900-1951* (1952), based on lectures he gave at the University of Chicago in 1951, was one of the most popular appraisals of twentieth century American foreign policy.

In 1960 President-elect Kennedy offered Kennan the ambassadorship to either Yugoslavia or Poland. Kennan accepted the Belgrade post and was officially designated ambassador on Feb. 8, 1961. A few days later Kennan and other former ambassadors to the Soviet Union met with the President for a reevaluation of U.S. policy toward the USSR in the light of Soviet Premier Nikita Khrushchev's conciliatory statements since Kennedy's election. Although Kennan—and perhaps the other ambassadors—were professionally skeptical about summit diplomacy, the immediate outcome of the meeting was an invitation to

Khrushchev for a face-to-face meeting with the President. (The meeting, held in Vienna June 3–4, 1961, increased tensions between the two countries.)

Kennan resumed his academic career in July 1963 but returned to the public spotlight in the mid-1960s as an important critic of American policy in Vietnam. In numerous articles and speeches and in testimony before several congressional committees, Kennan argued that Vietnam was not vital to American strategic or diplomatic interests. He warned that precipitous escalation of the war in Vietnam would destroy the possibility of a negotiated settlement and force a rapprochement between the Soviet and Chinese Communists.

Kennan's analysis received its widest hearing when Sen. J. William Fulbright (D, Ark.) [q.v.] invited him to testify before a nationally televised session of the Senate Foreign Relations Committee in February 1966. Kennan charged that because of the Administration's "preoccupation with Vietnam," Europe and the Soviet Union were not receiving proper diplomatic attention. Kennan argued that the U.S. had no binding commitment to South Vietnam and questioned whether American credibility or prestige would be seriously damaged by a withdrawal. Kennan counseled a minimal military effort to maintain a U.S. presence in Vietnam until a peaceful settlement could be reached. Always a European-oriented diplomat, Kennan "emphatically" denied the applicability of the "containment doctrine" to Southeast Asia while urging its retention in Europe. After the USSR invaded Czechoslovakia in August 1968, Kennan urged stationing 100,000 additional American troops in West Germany until the Russians left Czechoslovakia.

Kennan was a strong proponent of a professional diplomatic corps that could generally function without concern for momentary domestic political pressures. He thought highly publicized summit conferences among heads of state generally unproductive and often disruptive of long-standing diplomatic relationships. In the late 1960s Kennan was also a severe critic of the student left, which he considered moralistic and anti-intellectual. Throughout the 1970s, Kennan continued to argue that the U.S. should reduce its commitments abroad.

[JCH]

For further information:
George F. Kennan *On Dealing with the Communist World* (New York, 1964).
———, *Memoirs, 1925-1950* (Boston, 1967).
———, *Democracy and the Student Left* (Boston, 1968).

KENNEDY, JOHN F(ITZGERALD)
b. May 29, 1917; Brookline, Mass.
d. Nov. 22, 1963; Dallas, Tex.
President of the United States, January 1961-November 1963.

By the end of the 19th century both of John F. Kennedy's grandfathers were important figures in the world of Boston Democratic politics. His father, who was the first member of the Irish Catholic family to attend and graduate from Harvard, turned his considerable talents to business. In the 1920s Joseph P. Kennedy amassed a fortune in banking, securities speculation and the new motion picture industry. His social and financial success enabled the Kennedy children to penetrate the bastions of New England and New York society.

John F. Kennedy attended Choate, spent a year at Princeton and then went to Harvard, where he graduated in 1940. While John was still in college his father was appointed ambassador to Great Britain, and John Kennedy spent several vacations and part of a school year in England and on the continent. Out of these experiences came a senior thesis, which recounted and condemned England's prewar policy of appeasement. Published as *Why England Slept*, it became a best-seller in 1940.

After a brief attendance at Stanford Business School in 1941, Kennedy enlisted in the Navy. He served as the commander of a torpedo boat, which was sunk in a 1943 South Pacific engagement heavily publicized in Kennedy's subsequent political career.

Upon his discharge from the service, Kennedy worked for a few months as a journalist before he plunged into a campaign for Boston's 11th district U.S. House seat. Backed by his father, who had long held political ambitions for his sons, Kennedy waged a well planned, vigorous effort, which proved a prototype of his future campaigns. Elected with little difficulty from the predominantly Irish-Italian district, Kennedy usually voted with other Northern liberals in Congress. His tenure in the lower chamber was a conventional one, although he created a small furor in 1949 when he attacked President Harry S Truman [*q.v.*] and the State Department for what he considered the unnecessary loss of mainland China to the Communists.

In 1952 Kennedy ran against the popular incumbent senator from Massachusetts, Republican Henry Cabot Lodge [*q.v.*]. Despite Dwight D. Eisenhower's [*q.v.*] easy win in the state, Kennedy demonstrated remarkable popularity by defeating Lodge by approximately 70,000 votes.

During 1954 Kennedy opposed any attempt to aid the French, then under siege at Dien Bien Phu. He told the Senate in April that a French victory was impossible and that the American people should be "told the truth" that "no amount of military assistance" could prevent Communist takeover. He warned that the U.S. could prevent Communist expansion in Asia only by supporting independence.

Kennedy took an increasing interest in foreign affairs. In 1957 he edged out Kefauver to win a seat on the coveted Foreign Relations Committee. He was particularly prominent in urging a reorientation of U.S. policies toward underdeveloped nations. Keenly aware of the force of anti-colonialism in emerging nations, he pointed out in a 1957 article in *Foreign Affairs* that American leaders underrated the strength of nationalism in Asia and Africa and that the Administration lacked a definable Middle Eastern policy.

Kennedy caused a controversy in July 1957, when he brought the Algerian question to the Senate floor and urged that the civil war there be ended with Algerian independence. He offered a resolution proposing that the U.S. negotiate the conflict. Maintaining that nationalism was a prime ingredient in most rebellions, he warned that mere "economic and social reform" would not prevent the demise of colonialism. He was severely criticized by the Eisenhower Administration and members of both parties for antagonizing France. Kennedy also urged the U.S. give priority to economic over military foreign aid and proposed economic aid to some Soviet satellites.

Kennedy was a cold warrior who saw Communist expansion as a major threat to the U.S. In 1957 he supported the Eisenhower Doctrine which gave the President authority to use U.S. troops to protect Middle Eastern nations threatened by Communist take over. In August 1957, he introduced legislation providing funds for "educational materials" to inform the public of the nature of the Communist threat. He urged Americans to support increased military expenditures for defense against the Soviet Union, fearing that a "Maginot Line" mentality had developed in the U.S. which might prove fatal and "would not only have the effect of tempting the Soviet Union to initiate an all out attack, but would also affect the position of our diplomacy, the security of our basis. . . ." Beginning in 1958 he suggested a "missile gap" existed between the U.S. and the USSR, and predicted it would grow more serious in the 1960s. He claimed that *Sputnik* and other technological advances gave the USSR the advantage in the world balance of power and warned of a Russian attack that would destroy the world. Kennedy questioned the value of trying to appease the Soviet Union and urged a strong military stand to prevent a "second Munich."

Kennedy announced his candidacy for the Democratic Presidential nomination in January 1960. After a series of spectacular wins in the West Virginia and Wisconsin primaries, proving that his Roman Catholi-

cism was not a handicap to his candidacy, he won the Democratic nomination on the first ballot in Chicago and was narrowly elected President in November.

Kennedy considered the conduct of foreign affairs his most important responsibility and his most difficult challenge. In a inaugural address devoted almost exclusively to world affairs, he pledged the nation "to pay any price, bear any burden, meet any hardship, support any friend, oppose any foe, to assure the survival and success of liberty." Kennedy thought the Cold War was at its "hour of maximum danger," and he called for sacrifice and commitment by all citizens. In what became the most memorable line in a speech that many historians then considered the best since Lincoln's, Kennedy proclaimed, "Ask not what your country can do for you, ask what you can do for your country."

With his most influential foreign policy advisers, Gen. Maxwell Taylor [*q.v.*], McGeorge Bundy [*q.v.*] and Robert McNamara—"the best and the brightest" as David Halberstam [*q.v.*] would later call them—the President sought a new and more effective strategy for countering the Communist military and political threat. These New Frontiersmen held their fiscally conservative and ideologically rigid predecessors responsible for a dangerous overreliance upon the nuclear deterrent. Kennedy foreign policy strategists sought a more "flexible" response to the Communists, one that would counter the enemy regardless of the form its offensive took: local brushfire insurgencies, ideological warfare or diplomatic maneuver.

The Peace Corps, Food for Peace, the Alliance for Progress, economic aid for underdeveloped nations and for the dissident Communist regimes of Yugoslavia and Poland were programs inaugurated or increased by the Administration as part of its more flexible strategy in the Cold War. At the same time Kennedy favored an expanded military establishment possessing sufficient conventional, nuclear and counterinsurgency forces to effectively oppose any level of Communist aggression. During the first six months of his presidency, Kennedy asked for and received $6 billion in additional military appropriations from Congress. In all, the defense budget rose from $43 to $56 billion while Kennedy was in office. *to suppress Communism in forei-*

During his first year Kennedy faced a difficult series of diplomatic and military pressures and reverses. He accepted the neutralization of Laos in early 1961 as the most advantageous solution to a troublesome local situation. In April the President suffered a personal humiliation when a CIA-planned exile invasion of Cuba was routed at the Bay of Pigs. Later in the spring the Soviets stepped up their pressure on West Berlin and demanded that the West recognize as permanent the postwar division of Germany. When Kennedy met with Nikita Khrushchev in Vienna in June, the new President appeared shaken by the Russian leader's intransigence and believed he had failed to make a strong impression on the Premier.

While Kennedy could do little to rectify the American situation in Laos or Cuba, he was determined to demonstrate U.S. firmness in Berlin. In July the President reaffirmed the American will to defend West Berlin by ordering 250,000 reservists to active duty and asking Congress for another increase in the military budget. At the same time he outlined a sweeping civil defense program designed to show the Russians America's willingness to risk nuclear war over the German city. (The USSR responded to the crisis by building the "Berlin Wall" in August and letting the issue of a German settlement die by the end of the year.)

By the fall the Communist insurgency in South Vietnam had begun to seriously weaken the American-backed regime there. Kennedy sent two of his most trusted advisers, Walt W. Rostow [q.v.] and Maxwell Taylor, to survey the situation. Upon their return Kennedy agreed to sharply increase the level of American military and economic assistance and to dispatch an additional 400 military counterinsurgency specialists there. Most historians have concluded that the stalemate in Laos, the defeat at the Bay of Pigs and the Soviet pressure on Berlin contributed to Kennedy's determination to avoid a defeat in Vietnam. Although he never authorized a full-scale commitment of U.S. ground troops to Vietnam, the number of American military "advisers" there increased from 700 to over 15,000 during his term in office.

Kennedy confronted his most serious Cold War crisis in October 1962 when American intelligence discovered that the Soviets had begun to install offensive missiles in Cuba. Working closely with his brother Robert, Kennedy rejected the views of his advisers who favored an immediate air strike, but he also opposed an extended period of negotiations or a public tradeoff of Soviet missiles in Cuba for American rockets in Italy or Turkey. Instead, Kennedy and a special committee of the National Security Council, which met each day to "manage" the crisis, decided to impose a "quarantine" of the island, which went into effect on Oct. 24. On Oct. 28 the Soviets turned back from the potential naval confrontation and agreed to remove their Cuban missiles. We were "eyeball to eyeball," said Dean Rusk, "They blinked first." Kennedy thought the successful resolution of the missile crisis a triumph for the mode of cool, rational decision making characteristic of the New Frontier. Nevertheless, he had been sobered by the imminence of nuclear war. "I want no crowing and not a word of gloating," Kennedy told his staff.

When Khrushchev later suggested that negotiations be reopened toward a long-deferred nuclear test ban treaty, Kennedy quickly assented. Disagreement over on-site inspection of underground nuclear tests stalled the talks, but in a speech delivered at American University on June 10, 1963 Kennedy announced that he was sending Averell Harriman [q.v.] to Moscow to negotiate a more limited test ban agreement excluding the controversial underground tests.

The American University speech was one of Kennedy's most notable addresses. Avoiding the Cold War rhetoric he often had used in the past, Kennedy expressed his admiration for the Russian people and affirmed the common interest of both nations in avoiding nuclear holocaust. In July a limited nuclear test ban agreement was initialed in Moscow and, with surprisingly little domestic opposition, ratified by the Senate in September. Although the test ban treaty did nothing to stop the arms race, it ended the poisonous radioactive pollution of the atmosphere. It was Kennedy's most enduring achievement in foreign affairs.

While riding in Dallas motorcade early on the afternoon of Nov. 22, Kennedy was shot and killed with a high-powered rifle fired by Lee Harvey Oswald. A number of public and private investigations over the next decade found no conclusive proof that the President's assassin, a man of erratic political views, did not act alone.

In the aftermath of the assassination, Kennedy's popular reputation reached heights unsurpassed in the last century, except by Lincoln and Franklin Roosevelt. "He left a myth," wrote Richard Neustadt in 1964, "[of] the vibrant, youthful leader cut down senselessly before his time." Award-winning biographies by presidential aides Arthur Schlesinger and Theodore Sorensen ably defended Kennedy as a pragmatic liberal who used a powerful intellect and growing political sensibility to break a new and progressive path in American politics.

Although the public's warm remembrance of Kennedy hardly wavered over the next decade, scholarly estimates of his policies fell in the late 1960s. Escalation of the Vietnam war cast Kennedy's early military commitment to Indochina and his Administration's aggressive Cold War posture into an unfavorable light. In the early 1970s President Nixon's abuses of executive authority prompted many historians to reconsider Kennedy's own favorable attitude toward the expansion and use of presidential power. Finally, a series of revelations concerning illegal CIA and FBI activity during the early 1960s further diminished the luster of Kennedy's years in office.

[NNL]

For further information:
James T. Crown, *The Kennedy Literature: a Bibliographical Essay on John F. Kennedy* (New York, 1968).
Henry Fairlie, *The Kennedy Promise* (New York, 1973).
Roger Hilsman, *To Move a Nation: the Politics of Foreign Policy in the Administration of John F. Kennedy* (Garden City, 1967).
Lewis J. Paper, *The Promise and the Performance* (New York, 1975).
Arthur M. Schlesinger, Jr., *A Thousand Days* (New York, 1965).
Theodore C. Sorensen, *Kennedy* (New York, 1965).
Richard J. Walton, *Cold War and Counterrevolution* (New York, 1972).
Theodore White, *The Making of the President 1960* (New York, 1961).

KENNEDY, ROBERT F(RANCIS)
b. Nov. 20, 1925; Brookline, Mass.
d. June 6, 1968; Los Angeles, Calif.
Attorney General, January 1961-September 1964; Democratic Senator, N.Y., 1965-68.

Robert Kennedy was the seventh of nine children in a wealthy and politically ambitious Irish Catholic Massachusetts family. After naval service in World War II, he graduated from Harvard in 1948 and the University of Virginia Law School three years later. He served briefly as a Justice Department lawyer before resigning to manage his brother John F. Kennedy's successful 1952 Senate race.

In the early and mid-1950s, Kennedy served as assistant counsel and then chief Democratic counsel for the Senate Permanent Subcommittee on Investigations. In 1957 he was named chief counsel for Sen. John L. McClellan's (D, Ark.) Senate Rackets Committee, where he won national prominence for his investigations of Teamsters Union leaders James Hoffa and David Beck. He resigned in 1959 to manage his brother's presidential campaign.

Kennedy was appointed Attorney General

by the President-elect in December 1960. As the brother of the President, Robert Kennedy had influence and power not available to other high Administration officials. He had the full confidence of President Kennedy and the strong rapport, friendship and loyalty between the two made the Attorney General the President's alter ego and his closest adviser and aide. After the unsuccessful Bay of Pigs invasion of April 1961, President Kennedy included his brother in the decision-making process on all crucial foreign and domestic policy questions. Among other tasks, the Attorney General carried out diplomatic missions to Europe and the Far East, encouraged the development of a counterinsurgency force in the military, kept an eye on overseas intelligence operations, advised on civil rights policy and dealt with many state party chairmen and political bosses around the country.

The Cuban missile crisis of October 1962 supplied perhaps the best example of Robert Kennedy's influential advisory role. He was a member of Excom, the group that met to consider the U.S. response to the discovery of Soviet offensive missiles in Cuba. In the early deliberations the Attorney General strongly opposed proposals for a general air strike and invasion of Cuba and supported the idea of a "quarantine." Acting as unofficial chairman of the committee in the President's absence, Kennedy was a major force in securing a consensus within the group on the decision to blockade Cuba. On Oct. 26 a letter from Soviet Premier Nikita Khrushchev suggested a bargain in which Soviet missiles would be withdrawn from Cuba in return for an American pledge not to invade the island. It was followed the next day, however, by a second letter demanding the withdrawal of American missiles in Turkey in exchange for removal of the Cuban missiles. During a debate in ExCom over the American response to the second Khrushchev proposal, Robert Kennedy devised the idea of ignoring the second letter and responding favorably to the first. The Attorney General helped draft the President's reply and then personally delivered a copy of it, along with a strong warning, to the Soviet Ambassador to the U.S. The next day Khrushchev agreed to the American proposal for removal of the Cuban missiles in exchange for an end to the blockade and a promise that the U.S. would not attack Cuba.

While Kennedy initially supported the U.S. committment to Vietnam, he shared his brother's doubts about a viable, long-term solution. Nonetheless, Kennedy did not become a major dissenter until 1966, when he began to publicly criticize Johnson's escalation of the war. In February 1966 he recommended that the National Liberation Front (NLF) be "admitted to a share of power and responsibility in a future coalition South Vietnamese government." In March of the next year he proposed suspending U.S. bombing of North Vietnam as part of a three-point plan to help end the war, but his proposals were immediately rejected by the Administration. In November 1967 he made his strongest criticism of the war, asserting that the U.S. "moral position" in Vietnam had been undermined by the Johnson Administration. "We're killing South Vietnamese," he said, "we're killing women, we're killing innocent people because we don't want to have the war fought on American soil."

In March 1968 Kennedy announced his candidacy for the Democratic presidential nomination. His campaign ended in June when he was assassinated.

[CAB, FHM]

Robert Kennedy (New York, 1968).
Robert Kennedy, *Thirteen Days: A Memoir of The Cuban Missile Crisis* (New York, 1969).
Arthur Schlesinger, *Robert Kennedy and His Times* (New York, 1979).
William V. Shannon, *The Heir Apparent* (New York, 1967).
Theodore H. White, *The Making of the President 1968* (New York, 1968).

KISSINGER, HENRY A(LFRED)
b. May 29, 1923; Furth, Germany.
Special Assistant to the President for National Security Affairs, December

1968-November 1975; Secretary of
State, September 1973-January 1977.

Heinz Alfred Kissinger was born into
an Orthodox Jewish family. The family
fled Nazi Germany in 1938, going first to
England and then to New York City,
where Kissinger studied accounting at
City College and worked in a shaving
brush factory. He was drafted in 1943 and
worked in Army intelligence. After serving as a district administrator with the
military government of occupied Germany from 1945 to 1946, Kissinger enrolled
at Harvard. He received a B.A. summa
cum laude in 1950 and a Ph.D. in 1954.
His dissertation, later published as a
book, concerned European diplomacy
during the post-Napoleonic period. The
work sought to show how the archconser-
vative Prince Metternich brought order,
stability and an era of peace to Europe
through maintenance of a balance of power in which each country had a vested interest. Kissinger admired Metternich's
skillful use of personal and secret negotiations unhampered by the demands of
bureaucracy and public opinion and of
his occasional threat of force to preserve
order. Kissinger's study reflected his own
pessimism and fear of instability and
served as the basis for his approach to international power politics.

In 1954 Kissinger became study director of a Council on Foreign Relations
project seeking to explore alternatives to
the massive retaliation policy of the Eisenhower Administration. The project report, published in 1957, accepted Eisenhower's view that the Soviet Union was
an expansionist power seeking to undermine the stability of the West, but proposed a strategy based on the limited use
of nuclear weapons as an alternative to
massive retaliation.

In 1956 Nelson A. Rockefeller appointed
Kissinger a director of a Rockefeller Brothers
Fund special project formed to study the
nation's major domestic and foreign problems.
The project's final foreign affairs report,
published as *The Necessity for Choice: Pros-*

pects for American Foreign Policy (1961),
warned against optimism over prospects for a
Soviet-American detente and stressed the
need for a strategy centered on tactical
nuclear weapons. It called for an expanded nationwide civil defense system and
for a major increase in defense spending
to meet the expected Soviet challenge.

Kissinger returned to Harvard as a lecturer in the government department in
1957 and eventually became a professor
in 1962. From 1959 to 1969 he was director of Harvard's Defense Studies Program. Kissinger also served as a consultant to the Arms Control and Disarmament Agency from 1961 to 1967 and to the
State Department from 1965 to 1969. Between 1961 and 1962 he was an adviser to
the National Security Council. During the
late 1960s he visited South Vietnam as a
State Department consultant. On the basis of personal interviews with many non-
government Vietnamese, Kissinger concluded that an American victory was impossible, but that it was also unacceptable
to withdraw from Vietnam in a manner
that would cause the U.S. to lose its "hon-
or" and credibility in the eyes of its allies.

Kissinger wrote speeches for Rockefeller's bid for the 1968 Republican presidential nomination. He also produced a
peace plan that incorporated elements of
the plan he would pursue as Nixon's foreign policy adviser, including a proposal
for the gradual withdrawal of U.S. troops
and their replacement by South Vietnamese. In addition, the plan recommended the withdrawal of troops on both
sides, the imposition of an international
peace-keeping force, internationally supervised free elections and negotiations
for the reunification of Vietnam.

Rockefeller's failure to win the nomination upset Kissinger, who considered
Richard Nixon a demagogue without purpose or a sense of history and a man who
did not "have the right to rule." Nixon,
however, had been impressed by Kissinger's work and, through his aides, in-
duced the professor to act as a foreign policy consultant for the Republican campaign. In late November 1968 Kissinger

was offered the post of head of the National Security Council (NSC) and the position of special assistant for national security affairs.

Politically the offer was a clever move aimed at hurting Nixon's old rival Rockefeller: Rockefeller was not offered a post in the new Administration and at the same time one of his closest advisers was taken from him. Moreover, the appointment added an intellectual to the White House staff and won Nixon some rare praise from liberal and academic critics.

Kissinger quickly altered his opinion of Nixon. He discovered he and Nixon agreed on their approach to foreign policy and shared a contempt for the bureaucracy and a pessimism about the limits of American power. They both believed that there was need for more flexibility, more thorough planning and a better defined philosophy in the conduct of foreign affairs. Nixon realized that the American public was tired of the Cold War rivalry with the USSR and particularly of the Vietnam war. Both men wanted to maintain an active international role for the U.S. and subtly resist what they viewed as the new isolationist tendencies of Congress and the public.

The new President claimed expertise in foreign affairs and wanted to make policy himself, not delegate the task to the traditional departments, State and Defense, as it had been under Lyndon Johnson. Both men agreed that Johnson had been hampered in foreign affairs because he had delegated authority and only heard what his advisers thought he wanted to hear. The new President wanted Kissinger to coordinate the thinking and recommendations of the various departments and then present him with a reasonable array of alternatives for a given foreign policy issue. Nixon aimed to rationalize and centralize the foreign policy bureaucracy and to make Kissinger the channel through which recommendations from below were passed, criticized and refined. From the beginning Kissinger's position was clearly superior to those of the Secretaries of Defense and State. Subsequently his skill at political infighting, his capacity for hard work and the President's growing dependence on him amplified that superiority. He quickly recruited an NSC staff, appropriating some of the most highly regarded Pentagon and State Department personnel.

The contrast between Kissinger's mode of operation and that followed during Johnson's period was evident in one of his first tasks, preparation of an options memorandum on the progress of the Vietnam war. Identical questions were directed to second-echelon staffers of various departments. Thus many officials evaluated areas outside their field of expertise. In contrast, Johnson's information about military matters always came from top people in the Pentagon. One result of the Kissinger report, called the National Security Study Memoranda (NSSM), was a wider range of opinions and therefore greater accuracy and honesty. But a further result—and one Kissinger did not foresee—was the virtual ineffectiveness of cabinet departments in determining policy. The NSC, in fact, supervised studies on a wide range of policy issues, working through an Interdepartmental Group (IG) composed of assistant secretaries or their deputies from State, Defense, Commerce, Treasury and other relevant departments. The IG never made recommendations. It produced "area" options for NSC consideration. Kissinger himself chaired the committees that reviewed the defense budget, intelligence policy, clandestine intelligence operations, as well as the Washington Special Action Group (WSAG), the top-level crisis group, and the Verification Panel, which oversaw monitoring of the nuclear arms agreements with the Soviet Union. Thus, whatever went to the President had to pass through Kissinger. Unwittingly the Nixon White House became as isolated as Johnson's.

The Soviet Union was the centerpiece of Kissinger's foreign policy. In his view success in any other area of foreign policy was in some way dependent on the Administration's relations with the Soviets.

While he no longer thought of the Communist world as an aggressive monolith, he still believed that the USSR was a capricious power not yet reconciled to the international status quo. It was Kissinger's aim to get the Soviet Union to act as a responsible nation-state convinced that working with the U.S. to maintain an international balance of power was in its best interest. To accomplish this he developed the concept of "linkage." If the Soviets wanted American trade and technology, Kissinger argued, then they had to make concessions. Most importantly, the Soviets would have to put pressure on the North Vietnamese to negotiate an end to the Indochina conflict.

Nuclear weapons constituted another crucial issue dividing the two powers. Aside from the realization that nuclear war between the superpowers was unthinkable, Kissinger knew that neither the U.S. nor the Soviet Union could tolerate the costs of an accelerated arms race. He also believed that it was in the mutual interest to defuse tensions in central Europe and in other trouble spots. In addition the U.S. should share some of its heavy defense burden with its allies. This was essential not only in economic terms but also because Kissinger felt that American foreign policy since World War II had been too paternalistic. Without retreating into isolationism, the U.S. no longer needed to confront international crises single handedly, although in practice Kissinger himself acted unilaterally. Nixon was in agreement on the necessity for detente with the USSR and restraint on unilateral U.S. action in local conflicts.

Nixon and Kissinger, because of their emphasis on linkage, were less disposed to rush into the Strategic Arms Limitation Talks (SALT) than were many of their advisers, such as Secretary of State William Rogers [q.v.]. Nixon responded to early Soviet calls for SALT by saying that talks would be feasible "in a way and at a time that will promote, if possible, progress on outstanding political problems at the same time—for example, on the problem of the Middle East and other outstanding problems in which the U.S. and the USSR, acting together, can save the cause of peace." Meanwhile he supported the development of the Safeguard anti-ballistic missile and the MIRV (multiple independently targeted reentry vehicle) to strengthen America's bargaining position when talks began. The Russians took this expression of linkage to be a form of blackmail or extortion. Government bureaucrats and members of Congress, despite Kissinger's explanation of the concept, feared that it would endanger SALT's future and viewed support of weapons development as lack of interest in arms control.

Kissinger ignored early calls for wide-ranging discussions with the Soviets to give his staff time to prepare a study on the relative military strength of the two superpowers. One part of the study provided the basis for the President's approval of the nuclear nonproliferation treaty negotiated by the Johnson Administration. It was sent to the Senate in February 1969. The other part of the study put into question Nixon's campaign pledge to ensure "clear-cut military superiority" over the Soviet Union. Superiority was impossible in the decade ahead, especially in view of the Soviets' enormous defense budgets. Nixon accepted the findings and publicly substituted Kissinger's "sufficiency" for "superiority," asserting that the Administration would guarantee "sufficient military power to defend our interests and to maintain . . . commitments." The Helsinki SALT discussions did not begin until November 1969. Although the Soviets had not yet offered to satisfy U.S. demands in the Middle East and Vietnam, Kissinger hoped that progress in the negotiations would encourage greater Soviet accommodation.

Vietnam was the most pressing foreign—and domestic—problem inherited from the Johnson Administration. It also proved harder to resolve than Kissinger expected, because he underestimated the tenacity of Hanoi and the National Liberation Front (NLF). At the 1969 Paris peace talks, the North Vietnamese rejected Kissinger's "two track" formula, which projected a military settlement between Washington and Hanoi and a political settlement between Saigon and the NLF. Kissinger, as his former aide Roger Morris pointed out, was unable to understand the North Vietnamese position that the conflict was a civil war. It was for this reason that he insisted—until May 1972—on mutual withdrawal of troops, a proposition that Hanoi considered unreasonable and unacceptable.

Both Kissinger and Nixon recognized that a military victory was impossible in Vietnam. But they refused to consider a U.S. withdrawal, which they thought would be an ignominious act unworthy of a great power and a signal to enemies and allies that the U.S. could not be trusted to keep its commitments. Instead, in June 1969 they proposed a policy of Vietnamization, gradually giving the South Vietnamese Army the responsibility for conducting the war. But Kissinger had little faith in Saigon's military capacity and he ultimately placed his hopes in a combination of personal diplomacy and periodic "savage, punishing" military escalations. He initiated his personal diplomacy in secret Paris meetings in August 1969 and between February and April of the following year he met with Le Duc Tho, a member of Hanoi's politburo. Little was accomplished and even less was achieved in the official talks, which only served as a cover for the secret conferences. Meanwhile, the Administration pressured the North Vietnamese militarily. In March 1969 secret B-52 raids began over Cambodia, in spite of Washington's official recognition of that nation's neutrality, in an effort to keep enemy troops from moving across the border.

Kissinger's early efforts at diplomacy engendered criticism from several quarters and despite his efforts to end U.S. involvement in Vietnam, the anti-war movement remained active. As an academic in whom some intellectuals had put their hopes for a speedy settlement, Kissinger was especially subject to severe criticism from the left. His penchant for secrecy and tendency to show sympathy for the views of whatever groups or individuals to whom he was speaking earned him a reputation for duplicity. Members of Congress resented Kissinger's refusal to appear before their committees under the cloak of "executive privilege." (As a personal adviser to Nixon, he was not required to testify.) Kissinger's standing fell even further when he supported Nixon's decision to invade Cambodia in May 1970. With one exception his principal aides, who had tolerated his demanding regimen and abusive treatment because of their faith in him and in spite of their aversion to Nixon, quit. Academic colleagues advised Kissinger to resign; others asked him to "stop that madman."

That liberal critics came to view Kissinger as equally villainous as Nixon reflected a growing public awareness that Kissinger was, as some said, "the second most powerful man" in the country and that he, not Rogers, shaped U.S. foreign policy. Kissinger was deemed so important that the Harrisburg Six, a group of pacifists, were indicted in January 1971 for allegedly conspiring to kidnap him and put him on trial for war crimes. Kissinger sought to maintain contact with his critics and even spoke with members of the Harrisburg group, one of whom said, "The scary part of it is he really is a nice man."

Yet Kissinger was popular with the general public. With the exception of Nixon, he was the only member of the Administration to make the 10 "most-admired" persons list, which was compiled annually on the basis of a national poll. The admiration was due in part to the largely uncritical attitude of the national media, which was impressed by his intellectual credentials, charmed by his combination of arrogance and self-deprecating wit and aware of the marketability of his romantic secret shuttle diplomacy. Kissinger, unlike Nixon and his media-hating staff, cultivated the press. A divorced bachelor, Kissinger was photographed in the company of elegant women and was depicted as a cocktail party "swinger" who still found the time to unveil frequent diplomatic marvels. In November 1972 he ascribed his popularity to the "fact that I have acted alone. . . . The Americans love the cowboy . . . who comes into town all alone on his horse. . . ." It was not until after Watergate that the nonradical press would evaluate him somewhat more critically.

One of the least disputed triumphs of the Nixon-Kissinger era was the establishment of ties with the People's Republic of China. It was a case in which the initiative was clearly Nixon's. Both Kissinger and the President had long held the Cold War view of an irresponsible, fanatical China bent on world conquest. Kissinger, whose international bias was clearly European, admittedly knew almost nothing about China and was slower to change his views than Nixon. Yet he appreciated that an approach to China could exploit strained Sino-Soviet relations and be used as leverage in dealings with the Soviet Union, which was obsessed with a fear of the Chinese. Besides, it was consistent with Kissinger's philosophy to give powerful nations a stake in maintaining the international balance of power. Throughout 1969 Nixon put out diplomatic "feelers" to the Chinese via the French, Rumanians and Pakistanis. Kissinger applauded the President's diplomatic challenges to the Soviets—and to the cautious State Department as well—such as his August 1969 visit to Rumania, which was on bad terms with the Soviets and close to the Chinese. More substantive moves (e.g., easing restrictions on American travel to China and ending U.S. naval patrols in the Taiwan Strait) came at the same time border clashes broke out between the Russians and the Chinese. The first direct contacts with the Chinese were made in December 1969 in Warsaw, over the objections of both Soviet specialists in the State Department and hard-liners in the Chinese government. In October 1970 the White House publicly suggested that it was ready to adopt a two-China formula in the United Nations. After Chairman Mao Tse-tung and Premier Chou En-lai were convinced that the South Viet-

namese invasion of Laos in February 1971 was not the prelude to a U.S. invasion of China, they invited an American envoy to Peking, suggesting either Rogers or Kissinger. Nixon chose Kissinger.

With the exception of a group of Ping-Pong players, Kissinger was the first American to officially enter China since 1949. During a July 1971 Asian tour, he flew secretly to Peking via Pakistan. The meetings with Chou were marked by cordiality and apparently genuine personal rapport. The initial climate of goodwill that Kissinger fostered was considered to be his most important contribution to the successful approach to China. At the talks he also conceded that the Americans would now consider Taiwan a part of China, allowing its political future to be settled between the two Chinese governments. Kissinger also laid plans for Nixon's February 1972 visit.

Nixon's surprising announcement of the Peking visit won wide national support, with the exception of some extreme conservatives, and helped his popularity ratings. As Kissinger expected and even hoped, the Soviets were upset. But American allies, especially the Japanese and the Nationalist Chinese, resented not being consulted on the move. Nixon and Kissinger, however, enjoyed the theatricality of the trip and the impression it gave of diplomatic initiative and daring. The Administration proceeded to cut back its troop strength in Taiwan and supported the quest of the People's Republic for seats in the U.N. General Assembly and on the Security Council, although it publicly claimed it would oppose any effort to oust Taiwan from the international organization.

The Chinese breakthrough was combined with the adoption of a firmer policy towards the Soviet Union. Kissinger and the President had been battling with Rogers and the State Department over linkage and Nixon's hard-line approach to the Russians. In the autumn of 1970 Kissinger, over State's objections, orchestrated the threatening U.S.-Israeli military moves that appeared to stop Moscow's client Syria from toppling the pro-Western regime of Jordan's King Hussein. During the same period Kissinger, employing "tough" language, warned the Soviets not to construct a nuclear submarine base in Cuba, since it was a violation of the post-1962 missile crisis understanding between the U.S. and the USSR. According to CIA reports, the Soviets stopped construction of the base. The Soviets, besieged by problems with China and Warsaw Pact nations, finally agreed in May 1971 to link limitation of offensive and defensive weapons in any SALT accord. Two months after Kissinger's visit to Peking, the Americans and Russians began preparations for a May 1972 Moscow summit. In April 1972 Kissinger made a secret trip to Moscow to lay plans for the May summit and to get the Soviets to pressure the North Vietnamese to become more flexible in the Paris peace talks. The summit, so important to Kissinger's grand designs, produced a large number of cultural, scientific, environmental and trade agreements and eventually the first SALT treaty, which set a limit on certain defensive weapons. SALT gave a crucial boost to Nixon's reelection chances. Larger trade arrangements, including the grain sale to the Soviets, were negotiated by Kissinger in September. In addition, a few weeks after the summit Soviet President Nikolai Podgorny flew to Hanoi to recommend more flexible negotiations with the U.S., since Moscow felt that Nixon was actually ending American involvement and the fall of Saigon was inevitable anyway.

Kissinger's strategy did not always produce the desired results. His famous "tilt" toward Pakistan in the December 1971 India-Pakistan war, conditioned by his and Nixon's emotional dislike of Indira Gandhi and their gratitude to Pakistan for its help in making contact with Peking, was controversial. The U.S. was put in the position of supporting a military dictatorship against the world's largest democracy and opposing Bangladesh's struggle for independence. India won; Pakistan lost Bangladesh, formerly East Pakistan; and the Soviets, who supported the Indians, claimed a victory over the Americans and Chinese (who also supported Pakistan). Biographers Marvin and Bernard Kalb reported that the policy failure led Kissinger to briefly consider resignation. Records of secret meetings about the war were leaked to Jack Anderson who published parts of them in his column, proving a great embarrassment to Kissinger. He reportedly suspected that White House aides John Ehrlichman and H.R. Haldeman, who were jealous of his influence with the President, were responsible for the leaks.

During 1972 Kissinger focused his attention on ending the Vietnam war, which he regarded as a nuisance that kept him from more important business and which jeopardized Nixon's chances for reelection. In the months preceding the 1972 presidential election, he circled the globe in an effort to end the U.S. involvement in Vietnam. Nixon's critics, including his Democratic opponent for the presidency, Sen. George McGovern (D, S.D.) [q.v.], suggested that the President was "manipulating" public opinion and raising expectations by keeping Kissinger in the spotlight. Kissinger even appeared in a Republican campaign film in which he praised Nixon for making possible through SALT a "generation of peace." He also attended GOP contributors' dinners in a "nonpartisan" capacity. He met frequently—in highly publicized secret meetings—with Le Duc Tho, and before the election stated "peace is at hand," which many interpreted as an obvious ploy to improve the President's reelection chances. In October, Kissinger completed a peace settlement with the North Vietnamese. However, he was unable to get the North Vietnamese to accept changes that the South Vietnamese insisted on before agreeing to the proposal. In December, Nixon, with Kissinger's approval, resumed B-52 raids on the North to pressure Hanoi into resuming negotiations.

A peace agreement was signed in January 1973. It followed the one Kissinger had negotiated in October. The terms included: a cease-fire; the complete withdrawal of U.S. troops and the dismantling of U.S. bases within 60 days; and a prisoner-of-war (POW) exchange. The cease-fire allowed North Vietnamese troops to remain "in place," i.e., they were left in control of those areas in the south which they actually occupied. Foreign troops were to leave Laos and Cambodia and troop and supply movements through these countries were banned, but no deadline was set. The DMZ would be the provisional dividing line between north and south until reunification could be achieved peacefully. An international commission would deal with the release of POWs, elections, etc. and President Thieu would remain in office pending elections. After the Americans left Indochina, however, an increasingly contentious Congress obstructed Kissinger's plans for further involvement there. In March and April 1973 Kissinger pleaded unsuccessfully for the continued bombing of Cambodia in order to force Hanoi to abide by the Paris accords and bring about a cease-fire. His support of an aid program for Hanoi struck congressional conservatives as an admission that the United States owed reparations to the enemy. In June, Kissinger concluded a round of talks with Le Duc Tho about observance of the terms of the January agreement. The resulting communique did not provide for an end to the Cambodian and Laotian conflicts. The poor results of the talks, some analysts suggested, only reflected the condition of an Administration weakened by the Watergate scandal.

One of Kissinger's greatest triumphs was his handling of the delicate situation in the Middle East, an area that occupied much of his time during Nixon's final months in the White House and during the Ford Administration. In Nixon's first Administration, the area had been left largely to the State Department, because, as analysts noted, State needed something to do and it was thought that Kissinger's Jewish ancestry might prejudice the Arabs against him. However, during the mid-1970s Kissinger handled Middle Eastern diplomacy on a personal level. His ethnic background eventually became an asset because it proved difficult to accuse him of anti-Semitism when he showed sympathy for Arab interests.

In October 1973 Egyptian President Anwar Sadat precipitated the Yom Kippur war with Israel to force the return of Egyptian land lost to the Israelis six years before. For years the U.S. had been staunchly pro-Israel. Kissinger, though not possessed of strong emotional ties to that nation, saw Israel as a U.S. ally and the Arab states, with the exception of the conservative monarchies, as Soviet clients. He blamed the Soviets for supplying offensive arms to the Arabs and encouraging the attack on Israel. Their actions, he felt, were inconsistent with detente. Yet because of Defense Department hesitation, the U.S. only slowly matched the Soviet effort in supplying military aid to its ally. Secretary of Defense James Schlesinger [q.v.], a frequent critic of Kissinger's policies, hesitated to give Israel massive support because such aid might precipitate an oil embargo threatened by the Arabs. However Nixon finally overrode Schlesinger. In view of his Watergate problems, the President realized that failure to aid Israel would result in an overwhelmingly negative public and congressional reaction and what he saw as weakness in the face of a Soviet challenge. In response to the U.S. aid to Israel, the Arab nations instituted a total ban on oil exports to supporters of Israel.

American aid made possible a spectacular Israeli counteroffensive and the Soviet Union consequently called for a cease-fire. Kissinger went to Moscow with authorization from Nixon to sign anything in his name. The Secretary of State and Brezhnev worked out a cease-fire providing for direct Egyptian-Israeli talks. The cease-fire was precarious, however, and a few days after meeting with Brezhnev, Kissinger called for a worldwide nuclear alert of U.S. forces in response to what he claimed were Soviet military moves to intervene in the conflict on the side of the Arabs. Kissinger's action, some skeptics believed, was a dangerously reckless tactic to divert domestic attention from the President's role in Watergate. Military and political analysts at least thought that the Russians' behavior, though belligerent, did not warrant preparations for nuclear war.

Soviet unwillingness to pursue an active role in achieving a Middle East settlement worked in Kissinger's favor. He was able to personally direct the negotiations. His shuttle diplomacy, rather than multilateral discussions in Geneva, provided the basis for a series of agreements leading up to the Egyptian-Israeli peace treaty of 1979. U.S. influence in the Middle East and Kissinger's prestige benefitted from the new situation.

The embargo dictated a more evenhanded U.S. policy in the Middle East. It was Kissinger's aim, then, to keep Israel from winning complete victory. Israeli victory would make the oil embargo permanent and peace impossible, since the Arab states, especially Egypt, would never resign themselves to the loss of their territory. Without the return of Arab lands, there could be no peace, and without peace, it was likely that the oil producers would refuse to sell to the United States.

Kissinger's diplomatic offensive in the Middle East began in November 1973 and lasted through 1976. He developed an apparently warm and intimate relationship with Sadat, who had shown signs of desiring better relations with the U.S. since 1972, when he expelled Soviet advisers from Egypt. Kissinger arranged two Sinai disengagements, in January 1974 and September 1975, which gave Egypt back its land and some measure of pride and offered Israel a measure of security it had been unable to attain in four wars. He also produced a disengagement on the Golan Heights between Israel and Syria in May 1974, although relations between the two nations remained hostile. The Mideast oil embargo was ended and relations with Saudi Arabia were restored. Such triumphs were as much responsible for Kissinger's international "Super K" reputation as the opening of relations with China. However in some places his achievements were viewed more critical-

ly. Jewish-American opinion, already angered that detente ignored the plight of Soviet Jews, attacked Kissinger's sympathy for the Arab position. Israeli public opinion, too, reflected the view that Kissinger had forced the Israeli government into disadvantageous settlements as the price of continued U.S. support. Moreover, some analysts noted that Kissinger had been unable to moderate sufficiently the position of the more militant Arab states, particularly Syria. Most importantly, his diplomacy ignored the question of the stateless Palestinians, who were, in fact, the key to any permanent Middle East peace.

The Middle East oil embargo gave rise to further friction in the relations between the U.S. and its traditional allies, Western Europe and Japan. Ironically it was Kissinger's reputedly less-idealistic "European" style of diplomacy that contributed to the deterioration of the alliance with Europe, which had already been adversely affected by disagreements over trade, monetary and military policies. Kissinger had once criticized American policymakers for their failure to consult with the allies on world issues and to consider those countries in terms of their national interests. Yet in his diplomatic initiatives with the Soviets and the Chinese, Kissinger usually failed to advise the governments of Western Europe and Japan beforehand. The behavior was partly due to Kissinger's stress on secrecy, but it also arose out of the assumption that the U.S. was a great power with global interests. Europe, in contrast, was considered a regional power. Conscious of the neglect, Kissinger in April 1973 announced the "Year of Europe," proposing a new Atlantic Charter that would include the Japanese and require a cooperative comprehensive policy on energy, military, monetary and commercial issues. The proposal was spurned more than once. British Prime Minister Edward Heath and French President Georges Pompidou made it clear in May that they wanted issues considered separately. European Economic Community (EEC) spokespersons warned the U.S. that Europe would act as a "distinct unity" in world affairs.

The Arab oil embargo prompted Kissinger to propose in December 1973 a cooperative effort on the part of the industrialized nations to develop long-term energy planning. The proposal conflicted with a French call for an Arab-EEC summit. Kissinger continued arguing in favor of oil consuming nations' solidarity in the face of high prices imposed by the Organization of Petroleum Exporting Countries (OPEC). He noted, however, that the burden of high prices weighed most heavily on underdeveloped nations. Kissinger recommended vigilance to ensure that "petrodollars" invested in the industrial economies did not threaten the sovereignty and security of the individual nations. Another proposal suggested that oil-consuming nations establish a $25 billion lending facility to provide funds for nations unable to meet balance of payments obligations.

European unwillingness to cooperate with the U.S. exasperated Kissinger, who in March 1974 declared that the Europeans constituted the nation's biggest foreign policy problem. The statement irritated the Europeans, who believed that it was in their self-interest to cultivate closer ties with the Arab world. Kissinger, in their view, was taking an excessively hard line against the Arabs. Particularly unwise, they thought, were statements by Kissinger and other members of both the Nixon and Ford Administrations, suggesting that the Americans might be forced to occupy Arab oil fields in case the Arabs became unreasonable in their policy on petroleum exports. In addition, the Europeans shared with the Arabs concern over the Americans' inability or unwillingness to fortify the dollar. Kissinger was never able to mend relations strained during the oil crisis and Europe remained a source of tension throughout his tenure.

Despite his triumphs and reputation, Kissinger, like most members of the Nixon Administration was touched by Watergate and related issues. In May 1973 it was revealed that he had approved wire-taps of officials and newsmen in efforts to stem policy leaks. Kissinger admitted that he had authorized the taps, but he claimed that the idea had been suggested and put into operation by FBI Director J. Edgar Hoover and Attorney General John Mitchell. They assured him, he alleged, that the taps were legal. Besides, Kissinger argued, it was essential to stop the leaks to the press, which were damaging national security. Also harmful to Kissinger's image was information made available in 1973 and 1974 about his role in the secret bombing of Cambodia and efforts by the CIA and International Telephone and Telegraph to overthrow the democratically elected Marxist government of Salvador Allende in Chile. It appeared that Kissinger was as likely to resort to covert means to achieve his goals as were the political advisers who surrounded Nixon.

Watergate had a significant effect on Kissinger's conduct of foreign affairs. When he went to Moscow in late 1973, he found the Soviets uninterested in reaching any substantive agreements on arms control issues. They were evidently unwilling to deal with a lame-duck administration that might not be able to carry out its part of any bargain. Kissinger warned the American public that obsession with Watergate could damage the nation's international role and destroy the unique opportunity then available to ensure world peace. He privately urged the President to cut off all ties with Haldeman and Ehrlichman and to provide all the White House tapes requested by the Senate Watergate Committee and the special Watergate prosecutor. Kissinger reportedly considered resigning during the crisis, but soon decided that the best solution to a political nuisance—his view of Watergate—that was obstructing foreign policy was the resignation of the President.

Nixon made Kissinger Secretary of State in May 1973. Aside from a supposed desire to humiliate Rogers, Kissinger wanted the post to guarantee that he alone would control the direction of foreign affairs at a time when Nixon was, in his opinion, so desperate that he was liable to act irrationally. Moreover Kissinger hoped to strengthen his strategic position within the Administration against his newest White House rivals, White House Chief of Staff Alexander Haig and Secretary of the Treasury John Connally [*q.v.*]. The President also hoped that naming Kissinger Secretary of State would help lift his faltering position. Kissinger was Nixon's most prestigious aide, and his diplomatic triumphs had given luster to the Administration. The new appointment was designed to give the White House a measure of legitimacy. Without Kissinger, observers hypothesized, Nixon had no chance of survival.

In reaction to Watergate, the new Secretary of State promised that secrecy would no longer be as necessary in his work as it had been in the past. Secret diplomacy, he explained, had been essential in order to implement "some revolutionary changes," but the foundations had now been laid. The conduct of foreign policy in the future, he predicted, would be less secretive and less dramatic. Kissinger's reputation received another boost in October 1973 when he won the Nobel peace prize for his Vietnam negotiations, although the choice was not universally applauded.

Nixon, trying desperately to avoid confronting the question of his role in the Watergate cover-up, sought to take refuge in the less compromising realm of foreign policy in order to emphasize his indispensability. He specifically tried to take advantage of the enormous public acclaim Kissinger was winning through his Middle East shuttle diplomacy. In the spring of 1974, soon after Kissinger had worked out agreements between the Israelis and their Arab neighbors, Nixon toured the Middle East. The President traveled abroad as often as possible, even irritating foreign leaders by his desire to publicize the significance of routine conferences, which they thought unnecessary in the first place. The June 1974 summit meeting with Brezhnev produced nothing.

Kissinger resented Nixon's attempts to share the spotlight with him. He also feared that the President's frenetic travels could have undesirable effects on the work he had already done. Moreover, Kissinger felt that unless Nixon resigned, he too would be dragged irretrievably into Watergate.

In a June press conference in Salzburg the Secretary of State complained about "innuendos" that he had participated in illegal wiretapping. Speaking so emotionally that some critics called it a "tantrum," Kissinger said that he did not think it "possible to conduct the foreign policy of the United States under these circumstances when the character and credibility of the Secretary of State is at issue. And if it is not cleared up, I will resign." He requested that the Senate Foreign Relations Committee investigate charges against him. (In August the Committee cleared him of charges that he had perjured himself in testimony about his role in the wiretaps.) Although highly sensitive to criticism, Kissinger in this case appeared to be demanding that Nixon take responsibility for all illegalities and resign.

In Nixon's last days, however, Kissinger, whose relationship with the President had always been solely professional, sought to soothe his superior's vanity by assuring him that history would look favorably on Nixon's achievements, particularly in the area of foreign affairs. In a conversation between Nixon and Kissinger related in *The Final Days,* the Secretary of State reportedly knelt down in prayer beside the weeping President. Nixon resigned in August 1974. His successor, Gerald Ford [*q.v.*], asked Kissinger to remain.

Kissinger's last three years in government lacked the drama of the first five. Relations with China progressed slowly, in part because of internal political struggles in that country. The two nations agreed, however, to the establishment of liaison offices in Washington and Peking. Detente with the Soviets slowed too, and SALT II negotiations were not completed while he was in office. However, the Ford-Brezhnev Vladivostok summit of

November 1974 produced a tentative agreement on ceilings for strategic delivery vehicles and MIRV missiles. An effort to provide the Soviets with most-favored nation status in a trade treaty met with fierce congressional opposition. The legislators, led by Sen. Henry Jackson (D, Wash.) [q.v.] and supported by the American Jewish lobby, wanted any U.S. trade concessions tied to a Soviet agreement to liberalize their emigration restrictions on Soviet Jews. The furor embarrassed both Kissinger and the Soviets and led to Soviet cancellation of the treaty in January 1975. Conservatives began to regularly accuse Kissinger of "selling out" to the Russians and some extremists even referred to him as the "Jewish Communist." Liberals continued to attack what they considered his hardline attitude, and there was a wider consensus which believed that Kissinger was unconcerned about human rights and moral issues.

In 1975 the site of East-West confrontation shifted from Indochina and the Middle East to Africa. Both the State Department and the NSC had been unprepared for "destabilization" in Africa. They had not foreseen the Portuguese withdrawal from its African colonies nor the development of black liberation movements in areas controlled by whites. A 1971 NSC memorandum concluded that black insurgents were not "realistic or supportable" alternatives to white regimes. However the appearance of Cuban troops in the Angolan civil war in 1975 prompted Kissinger to employ threatening language against the Soviets and to reevaluate U.S. African policy.

In September 1975 Kissinger made a strong statement against apartheid and indicated American displeasure with South Africa's policy in Namibia, expressing support for Namibia's complete independence. He sought to identify the U.S. with the aspirations of black Africa. He realized that past American policy, exemplified by unstinting support for the Portuguese in Angola showed an inability to perceive the direction of the flow of power on the continent. A tour of black Africa in early 1976 gave evidence of the shift in U.S. sympathies. In a speech in Nairobi in May, Kissinger proposed a multibillion-dollar raw materials development program intended to benefit African nations. He also called for a $7.5 billion international drought-relief program for the sub-Sahara. Most importantly, Kissinger decided that the United States could no longer support the white supremacist regime in Rhodesia. He even promised aid to any south African nation that joined the campaign against Rhodesia. Together with the British, Kissinger put pressure on Rhodesian Prime Minister Ian Smith to agree to the end of white rule and preparations for a coalition government that would include moderate black leaders. To force Smith to accept the plan, he sought to persuade South Africa to stop supplying Rhodesia. The interim government plan for Rhodesia was accepted by Smith in November 1976.

It was not clear to political observers whether Kissinger under President Gerald Ford determined foreign policy as completely as he had in Nixon's last year in office. Ford depended on Kissinger, but he also saw the Secretary of State as more of a liability than Nixon ever had. In Ford's two years in office, there were repeated rumors that Kissinger would be replaced; the rumors were usually followed by denials from Ford and, in some cases, by a diplomatic coup that temporarily silenced Kissinger's critics. Nonetheless, in May 1976 Kissinger told a reporter that he expected to resign in 1977, even if Ford was elected to a full term. Kissinger's sins, in the opinion of his critics, were many. Even his biggest successes were interpreted as failures. Although the left remained hostile to Kissinger, particularly for his role in the overthrow of Salvador Allende's Marxist government in Chile, it was criticism from the Republican Party's radical right wing that most worried Ford.

Ironically, Kissinger, who had called the nuclear alert in 1973 and had advocated massive bombing of North Vietnam, was considered "soft" on Communism in the eyes of the right. Proponents of a big defense budget argued that SALT had given the Soviets an advantage over the United States and that Kissinger was fully conscious of what he had done. Secretary of Defense James Schlesinger [q.v.] claimed that Kissinger made too many concessions and was reluctant to accuse the Soviets of violating previous agreements. Schlesinger argued that the Vladivostok accord had set too high a limit on the number of MIRV's, thus failing to reduce the threat presented by Moscow's huge new missiles. The Kissinger-Schlesinger enmity led to the ouster of Schlesinger in November 1975. To give the appearance that Kissinger's authority was also being reduced, Ford replaced Kissinger as head of the NSC. However his successor in the NSC was known to be an adherent of Kissinger's policies and likely to carry out the recommendations of the former chief.

Congress also provided a forum for criticism of Kissinger's foreign policy. Senator Jackson, a supporter of both Israel and the defense establishment, led the attack on detente and the new Middle East policy. Supporters of Israel were especially angered by the United States condemnation in the U.N. of Israel's settlements on the West Bank of the Jordan River and its occupation of East Jerusalem. Just as the American Jewish community influenced congressional opinion, the nation's considerable Greek community stirred a sharp reaction against Kissinger's "tilt" toward Turkey on the Cyprus issue. In May 1975 Congress banned military aid to Turkey, justifying its action on the grounds that the law prevented the use of U.S. weapons for purposes other than defense (the Turks had used American weapons in the invasion of Cyprus).

Kissinger's handling of foreign policy became a major issue during the 1976 presidential campaign. Ronald Reagan, running against Ford in the Republican primary, argued that the Helsinki accords had recognized the status quo in Eastern Europe and thus abandoned the "captive" nations of the Warsaw Pact to perpetual Soviet domination. Reagan even attacked Kissinger's position on Rhodesia for favoring "revolutionaries" at the expense of legitimate governments. In March 1976 Reagan, relying on information provided by Adm. Elmo Zumwalt, claimed that Kissinger had once compared the United States to Athens and the USSR to Sparta. According to Reagan, Kissinger had said that the job of "Secretary of State is to negotiate the most acceptable second-best available." Reagan insisted that the United States could never be second best and that it should never abandon its ideals. Reagan was able to tap a strong chauvinist sentiment in the Republican Party that could not be reconciled to Kissinger's pragmatic approach to diplomacy. The Reagan wing of the Party still objected to relations with China and condemned Kissinger's efforts begun in 1973 to work out an agreement giving Panama control over the Panama Canal. The Democratic candidate, Jimmy Carter, hit on the idealism-morality issue when he charged that Kissinger's foreign policy was based on "the assumption that the world is a jungle of competing national antagonisms where military muscle and economic muscle are the only things that work."

While Kissinger was a frequent target of criticism by Congressional liberals and conservatives, most observers agreed that he achieved a number of diplomatic breakthroughs. Kissinger was the main negotiator of the two arms control agreements with the Soviet Union. He also helped to engineer the normalization of relations with Communist China. In the Middle East, he laid the foundations of the beginnings of a possible peace between Israel and its Arab neighbors. In Africa, he helped to bring majority rule to Zimbabwe-Rhodesia. Equally important perhaps, Kissinger sought to educate the United States about the subtleties of the European tradition of balance of power politics which was so alien to the American experience and tradition.

[JCH]

For further information:
Carl Bernstein and Bob Woodward, *The Final Days* (New York, 1976).

Marvin Kalb and Bernard Kalb, *Kissinger* (New York, 1974).

Henry Kissinger, *White House Years* (New York, 1979).

Bruce Mazlish, *Kissinger: The European Mind in American Policy* (New York, 1976)

Roger Morris, *Uncertain Greatness: Henry Kissinger and American Foreign Policy* (New York, 1977).

Michael Roskin, "An American Metternich: Henry A. Kissinger and the Global Balance of Power" in *Makers of American Diplomacy*, Frank J. Merli and Theodore A. Wilson, eds. (New York, 1974).

KNOWLAND, WILLIAM F(IFE)
b. June 26, 1908; Alameda, Cal.
d. Feb. 23, 1974; Oakland, Cal.
Republican Senator, Calif., 1945–58.

William Knowland was the son of a six-term California congressman. Following graduation from the University of California in 1925, he joined the editorial staff of his father's newspaper, the Oakland, Calif. *Tribune*. In 1933 Knowland won a seat in the California Assembly; two years later he moved to the state Senate. In 1938 Knowland was elected to the Republican National Committee and three years later became chairman of its executive committee. California Gov. Earl Warren appointed Knowland to finish the term of the deceased Sen. Hiram Johnson (R, Calif.) in 1945.

Knowland was primarily known as an ardent supporter of Nationalist China. As a spokesman for the "China Lobby," he defended Chiang Kai-shek's government against charges of corruption and demanded increased aid to the regime. Although he voted for much of the legislation enacting Truman's policy of containment toward the Soviet Union, Knowland initially opposed such measures as the Marshall Plan unless they were coupled with increased assistance to Chiang.

In 1949 Knowland described the White Paper on China, which blamed the fall of China on the Nationalists, as a "white-wash" of a "do-nothing-policy." With the possibility of a Communist invasion, Knowland publicly called on Truman to use the Navy to protect Formosa. The California Senator opposed recognition of the new Peking government and urged all-out military aid for Chiang to reconquer the mainland.

Knowland maintained that Communists and Communist sympathizers in the State Department were responsible for the fall of China. He pointed particularly to Owen Lattimore, a State Department adviser. In 1949 he charged Lattimore with advocating a "policy of appeasement" in Asia. The following year he maintained that the scholar was espousing the Communist Party line. Knowland was never able to generate national publicity for his charges until Sen. Joseph R. McCarthy (R, Wisc.) took up the campaign.

Knowland initially applauded Truman's intervention in Korea but soon joined Gen. Douglas MacArthur [*q.v.*] and his supporters in charging that the President's policies prevented a military victory. Of all the Republican critics of the Administration, Knowland was the most bellicose on the war. He even welcomed a full-scale war with the Chinese as an alternative to what he called a "Far Eastern Munich." Knowland opposed any truce that would lead to a permanent partition of the Korean peninsula.

When Senate Majority Leader Robert A. Taft (R, Ohio) [*q.v.*] died in April 1953, Knowland succeeded him. Following his Party's loss of the upper chamber in 1954, he became minority leader. But Knowland was never able to develop a close relationship with Eisenhower because of his strident stands. He vigorously opposed the admission of Communist China to the U.N. and supported the efforts of the Committee for One Million Against the Admission of Communist China to the United Nations to pressure the Administration to take a firm stand on the issue. On numerous occasions he attempted to get Senate passage of a resolution supporting U.S. withdrawal from the U.N. if Communist China were admitted. In April 1954 Chinese Premier Chou En-lai announced that his country desired peaceful relations with the

U.S. and asked for negotiations on outstanding issues. Knowland maintained that acceptance of the Chinese peace initiative would be "another Munich." Pressure from Knowland and from other Nationalist supporters prompted Secretary of State John Foster Dulles [q.v.] to announce that the Administration opposed Communist China's admission to the world body. Still unsatisfied, in July Knowland threatened to resign his majority leadership in the Senate if the Communists were admitted and to campaign for the U.S. withdrawal from the U.N.

Knowland was particularly concerned over the Geneva Conference on Indochina and Korea, scheduled for the spring of 1954. He believed that any negotiation with the Chinese would be tantamount to recognition of the Communist regime. With Dulles preparing to attend the conference in April, he warned against any "steps that could be interpreted as recognition." Knowland's pressure had an important effect on the Administration, which felt it had to placate the China Lobby. Dulles flew to Geneva for a brief time and at one session refused to shake hands with Chou En-lai. He then downgraded the U.S. delegation to the status of observer and instructed Undersecretary of State Walter Bedell Smith to take no part in the negotiations and ignore the Chinese.

When the Communist Chinese began shelling the offshore islands of Quemoy and Matsu during the fall of 1954, Knowland called for a vigorous response by the U.S. and advocated blockading the Chinese coast. The Joint Chiefs of Staff recommended bombing the mainland, while Dulles considered threatening the Chinese with a nuclear attack. Eisenhower resisted the pressure and took no military action.

In 1958 Knowland made an unsuccessful bid to be elected governor of California. After his defeat, he returned to his newspaper business but remained active in Republican national politics. In February 1974 Knowland died, an apparent suicide.

[JB]

LIPPMANN, WALTER
b. Sept. 21, 1889; New York, N.Y.
d. Dec. 14, 1974; New York, N.Y.
Journalist.

Lippmann was the son of well-to-do Jews. He graduated from Harvard in 1910 and worked briefly for Lincoln Steffens's *Everybody's Magazine.* In 1914 he joined Herbert Croly in founding *The New Republic,* a liberal journal supporting Woodrow Wilson's progressivism and internationalism. Three years later he was appointed assistant secretary of war and contributed to the formation of the Fourteen Points and Treaty of Versailles. After the war Lippmann joined the *New York World,* soon becoming its Washington correspondent. During the 1920s he also published a number of books expressing his growing pessimism with popular democracy.

In 1931 the journalist began his long association with the *New York Herald Tribune.* In his column "Today & Tomorrow," Lippmann analyzed contemporary issues in relation to the problems of American democracy. He initially supported Franklin D. Roosevelt but by 1935 increasingly criticized what he thought was the President's move toward socialism. Nevertheless, he applauded Roosevelt's foreign policy. He deplored the isolationism and pacifism of the nation in the face of Hitler's expansion and supported Roosevelt's attempts to aid U.S. allies.

During the war Lippmann outlined his goals for American diplomacy. In *U.S. Foreign Policy: Shield of the Republic* (1943) and *U.S. War Aims* (1944), he criticized the Wilsonian ideas of internationalism. Lippmann advised Americans to base their diplomacy on realpolitick. National interest, he asserted, was determined by geopolitical and economic factors, not abstract theories of right versus wrong. Lippmann proposed that the U.S., USSR and Great Britain recognize each others spheres of influence to prevent future conflict. These three nations could then form a coalition to check the rise of

Germany and Japan, the only two nations that could threaten the status quo. Lippmann ridiculed the idea of an international organization formed to keep the peace, maintaining that only treaties based on geopolitics could create a stable world.

The journalist warned the Western allies not to challenge the future Soviet hegemony in Eastern Europe. Lippmann acknowledged that Soviet repression in the area could strain his proposed coalition. However, he reasoned that the Soviet Union would not quickly move to suppress freedom because its foreign policy was not determined by ideology but by a desire to protect its western border. He hoped for a neutralized Eastern Europe under Soviet influence but not oppression.

During the postwar years Lippmann continued to oppose Truman's concentration on Eastern Europe. He also criticized the Administration's desire to build a strong Germany as creating an unnecessary source of tension in the Cold War. The only way to allay Soviet fears and introduce stability in Central Europe was, in his opinion, to keep Germany decentralized and neutralized. If the West pushed too hard for unification of Germany, he warned, the Soviets might use their military power to unite the nation under a Communist regime.

Lippmann believed America's major interest was in the Eastern Mediterranean, on the vital oil routes to Western Europe. In 1947 he endorsed the President's request to send aid to Greece and Turkey, then threatened by Communist rebels. However, he attacked the Truman Doctrine, promising American aid to nations fighting Communism, because it was couched in terms of a Wilsonian moral crusade.

During the latter half of 1947, Lippmann engaged in a major debate with George Kennan [q.v.] over foreign policy. The Soviet expert maintained that Russian diplomacy was based on Stalin's paranoia of capitalist encirclement and a desire to extend Communism. To meet Soviet aggression, Kennan recommended a policy of containment. By placing American power and aid in shifting areas of conflict, the West would soon show the Soviet Union its determination to prevent Communist expansion.

Lippmann dismissed irrationality as a motive for Soviet diplomacy, reiterating his belief that it was based on geopolitical considerations. He supported the Marshall Plan of economic aid to Europe but condemned containment because he thought it would lead to "unending intervention" and would allow the Soviet Union to maintain the initiative in the Cold War. Instead of containment, he proposed disengagement by both powers: a U.S. withdrawal from Western Germany to be matched by a Soviet withdrawal from the East. Disengagement, he predicted, would restore some democracy to Eastern Europe because Russia would not have to fear penetration from the West.

In the late 1940s and early 1950s, Lippmann devoted less time to foreign affairs. However, when the Eisenhower Administration came to power, he once again began to attack American foreign policy. He ridiculed the Administration's attempts to couch foreign policy in terms of a moral crusade and denounced John Foster Dulles's [q.v.] call for the liberation of Eastern Europe. Lippmann considered involvements in Southeast Asia and Quemoy-Matsu unnecessary overextensions of American power. Disengagement and the American willingness to cooperate with neutral nations, he maintained, were the best ways to ensure a pro-American stable world. Lippmann supported John F. Kennedy for President in 1960 but became increasingly disillusioned with his foreign policy. He was impressed with the early Johnson Administration but broke with the President over the war in Vietnam. From 1963 to 1968 Lippmann worked for *Newsweek* magazine. The dean of American journalists died in December 1974.

[JB]

For further information:
Marquis Childs and James Reston, eds., *Walter Lippman and His Times* (New York, 1959).

LODGE, HENRY CABOT

b. July 5, 1902; Nahant, Mass.
Ambassador to the United Nations, January 1953-August 1960; Ambassador to Vietnam, August 1963-April 1964, July 1965-April 1967. Chief Negotiator, Paris Peace Talks, January 1969-December 1969; Special Envoy to the Vatican, 1970-75.

Born into a distinguished New England family that dated back to the colonial period, Henry Cabot Lodge was raised by his grandfather, Sen. Henry Cabot Lodge, Sr., (R, Mass.) after the death of his father in 1909. Following his graduation from Harvard in 1921, Lodge began a career in journalism as a reporter and then editorial writer for the *New York Herald Tribune*. In 1933 he was elected to the Massachusetts House of Representatives. Three years later he defeated veteran Democratic politician James M. Curley for a seat in the U.S. Senate. With the exception of periods of service in the Army from 1941 to 1942 and 1944 to 1945, he remained in the upper house over the next 15 years.

In the Senate, Lodge became one of the leading spokesman for the internationalist wing of the Republican Party; and during the early 1950s he played an important role in persuading General Eisenhower to run for President.

Because of his preoccupation with Eisenhower's nomination, however, Lodge neglected his own senatorial race against 35-year-old Rep. John F. Kennedy (D, Mass.) [q.v.]. As a result of this, the ardent opposition of Taft Republicans in Massachusetts and Kennedy's superior campaign, he lost his bid for reelection by 70,000 votes out of 2.3 million cast.

Following his own election, Eisenhower made Lodge his personal liaison to arrange the transfer of power. He also appointed the Senator chief delegate to the U.N., a position which, he assured Lodge, was second in the State Department to that of Secretary of State. The President-elect also made him a member of the cabinet and of the National Security Council.

Lodge viewed himself not as the head of an embassy who was obliged to take directions from the State Department but as one of Eisenhower's senior policy advisers. According to Assistant Secretary of State for U.N. Affairs Robert Murphy, "The political influence and exceptional ability of Ambassador Lodge gradually transformed the American delegation at the U.N. until, as the years passed, [the] mission behaved less like an embassy than a second foreign office of the United States government." Lodge was permitted to speak in U.N. debates without prior clearance from Washington. President Eisenhower often remarked that his ambassador had articulated the position he would have taken had he been consulted.

At the U.N. Lodge played the role of a cold, unbending foe of Communism, while keeping the lines of communication open to the Soviets through his staff, particularly his assistant, James Wadsworth. He represented the U.S. at important debates during the Suez crisis and Hungarian revolt of 1956 and explained U.S. action in sending troops to Lebanon two years later. As Eisenhower's official representative, Lodge accompanied Soviet Premier Nikita Khrushchev on his 12 day tour through the U.S. in 1959. Ambassador Lodge was also with the two leaders during their talks at Camp David.

In 1960, Lodge was the Republican Vice-Presidential candidate in the campaign in which Kennedy defeated Nixon.

In June 1963 President Kennedy, anxious to gain bipartisan support for American involvement in Vietnam, appointed Lodge ambassador to Saigon. While at that post Lodge served not only as an executor but also as an important formulator of policy. The Ambassador arrived in Saigon on Aug. 22 during the crisis precipitated by the Diem regime's attack on Buddhist dissidents. This attack, carried out by President Ngo Dinh Diem's brother, Ngo Dinh Nhu, generated fierce criticism not only from foreign governments but also from elements within Vietnam. Several American observers also thought the attack threatened the military effort in that country. After assessing the situation, Lodge came to the conclusion that the war could not be won with the unpopular regime. In the ensuing months he worked to convince Washington that it should be replaced.

Two days after his arrival the Ambassador was instructed by State Department officials to tell Diem that he must "rid himself of Nhu" and to inform military leaders that if Diem did not, the U.S. would "give them direct support in any interim period [of the] breakdown [of the] central government." Lodge approved of the plan but proposed to forego what he believed to be a futile attempt to approach Diem and, instead, state the U.S. position only to the generals, thus throwing U.S. support behind a coup. However, the message, written by George Ball [q.v.], Michael Forrestal, Roger Hilsman and Averell Harriman [q.v.], had not been adequately studied by the Secretaries of Defense and State or the Chairman of the Joint Chiefs of staff, who, upon reflection, questioned the efficacy of a coup. The State Department sent Lodge a message canceling the previous communications and ordering him to 'work for the reform of the Diem regime. The suggested coup did not take place because the Vietnamese generals were unable to achieve a favorable balance of forces in the Saigon area and because several believed that the U.S. had leaked information about their plot to Diem and Nhu.

Despite Washington's decision Lodge remained convinced that the war would not be won with Diem, and he tried to persuade Washington that a new, more popular government was necessary. During September he carried on a secret correspondence with Kennedy in which he presented his pessimistic view of the situation and suggested the need for change. In addition, he gave Secretary of Defense Robert S. McNamara [q.v.] extensive briefings during the Secretary's September visit to undercut the military's uniformly optimistic reports to Washington.

In Saigon Lodge worked on what he re-garded as futile attempts to force Diem to reform. Through press leaks he informed the government that the U.S. would have to withdraw its support if Diem did not institute necessary changes. During the first week in October, Washington, on advice given earlier by Lodge, deferred approval of a portion of the foreign aid program as a threat of possible further cuts unless Nhu was removed. At Lodge's suggestion John Richardson, the Central Intelligence Agency chief in Saigon who had been a supporter of Diem, was returned to Washington on Oct. 5, ostensibly because his cover identity had been compromised. In a more controversial move Lodge, with the permission of Washington, informed the South Vietnamese government on Oct. 17 that U.S. aid for Diem's private guard, which had been used in August to put down the Buddhists, would be suspended until it was transferred to field combat.

South Vietnamese generals interpreted these actions as a green light for a coup and in the beginning of October approached Lodge's aides to ask about the U.S. stand on a change of government. On Oct. 5 the Ambassador indirectly informed them that the U.S. would not thwart any proposed coup. Whether this was done before or after receiving an Oct. 5 message from the President ordering him not to give active "covert encouragement to a coup" but to "identify and contact possible alternative leadership" is unclear.

As the coup took shape during the last days of October, Lodge worked to forestall any attempt by Washington to oppose it. On Oct. 30, when several of the President's advisers decided to make one last attempt to deal with Diem and asked Lodge to delay or call off the coup, he informed them that the matter was in Vietnamese hands and he could do nothing to prevent it. A successful coup took place on Nov. 1.

During the months following the coup, Lodge remained an important force in Vietnamese politics, attempting to aid in the establishment of a stable government and pushing for needed reforms. In May 1964 he resigned his post to return home to try to prevent the nomination of Sen. Barry

Goldwater (R, Ariz.) [*q.v.*] as the Republican presidential candidate.

At the request of President Johnson, Lodge toured North Atlantic Treaty Organization countries in August and September 1964 to acquaint their leaders with American policy in Vietnam. In February he became a presidential "consultant" on Vietnam and helped shape the decisions to launch an air war on North Vietnam and to make major ground troops commitments to the struggle. Lodge supported both of these measures on the grounds that the U.S. could not abandon a country it had promised to protect and that a defeat would encourage new Communist aggression in Asia.

In July 1965 Johnson asked Lodge to serve a second tour in Vietnam. The Ambassador, who had been a popular figure in that Southeast Asian country, replaced Maxwell Taylor [*q.v.*], whose relations with the government and the opposition leaders had become increasingly strained. Even before assuming his post Lodge attempted to convince Washington to reemphasize the pacification program, which had been stressed in 1962 but had been subordinated to military considerations during the early days of the Johnson Administration. Lodge insisted that the military situation could be settled if the government secured the political support of the people. This, he believed, could be achieved only by a program designed first to provide protection and then to carry out economic and social reforms that would raise the living standards of the rural population of South Vietnam.

By late 1965 both Washington and Saigon had acceded to Lodge's request. The South Vietnamese government established the Revolutionary Development Cadres, financed by $400 million in Agency for International Development (AID) funds. Once the program had been established, the Ambassador's involvement became inconsistent and irregular, particularly after February 1966 when Johnson put William Porter in complete charge of the effort. Lodge objected to a subordinate controlling the program and refused to support his recommendations or press for further Administration backing. Despite the embassy's optimistic reports on the success of pacification, the program floundered. After Lodge left Vietnam the effort was restructured in hopes of improving its effectiveness, but rural pacification eventually proved a failure.

While Lodge's emphasis on pacification was lauded by many for its stress on development rather than military destruction, such critics as Frances Fitzgerald believed that the results bore little relation to the enormous amount of money spent. She also questioned the techniques and statistical compilations used to evaluate the program, pointing out that the standardized reports used by the pacification cadres were skewed toward registering success and ignoring failure.

Because Lodge saw himself as a presidential adviser rather than as a manager of the American civil-military effort in Vietnam, he did not try to formulate an integrated program of U.S. involvement. He respected the American generals leading the war and so did not play an active role in making military decisions. Lodge concurred with the Pentagon's claim that intensified bombing of the North would raise South Vietnamese morale, and he recommended quick resumption of bombing raids after the December 1965-January 1966 bombing pause failed to lead to peace negotiations with the North Vietnamese government.

During the spring of 1966 Lodge became involved in efforts to end the conflict between the central government, led by Premier Nguyen Cao Ky, and the Buddhist-dominated Struggle Movement led by Tri Quang. Prompted by the regime's failure to set a definite date for elections and its dismissal of the leading Buddhist general, Nyugen Chanh Thi, the Movement demanded the overthrow of Ky and the installation of a civilian government. By the end of March anti-government Buddhists and sympathetic elements of the South Vietnamese Army had gained control of Hue and Da Nang. Although Lodge supported Ky and termed the Buddhists demands "a naked grab for power," he tried to prevent a head-on collision between the two groups.

When conciliatory efforts failed Lodge concurred in Ky's decision to use force. In early April the U.S. Military Assistance Command in Vietnam airlifted loyal South Vietnamese troops to Da Nang in an unsuccessful attempt to quell the disturbances.

To avoid heightening anti-American feelings, Lodge did not involve American men or equipment or use economic leverage in Ky's later attempts to end the protests. At the direction of the State Department, he maintained relations with both factions and urged moderation. When Ky again sent troops to the rebel cities against Lodge's advice, the U.S. gave no assistance and withdrew its military advisers from army units of both factions. The Movement was put down by a combination of force and negotiations in June 1966. Reacting to criticism that America should not be fighting for a country afflicted with petty political squabbles, Lodge defended American involvement, saying that the nation's strategic interest in the war lay "in avoiding World War III."

During the summer of 1966 the Ambassador opened secret negotiations with Hanoi that were designed to explore the North's reaction to a possible bombing pause. In November Lodge relayed communications from Washington suggesting that the U.S. would halt bombing North Vietnam in return for a secret commitment from Hanoi "after some adequate period" to reduce its infiltration of South Vietnam. The proposed delay in the North's reaction was designed to give the impression that its withdrawal of troops was not related to the bombing pause. In December Lodge received word that Hanoi seemed ready to negotiate on American proposals. However, during the following days the U.S. resumed heavy bombing near population centers around Hanoi. Despite Lodge's attempts to halt the air strikes, they continued and the talks collapsed. Lodge resigned his post in April 1967.

In March 1968 Johnson asked Lodge to become a member of the Senior Advisory Group on Vietnam convened to consider the military's request that over 200,000 additional troops be sent to Vietnam following the Tet offensive. During the group's meetings he was one of the men dissatisfied with current policy who were still reluctant to vote for a dramatic change. The panel recommended rejection of the troop increase request and favored adoption of a policy of de-escalation. Johnson announced this policy on March 31, 1968.

In January 1969 President Nixon appointed Lodge chief negotiator to the Paris peace conference, replacing veteran diplomat W. Averell Harriman [q.v.]. Lodge's credentials marked him as an ardent anti-Communist, meaning that the North Vietnamese could anticipate few concessions from the new Administration. New York attorney Lawrence Walsh and ambassador to Indonesia Marshall Green were named Lodge's assistants. The American proposals called for complete withdrawal of all outside forces within one year, a cease-fire under international supervision and free elections under international supervision. The North Vietnamese rejected consideration of these proposals and demanded the immediate and total withdrawal of all Americans from South Vietnam. Frustrated by Hanoi's "take it or leave it" attitude, Lodge asked to be relieved in October 1969. Nixon's failure to immediately replace Lodge upon his resignation Dec. 8, 1969, indicated that the Administration was momentarily downgrading the peace negotiations.

In July 1970 Lodge became President Nixon's special envoy to the Vatican, a position accepted without pay and not requiring residence in Rome. The post held significance because the Vatican was a center of worldwide information and provided an opportunity for possible peace negotiations with North Vietnam and inquiries concerning the fate of American prisoners-of-war there. Also in July 1970 Lodge was named chairman of a special presidential commission to study U.S. policy toward Communist China. After hearing testimony from 200 witnesses in six U.S. cities, the commission recommended in April 1971 that the United States seek Communist China's admission to the United Nations without the expulsion of Nationalist China.

During the 1970s Lodge maintained his home in Beverly, Mass., primarily tending to personal business. He attended the 1976 Republican National Convention but did not play a significant role.

[TML]

For further information:
Alden Hatch, *The Lodges of Massachusetts* (New York, 1973).
Henry Cabot Lodge, *The Storm Has Many Eyes* (New York, 1973).
William J. Miller, *Henry Cabot Lodge* (New York, 1967).

LOVETT, ROBERT A(BERCROMBIE)
b. Sept. 14, 1895; Huntsville, Tex.
Undersecretary of State, July 1947-January 1949; Deputy Secretary of Defense, October 1950-December 1951; Secretary of Defense, December 1951-January 1953.

Lovett's grandfather had been an officer in the Confederate Army. His father was a lawyer who eventually became president of the Union Pacific and Southern Pacific railways. Lovett entered Yale in 1914. In his junior year his studies were interrupted with U.S. entry into World War I. Lovett helped organize the Yale unit of pilots and commanded the first U.S. Naval Air Squadron. He returned to Yale after the war, in 1919, receiving his B.A. degree that summer. After college Lovett studied for one year at Harvard Law School and Harvard Graduate School of Business Administration. In 1921 he joined his father-in-law's banking firm, Brown Brothers, as a clerk and rose to become a partner in 1926. That year he was elected a director and member of the executive committee of the Union Pacific Railroad. In 1931 helped arrange the merger between Brown Brothers and the Harriman banking house to form Brown Brothers, Harriman & Co.

During the 1930s Lovett's chief business activity was in the field of international investments. Frequent trips to Europe gave him an insider's view of European industry and convinced him that Hitler was building up Germany in preparation for war. Convinced of the importance of air power in the coming war, during 1939 Lovett made a personal tour of most of the aircraft plants in the U.S. He recommended ways of improving production to Undersecretary of the Navy James V. Forrestal [*q.v.*], who passed these along to Undersecretary of the Army Robert Patterson. Patterson was so impressed that he asked Lovett to come to Washington as his special assistant in 1940. In April 1941 Lovett was made assistant secretary of war for air. He helped obtain for the air arm the preferential semi-autonomous status it enjoyed within the Army. He also pushed for priority on bomber production in the war effort. Lovett's chief responsibilities during World War II were in the area of procurement and production. He encouraged aircraft manufacturers to construct long-range bombers and was a key figure in approving B-36 development. Patterson was quoted as having said, "The fact that our air forces achieved their huge expansion in time was due more to Bob Lovett than to any other man." In November 1945 Lovett resigned from his government post to resume his banking career.

Two years later Secretary of State George C. Marshall [*q.v.*] asked Lovett, with whom he had become a close friend during the war, to be his undersecretary. Lovett began to serve in this position in July and became known as Marshall's "trouble-shooter." The two men worked well as a team. A Marshall aide once remarked, "he [Marshall] and Lovett were the perfect combination. Lovett was the best description I've ever seen of an alter-ego." With similar motives, intent and dedication, the two men guided the State Department during some of the most difficult years of the Cold War. Lovett helped administer the Department and served as acting Secretary of State during Marshall's frequent absences from Washington. During the summer of 1947 Lovett oversaw the preparation of the Marshall Plan, pressing for assistance based on self-help and mutual aid, and negotiating with Europeans on the rehabilitation of Germany. He was also responsible for getting the U.S. military government in Germany to accept its expanded role in administering the plan.

The following year Lovett became deeply involved in the efforts leading to the formation of the North Atlantic Treaty Organization. In response to growing Cold War tensions and the Berlin blockade, the U.S. moved to form a mutual defense alliance in Western Europe that would also include Germany. In order to overcome opposition from Republican members of Congress who opposed abolishing America's historic position of no entangling alliances and feared the rearmament of Germany, Lovett worked closely with Sen. Arthur Vandenberg (R, Mich.) [q.v.] to develop the plan. The result of the Lovett-Vandenberg talks was Resolution 329, the Vandenberg Resolution passed in June 1948. The measure gave senatorial approval to the establishment of a regional defense agreement by the U.S. with other countries under the U.N. Charter. During the summer of 1948 Lovett headed the American delegation at secret meetings with diplomats from the Brussels Pact countries and Canada in discussions that led to the signing of the North Atlantic Treaty in 1949.

When Marshall resigned as Secretary of Defense in September 1951, Truman nominated Lovett as his successor. The banker accepted the position only because Marshall had asked him to stay. One of Lovett's contributions to long-range defense strength was to firmly establish the preparation of a coordinated defense-wide budget. Lovett expanded research and development programs while in office to include missile development and biological and chemical warfare research. Under his direction production of the *Atlas* intercontinental ballistic missile, abandoned in the late 1940s, was started again.

With the coming of a Republican Administration in January 1953, Lovett left government service and worked in banking during the 1950s.

In 1960, Kennedy offered him his choice of the three top cabinet portfolios—State, Defense or Treasury. Lovett refused the appointments because of ill-health and never held a government post during the Kennedy Administration. Instead, Kennedy used him as an adviser on important appointments and counselor on foreign and defense policy.

During the months prior to the inauguration, the former Secretary of Defense served as a link between Kennedy and many of the prominent officials of the Marshall era. Lovett also introduced the President to sources of talent unknown to him because of the business community's coolness toward Kennedy and his family. Lovett was one of the major supporters of Dean Rusk's [q.v.] appointment as Secretary of State. When the offer was made Lovett convinced the Rockefeller Foundation to make Rusk, who was then Foundation president, a financial settlement that enabled him to accept the appointment.

As a former high-ranking government official, Lovett often testified at congressional investigations on the Administration's behalf. He appeared at the August 1961 Senate Foreign Relations Committee hearings on the formation of a disarmament agency where he spoke in favor of the measure. During the January 1962 Senate Preparedness Subcommittee probe of State Department censorship of high military officials, he testified in favor of departmental review of officials' speeches necessary for continuity in foreign policy.

Lovett was among the former high-ranking diplomats serving on Excom, the committee formed to advise the President following the discovery of Soviet missiles on Cuba in October 1962. Within that group he was a sharp critic of U.N. Ambassador Adlai Stevenson's [q.v.] proposal to give up the Guantanamo naval base and withdraw Jupiter missiles from Turkey and Italy in return for removal of Soviet missiles from Cuba.

In December 1962, following attacks by conservative senators on Kennedy's foreign aid program, the President formed a committee of conservative businessmen, headed by Lucius Clay [q.v.], to investigate the system and presumably recommend its continuance. As a prominent Wall Street investment banker, Lovett became a member of that body. According to Schlesinger, Lovett's chief contribution to its deliberations "lay in elegantly sarcastic phrases: 'There has been a feeling that we are trying to do too much for too many too soon, that we are overextended in resources and undercompensated in results, and that no end of foreign aid is either in sight or in mind.'" The committee stressed that the program was indispensable to American security, but it recommended that aid operations be improved and the level of assistance reduced.

Because Lyndon B. Johnson [q.v.] did not maintain close contacts with the Eastern business community, Lovett's influence declined during the last half of the decade. He did, however, serve on two committees created in 1964 to advise the President—a nonpartisan citizen's panel on foreign policy and a panel to study ways of halting the spread of nuclear weapons.

[EWS]

MacARTHUR, DOUGLAS
b. Jan. 26, 1880; Little Rock, Ark.
d. April 5, 1964; Washington, D.C.
Supreme Commander of Allied
Powers in the Pacific, 1945–51;
Commander, United Nations Forces
in Korea, 1950–51.

The son of a Union Army general, Douglas MacArthur followed his father in a military career. MacArthur ranked first in the 1903 West Point graduating class. He served in several stateside Army posts until United States entry into World War I in 1917. During the war he was decorated on 13 occasions and was cited seven times for bravery. In 1918 MacArthur was promoted to brigadier general. After serving as West Point superintendent from 1919 to 1922, MacArthur was assigned to the Philippines. In 1930 he became a four star general and Army Chief of Staff, the youngest in United States history. From 1935 to 1941 he served as military adviser to the Philippine government. In July 1941 MacArthur was named commander of United States Army forces in the Far East. From the outbreak of the war in December 1941 until March 1942, he directed the defense of the Philippines against the Japanese. Ordered to Australia by President Roosevelt, MacArthur became commander of Allied forces in the Southwest Pacific. Starting in late 1942 he opened a three year offensive against the Japanese, returning to the Philippines in October 1944. He became a five star general in December 1944 and in April 1945 received command of all Army forces in the Pacific. Following Japan's surrender in August, 1945 President Truman named MacArthur Supreme Commander of the Allied Powers in the Pacific (SCAP) with responsibility to accept the Japanese surrender on the battleship *Missouri* on Sept. 2, 1945.

President Truman approved the Allied occupation policy for Japan that month. Policy was to be determined by the Far Eastern Commission representing the 11 nations that had been at war with Japan. MacArthur was simply to carry out its decisions. The General, however, almost completely disregarded the Far Eastern Commission and paid little attention to advisers and directives sent from Washington. Instead he administered Japan's occupation with the help of trusted men who had been trained in war and experienced in military operations rather than government.

MacArthur's chief aims included the elimination of Japanese militarism in all its forms and the initation of political economic and social reforms to pave the way for a democracy. Rather than vindictive, as the Japanese expected, MacArthur's firm but fair leadership gained him much respect. The military was quickly disarmed, war industries rapidly destroyed and war crimes trials conducted for those deemed responsible for the war. A new constitution was passed by the old Diet and went into effect on May 3, 1947. It provided for a number of democratic rights, including free press and free speech. The document also stated that Japan renounced forever the right to make war and banned the maintenance of land, sea and air forces. Thereafter SCAP functioned through directives which were incorporated into law by the new Japanese Diet. The police force and school system were decentralized, large land holdings were broken up and some effort was made to destroy the large industrial combines (Zaibatsu). In late 1947 MacArthur referred to Japan as the "Switzerland of the Pacific."

As early as 1946 MacArthur had urged that the occupation last no longer than three years, but the Big Four wartime partners failed to conclude a Pacific peace accord. Following the fall of China in 1949, Russia militated against Japan's recovery. Following the outbreak of war in Korea in June 1950, MacArthur successfully encouraged the Japanese government to restrict Communist groups in the country. To guard against sabotage a 75,000 man police reserve was established. Without Russian participation, and as a bulwark against Communism in the Pacific, the United States completed a general peace treaty in September 1951, after MacArthur's departure.

An ardent anti-Communist, MacArthur was anguished by the fall of China in 1949. He was critical of the United States failure to provide adequate assistance to Chiang Kai-shek. He maintained that the Chinese Communist victory encouraged further Communist imperialism which would jeopardize United States security. His beliefs that the fall of China marked the beginning of America's crumbling power in Asia was later reenforced by its Korean war policy.

When the Republic of South Korea (ROK) was formed in August 1948, MacArthur's official connection with the peninsula ceased until North Korean forces invaded ROK in June 1950. MacArthur claimed that Washington officials ignored his intelligence reports that such an invasion was impending. With war at hand President Truman named him commander in chief of United Nations forces in Korea. Unprepared and undermanned, the U.N. army was quickly pinned to the Pusan perimeter. In a daring plan MacArthur directed a successful landing behind enemy lines at Inchon on Sept. 15, 1950. MacArthur was confident of victory by the year's end and also confident that the Chinese Communists would not enter the war. He reported this to President Truman at their Wake Island meeting in October 1950.

In late November 1950 U.N. forces were deep into North Korea and were caught with their overextended lines by contingents of Chinese Communist troops which had crossed the Yalu River. By early 1951 the Communists had regained much of North Korea. MacArthur charged "that there is no substitute for victory" and demanded that the Yalu River bridges and Manchurian supply depots be destroyed. He also urged that Chiang's Nationalist Army be permitted to invade the mainland. MacArthur related these views by letter to Rep. Joseph Martin (R, Mass.) on March 20, 1951. The Administration denied MacArthur's requests. Committed to European reconstruction, fearing Russian intervention if the Nationalist Chinese entered the war, Truman determined to keep the war localized in Korea. MacArthur's public statements on the matter strained his relations with the President. When Rep. Martin read MacArthur's letter on the floor of Congress on April 5, 1951, President Truman decided to dismiss MacArthur, which was done April 11, 1951.

The General received a tumultuous welcome upon his return to the United States. Although he told a joint session of Congress on April 19, 1951 "that old soldiers never die, they just fade away," MacArthur remained a public figure for some time. He delivered the keynote address to the Republican National Convention in 1952 and also was a candidate for the Party's presidential nomination. In the same year he became chairman of the board for Remington Rand. He spent his later years quietly living at New York's

Waldorf-Astoria. For service to his country, Congress ordered a gold medal struck for MacArthur in 1962 and in the same year he received West Point's Sylvanus Thayer Award. He died at the age of 84.

[TML]

For further information:
Herbert Feis, *Contest Over Japan* (New York, 1967).

MARSHALL, GEORGE C(ATLETT)
b. Dec. 31, 1880; Uniontown, Pa.
d. Oct. 16, 1959; Washington, D.C.
Secretary of State, January 1947 - January 1949; Secretary of Defense, September 1950 - September 1951.

The son of a coal merchant, Marshall attended the Virginia Military Institute, where he graduated in 1901. The following year he joined the Army. From 1902 to 1906 he was stationed in the Philippines and the American Southwest. Marshall attended the Infantry-Cavalry School from 1906 to 1907 and graduated from the School of the Line (the forerunner of the Command and General Staff School) in 1908. For the next two years, he served as instructor at the school. During World War I he held high administrative and planning posts with the American Expeditionary Force. In 1918, as chief of operations of the First Army, he helped prepare the Meuse-Argonne offensive.

Impressed with Marshall's ability, Gen. John Pershing appointed him aide de camp; Marshall served at that post from 1919 until the General's retirement in 1924. He saw duty in China from 1924 to 1927 and was stationed at the Infantry School at Fort Benning, Ga., from 1927 to 1932. As assistant commandant in charge of instruction, he strengthened the curriculum and revamped instruction techniques. His work influenced several generals, including J. Lawton Collins and W. Bedell Smith, who became prominent in World War II. During the 1930s Marshall organized Civilian Conservation Corps camps in South Carolina, Georgia, Washington and Oregon. Marshall became chief of the War Department's War Plans Division in 1938. The Brigadier General was appointed Army Chief of Staff a few months later. In September 1939 he was jumped in rank to full general.

At that post Marshall directed the American military buildup for World War II. Under his command the Army grew from 200,000 to 8.3 million men. He helped train an excellent fighting force, chose outstanding officers, and coordinated the procurement of material necessary for the war effort. An aloof, confident, self-disciplined man, Marshall impressed Allied military leaders with his air of command. He led the opposition to Churchill's Mediterranean strategy, pressing instead for a cross-channel invasion route for the conquest of the Axis powers. His diplomatic ability broke many deadlocks between the Allied leaders. Because President Roosevelt felt him too valuable to leave his post, Marshall did not lead the Normandy invasion. The campaign was headed by his protege, Gen. Dwight D. Eisenhower [*q.v.*]. During late 1944 Marshall was named General of the Army with rank over all other five star military men except Adm. William Leahy. Marshall emerged from the war a hero, representing to many the best in the nation's military tradition. Winston Churchill called him "the true organizer of victory." He retired as Chief in November 1945 at the mandatory age of 65.

On Nov. 27, a week after Marshall left the Army, President Truman asked him to go to China to try to bring peace in the growing civil war between Communists and Nationalists. Although anxious to leave government service, Marshall felt himself duty-bound to comply with the President's request. He was named Truman's special emissary with the personal rank of ambassador. Truman had chosen the General because of his own respect for Marshall, whom he publicly called "the greatest living American." The President thought that Marshall's wartime experience in dealing with military leaders would aid him in negotiations between Mao Tse-tung and Chiang Kai-shek. More importantly, the President believed that Marshall's stature and reputation for objectivity would blunt already growing criticism by the China Lobby that the Administration was willing to "sell out" China to the Communists.

Marshall played a major role in drafting the instructions for his own mission. He was to form a coalition government composed of representatives from all political parties but dominated by the Nationalists. In addition, he was to develop a comprehensive and impartial economic assistance program to aid all of China. Privately, he won Truman's acknowledgement that if unification were impossible, he would have to continue military aid to Chiang. During 1946 Marshall, against difficult odds, worked to assemble the coalition. Each side deeply distrusted the other. The Nationalists refused to accept Communists into the government until Mao disbanded his army. The Communists, in turn, refused to disarm without guarantees of their status in the government. Nevertheless, by late February Marshall had negotiated a truce, set up a date for convening a National Assembly and a council to draft a constitution, and secured agreement from both sides to a plan for integration of their armies.

In March 1946 Marshall returned to Washington to consult with Truman and work out a Chinese aid program with various government agencies. In his absence the shaky accord disintegrated. Conservative Kuomintang elements rejected coalition with the Communists. In addition, when Mao's forces moved into areas of Manchuria abandoned by the Soviet Union, the Nationalists attempted to prevent the takeover. Warning that Chiang was overextending his supply lines, Marshall attempted to stop the offensive and negotiate a truce. His efforts failed. Both Communists and Nationalists stiffened their attitudes, forcing him to conclude that his peace efforts had reached an impasse and that he should be recalled. Truman ended

the mission in January 1947. In his reports Marshall warned that if the U.S. would try to save Chiang it would "virtually [have] to take over the Chinese government. . . . It would involve [the U.S.] in a continuing commitment from which it would practically be impossible to withdraw." Anxious not to become pulled into such a war, the President gradually withdrew American aid, granting only token assistance in response to domestic criticism.

While Marshall was still in China, Truman asked him to accept the post of Secretary of State. Marshall did not desire the prestigious position. He would have preferred retirement. However, he accepted it, as he had the China mission, out of a sense of duty. The Senate, disregarding precedent, unanimously approved the nomination without a hearing on Jan. 8. Marshall became the first military leader to head the State Department.

Most Americans praised Truman's choice, but a few criticized the appointment of a career officer to the senior cabinet post and warned of a trend towards militarism in the conduct of foreign affairs. To these doubters Marshall retorted, "It is not with brass hats but with brass heads that the danger to our country lies." He quickly stopped speculation that he might use his position to run for high elective office, arguing that his cabinet post was not political and assuring the nation that he would not become involved in partisan matters.

Marshall's appointment gave the Administration prestige at a point when its popularity was low and aided Truman's drive for a bipartisan foreign policy. He had immense authority with Congress and received the support of many conservative Republicans who had opposed the Administration's conduct of foreign affairs. The public admired him as a man of integrity and wisdom who stood above politics. Foreign leaders, many of whom he had dealt with during the war, respected him. Marshall quickly developed a close working relationship with Truman, who in the words of historian Alexander

DeConde, "virtually adored him." Truman was so in awe of the man that he never seemed relaxed with Marshall. The President placed such trust in Marshall's judgment that the Secretary later admitted he found it frightening. In the General, Truman found a man of ability and prestige who was deeply loyal even when others deserted him. During 1948, when Truman's popularity was low, Marshall resisted suggestions by his subordinates that he divorce foreign policy from the President. Even though the two men occasionally differed on details of foreign policy, they never quarreled over fundamental issues.

One of Marshall's first tasks as Secretary was the reorganization of the Department to clarify the lines of authority. He developed a structure similar to that of the military with the undersecretary of state acting in effect as a chief of staff. He did not concern himself with the day-to-day workings of the bureaucracy or the details of foreign policy planning. Only major policy questions came to his desk. Most recommendations were made by his undersecretaries, Dean Acheson [q.v.] and later Robert Lovett [q.v.]. Marshall thought his function was to determine broad policy objectives. To advise him, he created a Policy Planning Staff outside the Department hierarchy. Its task was to analyze trends in foreign affairs and make long-term policy suggestions.

The selection of Marshall as Secretary of State signaled a firmer Administration policy toward the Soviet Union. Marshall shared Truman's growing belief that Soviet Communism was a threat to the Western world and that the United States had a responsibility to resist Soviet expansion. Marshall was oriented toward Europe and recommended that the U.S. stop Soviet expansion there before directing attention toward Asia. Endorsing the concept of a bipartisan foreign policy, he criticized the lack of American intensity and unity of purpose to meet the Soviet challenge.

Marshall was away at conferences during much of the time and could not give close attention to molding the Administration's containment policy toward the Soviet Union. Dean Acheson, therefore, played a major role in policy formulation. Nevertheless, Marshall determined broad policy objectives and offered suggestions on specific proposals when he thought necessary. In early 1947, following the British announcement of their withdrawal from Greece and Turkey, Marshall recommended a program of American aid to prevent a Communist takeover in the area. Because he was preparing for the Moscow Conference of foreign ministers, he entrusted the formulation of the plan to Acheson. The Undersecretary proposed a $400 million program of assistance to the two nations. Anxious to win approval of a measure from the conservative dominated Congress, Acheson couched the request in terms of a world crusade against Communism. Marshall opposed the ideological tone and the open-ended American commitment of Acheson's proposal. Nevertheless, on the advice of congressional leaders, Truman overrode him and delivered the speech Acheson had recommended. Despite his opposition to the manner in which the plan was presented, Marshall lobbied for the proposal, which was passed in May.

The Moscow Conference, held in March and April 1947, reinforced Marshall's growing belief that hopes for cooperation with the Soviet Union were useless. At the meeting, called to discuss the future of Germany, the Russians proposed the political centralization of that defeated nation. They asked for Russian participation in the control of the Ruhr and settlement of reparation issues favorable to Moscow. When no compromise could be reached, Marshall, who stressed the importance of Germany in rebuilding Europe, became convinced that the Russians wanted Western Europe reduced to economic and political chaos.

On April 28, two days after his return, Marshall delivered a national broadcast address on the conference. Europe, he said, was not recovering from the war as quickly as expected and would need immediate U.S. aid. "The patient is sinking," he said, "while the doctors deliberate." The following day, working on ideas advanced by planners in the State, War and Navy departments, he asked George F. Kennan [q.v.], head of the Policy Planning Staff, to begin formulation of an aid proposal. Kennan, Acheson, and Undersecretary of State for Economic Affairs William L. Clayton worked through the spring to develop the plan. Kennan recommended a long-term aid program directed primarily by Europeans. Clayton, on the other hand, urged immediate aid under the control of the U.S. Both men insisted that the participation of Germany was vital even though it might make permanent the division of that nation and increase tensions with the USSR. Marshall agreed with Kennan's insistence on European initiative. He also accepted Kennan's recommendation that the Soviet bloc be invited to join the plan despite the risk that the Russians might try to block German economic resurgence with demands for a joint administration of the Ruhr. And he and Kennan agreed on strict controls over Soviet entrance. These controls eventually prevented Russian acceptance of the proposal.

Marshall carefully timed the public announcement of the plan. It must, he insisted, break with "explosive force" to overcome isolationist opposition. "It is easy to propose a great plan," he maintained, "but exceedingly difficult to manage the form and procedure so that it would have a fair chance of political survival." Although many details remained undeveloped, Marshall announced the European Recovery Program (ERP) during a commencement address at Harvard in June of that year. "It is logical that the U.S. should do whatever it is able to do to assist in the return of normal economic health in the world, without which there can be no political stability and no assured peace," he said. "Our policy is directed not against any country or any doctrine but against hunger, poverty, depression and chaos." Marshall then invited the Europeans to draft a joint proposal for economic aid that would "provide a cure

rather than a mere palliative." Europeans responded enthusiastically to the plan, eventually requesting a four-year program of $17 billion in aid.

Marshall's belief that the Soviets intended to wreck European recovery was reinforced during the fall of 1947, when Moscow initiated a propaganda campaign against the ERP, recreated the Cominform and approved Communist-inspired violence in Western Europe. The final breakdown of East-West cooperation came at the London Conference in December 1947. Marshall was weary of continued Russian demands for German reparations, abolition of the joint British-American sectors called Bizonia in western Germany and participation in the occupation of the Ruhr. He, therefore, abruptly asked for adjournment of the meeting. No plans were made to call another one.

During the first half of 1948, Marshall worked for the passage of the ERP. He encountered intense opposition from a hostile Congress dominated by Republicans unwilling to give the Administration a major diplomatic triumph during the election year and reluctant to grant large amounts of foreign aid. With the help of Sen. Arthur Vandenberg (R, Mich.) [q.v.], Marshall gradually gained acceptance of the proposal. An effective witness before committees and an excellent impromptu speaker, he convinced Congress of the need for the plan. His reputation as a nonpartisan also helped the proposal on Capitol Hill. Marshall explained that an economically stable Western Europe would correct adverse socio-economic conditions that had served to breed Communism. To congressmen fearful that German participation might lead to a return of militarism, he pointed out that the plan contained controls to insure use of German natural resources and industrial capabilities solely for Europe's economic rehabilitation. Marshall disagreed with those who warned that the program would be a drain on the U.S. economy. Rather, he maintained that a revitalized Western Europe would stimulate U.S.

production and trade. He expressed concern over continued Russian expansion westward, fearing the collapse of Western civilization if Soviet aggrandizement were not checked. Marshall rejected Sen. William Fulbright's (D, Ark.) [q.v.] suggestions that the European nations be required to create a continental federation before becoming eligible for aid. Although he hoped that economic integration might eventually lead to political unity, Marshall counseled caution. He noted that European nationalism might prove an insurmountable obstacle. Forcing the issue might bring accusations of American imperialism. By the spring of 1948 Marshall had convinced a majority in Congress to back his plan. Events in Europe coalesced support. The Communist coup in Czechoslovakia during February convinced many of the need to take action on the proposal. Congress passed the Marshall Plan in March.

Because of his respect for the man, Truman rarely acted against Marshall's advice. One of the few times he did so concerned the division of Palestine and the recognition of Israel. The President favored partitioning Palestine between Jews and Arabs. Marshall, on the other hand, opposed immediate although not ultimate independence for Israel. Influenced by State Department advisers, including the Policy Planning Staff, he warned the President that Israel would be too weak militarily to fight the war that would surely break out upon independence. The U.S. might, therefore, be forced to protect the fledgling nation. Marshall also observed that recognition would alienate the Arab states, which had important oil reserves.

By March 1948 he had convinced Truman to acquiesce to the continuation of trusteeship status in the area if negotiations over partition failed. However, in early May, days before the British mandate terminated and the Jews declared independence, Truman reversed himself. On the advice of Clark Clifford [q.v.], who warned the President that he would need the Jewish vote in the November election, Truman came out for immediate recognition. After a meeting with Marshall on May 12, he resumed his support for the Secretary's position. He told Clifford that he wanted recognition but not immediately. Clifford persuaded Truman to reconsider, and just minutes before Israel declared independence on May 14, the President granted recognition.

Marshall successfully clashed with Truman's political advisers over the handling of the Soviet blockade of Berlin in June 1948. He rejected the suggestion of such military leaders as Gen. Lucius Clay [q.v.] that the U.S. force entrance into Berlin with armed convoys. Marshall convinced Truman to support an airlift to supply the beleaguered city. As fear of war increased and criticism of the President's handling of foreign policy mounted during the election year, Truman's policy advisers urged him to take dramatic action on Berlin to gain support. They were concerned that the public considered Marshall the dominant force in foreign affairs. Marshall, one of Truman's advisers said, was always associated with diplomatic victories, Truman with defeats. They suggested that Truman send Chief Justice Fred Vinson to Moscow to conduct direct talks with Stalin on Berlin. Truman agreed. Marshall, however, opposed the mission, arguing that it would undercut negotiations on the issue at the U.N. Truman cancelled the mission. His advisers tried to convince him that the Secretary did not understand the political importance of the move but the President refused to ignore Marshall's advice.

Although Marshall focused much of his attention on Europe, he played a major role in developing policies toward other areas. His actions were shaped, in part, by the growing Cold War. Marshall pushed for the unification of the armed services and the establishment of an agency to coordinate military and foreign policy. Some of his suggestions were incorporated into the National Security Act of 1947, which created the National Security Council. The body was composed of the President and the Secretaries of State, Defense, Army, Navy and Air Force. It was to advise and coordinate defense and foreign policy. Marshall advocated universal military training to expand the Army, thus increasing its effectiveness as a diplomatic weapon. He also championed rearming Western Europe to bolster the region against potential Soviet aggression. Just one month after becoming Secretary of State, Marshall had spoken in favor of international control of atomic energy and supported the Baruch Plan, which called for U.N. control and inspection of atomic sites. When it became apparent in 1948 that the Russians had no interest in atomic controls, Marshall expressed no reservations about increasing U.S. experimentation with atomic weapons and cautioned against unilateral atomic disarmament.

Marshall had little interest in Latin America, and according to one critic, during his tenure Latin American affairs temporarily fell in eclipse. He did, however, initiate a series of alliances designed to prevent Communist expansion in the area. In 1948 he persuaded the Latin American nations to join together in the Rio Pact. The treaty stipulated that an attack against any hemispheric nation would be considered an attack against all but that members would not be required to use their armed forces without their consent. It also defined the Pact's security zone to include all the Americas. The following year Marshall helped formulate the Pact of Bogota, establishing the Organization of American States. The meeting reaffirmed the principle that an attack against one member was aggression against all.

While the political and military needs of the hemisphere were central to Marshall's thinking, the economic problems resulting in part from the end of the war received only verbal attention. American wartime investment contributed to the Latin American economic boom, which abruptly ended after the armistice. By 1947 Latin American political leaders were seeking U.S. economic assistance. Speaking for the Administration in 1947 at the Rio Conference, Marshall explained that Europe, being "threatened with starvation and economic chaos" must receive attention first, and he predicted that European rehabilitation would contribute to "the economy of this hemisphere." At the 1948 Bogota meeting, Marshall asked for Latin Americans to understand that the U.S. alone was carrying almost the entire burden of world recovery and reiterated a promise for future economic aid.

During his tenure Marshall began discussions on the formation of a North Atlantic alliance, which he thought necessary in light of Soviet intransigence at the U.N. and Russian conduct in Europe. The result was the Brussels Pact, a 50-year mutual defense agreement signed in March 1948 by Britain, France and the Benelux countries. Although Marshall advocated supplying American arms and reviving lend-lease to assist in meeting the alliance's military needs, Congress refused funding. In the spring of 1948 he held secret meetings with Sens. Henry Cabot Lodge (R, Mass.) [q.v.] and Arthur Vandenberg on possible U.S. involvement in a European defense pact. The result of these conversations was Senate Resolution 239, which supported the principle of U.S. participation in regional collective arrangements. Throughout the summer and fall of 1948, at Marshall's direction, Robert Lovett held secret talks with Brussels Pact representatives over U.S. involvement in the organization. The result was the North Atlantic Treaty signed in 1949, after Marshall had left office.

As Secretary of State, Marshall was careful to avoid increasing U.S. involvement in the Chinese civil war. He made no policy statements on China and resisted demands from the powerful China Lobby to increase aid to Chiang, fearing that such a commitment would jeopardize the U.S. position in Europe. Neither Truman nor Marshall believed that increased aid would save Chiang. Marshall had told the Chinese leader that "the fundamental and lasting solution to China's problems must come from the Chinese themselves."

Nevertheless, Marshall was forced to make some concessions to right-wing pressure. In July 1947 he sent Gen. Albert Wedemeyer to China to investigate the situation and to make policy recommendations. Wedemeyer's report suggested increasing aid to the Nationalist regime. Believing the General's assessment inadequate and impractical, Marshall urged the report's suppression. Truman agreed. Nevertheless, during the debate on the European Recovery Program, the Administration, seeking to placate critics, asked for a slight increase in aid to China. At the same time Marshall abandoned advocacy of a coalition government although he would not acquiesce to Republican calls for intervention in the war.

Despite Republican opposition to the Administration's China policy, Marshall escaped personal criticism while at the State Department. Conservatives vigorously attacked Truman and other high officials in the Department. Vandenberg, while denouncing Administration policy, refused to say anything that reflected on Marshall's personal role. He merely stated that he thought Marshall was "somewhat misled by the boys on the Far East desk." However, after China fell to the Communists in 1949, Republican conservatives pointed to Marshall as one of those responsible for Mao's victory. Sen. William Jenner (R, Ind.) [q.v.] described him as "either an unsuspecting stooge or an actual co-conspirator with the most treasonable array of political cut-throats ever turned loose in the executive branch of government."

The stress of his position and the continual round of conferences eventually undermined Marshall's health. He underwent a kidney operation in December 1947 and resigned one month later. In order to keep Marshall close to the Administration, Truman arranged Marshall's appointment as head of the American Red Cross. Marshall crisscrossed the country promoting the agency and investigating

its extensive bureaucracy.

In July 1950, while vacationing in Michigan, Marshall received a call from Truman asking him to become Secretary of Defense. Once again out of a sense of duty Marshall agreed. Truman again turned to Marshall during a period of crisis. The Administration was under extreme criticism for its handling of the Korean conflict. Morale in the Army was low. Military strength had not reached the numbers needed, many units were staffed by poorly trained draftees, and soldiers were fighting with antiquated weapons which were in short supply. Officers decried the limited defense budgets of the late 1940s and the lack of coordination between military plans and foreign policy. Many, most notably Gen. Douglas MacArthur [q.v.], bridled against carrying on a limited war.

Marshall's appointment lifted morale in the Department. He was a symbol of past military victory, of stability and of achievement. As he had done in the State Department, the new Secretary reorganized the Pentagon, forming the same kind of hierarchical structure he had utilized before. He gradually eased out many political appointees and brought in such experienced men as Robert Lovett with whom he had established a good working relationship. Marshall also reopened communications between the State and Defense departments at the lower levels to coordinate policy.

Marshall's immediate task was to rebuild America's military posture. He thought it useless to rely exclusively on atomic weapons. Ground troops, he believed, were the deciding element in any conflict. In 1950 he asked Congress to place 2.7 million men under arms by June 1951 and requested a $6.5 billion military program to meet the needs of his Department. He continued to advocate universal military training, which Congress approved in June 1951.

Marshall supported the Administration's limited war policy in Korea, although shortly after MacArthur's successful invasion at Inchon in September 1950, he wavered. On Oct. 1, in one of his first acts as Secretary, he cabled MacArthur to "let action determine the matter." Nevertheless, he ultimately backed Truman's decision to repel the Communist invasion of South Korea and not extend the war into China. His stand was consistent with the "Europe first" policy he had advocated while Secretary of State.

Following Communist Chinese intervention in Korea in late 1951, MacArthur called for the bombing of Communist sanctuaries in Manchuria and the "unleashing" of Chiang Kai-shek's Nationalist troops against mainland China. MacArthur reasoned that the defeat of Asian Communism would persuade the Soviets to abandon their European ambitions. Marshall and the Administration disagreed. They maintained that Chiang's small force offered little promise of success, while expansion of the war increased possibilities of Russian intervention and left Western Europe vulnerable to attack.

By the spring of 1951 MacArthur's policy disagreements with the Administration had become public. The General openly criticized Truman's decision to fight a limited war and, in essence, challenged the President's position as spokesman on foreign policy. With Marshall's approval Truman relieved MacArthur of his command in April 1951. The nation was shocked by the action. Although the Joint Chiefs of Staff had also supported the action, critics contended that the firing was a result of a feud between Marshall and MacArthur that could be traced back 40 years. In May 1951 Marshall testified at congressional hearings on the dismissal. Through almost a week of questioning, he reiterated the theme that MacArthur had been called home for publicly disagreeing with the foreign and military policy of the U.S. Marshall's explanation quieted most congressional criticism. However, the Republican right vigorously attacked him and the Administration for the failure of policy in Asia. Sen. Joseph R. McCarthy (R, Wisc.) was the most vociferous of these critics. He alleged that Truman,

Marshall and Acheson had permitted the fall of China to the Communists and had tolerated known Communists in the State Department. He also implied that Marshall and Truman should be impeached. Congress ignored his advice.

In September 1951 Marshall retired to Leesburg, Va. He spurned a lucrative offer to write his memoirs. In 1953 President Eisenhower gave Marshall the honor of representing the U.S. at the coronation of England's Queen Elizabeth II. That same year he won the Nobel Peace Prize for having developed the European Recovery Plan. Marshall took no part in foreign or defense affairs during the 1950s. He received, however, the brunt of criticism from the China Lobby and right-wing Republicans who accused him of harboring Communists in government. He died in Washington D.C. in October 1959.

[EWS]

For further information:
Dean Acheson, *Present at the Creation* (New York, 1969).
Stephen E. Ambrose, *Rise to Globalism* (New York, 1971).
Robert H. Ferrell, *George C. Marshall* (New York, 1966).
Norman Graebner, *Uncertain Tradition: American Secretaries of State in the Twentieth Century* (New York, 1961).

McCARTHY, EUGENE J(OSEPH)
b. March 29, 1916; Watkins, Minn.
Democratic Senator, Minn., 1959-71.

Eugene McCarthy rose to unexpected prominence in the late 1960s as the foremost critic of President Johnson's Vietnam policy. The early successes of his unorthodox campaign for the presidency in 1968 helped drive Johnson from office and brought a corps of idealistic young volunteers from the anti-war movement into the Democratic Party, where they had a significant impact on American politics.

In the 13 years following his graduation from St. John's University in Minnesota in 1935, McCarthy taught economics and sociology at Catholic high schools and colleges. He also spent nine months in a monastery as a Benedictine novice in 1942 and 1943. McCarthy was teaching sociology at St. Thomas College in St. Paul when he first entered politics as a supporter of Hubert Humphrey's fight against the Communist-led wing of Minnesota's Democratic Farmer-Labor Party (DFL). After leading a successful drive to take control of the DFL in St. Paul and Ramsey County, McCarthy won election to the House of Representatives in 1948.

He was elected to the Senate in 1958 and in 1964 his assignment to the seat on the Foreign Relations Committee vacated by Humphrey gave him the long-desired opportunity to have a greater voice in the making of foreign policy. McCarthy stood out as a critic of U.S. policy in several important areas. Long an advocate of closer congressional oversight of U.S. intelligence agencies, he called for a "full and complete investigation" of the Central Intelligence Agency (CIA) in November 1965. "The role of the CIA in the Dominican Republic, Vietnam, Cuba and a number of other critical areas has raised serious questions about the relationship of the Agency to the process of making and directing foreign policy," he said, adding that there was some evidence that the CIA had gone beyond its statutory purpose of collecting and evaluating intelligence.

McCarthy was also a veteran critic of the large volume of U.S. arms sales to undeveloped nations. He charged that such sales undermined other foreign policy goals, such as peace and disarmament, exacerbated world tensions and led to the dangerous militarization of the Third World. Criticizing the Pentagon's effort to promote sales of U.S. weapons abroad, he warned in January 1967 that "we may be subsidizing weapons manufacturers to a dangerous and undesirable extent."

Through his opposition to the Vietnam war, McCarthy exerted a profound and dramatic impact on the course of American foreign policy. He was not an early dissenter, having voted for the Gulf of Tonkin Resolution in August 1964 and avoided any public criticism of Johnson's war policy until January 1966. At that time he joined 14 other senators in sending a letter to the President calling for continued suspension of air strikes against North Vietnam. The bombing, which had been halted during the holiday truce period, was resumed on Jan. 31. McCarthy maintained that the bombing had not had a "beneficial political or diplomatic effect" in the past. He suggested that the war in Vietnam called for "a national debate . . . and a real searching of the mind and the soul of America."

Whatever his private doubts about U.S. policy, McCarthy remained mild and hesitant in his dissent throughout 1966. In March he said, "I think that the kind of escalation we now have, in which we're sending in more troops, is defensible on the part of the Administration," while "bombing civilian areas in North Vietnam" is a "change of substance" and "should be challenged." McCarthy indicated in May that the U.S. should stay in South Vietnam even if a newly elected government opposed the American presence.

In early 1967 McCarthy became more vocal in his opposition. "We should hesitate to waste our strength—economic, military, and moral—in so highly questionable a course," he said on Feb. 25. Three days later he told a student audience that the war was "morally unjustifiable." In April he criticized President Johnson's use of Gen. William Westmoreland as a spokesman for his Vietnam policy as a "dangerous practice" and an "escalation of language, method and emotions." He was particularly upset by Undersecretary of State Nicholas Katzenbach's August 1967 defense of the Johnson Administration's broad interpretation of the Gulf of Tonkin Resolution and Katzenbach's dismissal of the lack of a congressional declaration of war in Vietnam as a matter of "outmoded phraseology." An angry McCarthy was quoted by a *New York Times* reporter as saying, "This is the wildest testimony I have ever heard. There is no limit to what he says the President can do. There is only one thing to do—take it to the country." In October

McCarthy published *The Limits of Power*, a strong critique of U.S. foreign policy.

After persistent urging by anti-war liberals, McCarthy announced on Nov. 30 that he was running for the Democratic presidential nomination in order to further the campaign for a negotiated settlement of the war. "I am concerned," he declared, "that the Administration seems to have set no limit to the price which it's willing to pay for a military victory." He also voiced his hope that his campaign might alleviate "this sense of political helplessness and restore to many people a belief in the processes of American politics."

Dismissed by many as a futile and quixotic venture, McCarthy's New Hampshire primary campaign slowly gained momentum and climaxed in a strong showing in the state's primary. As a result, Sen. Robert Kennedy (D, N.Y.) declared his own candidacy two days later and President Johnson announced that he would not seek reelection several weeks later. McCarthy's campaign, however, was soon overshadowed by Kennedy's and Vice-President Hubert Humphrey's. At the Democratic convention in Chicago, McCarthy was easily defeated by Humphrey.

McCarthy unexpectedly resigned from the Foreign Relations Committee in 1969 and retired from the Senate in 1971. He made lackluster runs for the presidency in 1972 and 1976, but he never ignited the enthusiasm he had fired in 1968, partly because of his occasional indifference and enigmatic behavior. Even while he personally was attracting little support, however, national party politics revealed the far-reaching effects of the movement he had crystalized: the reform of Democratic Party procedures, the introduction of thousands of young people as a potent factor in electoral politics, and eventually the ending of the Vietnam war.

[TO]

For further information:
Albert Eisele, *Almost to the Presidency: A Biography of Two American Politicians* (Blue Earth, Minn., 1972).
Eugene McCarthy, *The Year of the People* (New York, 1969).

McCLOY, JOHN J(AY)
b. March 31, 1895; Philadelphia, Pa.
Assistant Secretary of War, April 1941-November 1945; President, International Bank for Reconstruction and Development, March 1947-May 1949; Military Governor for Germany, May 1949-June 1949; High Commissioner for Germany, June 1949-August 1952; Presidential Disarmament Adviser, January 1961-October 1961; Director, U.S. Arms Control and Disarmament Agency, September 1961-October 1961.

McCloy graduated from Amherst College in 1916 and entered Harvard Law School. He left in May 1917, after the U.S. entered World War I, to enlist in the Army. McCloy returned to Harvard two years later and, upon graduating in 1921, practiced law in New York City. His work took him to Europe frequently, and between 1930 and 1931, he headed Craveth, DeGersdorff, Swaine & Wood's Paris office. Between 1930 and 1939 he was associated with the famous Black Tom Case, involving a 1916 explosion at a munitions plant in New Jersey. McCloy's investigation helped establish that German secret agents had sabotaged the factory. His work in this case gave him an expert knowledge of German espionage techniques and brought him to the attention of Secretary of War Henry L. Stimson. Stimson appointed him a consultant on counterespionage in October 1940. In December he promoted McCloy to special assistant to the Secretary and five months later made the lawyer assistant secretary of war. Over the next four years McCloy played an important role in the development of lend-lease, the internment of Japanese Americans, and the establishment of the Nisei units in the Army. He was also one of the few members in the Administration to know of the existence of the atomic bomb and the plans for its use before it was actually dropped on Hiroshima.

During World War II McCloy was deeply involved in the debate over policy toward Germany after the victory had been achieved. He and his colleagues in the War Department anticipated a brief period of military government followed by a civilian controlled occupation. They found the prospect of prolonged military government distasteful because of the inability of the Army to deal with the economic and social problems of postwar Germany. The war had brought glory to the military. Its leaders did not want to risk this prestige in an operation for which none had a background.

Despite this sense of its own limitations, the War Department did not want any civilian interference during the period of military government. McCloy effectively blocked all attempts by the State Department and other civilian agencies to develop long-range policies for the occupation. He received passive support from the White House. As a consequence, when the German government began to disintegrate in late 1944, the only issue that had been settled was the delineation of Allied zones.

After the war McCloy and the War Department joined the State Department in opposing Secretary of the Treasury Henry Morgenthau's plan for the "pastoralization" of Germany. Between September 1944 and May 1945 McCloy, representing the Army, negotiated with various members of the Treasury and State departments on the character of the military occupation. He ultimately agreed to a restricted form of the Morgenthau plan. The Army was to take no role in bolstering the German economy; that task was to be left to the Germans. It was to do all it could to arrest former Nazis. No Nazi was to remain in any government position, and the German military establishment was to be disbanded. Other than these provisions, the Army was directed not to become involved in German political affairs although it was to administer the territory "with a view to political decentralization." The agreement limited the Army's liability, as McCloy, Stimson and the military wanted. However, it virtually insured economic and political chaos in Germany. As the Cold War developed this policy was gradually abandoned. Working closely with McCloy Gen. Lucius Clay [q.v.], the military governor carried out policies designed to revive the German economy and rebuild its industrial base.

During the same period McCloy participated in the formulation of policies toward Latin America, Europe and the Far East. In May 1945, in conjunction with Stimson, he pursued sanctions within the U.N. Charter allowing mutual security groups. These provisions were designed, in part, to protect American "preclusive rights" in the Western Hemisphere. The following month he took part in discussions leading to establishment of the 38th Parallel as the line delineating Communist controlled North Korea from the South.

In May 1949 Truman appointed McCloy military governor and U.S. high Commissioner for Germany. McCloy took an active role in the negotiations between Germany and France that led to the adoption of the Schuman Plan and to the formation of the European Coal and Steel Community. The Germans had resisted proposals to prohibit a steel producer from owning coal mines that supplied more than 75% of his coal requirements. McCloy broke this impasse by threatening to reclaim supervision of decartelization and impose even stricter measures against German industrial combinations. His implied threat of continued international occupation of the Ruhr gave the Germans another powerful incentive to come to terms. Upon concluding the agreement, both the Germans and French praised McCloy's role as mediator. During the same period he acted as mediator in talks on the establishment of a European defense force.

McCloy proved himself an attentive politician during his service in Germany. He paid little attention to the administrative aspects of occupation and spent most of his time with German political leaders. McCloy worked with both the Christian Democrats and the Social Democrats, although he seemed to favor the more conservative Christian Democrats if only because their leader, Conrad Adenauer, was the head of the new German government.

McCloy returned to private life in 1951 and served as director of a number of major corporations during the 1950s. But he also remained active in politics and advised President Eisenhower on arms control strategies and served as chairman of the Ford Foundation and the Council of Foreign Relations. In fact, the journalist Richard Rovere wryly referred to McCloy as the "chairman of the Establishment."

In January 1961 President-elect Kennedy appointed McCloy, a Republican, his principal disarmament adviser and negotiator. While at that post McCloy drafted the bill that led to the establishment of the U.S. Arms Control and Disarmament Agency in September 1961. The Agency was designed to coordinate government policy on disarmament and nuclear testing free from the influence of other federal bodies.

McCloy's primary responsibility during 1961 was to negotiate conditions under which the stalemated East-West disarmament talks could resume. Working through the summer of 1961, he finally got the Soviet Union to agree to a declaration of principles to govern formal negotiations. This agreement was submitted to the U.N. in September. However, the ensuing disarmament discussions proved futile. In October McCloy resigned his post, terming his diplomatic activity "the most discouraging exercise in disarmament negotiations" since World War II. Six months later he was appointed to the General Advisory Committee of the U.S. Arms Control and Disarmament Agency.

Following President Kennedy's October 1962 announcement of a Cuban blockade to force the removal of Soviet missiles from that island, McCloy was asked to take part in U.N. negotiations on the terms of inspection for the weapons' removal. Kennedy, anxious to have bipartisan support for his policy and fearing that U.N. Ambassador Adlai Stevenson [q.v.] would be too conciliatory, wished the tough-minded Republican to be part of the three-man team pressing American demands for the withdrawal of both Soviet missiles and bombers under supervised conditions. The talks proved unproductive and the question of inspection was solved only in December, when Nikita Khrushchev agreed to remove the missiles and bombers and permit aerial observation and counting of the weapons as they left.

In 1968 McCloy became a member of the Senior Advisory Group on Vietnam, convened to consider the military's request that over 200,000 additional troops be sent to Vietnam. During the committee's meetings McCloy was among those men, along with Henry Cabot Lodge [q.v.], Arthur Dean and Gen. Omar Bradley, who were dissatisfied with the existing policy but were reluctant to declare for a dramatic change. Nevertheless, the majority of the group recommended rejection of the troop buildup request and the de-escalation of the war. Johnson announced this policy on March 31, 1968.

Despite his advanced years and the fact that he held no official public posts under the Nixon and Ford administrations, McCloy maintained an intensive activity at the highest levels of business and government, particularly as the legal representative of the major U.S. oil producers. Much of McCloy's behind-the-scenes activity became known through his 1974 testimony before the Church committee investigation of the oil crisis. McCloy told the committee that since 1961 he had been regularly advising U.S. presidents on how to confront the growing power of the Organization of Petroleum Exporting Countries (OPEC), which was founded in 1960. More importantly, from 1961 to 1971, McCloy had been the legal representative of U.S. oil companies in dealings with the U.S. Department of Justice over antitrust questions. McCloy felt that U.S. antitrust laws were a useless obstacle to a united front of U.S. oil majors against OPEC. McCloy's lobbying efforts to gain acceptance for joint company actions, however, came to naught.

At his 1974 Senate committee testimony, McCloy argued that the U.S. had been "living in a sort of fool's paradise" where oil was concerned. Referring to the massive public criticism of the U.S. oil companies after October 1973, and the calls for the very antitrust actions he had worked to avoid, McCloy said that "it seems that it is only in the United States that an almost masochistic attack on the position of its own oil companies persists."

In 1978 McCloy was an author of an American Bar Association report on the oil crisis. He also remained active as a director of the Olin Foundation, a private firm with a significant impact on major policy questions.

[LG]

For further information:
Anthony Sampson, *The Seven Sisters* (New York, 1975).

McCONE, JOHN A(LEX)
b. Jan. 4, 1902; San Francisco, Calif.
Director of Central Intelligence,
November 1961-April 1965.

John McCone was born into a prosperous San Francisco family. He graduated from the University of California in 1922 and over the next 25 years amassed a fortune in the steel and shipbuilding industries. During the Truman Administration McCone held several high posts in the Defense Department, where he helped James Forrestal in the creation of the Central Intelligence Agency (CIA). From 1958 to 1961 he served as chairman of the Atomic Energy Commission.

In September 1961 President Kennedy appointed McCone director of the CIA to succeed Allen Dulles [*q.v.*], who had retired following the abortive Bay of Pigs invasion. Kennedy chose the conservative Republican not only because of his reputation as a good manager but also because the President felt vulnerable to an attack from the conservative wing of the Republican Party following the Bay of Pigs fiasco. McCone's appointment was intended to quiet these critics and ensure approval of future CIA actions on Capitol Hill. However, liberals within the Administration were appalled by the choice and were convinced that McCone's reporting would reflect a right-wing bias.

McCone proved himself an able administrator even in the eyes of such liberals as Roger Hilsman. Reversing his predecessor's stand, McCone did not try to make the Agency dominant in foreign policy formation and instead worked to repair relations with the State Department and Congress. He also succeeded in improving Agency morale, which was low following the Cuban invasion.

Although conservative on many issues, McCone did not let his personal attitudes bias intelligence estimates. He was not, however, above using his official position to further his views outside the Agency. According to David Halberstam, McCone secretly opposed the nuclear test ban treaty of 1963 and lent CIA atomic energy experts to conservative Sen. John Stennis (D, Miss.) to help him make a case against the agreement. In public, however, the Director testified in favor of the treaty, which was ratified by the Senate in September 1963.

McCone became one of Kennedy's advisers during the 1962 Cuban missile crisis. As early as August 1962 he had received reports that Soviet anti-aircraft missiles were being introduced into Cuba and had ordered intelligence flights over the island stepped up. On Aug. 22 McCone told the President that he believed the USSR was installing offensive missiles on the island. Kennedy, however, dismissed this warning as the fears of an overzealous anti-Communist.

Having voiced his suspicions McCone, who had just remarried, left on a wedding trip to Europe. During his absence several U-2 spy planes strayed or were shot down over Russia and China. Consequently, flights over western Cuba were stopped to reduce the probability of loss and a resulting public outcry. While in Europe and after his return, McCone lobbied for resumption of the overflights. They were finally resumed on Oct. 4. Ten days later flights over western Cuba revealed the presence of offensive missiles.

In the policy debate that followed this revelation, McCone was a member of Excom, the special group formed to advise the President and gain bipartisan support for Administration action. In conjunction with Paul Nitze [q.v.], Dean Acheson [q.v.] and the Joint Chiefs, McCone recommended the use of air strikes to remove the missiles, but Kennedy rejected the idea and instead instituted a "quarantine" of Cuba on Oct. 23.

As the U.S. became increasingly involved in Vietnam, a larger portion of McCone's time was devoted to activities in that country. In the policy meetings that followed the Diem regime's crackdown on Buddhists in August 1963, McCone was among the Kennedy advisers who cautioned against support of a coup. Instead he suggested that the U.S. maintain Diem but insist on reforms. This policy was carried out while conditions were established that would permit a successful coup without direct American intervention.

In 1974 and 1975 a Senate investigation revealed that while McCone was head of the CIA the Agency had carried on the illegal surveillance of over 10,000 American citizens and had made several unsuccessful attempts to assassinate foreign leaders, including Patrice Lumumba and Fidel Castro. Because the system of executive command and control was purposely ambiguous to permit "plausible denial," McCone's exact role in these plots remained undetermined. In 1975 hearings before the Senate Select Committee on Intelligence, McCone testified that he had not been aware of the efforts and had not authorized plots against the Cuban dictator. The Committee report attributed the assassination attempts to vague orders that were subject to differing interpretations by the subordinates responsible for carrying them out.

As Johnson's chief intelligence officer, McCone became increasingly involved in Vietnam policymaking. Although personally hawkish on the war, McCone was fair in presenting the views of more dovish experts in the Agency. McCone was reportedly one of the few high Administration officials willing to give Johnson unbiased, often pessimistic reports on the progress of the war. During the debate on the possible intro-

duction of combat forces in Vietnam in the spring of 1965, McCone cautioned against the move unless it was accompanied by an expansion of bombing in the North. He believed that the war could not be won in the South. The U.S. could achieve victory only by inflicting such serious injury on North Vietnam that it would be forced to negotiate. Therefore, McCone said, the number of bombing raids would have to be vastly increased and targets expanded to include airfields, power stations and military compounds. McCone's advice went unheeded. U.S. Marines began offensive operations in April. Although raids were increased during May and June, they did not reach the high levels advocated by the Director.

In April 1965 McCone resigned as director of the CIA because Johnson did not support his efforts to centralize intelligence operations and returned to private business.

[EWS]

For further information:
David Halberstam, *The Best and the Brightest* (New York, 1972).
U.S. Senate Select Committee on Intelligence Activities, *Alleged Assassination Plots Involving Foreign Leaders* (Washington, 1975).
———, *Foreign and Military Intelligence* (Washington, 1976).
———, *Intelligence Activities and the Rights of Americans* (Washington, 1976).
David Wise and Thomas B. Ross, *The Invisible Government* (New York, 1964).

McGOVERN, GEORGE S(TANLEY)
b. July 19, 1922; Avon, S.D.
Democratic Senator, S.D. 1963-.
Democratic Presidential Nominee, 1972.

The son of a Methodist minister, George McGovern attended Dakota Wesleyan University and served in the Army Air Corps during World War II. He received his doctorate at Northwestern University in 1953, while also teaching at Dakota Wesleyan from 1949 to 1953. He resigned his professorship to become executive secretary of the Democratic Party in South Dakota and built it into a viable statewide organization. McGovern was elected to the House of Representatives in 1956 and in his two terms established a reputation as a liberal. In 1960 he unsuccessfully challenged Republican incumbent Karl Mundt for a Senate seat.

In January 1961 President John F. Kennedy appointed McGovern director of the newly created Food for Peace program. McGovern worked to develop the program as a humanitarian instrument of U.S. foreign policy. He resigned in July 1962 to run for the Senate once again and won a narrow victory becoming South Dakota's first Democratic Senator in 26 years.

McGovern's maiden Senate speech in March 1963 was a critique of U.S. Latin American policy, and he continued throughout the decade to denounce what he considered the militaristic bent of U.S. foreign policy and the burgeoning defense budget. He regularly voted to reduce defense appropriations and opposed much of the Pentagon's expensive new weaponry, including the Air Force's advanced manned bomber and the anti-ballistic missile system. He also sought to reduce military assistance to foreign countries.

McGovern was most conspicuous as an early, outspoken foe of the Vietnam war. He first criticized U.S. involvement in September 1963, although he did vote for the Gulf of Tonkin resolution the following August. (The next day he inserted some second thoughts in the *Congressional Record*: "I do not want my vote for the resolution to be interpreted as an endorsement for our long-standing and apparently growing military involvement in Vietnam.") In January 1965 he called the war "a South Vietnamese problem . . . not basically a military problem but a political one." He proposed a negotiated solution, leading to gradual withdrawal of U.S. troops and the neutralization of Vietnam protected by a U.N. presence. He visited Vietnam in November

1965 and returned to call for a bombing halt and recognition of the National Liberation Front. In April 1967 he castigated U.S. policymakers for "distorting history to justify our intervention" and "backing a dictatorial group in Saigon against a competing group backed by a dictatorial group in the North."

McGovern immediately became an outspoken critic of Nixon Administration policies. He opposed deployment of the Safeguard anti-ballistic missile (ABM) and was one of only nine Senators in November 1969 who voted against a military appropriations bill that included funding for the ABM. While other Democratic critics were willing to give Nixon a chance to develop his own policy, McGovern attacked him as early as March 1969 for persisting in the "tragic course" set by Johnson. When Nixon announced in June 1969 his first troop withdrawals, McGovern labeled the action "tokenism." In July McGovern revealed that he had conferred with North Vietnamese and Vietcong representatives in Paris during May and that they had specified a commitment to "unconditional" withdrawal of all U.S. troops as essential for a peace agreement. McGovern called for a unilateral 30-day ceasefire by the United States.

In October he spoke before the Vietnam Moratorium rally in Boston and the following month addressed a massive antiwar demonstration in Washington, D.C. During Senate Foreign Relations Committee hearings in February 1970 on the war, McGovern called Vietnamization a "political hoax" designed to "tranquilize the conscience of the American people while our government wages a cruel and needless war by proxy."

After the invasion of Cambodia by U.S. troops in April 1970, McGovern joined in legislative efforts to mandate an end to the war. In June he voted for the Cooper-Church Amendment to cut off funds for U.S. operations in Cambodia. In July he cosponsored legislation to end the draft and to establish an all-volunteer army. With Sen. Mark Hatfield (R. Ore.) he introduced an "end-the-war" amendment to a military appropriations bill that would have legislated the withdrawal of all U.S. combat troops from Southeast Asia by the end of 1971. After heated debate the Senate rejected the amendment on Sept. 1 by a vote of 55–39. Although the vote was interpreted by many as an Administration victory, McGovern thought otherwise. "It is remarkable," he said, "that for the first time in history more than one-third of the U.S. Senate has voted to cut off funds for a war while we are still in battle." In January 1971 he and Sen. Hatfield reintroduced the "end-the-war" legislation, but in June the Senate again rejected it. McGovern participated in the Senate filibuster to block extension of the Selective Service Act and voted against the bill in September.

In 1971 McGovern also launched his successful campaign for the Democratic presidential nomination. His major themes were an immediate end of the Vietnam war and a major shift of government spending from defense to anti-poverty programs. Thanks to these two themes, McGovern won the nomination of his party the following year, but was decisively defeated by President Nixon in the November election.

Following his presidential defeat, Mc-Govern took a leading role in urging the normalization of relations with Cuba. After visiting the island in May 1975 at the invitation of Fidel Castro, McGovern called for an immediate end to the U.S. trade embargo. In August McGovern praised the Ford Administration's decision to allow foreign subsidiaries of U.S. firms to trade with the Castro regime. McGovern visited Cuba a second time in April 1977.

Initially a supporter of Arizona Rep. Morris Udall's candidacy for the 1976 presidential nomination, McGovern switched to Jimmy Carter in June 1976. However after the election he attacked the "Republican economics" of the Carter Administration in May 1977, and the following year was vocal in his criticism of Carter's proposed cuts in domestic social welfare programs in order to expand the defense budget.

[JD]

For further information:
George Stanley McGovern, *Grassroots: The Autobiography of George McGovern* (New York, 1977).
Robert Sam Anson, *McGovern: a Biography* (New York, 1972).

McNAMARA, ROBERT S(TRANGE)
b. June 9, 1916; San Francisco, Calif.
Secretary of Defense, January 1961-February 1968.

Robert S. McNamara, Secretary of Defense under Presidents Kennedy and Johnson, was one of the most controversial cabinet members of the postwar era. During the Kennedy years he won recognition for his efforts to bring the armed forces under strong civilian control. Under President Johnson he became a leading architect of American strategy in Vietnam.

McNamara, son of the sales manager of a wholesale shoe business, was raised in a middle-class section of Oakland. From grammar school to the University of California, Berkeley, to the Harvard Business School, McNamara was an outstanding student. After taking his M.B.A. in 1939, McNamara worked briefly for a San Francisco accounting firm. The next year he returned to Harvard to accept a teaching post in the business school.

McNamara was rejected for service in World War II because of poor vision. He remained at Harvard to instruct Army Air Corps officers in statistical techniques useful for the management of the war effort. After a year of teaching McNamara flew to England to aid the Air Corps in directing the planning and logistical effort that supported bomber operations. In March 1943 he was assigned the rank of captain in the Air Corps and subsequently was promoted to lieutenant colonel. While serving in the Far East at the end of the war, McNamara won praise for his pioneering efforts in the assessment of the effects of B-29 bombing raids on Japan.

In 1945 McNamara joined a group of young Army officers, later dubbed the "whiz kids," who offered their managerial services to the financially troubled Ford Motor Company. As general manager and vice president of the automotive division of Ford in the 1950s, McNamara supported the development of the Falcon, a compact economical automobile, and the four-door version of the Thunderbird, a luxury car, both of which were financial successes. In November 1960 McNamara was named company president, the first man outside of the Ford family to hold that position.

McNamara, a registered Republican, had held his new post for only a month when President-elect John F. Kennedy invited him to take a high cabinet post in the new Administration. McNamara had been suggested to Kennedy by Robert Lovett [q.v.], a leading New York banker upon whom Kennedy relied for advice on staffing many of his top policymaking positions. Offered the choice of either the Treasury or the Defense Department, McNamara chose the latter because he considered it the greater challenge.

Shortly after he assumed office in January 1961, McNamara made it plain that he would not, as had most of his predecessors, serve passively as a referee mediating between the conflicting interests of the Army, Navy and Air Force. McNamara argued that many operations of the Pentagon were grossly inefficient because the three armed services were working at cross purposes, duplicating efforts that cost the taxpayers billions of dollars. McNamara enlarged his personal staff and moved to centralize decision making authority, thereby undercutting the power of the subordinate Army, Navy and Air Force Secretaries. He also created several new divisions controlled by civilians to deal with the common needs of the armed services. McNamara created a Defense Intelligence Agency to evaluate the intelligence operations of all three services and a Defense Supply Agency to purchase standardized items for use by the Army, Navy and Air Force.

One of McNamara's major goals was to develop a large and highly mobile striking force, which would permit the U.S. to deal with guerrilla or conventional wars without having to resort to nuclear weapons. The Eisenhower Administration's doctrine of "massive retaliation," he suggested, had limited American foreign policy options and increased the probability of a nuclear confrontation. In developing a "flexible response" capability, McNamara won approval for a 300,000-man increase in U.S. fighting strength and authorization for a vast buildup in U.S. capacity to airlift troops.

McNamara considered the Administration's handling of the Cuban missile crisis in October 1962 an example of the successful use of a "flexible response" strategy. When the Pentagon learned that the Soviet Union was erecting long-range missile sites in Cuba, the Administration did not immediately attack the launch pads as some military officers proposed. Instead, it demanded that the sites be dismantled and imposed "quarantine" around the island to turn back Soviet missile transport ships. McNamara carefully supervised the deployment and conduct of the blockade ships to ensure that unnecessary clashes with the Soviets would be avoided. After the U.S. Navy intercepted two ships on the high seas, the Russians agreed to withdraw their missiles from Cuba.

As a result of the buildup of conventional armed forces and development of contingency plans for brushfire wars, McNamara was reasonably confident of his Department's ability to deal with Communist guerrilla activity in Vietnam. The Defense Department rather than the State Department assumed primary responsibility for Vietnam affairs, because President Kennedy had greater confidence in the abilities of McNamara than in those of Secretary of State Dean Rusk [q.v.]. In addition, McNamara had already assumed important diplomatic responsibilities, particularly in his efforts to shore up the divided North Atlantic Treaty Organization. Finally, throughout the 1950s U.S. relations with Vietnam had been considered more of a military than a political problem, and the same attitude prevailed in the 1960s.

At the end of 1961 there were an estimated 2,000 American troops in South Vietnam training Vietnamese military personnel and operating aircraft, transport and communications facilities. In the spring of 1962 McNamara stated that the U.S. had no plans for introducing combat forces into South Vietnam, although Americans already there were authorized to fire if fired upon. In the fall of 1963 McNamara and Gen. Maxwell D. Taylor [q.v.] visited Saigon and then advised President Kennedy that the main U.S. military role in Vietnam could be completed by the end of 1965, although there might be a continuing need for U.S. advisers for some time thereafter. At the time of President Kennedy's death, there were some 15,000 American advisers in South Vietnam.

Within a year, however, it had become clear to McNamara that the war against the Communist guerrillas and their North Vietnamese allies could not be won quickly or easily. Vietnam soon became his overwhelming preoccupation. In March 1964 McNamara again visited South Vietnam. His report was pessimistic. The Communist position remained very strong; plans for the reduction in the number of U.S. advisers in South Vietnam had been dropped. Responding to congressional criticism that U.S. advisers were forced to use inferior equipment, McNamara replied that U.S. forces in Vietnam had a "blank check" on arms, manpower and funds. The statement startled some reporters who had long associated McNamara with "cost effectiveness," but President Johnson supported his Defense Secretary. (Between 1965 and 1967, when McNamara left office, defense spending for Vietnam rose from $1 billion to $20.6 billion.) By April 1964 McNamara was so closely identified with Vietnam policy that Sen. Wayne Morse (D, Ore.) dubbed the conflict "McNamara's war." "I think it is a very important war," replied McNamara, "and I am pleased to be identified with it and do whatever I can to win it."

By 1964 U.S. aircraft were aiding the South Vietnamese armed forces in carrying out covert raids on North Vietnam's coastal installations and attacks on infiltration routes in Laos and Cambodia. Despite these actions Communist forces threatened to overwhelm South Vietnam. Consequently, Pentagon strategists began drawing up plans for possible direct U.S. intervention.

An opportunity to implement those plans came on Aug. 4, 1964, when two U.S. destroyers were allegedly attacked by North Vietnamese gunboats in the Gulf of Tonkin. Adm. Ulysses S. Grant Sharp, commander-in-chief of U.S. Pacific forces, and members of the Joint Chiefs of Staff urged immediate retaliation against North Vietnam. President Johnson agreed. McNamara, however, delayed action for several hours. Evidence of the night attack, based largely on radar and sonar readings, was ambiguous; consequently, McNamara telephoned Sharp in Honolulu advising him to "make damned sure what happened." Despite the fact that only one shell from the alleged skirmish was discovered, Sharp remained convinced of the attack. Therefore President Johnson, with the approval of McNamara, ordered air strikes against North Vietnamese shipping and coastal installations. McNamara presented evidence of the attack to Congress, which on Aug. 7 approved the Tonkin Gulf Resolution, giving the President broad power to "take all necessary measures to repel . . . further aggression" throughout Southeast Asia.

Throughout the fall of 1964 McNamara received reports of significant gains by Communist forces in South Vietnam. Gen. William Westmoreland commander of U.S. ground advisers in Vietnam, and Gen. Maxwell Taylor [q.v.] urged the President to permit systematic bombing of North Vietnam to destroy its will to make war. McNamara argued against such a course, suggesting that the bombing of the North might escalate the conflict and that it could in no significant way force the North to abandon its support of Communist guerrillas in the South. President Johnson deferred the bombing decision until after the 1964 presidential election.

In February 1965, following Communist attacks on U.S. bases at Pleiku and Qui Nhon in South Vietnam, McNamara joined other members of the National Security Council in approving retaliatory air strikes. By the beginning of March, the U.S. was carrying out systematic bombing of the North. At the request of Gen. Westmoreland, 3,500 Marines were also sent to help defend the airbase at Da Nang. Despite these actions South Vietnamese forces appeared unable to stay the Communist advance. In April McNamara reported that "the intensification of infiltration [by North Vietnamese troops] has grown progressively more flagrant. . . ." After another meeting with Westmoreland in July, McNamara approved the General's request that 185,000 troops be sent to Vietnam by the end of the year. Johnson granted the request but rejected, as politically unpalatable, McNamara's proposal for calling up the reserves and a tax increase to pay for the war.

By November U.S. troops were engaged in major battles against North Vietnamese regulars in the Central Highlands. That month Westmoreland recommended that up to 400,000 troops be sent to Vietnam by the end of 1966. McNamara concurred but cautioned that "deployments of the kind I have recommended will not guarantee success. U.S. killed in action can be expected to reach 1,000 a month, and the odds are even that we will be faced in early 1967 with a 'no decision' at an even higher level." What McNamara had come to realize was that North Vietnam would counter a U.S. troop buildup by sending more of its own troops South.

At McNamara's request, the U.S. initiated a halt in the bombing of North Vietnam in December 1965. The Secretary argued that the bombing halt might induce North Vietnam to enter peace negotiations with the U.S. If not, then more intensive bombing could be justified. Gen. Westmoreland and the Joint Chiefs opposed the halt because they feared the North Vietnamese would take advantage of the lull to resupply their troops. The pause proved unproductive, and the bombing was renewed on Jan. 31, 1966.

Bombing strategy was a continual source of conflict between McNamara and the military. The President, McNamara, Secretary of State Dean Rusk [q.v.] and McGeorge Bundy [q.v.] retained the right to review all proposed bombing targets in North Vietnam. McNamara and his staff charged that the Joint Chiefs too often selected targets that were of dubious military significance. The Joint Chiefs, in turn, argued that McNamara placed unnecessary restrictions on U.S. air power.

In October 1966 McNamara visited South Vietnam for the eighth time. Publicly he was optimistic, stating that military progress "exceeded our expectations." Privately he had growing doubts. The air war had not forced North Vietnam into peace negotiations; U.S. troops had prevented a Communist victory but were now stalemated; casualties were high and prospects for a quick end to the war were nil. He was becoming increasingly sensitive to anti-war opinions, particularly those of Sen. Robert F. Kennedy (D, N.Y.) [q.v.]. In a speech delivered in Montreal in the spring of 1966, McNamara seemed to question the wisdom of the U.S. military commitment. Referring to the government of South Vietnam, he stated, "We have no charter to rescue floundering regimes, who have brought violence on themselves by deliberately refusing to meet the legitimate expectations of their citizens."

Such statements were rare. For the most part McNamara continued to urge Americans to remain firm in their resolve to resist Communist aggression. He was, in turn, denounced by anti-war leaders, who considered his references to "body counts" and "search-and destroy missions" ruthless and cold-blooded. McNamara, who had enjoyed his student days and brief career as a college teacher, was no longer welcome on many campuses. In a November 1966 visit to Harvard University, he was challenged to debate the war and was then hooted down. Yelling above the crowd, he recalled his student days, "I was a lot tougher and a lot more courteous than you. I was tougher than you and I am tougher today."

During 1967 McNamara became openly

skeptical over the effectiveness of bombing the North to prevent resupply of Communist troops in the South. Hoping to find a more effective means of preventing infiltration by North Vietnamese regulars, McNamara announced that the U.S. would construct a barrier of barbed wire, mines and electronic sensors south of the demilitarized zone. The barrier proved ineffective and was abandoned in 1969.

While concerned about the military conduct of the war, McNamara became increasingly interested in finding a way to end the conflict through a negotiated settlement. During the summer of 1967 McNamara, Paul Warnke and Paul Nitze [q.v.] drew up the "San Antonio Formula," a peace proposal offered privately to North Vietnam in August. The plan was a significant change in the U.S. terms for ending bombing and beginning negotiations. Prior to the communication the U.S. had offered to end the bombing if North Vietnam would stop its infiltration of the South. The San Antonio Formula modified this demand. It asked only for productive discussions in exchange for an end to the bombing. The U.S. requested no specific guarantee from Hanoi that it would end its infiltration. The only condition made was that the U.S. reserved its right to act if it concluded that the North Vietnamese were taking advantage of the bombing lull. The proposal, made public in September, was rejected by North Vietnam in October.

By the fall of 1967 McNamara was losing his influence within the Administration. His doubts about the bombing and his desire for a negotiated settlement conflicted with Johnson's hopes for a decisive military victory. Johnson, consequently, began to accede to the generals, who demanded more intensive bombing, increasing the number of available bombing targets in Vietnam. In November 1967 McNamara submitted a memorandum to the President in which he recommended that the U.S. freeze its troop levels, end the bombing of the North and turn over major responsibility for ground combat to the South Vietnamese Army. Johnson rejected the recommendations.

In November McNamara announced that he would resign in February to become the president of the World Bank. In January 1968, a few weeks before McNamara left office, Communist forces launched a major offensive against Saigon, Hue and other South Vietnamese cities. After intense fighting the Communists were driven out of the cities, but the Tet offensive seemed to confirm McNamara's pessimistic assessment of the war.

In response to the Communist offensive, the military requested more than 200,000 additional troops for the war. Johnson, concerned about the possible reaction to another increase, convened a senior advisory group on Vietnam to study the request. The panel, which included McNamara's successor, Clark Clifford [q.v.], recommended de-escalation. Johnson accepted their recommendations and at the end of March announced restrictions on future bombing of the North and a renewed bid for negotiations.

McNamara remained at the World Bank through the 1970s and worked for economic development in the third world.

[JWL]

For further information:
Leslie Gelb, *The Irony of Vietnam* (Washington, 1979).
James M. Roherty, *Decisions of Robert S. McNamara: A Study of the Role of the Secretary of Defense* (Miami, 1970).
Henry L. Trewhitt, *McNamara: His Ordeal in the Pentagon* (New York, 1971).

MORGENTHAU, HANS J(OACHIM)
b. Feb. 17, 1904; Coburg, Germany.
d. July 19, 1980; New York City.
Political scientist.

Morgenthau received a Juris Utriusque Doctor (doctorate of canon and civil law) from the University of Frankfurt in 1929 and two years later was appointed assistant to its faculty of law. In 1932 he went to Switzerland to teach German public law at the University of Geneva. He came to the United States in 1937 and taught law, history and political science at Brooklyn College and the University of Kansas City before becoming a visiting professor of political science at the University of Chicago in 1943. He became a full professor at that university six years later. In 1950 Morgenthau was appointed director of the Center for the Study of American Foreign and Military Policy at the University of Chicago.

In the late 1940s and the 1950s Morgenthau, through the publication of *Politics Among Nations* (1948), *In Defense of the National Interest* (1951) and other books, became known as a proponent of the "realist" approach to foreign policy. Rejecting Wilsonianism, he argued that America should not seek to transform the world according to its own political ideals but should instead concern itself with the promotion of vital national interests. Believing that popular passions often interfered with patient pursuit of the fixed designs required in diplomacy, Morgenthau felt that democratic societies like the United States found it difficult to pursue a coherent, rational foreign policy founded upon a consistent sense of the national interest.

Morgenthau's realist approach to world politics placed him in neither the conservative nor liberal camp.

Writing in the November 1962 issue of *Commentary*, Morgenthau advocated the employment of any necessary means, including an invasion, to remove Soviet missiles from Cuba. He wrote that since the promulgation of the Montoe Doctrine, America had claimed Latin America as a sphere of influence and stated that "if the United States is unwilling—nobody doubts its ability—to protect one of its vital interests, regarded as such for a century and a half, is it likely to protect interests elsewhere. . . ? Mr. Khrushchev, in particular, cannot help but ask himself that question."

Regarding Southeast Asia as beyond the American sphere of influence, Morgenthau criticized escalating United States intervention in Vietnam as contrary to the national interest during the mid and late 1960s. In an April 1965 *New York Times Magazine* article, he asserted that China rather than America would inevitably exert the predom-

inant cultural and political influence on the Asian mainland. Morgenthau contended that, nevertheless, Vietnam might retain considerable independence as a Communist state of the Titoist variety because of its historical enmity towards China. He concluded that American intervention in an unwinnable war would merely force the Vietnamese Communist leaders into a closer relationship with China.

Morgenthau was a prominent participant in a number of the early university teach-ins on the Vietnam war. On May 15, 1965 he criticized Administration policy at a Washington, D.C. teach-in sponsored by the Inter-University Committee for a Public Hearing on Vietnam. His talk was transmitted via a special radio hookup to over 100 campuses. McGeorge Bundy [*q.v.*], special assistant to President Johnson on national security affairs, was scheduled to be the major defender of the Administration, but he announced that he was unable to attend because of official business. Morgenthau told the teach-in audience that the government was creating a myth of North Vietnamese subversion of South Vietnam to justify American involvement in a civil war there. Two months later he finally debated Bundy on a special CBS television broadcast. Bundy contended that escalation or complete and immediate withdrawal were the only alternatives to the President's policy. Morgenthau declined to endorse withdrawal, asserting that the Administration could find a face-saving way of extricating America from the conflict without overt surrender.

In November 1965 Morgenthau addressed a New York meeting of Clergy Concerned About Vietnam, and the following March he appeared before the Senate Foreign Relations Committee to urge abandonment of the policy of military containment of China. As the anti-war movement became increasingly radical during the late 1960s, Morgenthau's prominence as an Administration critic receded. In 1968 he served as a foreign policy adviser to anti-war presidential candidate Sen. Eugene J. McCarthy (D, Minn.) [*q.v.*].

In 1968 Morgenthau joined the faculty of

the City College of New York. Concerned with the problems of Soviet Jews, he attended the Brussels Congress on Soviet Jewry in February 1971. In 1974 he became a professor at the New School for Social Research in New York City. Morgenthau died in 1980.

[MLL]

For further information:
Hans J. Morgenthau, *Truth and Power: Essays of a Decade, 1960-70* (New York, 1970).

NITZE, PAUL H(ENRY)
b. Jan. 16, 1907; Amherst, Mass.
Chairman, Policy Planning Staff, State Department, 1950-53; Assistant Secretary of Defense for International Security Affairs, January 1961-October 1963; Secretary of the Navy, November 1963-June 1967; Deputy Secretary of Defense, June 1967-January 1969.

The son of a professor of romance languages, Nitze graduated from Harvard in 1928. The following year he entered the banking firm of Dillon, Read, and Co. With the exception of the years 1938 to 1939, when he headed his own company, he remained there until 1941 when he entered government service as a financial director of the office of the coordinator of inter-American affairs. From 1942 to 1944 he held top administrative posts in the Board of Economic Warfare and the Foreign Economic Administration. Nitze served as vice chairman of the U.S. Strategic Bombing Survey from 1944 to 1946. After the war he accepted the post as deputy director of the office of international trade policy in the State Department. During 1947 he took part in discussions on European cooperation in the Marshall Plan and played a role in formulating the legislation formally establishing the aid program. Nitze became deputy to the assistant secretary of state for economic affairs in 1948.

During 1949 he became assistant to George F. Kennan [*q.v.*], director of the State Department's Policy Planning Staff. Before the end of the year, Kennan had resigned in a dispute with Secretary of State Dean Acheson [*q.v.*]. The Soviet expert opposed the formation of a military alliance with Western Europe, believing that it would antagonize the USSR and provide little protection in a nuclear age. Nitze, a long time advocate of a hard-line position towards the Soviet Union and a supporter of the alliance, took his place. He helped formulate the basic structure for the North Atlantic Treaty Organization (NATO) and pushed for the passage of the North Atlantic Treaty in Congress.

In response to the Soviet Union's successful detonation of an atomic bomb and the fall of China to the Communists in 1949, Acheson asked Nitze in January 1950 to head an inter-departmental study group to review American foreign and defense policy. Given to the President in April, the report, NSC-68, was the first comprehensive review of U.S. national security policy. Nitze's analysis was based on the assumption that the Soviets were dedicated to world conquest and would, by 1954, have the nuclear capability of destroying the United States. To meet the challenge, the U.S. would have to accept primary responsibility for the security of the non-Communist world. NSC-68 recommended a massive development of free world military capabilities "with the intention of righting the power balance and in the hope that through means other than all-out war [the U.S.] could induce a change in the nature of the Soviet system." The report recommendation a two-to-four fold expansion of American arms spending to strengthen NATO'S conventional forces and develop nuclear weapons. This increase would enable the alliance to meet a full-scale invasion and permit the U.S. to engage in peripheral limited conflicts. NSC-68 argued that because of its wealth, the U.S. could afford the increased expenditures, estimating that 20% of its gross national product could be used for arms without suffering severe economic dislocation.

Nitze also asserted that the U.S. had to rebuild the West until it surpassed the Soviet bloc. Only then could it stand at the "political and material center with other free nations in variable orbits around it."

Truman was initially reluctant to accept the program and refused to allow publication of the report. However, after the Korean war began, he started implementing its recommendations. NSC-68 fell from favor during the Eisenhower years, when the Administration attempted to cut the defense budget and rely on strategic nuclear weapons as America's first deterrent.

Nitze was originally slated for a top defense post in the Eisenhower Administration, but his name was dropped because of protests by the Republican right. During the 1950s he lectured and wrote on foreign policy. In 1957 he advised the Gaither Committee, formed to study U.S. defense needs. Two years later Nitze served as an adviser to the Senate Foreign Relations Committee.

In 1961 Nitze headed John F. Kennedy's pre-election task force on national defense problems. In both the Committee and task force reports, Nitze reiterated his belief that the U.S. had to assume a more diversified defense posture to provide a real alternative to the massive nuclear deterrent strategy of the Dulles era.

On Dec. 24, 1960 Kennedy appointed Nitze assistant secretary of defense for international security affairs. In this position Nitze urged NATO to move away from reliance on American nuclear power and organize a multilateral conventional and nuclear force (MLF) of its own.

During the Berlin crisis of 1961, Nitze headed the Berlin task force created to handle strategy in a possible showdown with Russia. As chairman, Nitze warned the Russians that the West would use "all their strategic capabilities" to protect Berlin.

A member of the Executive Committee of the National Security Council charged with policy analysis during the Cuban missile crisis of October 1962, Nitze was one of the advisers who advocated immediate military action to rid Cuba of Soviet missiles.

He opposed the Cuban blockade suggested by the more moderate Attorney General Robert F. Kennedy [q.v.] and Secretary of Defense Robert S. McNamara [q.v.]. Believing that military action was inevitable, Nitze and some of Kennedy's other advisers urged air strikes before the Soviet missiles were operational, when attempts to remove them would necessitate a massive attack that could lead to nuclear war.

In February 1963 Nitze, along with special presidential assistant Walt W. Rostow [q.v.], was assigned the task of analyzing the government's response to the crisis. Nitze concluded that his previous position had been in error because it overestimated the possibility that nuclear war would have resulted from a delay in air strikes.

In October 1963 Kennedy appointed Nitze Secretary of the Navy. Believing that one of the keys to a successful defense policy was the effective management of the service's extensive technological capability, the Secretary reorganized the Department of the Navy in 1966. His chief reform was creating the Office of Chief of Naval Material to direct the allocation of manpower and material resources.

During April 1967 Nitze worked closely with Secretary of Defense Robert McNamara [q.v.] in the Secretary's attempts to de-escalate the bombing of North Vietnam. They proposed that the Administration cease bombing above the 20th parallel, a plan rejected by President Johnson in the absence of what he considered enemy willingness to reciprocate.

In June 1967 President Johnson appointed Nitze deputy secretary of defense. Two months later Nitze again joined McNamara in writing a conciliatory proposal modifying the Administration's previous demand for North Vietnamese de-escalation before peace negotiations could begin. The "San Antonio Formula," sent privately to Hanoi, stated, "The United States is willing immediately to stop all aerial and naval bombardment of North Vietnam when this will lead promptly to productive discussions." On Oct. 3 North Vietnam emphatically rejected the plan.

During the first days of March 1968,

Nitze was a member of the Ad Hoc Task Force on Vietnam formed to study the military's request for over 200,000 additional ground troops following the Communist Tet offensive. Within this group Nitze was a strong opponent of further escalation. Arguing that the Administration should view U.S. involvement in Vietnam in the wider context of U.S. interests elsewhere in the world, he cautioned that further troop increases could lead to direct military confrontation with China or jeopardize military commitments elsewhere. Instead of continued escalation he advised a policy of strengthening the South Vietnamese Army and withdrawing American troops. After deliberation the committee rejected Nitze's recommendation and supported the request for ground troops. Most of the additional troops, however, were never sent to Vietnam. On March 31 President Johnson, on the advice of a group of senior statesmen and counselors, announced a policy of gradual de-escalation.

As deputy secretary, Nitze strongly supported the development of a limited anti-ballistic missile system, known as Sentinel, to protect the United States from a potential attack by Communist China. Nitze served as deputy secretary until January 1969. In November 1969 he went to Helsinki as a member of the U.S. delegation to the Strategic Arms Limitation Talks. In 1976, Nitze helped to found a conservative organization, The Committee on the Present Danger. During the 1980 presidential campaign, he acted as an advisor to the Republican candidate, Ronald Reagan.

[EWS]

NIXON, RICHARD M(ILHOUS)
b. Jan. 11, 1913; Yorba Linda, Calif.
President of the United States,
1969-74.

Born into a Quaker family of modest means, Richard Nixon grew up in Yorba Linda and Whittier, Calif. To supplement the family income, Nixon worked in his father's grocery store and held other jobs.

He excelled as a student in public schools and received his B.A. from Whittier College in 1934. Nixon graduated from Duke University Law School in 1937. After rejecting a position in a New York City law firm and failing to receive an appointment as an FBI agent because of the Bureau's limited budget, Nixon returned to Whittier to start his own practice. At the outset of World War II, he worked for eight months in the Office of Price Administration (OPA); that experience forever left him distrustful of government bureaucracy. From 1942 to 1945 Nixon served as a noncombat Navy officer in the South Pacific. Upon his return he won election to the House of Representatives as a Republican, his family's Party. During his term in the House from 1947 to 1950, Nixon established a national reputation as an investigator of Communist subversives in the federal government. That image helped to secure him election to the U.S. Senate in 1950.

From 1953 to 1960 Nixon served as vice president under Dwight D. Eisenhower.

Throughout the Eisenhower presidency, Richard Nixon advocated a hard-line policy towards Communist expansion. In 1954 he suggested, off-the-record, the possibility of sending American troops to Indochina if the French pulled out. (Some observers believed that this was an Administration trial balloon rather than Nixon's personal view.)

During Eisenhower's second term Nixon's political stock was greatly enhanced by his foreign travels. His South American tour in May 1958 was plagued by leftist violence. In Lima, Peru, Nixon faced down a stone-throwing crowd at San Marcos University. In Caracas, Venezuela, the windows of his automobile were smashed by a raging mob, and troops arrived just in time to prevent him from being dragged from the car and killed. His fortitude and calmness in the face of great physical danger earned him considerable admiration throughout the Western Hemisphere.

In July 1959 Nixon went to Moscow to open the American National Exhibition at Sokolniki Park. He was the highest-ranking American official to visit the Soviet Union since Premier Nikita S. Khrushchev's rise to power. On the day after his arrival, Nixon and Khrushchev engaged in a debate over the respective merits of capitalism and Communism. Part of the discussion took place in the model kitchen of the exhibition, and it became known as the "kitchen debate." Many Americans believed that Nixon had effectively "stood up" to the Soviet Premier.

Despite Nixon's extensive experience in foreign affairs as Vice President, he narrowly lost the 1960 presidential election to John Kennedy. This was followed by another defeat in the 1962 race for governor of California. Despite the two defeats, Nixon remained active in Republican national politics and campaigned extensively for Congressional candidates. His efforts were rewarded in 1968 when he won his party's presidential nomination and went on to win the national election in November.

Nixon's first priority as President in 1969 was to shift U.S. strategy in Vietnam. The President ruled out speedy withdrawal in favor of a more calculated plan designed to preserve the regime of South Vietnamese President Nguyen Van Thieu, an anti-Communist and ally of the U.S. More importantly Nixon and his chief foreign policy adviser, Henry A. Kissinger [q.v.], considered it vital to bolster U.S. relations with other powers, large and small, by demonstrating America's firm stand against the threat of Communist aggression. In early 1969 Nixon directed Gen. Creighton Abrams, Jr., commander of U.S. forces in South Vietnam, to limit offensive operations by American land forces so as to reduce casualties. Simultaneously the President ordered U.S. air forces to escalate bombings of North Vietnam after a vigorous offensive by the North Vietnamese in February.

Perhaps most significantly, the President and Defense Secretary Melvin R. Laird formulated a policy of "Vietnamization" of the conflict, first suggested by Nixon during the spring of 1968. From 1969 to 1972 the U.S. gradually withdrew 555,000 armed personnel on the assumption that the well-trained and well-equipped South Vietnamese Army could take over America's vast military role. But the U.S. continued massive air strikes. Nixon assured Thieu at a June 1969 meeting on Midway Island that the U.S. would not abandon South Vietnam altogether.

At the same time, in an effort to cut off Communist infiltration and supplies into Vietnam, Nixon widened the war. Beginning in 1969 he launched secret air bombing missions over the border provinces of the neutral nations of Laos and Cambodia, where the North Vietnamese maintained supply centers. This government soon lapsed into a corrupt and unpopular military dictatorship. On April 30, 1970, Nixon announced that U.S. and South Vietnamese troops had crossed into Cambodia to wipe out enemy sanctuaries. The President asserted that the short-term action was really "not an invasion of Cambodia" because the areas entered were under North Vietnamese control.

To quiet domestic criticism of the war, the President enunciated the "Nixon Doctrine," which promised that the U.S. would restrict its use of military intervention in future international crises. The President also reformed the Selective Service System to abolish discriminatory deferments and in 1973 ended the draft entirely. He assumed that the large reduction in the number of troops and the lower casualty rates in Vietnam combined with these other reforms would satisfy those segments of the American public concerned over escalation of the fighting between 1965 and 1968, "graphically demonstrating," Nixon recalled in his memoirs, "that we were beginning to wind down the war."

Despite the President's altered approach, the mass movement against the Vietnam conflict gathered greater force in 1969 and 1970. During that period colleges were torn apart by student protests of the war, while anti-war moratoriums, mass marches and meetings were held in major U.S. cities. The greatest turbulence, however, followed Nixon's announcement of the U.S. incursion into Cambodia. Violence between police authorities and students culminated at Kent State University when Ohio National Guardsmen fired on a crowd and killed four unarmed students. The Kent State shootings rocked the nation, as did a similar incident at Jackson State College in Mississippi. Initially Nixon dubbed his young critics "bums." However early on the morning of May 9, he made an attempt to ameliorate students at the Lincoln Memorial who were preparing to march against the war. The gesture proved fruitless.

Nixon and his aides responded to mass protests by developing a "seige" mentality. Since the beginning of his Administration, Nixon's assistants had regarded violent anti-war dissidents as potential revolutionaries. Secret data gathering by the federal government commenced against anti-war groups and eventually against less strident politicians and social groups critical of the Administration's Vietnam strategy. Concerned that members of anti-war coalitions and later more moderate critics of the President might succeed in crippling Nixon's presidency and in forcing his ouster, White House aides requested government agencies to keep secret files on such individuals. Furthermore, as in the Johnson years, the Nixon foreign policy leadership worried that domestic protest of diplomatic determinations would hurt America's prestige abroad; that in the eyes of foreign leaders, the U.S. could not be relied upon in crisis situations. Thus Nixon, Kissinger and other Administration officials not only felt free but obligated to adopt, out of concern for "national security," illegal or extralegal tactics against their more resolute and radical foes.

From the time of this 1968 campaign, Nixon had sensed a shift in the global balance of power. China emerged from its "cultural revolution" likely to assume a leadership role in the world, yet it was still suspicious of the Soviet Union; sporadic armed border clashes occurred along the Sino-Soviet border in 1969. Although Nixon had long been among those who opposed U.S. diplomatic recognition of China and its admission to the United Nations, the President now felt that Chinese leaders must be approached. As a Republican President with indisputable anti-Communist credentials, Nixon could slowly begin to "normalize" U.S.-Chinese relations with little fear of domestic political repercussions. Tentative discussions began soon after Nixon's inauguration. In July 1971 Kissinger secretly flew to Peking to arrange a presidential visit to China the following year. Announced officially in August, Nixon's trip in February 1972 laid the groundwork for formal relations, which were realized under President Jimmy Carter in December 1978.

U.S. relations with the Soviet Union improved markedly during Nixon's Administration. From the outset, Nixon favored the Strategic Arms Limitation Talks (SALT), begun under President Johnson, as a means of containing the arms race. Yet he supported continued increases in new military weapons procurement, notably during the congressional debate over the appropriation for the anti-ballistic missile system in 1969. The SALT negotiations were designed to culminate not in an overall reduction of U.S. military spending as much as a lessening in the growth rate of military expenditures. The talks ran from 1969 to 1972, when the Soviet leaders agreed to the first of several treaties to limit new armaments. When he went to Moscow in May 1972 to sign the accord, Nixon became the first President to visit the Soviet Union since 1945.

President Nixon fostered a U.S.-Soviet "spirit" of cooperation, or "detente," as Cold War tensions between the two great powers lessened. Pushed by Soviet Party Chairman Leonid Brezhnev, the USSR aggressively sought America's trade and its high technology and investment for mining Soviet natural resources. In addition a poor grain harvest forced the USSR to request the right to purchase U.S. grain in 1972. The grain transaction taxed the resources of the Agriculture Department and had the unexpected effect of raising

U.S. food prices the following year. That and the question of Soviet domestic repression raised concerns about the gains to accrue from the deal. Sen. Henry M. Jackson (D, Wash.) [q.v.] delayed approval of SALT-I over the issue of Soviet denial of emigration rights to Russian Jews.

Detente or the new China policy did not, however, resolve the problem of Vietnam. From 1968 to 1972 the U.S., North and South Vietnam and the National Liberal Front (the South Vietnamese Communist faction) continued fruitless negotiations in Paris. As the U.S. de-escalated its military operations, the governments of North and South Vietnam—the one hopeful, the other terrified over what withdrawal portended—hesitated to concede much. Nixon's patience wore thin, especially in light of the upcoming 1972 election and his inability to end the conflict. Continued North Vietnamese offensive operations in early 1972 provoked expanded U.S. air missions over North Vietnam and the mining of Haiphong, the major port city.

In late December the President again ordered a "reseeding" of mines in Haiphong harbor and the most intensive bombing ever of North Vietnam. "The order to renew bombing the week before Christmas," Nixon recalled, "was the most difficult decision I made during the war." It provoked a large outcry from both anti-war spokespersons and others, such as Sen. William B. Saxbe (R, Ohio), who normally supported the Administration. Nevertheless the "Christmas bombing" forced Hanoi's hand. In early January, Kissinger flew to Paris to effect an agreement. On Jan. 15 all bombing and mining operations against the North ceased. North Vietnam provided for the return of U.S. prisoners of war (mainly bomber pilots). On Jan. 23 a cease-fire was announced. Nixon had "won the peace," as he liked to phrase it, and rested on a high crest of popularity. The *Wall Street Journal* reported of an effort to repeal the constitutional limit of two presidential terms so that Nixon could run again in 1976.

Nixon's stunning triumph soon turned into a disaster, however, as the Watergate scandal began to emerge in 1973. In addition to undercutting his authority as President, the crisis proved to be so time-consuming that Nixon spent less and less attention on foreign affairs. As he became increasingly withdrawn, he delegated more authority to Secretary of State Kissinger who proved to be the prime figure in the Arab-Israeli negotiations of 1973-74.

Nixon finally resigned from office in August 1974. While the domestic illegalities of his administration were universally condemned, opinions about his foreign policy were more mixed. Liberal critics contended that he could have ended the Vietnam war more quickly and that he sometimes allied the U.S. too closely with unpopular rulers, like the Shah of Iran. Other critics also felt that Nixon too often saw regional conflicts in the Third World primarily in terms of the U.S.-Soviet rivalry. But most critics did agree that Nixon had made historic breakthroughs in creating a more normal relationship with the Soviet Union and Communist China. As President, Nixon rejected his former 1950s Cold War outlook in favor of the more classical balance of power approach.

[JLB]

For further information:
Henry Kissinger, *The White House Years* (New York, 1979).
J. Anthony, Lukas, *Nightmare: the Underside of the Nixon Years* (New York, 1976)
Richard Nixon, *RN; The Memoirs of Richard Nixon* (New York, 1978).
Jonathan Schell, *The Time of Illusion* (New York, 1976).

OPPENHEIMER, J. ROBERT
b. April 22, 1904; New York, N.Y.
d. Feb. 18, 1967; Princeton, N.J.
Physicist; Chairman, General

Advisory Committee, Atomic Energy Commission, 1947-52.

The son of a German-born textile importer, J. Robert Oppenheimer graduated from Harvard summa cum laude in 1925 and went on to pursue graduate studies at Cambridge. He received his doctorate in physics from the University of Goettingen in 1927. In 1929, after additional studies in Leyden, Zurich and at Harvard, Oppenheimer began teaching concurrently at the University of California at Berkeley and the California Institute of Technology at Pasadena. He was highly respected for his comprehensive mastery of atomic physics and his theoretical work during the 1930s on the positron and the theory of "gravitational collapse." Oppenheimer was nevertheless most noted for his inspirational and lucid teaching.

Oppenheimer first became interested in the possibility of an atomic bomb in 1939 after hearing Niels Bohr's explanation of the vast amount of energy that could be liberated during uranium fission. He spent much of his spare time making rough calculations of the critical mass that could cause an explosion, and in 1941 he began on his own initiative to work on the problems of fission at the Lawrence Radiation Laboratory in Berkeley. Because of his impressive work there, Oppenheimer was asked by scientist Arthur Compton to devote himself full time to the Manhattan District Project, the atomic bomb research project Compton had helped organize. Oppenheimer's suggestion that all Canadian and U.S. atomic research efforts be concentrated in one spot led to the creation of a "super" laboratory at Los Alamos, N.M., in March 1943. Appointed director of the laboratory, Oppenheimer used his personal magnetism to persuade top nuclear physicists to join the Project, despite the stringent security regulations to which they had to submit.

During 1944 and 1945 the development of the atomic bomb progressed at Los Alamos under Oppenheimer's supervision.

In April 1945, before the first bomb had been tested, Oppenheimer was appointed to a panel of scientists to advise President Harry S Truman's Interim Committee on atomic policy. Despite the hope of many of the Manhattan Project scientists that the bomb would be given a purely technical demonstration, Oppenheimer and the other panel scientists advised "direct military use" of the weapon against Japan to end the war quickly and save American lives. They recommended that a dual military and civilian target be chosen to demonstrate the bomb's destructive power and suggested it be dropped without prior warning. On July 16, 1945 the first atomic bomb was successfully tested in the desert near Los Alamos, shocking Oppenheimer and other scientists present with the magnitude of the explosion. The U.S dropped the A-bomb on Hiroshima on Aug. 6. Criticized for the failure of the advisory panel to protest the use of the weapon without warning on a civilian target, Oppenheimer later wrote, "What was expected of this committee of experts was primarily a technical opinion. . . ."

In 1947 Oppenheimer returned to the academic world as director of the Institute for Advanced Study at Princeton. He also continued to advise officials of the State Department and the Pentagon. That year he was appointed chairman of the General Advisory Committee (GAC) to the Atomic Energy Commission (AEC). After the successful test of the first Russian atomic bomb in 1949, the GAC was asked for recommendations on the advisability of producing a hydrogen or fusion bomb, a project abandoned during the war due to technical difficulties. Edward Teller [q.v.], who had worked under Oppenheimer on the Manhattan Project, urged a crash program to develop the weapon. However, the GAC scientists felt that such a move was both morally and economically unjustifiable and advised against production. Nevertheless, Truman approved the project. When, in 1951, Teller presented new ideas that made the bomb technically feasible, the GAC became enthusiastic. Attempting to explain this reversal, Oppenheimer later wrote that when a project becomes "technically sweet," you go ahead with it and worry about what to do with it "only after you have had your technical success."

After 1952 Oppenheimer's influence in the government waned. He served only occasionally as a special consultant, though he maintained top level security clearance, allowing him access to atomic secrets. In 1953, however, in the midst of Sen. Joseph R. McCarthy's (R, Wisc.) anti-Communist crusade, William L. Borden, former executive director of the joint Committee on Atomic Energy, sent FBI Director J. Edgar Hoover a letter indicating that Oppenheimer was probably a security risk. As a result, President Dwight D. Eisenhower suspended Oppenheimer's security clearance pending a review of his past Communist associations. In April 1954 Oppenheimer received a hearing before a special board appointed by the AEC. Almost all of his former colleagues at Los Alamos attested to his loyalty. However, his leftist ties during the 1930s and his ambivalence toward the production of the hydrogen bomb led the board to uphold the suspension of his security clearance. When Oppenheimer filed an appeal with the AEC, the Commission upheld the decision.

After the 1954 hearing Oppenheimer devoted himself to directing the work at the Institute for Advanced Study and to investigating the spiritual and intellectual problems raised by modern nuclear physics. In December 1963 President Lyndon B. Johnson, acting on the wishes of President John F. Kennedy, presented Oppenheimer with the Enrico Fermi Award. Oppenheimer died of cancer in 1967.

[DAE]

For further information:
Robert Gilpin, *American Scientists and Nuclear Weapons Policy* (Princeton, 1962).
Robert Jungk, *Brighter Than A Thousand Suns* (New York, 1971).

RADFORD, ARTHUR W(ILLIAM)
b. Feb. 27, 1896; Chicago, Ill.

d. Aug. 18, 1973; Bethesda, Md.
Chairman, Joint Chiefs of Staff, May 1953-August 1957.

At the age of 16 Radford entered the U.S. Naval Academy at Annapolis after having been refused admission to West Point. He graduated in 1916 and then saw action as an ensign on the battleship *South Carolina* during World War I. Following the War Radford moved up in rank as a naval aviator, eventually becoming a fighter squadron commander aboard the aircraft carrier, *Saratoga*. In 1941 he was selected to expand and centralize the Navy's pilot training program. During World War II Radford was promoted to rear admiral and commanded a carrier attack group in the South Pacific. After the War he became deputy chief and then vice chief of naval operations. In 1949 Radford took command of the Pacific fleet. A vigorous anti-Communist who declared that the U.S. would not be secure as long as Communists controlled mainland China, the Admiral gained the support of powerful congressional Republicans such as Sen. Robert Taft (R, Ohio) [q.v.]. At their urging Eisenhower selected Radford to be chairman of the Joint Chiefs of Staff in May 1953.

Radford was one of the chief architects of the Eisenhower Administration's "New Look" plan, hailed as a major departure in American defense policy. The failure of the U.S. Army to win the Korean war revealed what he believed was the futility of engaging in conventional ground warfare. He also questioned the need to have American troops in Western Europe when the U.S. had nuclear superiority over the Soviet Union. With these two facts in mind, Radford, his fellow Chiefs of Staff and Secretary of State John Foster Dulles [q.v.] formulated a policy stressing reliance on strategic nuclear weapons as America's first line of defense. Radford believed his New Look had many advantages. In the first place, American troops would not be called upon to fight unpopular wars such as that in Korea. In the second place, Radford argued, having supersonic bombers armed with nuclear weapons ready to attack at any moment would deter Soviet and Chinese aggression. The New Look also appealed to Administration budget cutters who believed it would reduce the cost of maintaining expensive conventional forces around the world. Critics such as Dean Acheson [*q.v.*], however, argued that the policy meant a return to unilateralism at the expense of American allies. They also believed that the threat of nuclear attack would prove irrelevant in the face of guerrilla warfare. Finally, they pointed out that the New Look was meaningless because the U.S. would never be the first nation to unleash a nuclear holocaust.

Radford took a hardline military stand toward Asian Communism that was often at odds with Eisenhower's own policies. In March 1954 French Chief of Staff Gen. Paul Henry Ely requested immediate U.S. aid to lift the Communist siege of Dien Bien Phu in northern Vietnam. At Eisenhower's request Radford outlined a proposal that included the use of American B-29 bombers to help relieve the embattled garrison. Ely hoped to use only enough air strikes to pressure the Communists to negotiate a face-saving withdrawal for the French from Southeast Asia. Radford, however, viewed American intervention as an open-ended commitment to stem the spread of Communism in Asia.

On April 3, 1954 Dulles called a secret meeting at the State Department between Radford and eight senior senators. Radford outlined his intervention plan but admitted he did not have the unanimous support of the other Chiefs and that the bombings could bring China into the war. Army Chief of Staff Gen. Matthew Ridgway [*q.v.*] issued a strong dissent to the Radford plan in which he maintained the bombings would be inconclusive and could lead to the introduction of American troops. The senators shared Ridgway's skepticism toward the operation. The following day Dulles and Radford met with Eisenhower, who overruled the Admiral's proposal. Until the fall of Dien Bien Phu on May 7, Radford persisted in calling for U.S. entry into the war.

On Sept. 3, 1954 Communist Chinese shore batteries began shelling the Nationalist-held islands of Quemoy and Matsu. Three days later the Joint Chiefs, headed by Radford, voted three-to-one (with Ridgway again dissenting) that Eisenhower authorize Chiang Kai-shek to bomb the mainland. If the Communists retaliated, the group suggested that the U.S. join the attack. Radford believed that war between the U.S. and Communist China was inevitable and that it would be better to fight China when it was weak than wait until it had grown in strength. However, Eisenhower, believing that the islands had little strategic value and fearing a general war with China, gave the plan no support. In January 1955, when the Chinese shelled the Tachen Islands 200 miles north of Taiwan, Radford once again urged the U.S. bomb the mainland. Eisenhower rejected this suggestion and convinced Chiang to withdraw from the islands. In the spring of 1955 Eisenhower tried to defuse the crisis further by suggesting that Chiang reduce his troops on Quemoy and Matsu in hopes of a reciprocal gesture from Peking. He sent Admiral Radford and Assistant Secretary of State Walter Robertson to present the plan to the Nationalist leader. Chiang rejected their proposal. The Communists continued shelling the islands, although with less frequency.

Radford publicly opposed any attempt at disarmament with the Soviet Union. In May 1957, shortly before Radford retired, Eisenhower publicly rebuked the Admiral for declaring that "we cannot trust the Russians on this or anything." A man with a tough no-nonsense manner, Radford remained a controversial figure throughout his career. Although praised as a brilliant naval officer, he was often criticized for his tendency to dominate those around him and to portray his views as those shared by the other Chiefs of Staff. His critics charged that he "abrogated more authority than he had."

Following his retirement in 1957, Radford continued to advise the Administration on military matters. He was Vice President Richard Nixon's [q.v.] military adviser during the 1960 presidential campaign and continued to recommend the defense of Quemoy and Matsu. In 1964 Radford served as an adviser to Republican presidential candidate Sen. Barry Goldwater (R, Ariz.) [q.v.].

[JB]

RIDGWAY, MATTHEW B(UNKER)
b. March 3, 1895; Fort Monroe, Va.
Army Chief of Staff, August 1953-June 1955.

Matthew B. Ridgway, the son of an Army colonel, was raised on various Army posts. Following his graduation from West Point in 1917, he taught languages there and then served on numerous assignments in Central America, the Far East and the United States. From 1939 to 1942 Ridgway was assigned to the War Department general staff, war plans division. During World War II Ridgway played an important role in the creation of Army airborne units and, as commanding general of the 82nd Airborne Division, participated in the invasion of Sicily, the Italian campaign and the invasion of Normandy. From 1945 to 1948 he had extended assignments with the Military Staff Committee of the United Nations and the Inter-American Defense Board. After the dismissal of Gen. Douglas MacArthur as leader of the U.N. forces in Korea, Ridgway took his place. In 1952 he replaced Gen. Dwight D. Eisenhower as supreme commander of Allied forces in Europe.

President Eisenhower appointed Ridgway Army Chief of Staff in August 1953. Ridgway soon clashed with the Administration over its decision to implement the "New Look" defense policy. This plan, prompted in part by a desire to reduce expenditures, called for primary reliance on strategic nuclear weapons, or "massive retaliation," for defense. In 1954 he joined Gen. James M. Gavin in protesting the cutbacks in the defense budget and the reductions in Army personnel which the policy entailed. He objected to a defense policy based on what he thought were principally political decisions and called for one based on the ability to fight small-scale, guerrilla-type wars as well as all-out nuclear attacks.

In debates over a military policy, Ridgway often served as a voice of moderation, countering the more bellicose policies of Chairman of the Joint Chiefs of Staff Adm. Arthur Radford [q.v.]. During the spring of 1954, when the Administration was considering a French request for U.S. military intervention in Vietnam, Ridgway opposed Radford's plan to use air strikes. The General feared that if bombing failed to achieve its objective, there would be a strong temptation to send U.S. ground troops to maintain U.S. prestige. Ridgway ordered a team of experts to evaluate the situation in Vietnam. A subsequent report concluded that the U.S. was not ready to fight a guerrilla-type war similar to the ones in that area. Eisenhower eventually accepted Ridgway's advice and refused direct American aid.

Ridgway again opposed Radford's recommendations following the shelling of the Nationalist Chinese islands of Quemoy and Matsu by the Communist Chinese during the fall of 1954. Radford and the majority of the Joint Chiefs argued that, although the islands had no strategic value to Taiwan, their loss would bring on a collapse of Nationalist morale, which, in turn, was important for the defense of Asia. Therefore, they recommended that Eisenhower permit Chiang Kai-shek to bomb the mainland. If Quemoy were attacked, they urged direct U.S. military intervention. Ridgway, the only dissenter among the Joint Chiefs, argued that it was not the military's responsibility to judge the psychological value of the island and urged restraint. Eisenhower, determined not to exacerbate the crisis further, ruled out American military intervention.

Ridgway retired as Army Chief of Staff in June 1955 and became director of Colt Industries. A few days before his departure, he elaborated his views on the need for a "viable strategy for Cold War situations" to meet aggression in the "mountains of Greece and Korea or the jungles of Indochina."

After leaving the military Ridgway continued to oppose the Administration's emphasis on nuclear air power and criticized the placing of politics above the national interest. As a member of the Association of the U.S. Army, he worked for acceptance of his "limited strategy" views, which gained wider support among congressional, academic and public leaders, especially after 1957, when the launching of the Soviet satellite *Sputnik* convinced many that the USSR was gaining superiority in missiles. In a committee report for the Association in 1960, Ridgway outlined a proposal for the reorganization of the Army into a "mobile ready force" capable of fighting small wars. The plan was eventually implemented as the "flexible response" policy of the Kennedy Administration.

During the Johnson years Ridgway was one of a number of military men, including Gen. James M. Gavin and U.S. Marine Corps Commandant David M. Shoup, who attempted to persuade the Administration to limit U.S. involvement in Vietnam. In an article published in *Look* magazine in April 1966, Ridgway proposed that the U.S. maintain a middle course between unilateral withdrawal from Vietnam and "all-out war." He believed that the U.S. should press for a negotiated settlement that would guarantee South Vietnamese security. Ridgway feared that increasing U.S. military involvement would lead to direct Chinese intervention. He opposed the suggestion of Air Force Gen. Curtis E. LeMay that the U.S. bomb North Vietnam "back into the Stone Age." Ridgway wrote that "there must be some moral limit to the means we use to achieve victory." The use of nuclear weapons against North Vietnam, he said, would be "the ultimate in immorality." Instead of a dramatic expansion of the war, he supported Gavin's plan for a permanent halt in air strikes against North Vietnam and the limitation of U.S. troop operations to coastal enclaves in the South.

In March 1968 President Johnson invited Ridgway and a number of prominent former government officials and military men to the White House to advise him on Vietnam strategy. The panel, known as the Senior Advisory Group, argued that the U.S. could not achieve victory in Vietnam even with increased troop strength and stepped-up bombing of the North. The group advised the Administration to seek a negotiated settlement with North Vietnam. Johnson heeded this advice. At the end of March he announced his decision to de-escalate the conflict and begin negotiations.

[JLW]

ROGERS, WILLIAM P(IERCE)
b. 23 June 1913, Norfolk, N.Y.
Secretary of State, January
1969-September 1973.

William P. Rogers moved from his small-town, upstate New York beginnings through positions as assistant attorney general to a racket-busting Thomas Dewey of New York in 1938, and as counsel to the Senate Special Committee to Investigate the National Defense Program in 1947 to serve in the Eisenhower Administration as deputy attorney general from 1953 to 1957 and then as Attorney General until 1961.

As a close friend of the then vice president, Richard Nixon, Rogers had been at Nixon's side for three of his "Six Crises"—in the Alger Hiss case he had counselled Nixon to pursue his inquiry, in the 1952 "slush fund" affair he had helped Nixon arrange his "Checkers" speech defense, and after Eisenhower's 1955 heart attack he had advised Nixon to "act scrupulously like a Vice-President—not like an Acting President." In short, William Rogers was a man Richard Nixon regarded as "a cool man under pressure . . . [with] . . . excellent judgment, a good sense of press relations, 'and one to whom I could speak with complete freedom."

After acting as a policy adviser during Nixon's 1960 presidential campaign, Rogers decided to drop out of politics for the first time in 15 years and to pursue the practice of law in earnest. An ambitious, self-made, and rather independent individual, Rogers felt he wanted to make it "on his own." He purposely interjected a sense of distance between himself and his old friend, Nixon, in order to dispel the notion that he was simply a Nixon crony. During the eight years of the Kennedy-Johnson presidencies, he proved himself and prospered as a senior partner in the prestigious New York-Washington-Paris law firm of Royall, Koegel, Rogers, and Wells. He did not even return to play an important role in Richard Nixon's second bid for the presidency in 1968.

Despite the drifting apart that had occurred between Rogers and Nixon during the 1960s, Nixon once again turned to his old friend in 1968, insisting that he accept the ranking cabinet position of the Secretary of State. In light of Rogers's meager experience in foreign affairs, the appointment was regarded as somewhat surprising and indicative of Nixon's intention "to call the turn" on foreign affairs. Indeed, Rogers' diplomatic experience consisted of having been representative at the independence celebrations of Togo in 1960, a member of the delegation to the United Nations in 1965, and a 10-week special representative on the Ad Hoc Committee on Southwest Africa in 1967.

His supporters maintained that since he was free of "any commitments or emotional attachments to past policies or procedures," he would be less righteous, doctrinaire or crusading than his two immediate predecessors, John Foster Dulles and Dean Rusk. In addition his reputation as one of the most glittering of the "diplomatic yet plain-spoken Hill-crawlers" was viewed as an asset to the Administration in soothing the Senate Foreign Relations Committee and thus easing the course of the new Administration's Vietnam policy. One lawyer-turned-diplomat, Nicholas Katzenbach, argued that "technical expertise" was not required in a Secretary of State and that "the Secretary's job . . . is pulling the government together on foreign problems, dealing with Congress, and . . . dealing with representatives of other governments. All [of which] falls quite naturally in the domain of any successful lawyer. Legal training—questioning, getting at the facts, looking at alternatives—is the greatest possible training."

From the President's perspective, Rogers's appointment had the advantages of bringing in a comfortable and trusted friend, an individual who would not compete with him for the diplomatic spotlight, and a Progressive-Republican from the party's Eastern, internationalist wing.

Once confirmed, Rogers quickly began to establish good relations with Congress, soliciting the advice of influential senators and representatives and, in turn, being seen as a "force for moderation" within the Administration. He also gave more attention than any postwar Secretary of State to structural reform. In an effort to modernize and streamline bureaucratic procedures and internal communications, Rogers installed a sophisticated computer system for information storage and retrieval and initiated new personnel, training and advancement programs designed to develop and keep highly qualified specialists.

By the end of President Nixon's first term, Rogers could claim, probably justifiably, that the Department had never been in better shape. Yet management alone was not the solution, since the Department's workload was growing. The Secretary pointed out that "apart from the everyday business of diplomacy . . . we've just recently had to become involved in problems that were formerly domestic but have become international. We're dealing now with the environment, communications satellites, air-traffic control, hijacking and drug suppression."

Early in his tenure, Rogers demonstrated that his talents as a negotiator would, at least partially, compensate for his lack of substantive expertise in foreign affairs. In early trips to Europe and the Far East, Rogers created a favorable impression with his "ability to gain the quick trust of foreigners by conveying goodwill and personal warmth." However, it was soon apparent that the President looked to Rogers for guidance on the public-relations implications of his decisions rather than on policy itself.

Indeed speculation maintained that Henry Kissinger [q.v.] at the National Security Council and Melvin Laird at the Pentagon were more influential in formulating foreign and national security policy than Rogers and the State Department. Certainly Defense Secretary Laird and Presidential Assistant Kissinger were more conspicuous and were more aggressive bureaucratic politicians than Rogers. Both Laird and Kissinger also had more extensive backgrounds in their fields than Rogers.

By inclination disposed towards keeping a rather low profile, Rogers did not attempt to be a moderating counterweight to Laird. Although rumor and bureaucratic reality pitted Rogers against Kissinger, Rogers seemed content to serve as the top-level confidant while Kissinger acted the part of the stimulator and sifter of policy ideas. While this stance may have resulted in peace among the President's foreign affairs/national security counsellors, it also had the effect of lowering public esteem for the State Department and of demoralizing the Foreign Service. One reporter commented that under Rogers, the Department's personnel seemed "consumed by self-doubt, as if they [were] constantly asking themselves whether what they do really matters."

There is considerable controversy over the extent of Rogers' influence in formulating American foreign policy during his four and a half years as Secretary of State. Part of this debate can be attributed to Rogers contention that he and the President thought "a lot alike." Thus, according to Rogers, he and the President were usually in agreement, so the Secretary seldom had to fight for his position. This natural agreement may have given the appearance that Rogers lacked significant policy influence.

Within this likemindedness, however, it is probable that Rogers exerted a cautious and moderating influence. For instance, in April of 1969, when North Korean jets shot down an American EC-121 intelligence plane over the sea of Japan, Rogers was the voice of caution, speaking against the retaliation urged by the Defense Department and urging a diplomatic resolution saying that "in international affairs, the weak can be rash, the powerful must be restrained."

Rogers also succeeded in curbing the Administration's response to the Peruvian expropriation of American oilfields and installations in the spring of 1969. Instead of provoking a confrontation with Peru (and by extension, with Latin America generally) by a retaliatory cut-off of American foreign aid, Rogers found a loophole in the Hickenlooper Amendment to avoid applying such economic sanctions and implemented a cautious response of diplomatic negotiation.

On policy regarding Vietnam, Rogers generally supported the Administration's goal of finding a political solution for South Vietnam based on free elections and went along with the military strategy of maintaining a degree of offensive pressure on enemy forces in South Vietnam. Within this context, however, he strenuously objected, without apparent effect, to the 1970 invasion of Cambodia and was a strong proponent for the withdrawal of American forces and for the policy of "Vietnamization."

Although Rogers was clear in expressing the administration's disappointment in the 1971 expulsion of Nationalist China from the United Nations in order to admit Communist China, he was also a potent administration advocate of improving U.S. relations with Peking.

In most of the dramatic foreign policy issues of the first Nixon administration, Rogers played a low-keyed, unspectacular role. The one area in which he took a prominent initiative—perhaps the issue he is principally known for—was the Rogers Plan for the Middle East.

Initially proposed to the Soviets in October 1969, Rogers publicly offered his peace proposals to the Middle Eastern belligerents in December. His plan called on Israel to withdraw from Arab territories occupied in the 1967 war in return for

Arab assurances of a binding commitment to peace. Although this initial proposal was rejected by both Arabs and Israelis, Rogers persevered in his efforts and during 1970 succeeded in securing Egyptian, Jordanian, and Israeli agreement to a cease-fire and a resumption of negotiations under the auspices of UN Ambassador Gunnar Jarring. Eventually Rogers' efforts in the Middle East were eclipsed by his successor's (Henry Kissinger's) "shuttle diplomacy."

Following Nixon's reelection in 1972, rumor began to predict Rogers' imminent departure. Thus, the announcement of his resignation in September 1973 came as no surprise. Apparently everyone concerned was happy with the change—Rogers was eager to get back to his New York law practice, the President continued to regard him as a man of "unwavering good spirits, good judgment and good sense." Kissinger, who had been called the "Secretary of State in everything but title," was finally accorded that formal rank.

Rogers returned to the law firm of Rogers and Wells of New York City and effectively retired from politics.

[MJW]

ROSTOW, WALT W(HITMAN)
b. Oct. 7, 1916; New York, N.Y.
Chairman, State Department Policy Planning Council, December 1961-April 1966; Special Assistant to the President for National Security Affairs, April 1966-January 1969.

Rostow was one of three sons of a Russian-Jewish immigrant family. He attended Yale as an undergraduate and, following two years as a Rhodes Scholar at Oxford, received his Ph.D. from Yale in 1940. Following wartime service in the Office of Strategic Services, he worked briefly in the State Department and then spent two years as assistant to the executive secretary of the Economic Commission for Europe. He returned to academic life in 1950, when he received a teaching appointment at the Massachusetts Institute of Technology (MIT). From 1951 to 1960 he was associated with MIT's Central Intelligence Agency (CIA)-backed Center for International Studies.

Rostow wrote extensively on foreign policy and international developments and on economic history. His best-known book, *The Stages of Economic Growth: A Non-Communist Manifesto*, published in 1960, argued that economic growth was a multi-staged process, stimulated by a widespread desire for the improvement of life as well as the search for profits. This "modernization" process, Rostow said, was characterized by a crucial "takeoff" period of rapid growth stimulated by the expansion of a few key economic sectors. Rostow counterposed his model to that of Marx and used it as the ideological underpinning for his policy approach towards the developing countries of Asia, Africa and Latin America.

Rostow began advising Sen. John F. Kennedy (D, Mass.) on foreign policy in 1958 and was active in Kennedy's 1960 presidential campaign. Kennedy appointed Rostow deputy special assistant to the President for foreign security affairs in the incoming Administration. Rostow was a participant throughout 1961 in the formulation of U.S. policy towards Laos and Vietnam, generally advocating a strong U.S. diplomatic and military role in fighting Communist insurgencies.

As part of a general November 1961 shuffle of foreign policy officials, Rostow was moved to the State Department as counselor and chairman of the Policy Planning Council. In his new post he was in charge of long-range analysis and planning in a broad range of foreign policy areas, but was no longer centrally involved in the White House decision-making process.

In May 1964 President Johnson appointed Rostow to the additional post of U.S. representative to the Inter-American Committee on the Alliance for Progress (CIAP). Created in November 1963, CIAP was a special committee of the Organization of American States intended to provide

Latin American countries with a greater say in the direction of the Alliance for Progress.

Although at this time Rostow did not directly participate in making high-level decisions on Southeast Asia, he exerted continued influence through State Department memoranda and—starting in June 1964—through direct access to the President. His most important contribution in this period was a presentation of his general perspective on Vietnam-like situations, which came to be called the "Rostow thesis." It was prepared in December 1963 but was not widely circulated until the following summer. Rostow restated his long-standing belief that externally-supported insurgencies could be stopped only by military action against the source of external support. A series of escalating military measures, designed to impart the maximum possible psychological blow, would, he argued, make it clear that continued support of insurgency would result in heavy costs. This in turn would lead to a cessation of the support.

This policy approach flowed from Rostow's belief that modernization created certain dislocations and discontents, which although transitional, could be used by Communists to gain support. It was therefore necessary to hold off any Communist challenge until full modernization was achieved, eliminating the problems that fed insurgency.

Consistent with this general framework, Rostow argued in February and April 1964 that it was crucial that the U.S. take action to force North Vietnam to abide by the provisions of the 1958 and 1962 Geneva Accords forbidding foreign troops in Laos or South Vietnam. In June he advocated increased military pressure against North Vietnam combined with a strong public stance against their support for rebel forces in Laos and South Vietnam.

In August 1964 the "Rostow thesis" was widely circulated inside the Administration. A detailed critique was prepared by the Defense Department. It concluded that serious difficulties were involved in attacks on North Vietnam and questioned whether domestic and international support could be rallied for such a program. Therefore, the report argued, acceptance or even public dissemination of the Rostow position was probably unwise. But, according to the authors of the *Pentagon Papers:* "These reservations notwithstanding, the outlook embodied in the 'Rostow thesis' came to dominate a good deal of Administration thinking on the question of pressures against the North in the months ahead."

As a National Security Agency working group was again reexamining the future direction of U.S. policy in Vietnam, Rostow contended in November 1964 that the U.S. had to convince the North Vietnamese of American determination to apply limited but sustained military pressure upon them until they ceased support of the National Liberation Front in South Vietnam. He urged the movement of a large retaliatory force to the Pacific area, the introduction of some U.S. ground troops in Laos and South Vietnam and the initiation of a naval blockade and bombing against North Vietnam. (Although all of these steps were eventually taken, the immediate White House decision favored more limited military action.)

Rostow became increasingly and publicly identified with the Administration's Vietnam policy in 1965. On arriving in Tokyo in April for a series of speaking engagements, he was met by 1,000 anti-American demonstrators. During this period of rising campus opposition to the war, Rostow defended the Administration's position at a May 15-16 national teach-in on Vietnam, broadcast to over 100 colleges.

On March 31, 1966 President Johnson appointed Rostow special assistant to the President for national security affairs, succeeding McGeorge Bundy [q.v.], who had resigned to become president of the Ford Foundation. In this post Rostow worked closely with Johnson for the remainder of the Administration on virtually all foreign policy issues. He selected the information to be presented to him, accompanied him on his foreign travels and sat in on meetings with foreign leaders. Rostow genuinely admired the President, and as criticism of U.S. policy in Vietnam grew, Rostow's continued optimism about the war and his willingness to defend it publicly led to an increasingly close relationship with President Johnson. (In September 1966 Johnson appointed Rostow's older brother, Eugene V. Rostow, undersecretary of state for political affairs.)

Although sustained U.S. bombing of North Vietnam began in March 1965, the targets were limited in nature. In September 1965 the Joint Chiefs of Staff began urging the bombing of more "lucrative" targets, including petroleum and oil facilities. A debate over the expansion of bombing targets went on for several months. In May 1966 Rostow came out in strong support of "systematic and sustained bombing" aimed at destroying the petroleum and petroleum-product facilities of North Vietnam. Rostow argued that a similar program—on which he had worked— had been effective against the Germans in World War II and would be equally effective against North Vietnam. Others, including the CIA, disagreed. After a period of hesitation in late May, Johnson approved the new air strikes, which included targets in the Hanoi-Haiphong area. In spite of initial reports of success, however, the program failed to limit the ability of the North Vietnamese to support the war in the South.

Throughout 1967 there was renewed conflict within the Administration over the bombing campaign against North Vietnam. Most military leaders urged an extension of bombing and the elimination of existing restrictions. Many civilian officials, particularly Assistant Secretary of Defense for International Security Affairs John T. McNaughton and Secretary of Defense Robert S. McNamara [q.v.], urged limiting the bombing to the southern panhandle of North Vietnam. In May Rostow, who attended the regular Tuesday meetings at which the President chose specific bombing targets, wrote an important memorandum indicating basic support for the McNamara-McNaughton position, although he argued that the option of future strikes in the Hanoi-Haiphong area had to be kept open. The President took a middle course and in July ordered a continuation of the "Rolling Thunder" bombing program along essentially existing lines, with only sporadic raids in the Hanoi-Haiphong area.

In June 1967 Rostow accompanied the President at the Glassboro, N.J., meeting with Soviet Premier Aleksei N. Kosygin. The following month he worked closely with Johnson during the Arab-Israeli war. He also served on a special group headed by Bundy that Johnson established to work on both the immediate crisis and long-range solutions to the Middle East situation.

On Nov. 1, 1967 an increasingly skeptical McNamara prepared a memo to the President in which he called for "stabilizing" the U.S. war effort in Vietnam, reexamining the ground fighting to try to reduce U.S. casualties and shift a greater burden of fighting to the South Vietnamese Army and instituting a bombing halt before the end of the year. Johnson gave the memo to Rostow and other senior advisers for comment. Rostow supported the first two proposals but opposed an unconditional bombing halt. His position was similar to that Johnson himself soon took.

Following the Tet offensive in late January and early February 1968, Johnson established a new group under incoming Secretary of Defense Clark Clifford [q.v.] to thoroughly reexamine Vietnam policy. Rostow drafted the directive to the group and participated in its deliberations. He apparently continued to oppose any new restriction on the bombing of North Vietnam. (By the end of March, however, Johnson decided on a partial bombing halt as a step towards negotiations.)

In the final months of Johnson's term of office, overtures were reportedly made in Rostow's behalf to MIT and several other leading universities to secure for him a teaching position after the Administration's end. These feelers were apparently rebuffed, partially due to Rostow's role in the planning and conduct of the war in Vietnam. Rostow eventually accepted a position as professor of economics and history at the University of Texas at Austin, where a Lyndon B. Johnson School of Public Affairs was planned. In the final hours of his presidency, Johnson awarded Rostow and 19 others the Medal of Freedom, the country's highest civilian honor.

In Texas Rostow resumed teaching and writing and helped Johnson organize his foreign policy papers for inclusion in his presidential library. Rostow continued to defend U.S. military involvement in Vietnam. Rostow published *The Diffusion of Power, 1957-1972,* an account of the U.S. role in world affairs which included some material on his own activities in the period covered.

[JBF]

For further information:
W.W. Rostow, *The Diffusion of Power, 1957-1972* (New York, 1972).
U.S. Department of Defense, *The Pentagon Papers,* Senator Gravel edition (Boston, 1971), Vols. III and IV.

RUSK, (DAVID) DEAN
b. Feb. 9, 1909; Cherokee County, Ga.
Secretary of State, January 1961-January 1969.

Dean Rusk, Secretary of State during most of the 1960s, spent his early years in poverty. He was the son of an ordained Presbyterian minister who had left the ministry because of ill-health and was forced to eke out a living as a farmer and mail carrier. Rusk worked his way through Davidson College and, following his graduation in 1931, studied at Oxford on a Rhodes Scholarship. Returning to the U.S. in 1934, he joined the political science department of California's Mills College. Rusk became dean of the faculty in 1938.

In 1943 Rusk served with the infantry in the China-Burma-India theater and eventually became deputy chief of staff to Gen. Joseph Stilwell. While in the Army he became a protege of Gen. George Marshall who admired the young man's diplomatic ability. After his discharge in 1946 Rusk, at the behest of Marshall, joined the State Department as assistant chief of the division of international security affairs. Several months later he became special assistant to Secretary of War Robert P. Patterson. In 1947 he returned to the State Department as director of the office of special political

affairs. During the next five years Rusk served as a close aide to Robert Lovett [*q.v.*] and Dean Acheson [*q.v.*]. In 1950 he was appointed assistant secretary of state for Far Eastern affairs. In this position Rusk helped formulate policy during the Korean conflict, supporting military action in Korea but opposing the expansion of the war into Communist China.

Rusk left the State Department to become president of the Rockefeller Foundation in 1952. During his tenure he helped expand the Foundation's projects to aid underdeveloped nations in Asia, Africa and Latin America in solving agricultural and public health problems.

Following his election in 1960 President Kennedy appointed Rusk his Secretary of State. Kennedy, who considered foreign affairs his personal responsibility, was determined to dominate foreign policy formulation during his Administration. He did not want a Secretary who might overshadow him and so rejected such prominent individuals as Adlai Stevenson [*q.v.*] and Chester Bowles for the position. Instead, he selected the relatively obscure Dean Rusk, a man, moreover, who agreed with the President's conception of policymaking. In addition, Rusk's appointment had the support of members of the powerful New York-based Eastern establishment with whom Kennedy wanted to develop close connections.

Rusk inherited an organization beset by problems. The postwar growth of the State Department had resulted in the development of an unwieldy bureaucracy that by 1961 threatened the effectiveness of U.S. policy. In addition, rivalry between the State and Defense Departments for dominant influence in foreign affairs had often crippled policymaking. More importantly, the McCarthyite anti-Communist crusades of the 1940s and 1950s had driven many capable men, particularly those knowledgeable about the Soviet Union and China, from the Department. These attacks had also bred timidity and political orthodoxy in those who remained. Consequently there was little creativity within the Department. (Kennedy considered State a "bowl full of jelly.")

During the Kennedy Administration Rusk attempted to make the Department more responsive to new policy trends and to the wishes of the President. Although he had only limited success in reforming the bureaucracy, Rusk, at the urging of the President, did permit such subordinates as Roger Hilsman, G. Mennen Williams and Theodoro Moscoso to tentatively explore new policies toward Asia, Africa and Latin America. In addition, Rusk quietly improved relations between State, Congress and the Central Intelligence Agency and moderated the rivalry between the State and Defense Departments. Critics claimed, however, that Rusk's cooperation with Defense was not so much the result of a conscious effort as it was of his inability to assert himself.

Despite his position and long tenure—he served the second longest term of any Secretary of State in the 20th Century—Rusk had little impact on foreign policy formulation. Because Kennedy sought to be his own Secretary of State, he personally directed day-to-day policymaking on many major issues, such as the East-West conflict over Berlin in the summer of 1961. Kennedy was also reluctant to rely on the traditional Department bureaucracy and instead appointed task forces made up of men both from in and out of government to deal with particular problems. Often these groups were composed of close personal friends and aides. Rusk, neither close to Kennedy nor constitutionally equipped to bypass the bureaucracy, was rarely given a role in these task forces.

Rusk's lack of impact can also be attributed to his personality and his conception of the role of Secretary of State. Rusk was by nature a reserved, unassertive man whose chief virtues were patience, the ability to handle detail and express himself clearly. These qualities served him well during private negotiations and earned him praise, even from his critics, as a supreme "technical diplomat." However, those who worked with Rusk also complained of his lack of imagination, creativity and qualities of leadership.

To a great degree, these qualities were not vital for the role that Rusk envisioned for himself as Secretary of State. Rusk believed that the Secretary should be the personal adviser of the President. It was the President who defined the nation's overall goals and objectives. The assistant secretaries of state with their expert knowledge of particular regions were the formulators and advocates of specific policies and the managers of the Department. The Secretary's job was to stay above the daily business of the Department and remain at the President's side as a judge of policy alternatives.

Consequently Rusk refused to advocate specific policies during most of the important crises of the Kennedy Administration. During the March 1961 debates over the proposed invasion of Cuba by U.S.-trained Cuban exiles, Rusk, in the words of Arthur Schlesinger, Jr. [q.v.], merely listened "inscrutably through the discussions, confining himself to gentle warnings about possible excesses." The Secretary, however, did caution that the invasion might result in a national and international loss of faith in the new President. To avoid this he suggested that someone make the decision to launch the invasion in the President's absence— someone who could be sacrificed if the plan failed. Although several aides urged Rusk to clearly voice his doubts about the invasion, the Secretary took no action. The invasion was launched on April 17 and was crushed two days later.

Rusk again played little part in the policy discussions that followed the discovery of Soviet offensive missiles in Cuba in October 1962. The Secretary did not join the early meetings of the Excom, the group formed specifically to advise the President in the crisis. At the meetings he did attend, Rusk advocated no particular response but opposed informing the Russians of U.S. knowledge of the missiles. He believed that such a step would permit the Soviets to act before the U.S. had formulated policy. Only at the Oct. 18 meeting did Rusk suggest a course of action, but his stand was extremely inconsistent. At the morning meeting he argued against an air strike to destroy the weapons. However, at the evening session he urged a limited air attack after informing U.S. allies. By the end of the meeting he had backed away from that position as well. On Oct. 23 Kennedy, at the suggestion of Attorney General Robert Kennedy [q.v.] and Secretary of Defense Robert McNamara [q.v.], instituted a "quarantine" of the island to force the removal of the missiles.

During the Kennedy Administration Rusk attempted to keep the State Department out of Vietnam affairs, believing that American involvement in that country was primarily a military problem. However, by 1963 he had become entangled in the conflict that would occupy his attention for the remainder of the decade.

Following the Diem regime's attack on dissident Buddhists in August 1963, American foreign policy advisers began a reevaluation of U.S. support of the regime. The President's highest advisers were divided on possible courses of action. Some, such as McNamara, wished to press Diem for reform. Others, such as Rusk, believed that a change of government might be necessary. The initial instructions sent to Ambassador Henry Cabot Lodge [q.v.] on Aug. 24, 1963 reflected the State Department's position. Lodge was told that Diem should be given every chance to "rid himself" of elements hostile to reform but that if he remained obdurate the U.S. "must face the possibility that Diem himself cannot be preserved." The Ambassador was also instructed to privately inform military leaders that the U.S. would not continue to support the government of South Vietnam unless reforms were made. At the insistence of Rusk, he was also given permission to tell the generals that the U.S. "would give them direct support in any interim period of breakdown [of the] central government."

Because of dissension among the President's advisers, these instructions were canceled on Aug. 30, and Lodge was ordered to work for reform of the regime. The policy debate continued throughout the fall of 1963. However, Rusk remained a shadowy figure in these discussions, leaving subordinates such as Lodge and Hilsman to expound the need for change. South Viet-

namese generals overthrew the Diem regime on Nov. 1.

Rusk's influence increased during the last half of the decade. According to Presidential Assistant W.W. Rostow [q.v.], Johnson built his advisory system around Rusk, Secretary of Defense Robert McNamara [q.v.] and Presidential Assistant McGeorge Bundy [q.v.], with Rusk as the central figure. He counseled the President on all important foreign policy matters, including the 1965 decision to send Marines to the Dominican Republic to evacuate Americans and keep peace between feuding factions in that nation's civil war.

In late May and early June 1967, following Egypt's deployment of troops on Israeli borders and its closing of the Gulf of Aqaba to Israeli shipping, Rusk worked closely with Johnson in an attempt to prevent a Middle East war. Fearing congressional disapproval of American unilateral action, Rusk counseled Johnson against an attempt to use American troops to force open the canal and attempted to gain support for allied action to pressure Egypt into changing its policy. His efforts failed; war broke out in the Middle East on June 6.

Rusk became one of the President's chief advisers on the Vietnam war. He helped Johnson make important decisions on the escalation of the conflict and, just as importantly, reinforced the President's own commitment to the American effort there. Rusk saw the conflict in Southeast Asia as an attempt by a militant Chinese government, prompted by the Marxist theory of world revolution, to expand its influence throughout Asia by means of "wars of liberation." Consequently, he argued, the U.S. was not in Vietnam simply because of its treaty commitments but because of the need to show that such expansion was doomed to failure. Although asserting that a victory in Vietnam was necessary for American security, Rusk did not define the war primarily as a battle for a strategic area but rather emphasized that it was a "psychological struggle for the conquest of minds and souls." The loss of Vietnam would mean "a drastic loss of confidence in the will and capacity of the free world to oppose aggression" and would bring the world considerably closer to a great power conflict, according to Rusk.

Because of his belief in the need for a military victory in Vietnam, Rusk consistently supported the Administration's escalation of the war. In August 1964 he backed Johnson's decision to stage retaliatory raids against North Vietnam for that nation's alleged attacks upon U.S. ships in the Gulf of Tonkin. He also supported systematic bombing of the North, begun in March 1965, as a means of forcing Hanoi to end infiltration of the South.

During 1964 and 1965 Rusk opposed attempts to negotiate a settlement. With the National Liberation Front controlling more than half of South Vietnam and the Saigon government crumbling, the U.S. could not bargain from a position of strength. Until military pressure on Hanoi tilted the balance of power toward the South, Rusk asserted, the North would have little incentive to negotiate and that whatever talks could be started would have little value. Rusk opposed the bombing halt of December 1965-January 1966 for the same reasons. Believing that a pause could be effectively employed only once, he recommended that the halt be postponed until the bombing had escalated to the point where North Vietnam could no longer tolerate the damage and would be forced to accept a settlement favorable to the U.S.

During the Johnson years Rusk emerged as the chief public defender of the Administration's position. In February 1966 he appeared at televised hearings of the Senate Foreign Relations Committee, chaired by Sen. William Fulbright (D, Ark.) [q.v.], to explain Administration policy. Rusk sought to refute Fulbright's charge that the conflict was a civil war in which the U.S. had no strategic interest by describing what he believed to be a long-term pattern of Communist Chinese aggression. One year later, in an October 1967 press conference, he justified the U.S. presence as necessary to protect the region from the future threat of "a billion Chinese on the mainland, armed with nuclear weapons." Rusk often used the analogy of Munich to explain the American

war effort in Vietnam. In a January 1967 letter to 100 student leaders, he maintained that the failure of the world community to stop aggression in Ethiopia, Manchuria and Central Europe during the 1930s had resulted in World War II. "In short," he wrote, "we are involved in Vietnam because we knew from painful experience that the minimum condition for order on our planet is that aggression must not be permitted to succeed. For when it does succeed, the consequence is not peace, it is the further expansion of aggression. And those who have borne responsibility in our country since 1945 have not for one moment forgotten that a third world war would be a nuclear war."

According to journalist David Halberstam, as Secretary of Defense Robert McNamara [q.v.] began to question U.S. policy during 1967, Rusk felt it his duty to be more steadfast in his support of the President's actions. In Halberstam's words, Rusk "became a rock, unflinching and unchanging and absorbing, as deliberately as he could, as much of the reaction to the war as possible."

Following the Communists' Tet offensive of February 1968, the military requested over 200,000 additional troops for the war. Rusk recommended that the President approve the increase. However, a bipartisan panel of statesmen specially convened to advise Johnson on the proposal opposed a further increase because of the detrimental effects it could have on the U.S. economy and society. Johnson accepted the panel's advice and on March 31 announced a policy of de-escalation. He hoped that the step would prompt Hanoi to enter negotiations. Hanoi quickly accepted the offer with the provision that initial meetings deal only with conditions for a total bombing halt. According to Undersecretary of the Air Force Townsend Hoopes Rusk "tried to slow down, and if possible avoid altogether" the initial talks. He emphasized the limited purpose of the discussions and denigrated the possibility of a complete bombing halt. Preliminary peace talks began in

Paris in May 1968. Rusk played little part in them; the American delegation was headed by W. Averell Harriman [q.v.].

Rusk left office in January 1969. After a few months in semi-retirement, he became professor of international law at the University of Georgia.

[EWS]

For further information:
David Halberstam, *The Best and the Brightest* (New York, 1972).
Townsend Hoopes, *The Limits of Intervention* (New York, 1969).
U.S. Department of Defense, *The Pentagon Papers*, Senator Gravel Edition (Boston, 1971), Vols. III and IV.

SCHLESINGER, ARTHUR M(EIER) JR.
b. Oct. 15, 1917; Columbus, Ohio.
Historian.

Following a brilliant academic career at Harvard and Oxford, Schlesinger joined his father in the Harvard history department in 1946. A leading spokesman for American liberalism in the postwar era, Schlesinger also wrote award-winning biographies of Andrew Jackson and Franklin D. Roosevelt, which cast both presidents as pragmatic and successful proponents of progressive social change.

After backing Adlai Stevenson [q.v.] in 1952 and 1956, Schlesinger switched his allegiance to John F. Kennedy in 1959 and helped recruit a liberal "brain trust" for the new President's administration. Kennedy appointed Schlesinger a special assistant in January 1961 and assigned him, among other tasks to work on Latin American affairs. Schlesinger toured South America with Food for Peace Director George McGovern [q.v.] early in the year and argued for the Alliance for Progress as a means both to promote progressive democracy in the hemisphere and to counter the influence of Cuban-backed Communist movements. Although he opposed the Bay of Pigs invasion of Cuba as unwise, Schlesinger helped develop U.S. efforts to economically and politically isolate Fidel Castro's regime from other Western Hemisphere governments.

Two months after Kennedy's assassination Schlesinger resigned his post as a White House special assistant and began work on a history of the Administration. His best-selling book, *A Thousand Days: John F. Kennedy in the White House*, was published in 1965 and won the Pulitzer Prize for biography the next year. The work celebrated the youth and vigor of the late President, his unsentimental liberalism and the sophistication of Administration policymakers. In 1966 Schlesinger was appointed Albert Schweitzer Professor of Humanities at the City University of New York.

During the same year, he began to oppose the Vietnam War and published *The Bitter Heritage: Vietnam and American Democracy*, which argued that the war must be stopped because of its "ugly side-effects" at home: "inflation, frustration, indignation, protest, panic, angry divisions within the national community, premonitions of McCarthyism." Schlesinger favored a gradual de-escalation of the war, with an immediate halt to the bombing. In April 1967 he joined with liberals Joseph Rauh and John Kenneth Galbraith to form Negotiations Now, a group seeking a million signatures on a stop-the-bombing petition.

Although aligning himself with the growing movement against the war, Schlesinger was careful not to lend his prestige to those in the New Left who attacked the entire thrust of the United States postwar foreign policy. Schlesinger argued that American involvement in Vietnam resulted not from an inherently expansionary American foreign policy but out of a series of mistakes leading to a military-political quagmire. Writing in the journal *Foreign Affairs* in October 1967, Schlesinger attacked the revisionist historians and argued that because of the character of the Soviet state, the "most rational of American policies could hardly have averted the Cold War."

In 1967 Schlesinger first advised Sen. Robert F. Kennedy (D, N.Y.) [q.v.] to avoid a primary battle with President

Johnson, instead urging that he throw his weight behind a peace plank at the Democratic National Convention. However, the historian-adviser reversed his position in November after Sen. Eugene McCarthy (D, Minn.) [q.v.] announced his candidacy for the Democratic presidential nomination. Schlesinger strongly supported Kennedy when he began his campaign in March. After Kennedy's assassination three months later, Schlesinger was among those former Kennedy aides who threw their support to Sen. George McGovern's (D, S.D.) [q.v.] short-lived bid for the Democratic nomination.

During the early 1970s Schlesinger was a leading academic critic of the Nixon Administration. His influential 1973 work, *The Imperial Presidency*, attacked the growing centralization of power in the executive branch and cast into a somewhat darker light the increasing power exercised by such liberal presidents as Roosevelt, Kennedy and Johnson.

[NNL]

For further information: ,
————, "Origins of the Cold War" *Foreign Affairs* XLVI (October 1967), pp. 22-52.
Arthur Schlesinger Jr., *A Thousand Days: John F. Kennedy in the White House* (New York, 1965).
————, *The Bitter Heritage: Vietnam and American Democracy* (New York, 1966).
————, *The Imperial Presidency* (New York, 1973).

SCHLESINGER, JAMES R(ODNEY)

b. Feb. 15, 1929; New York, N.Y.
Chairman, Atomic Energy Commission, August 1971-January 1973; Director, Central Intelligence Agency, January-June 1973; Secretary of Defense, June 1973-November 1975

Schlesinger graduated summa cum laude from Harvard in 1950. After extended travel abroad, he resumed his graduate studies at Harvard, taking his M.A. in economics in 1952 and his Ph.D in 1956. He began teaching at the University of Virginia in 1955 and at the Naval War College two years later. In 1960 Schlesinger's first book, *The Political Economy of National Security*, impressed the staff of the RAND Corp., a defense-oriented "think tank," and consequently, Schlesinger worked from 1963 to 1967 at RAND as director of strategic studies. He left RAND in 1967 to serve as assistant director of the Bureau of the Budget. When the new Nixon Administration reorganized the Bureau into the Office of Management and Budget (OMB), Schlesinger served as acting deputy director during the transition and thereafter as assistant director.

In December 1972, on what many observers believe was the urging of Henry Kissinger [q.v.], President Nixon appointed Schlesinger to succeed Richard Helms [q.v.] as director of the Central Intelligence Agency (CIA). In spring 1973 Nixon once again reshuffled his cabinet in the deepening Watergate crisis. Schlesinger was appointed Secretary of Defense, succeeding Elliot Richardson, who became Attorney General. Schlesinger had no difficulty establishing himself as a hardliner on military and security questions, defending in early speeches the tactical bombing of Cambodia in the Indochina conflict and the 1960-70 secret raids in that country as necessary to "defend U.S. servicemen."

The weakening of the North Atlantic Treaty Organization (NATO) and its alleged lack of preparedness for war with the countries of the Warsaw Pact was a major theme for Schlesinger before and after his move to the Department of Defense. He consistently opposed NATO troop cuts and the withdrawal of U.S. military personnel from Western Europe. These concerns were further aggravated during the October 1973 Mideast crisis when the European allies of the U.S. refused to collaborate openly in the defense of Israel for fear of alienating the Arab countries on which they depended for oil. Schlesinger stated in late October that the actions of these allies would cause the U.S. to "reflect" on its concepts of military strategy. In June 1974 Schlesinger attended NATO talks in Vienna and then went on to Moscow to participate in talks on strategic arms limitation. In December of that year he warned NATO ministers not to undertake military spending cuts for reasons of economy in the belief that the U.S. would bail them out militarily. In April 1975, however, as the U.S.-backed regime in Saigon was collapsing, Schlesinger assured America's allies that they would not be abandoned.

One of Schlesinger's attempts to reshape U.S. military strategy in the post-Vietnam world, and one linked to his downfall in October 1975, was his sponsorship of the concept of "limited nuclear warfare." In his view, growing Soviet nuclear capacity had rendered previous U.S. strategy obsolete. He expressed the fear held by many that the Soviets had reached a point where they could withstand a U.S. counterattack and still have the missiles necessary to devastate the U.S. mainland, and stated that "we are seeking to forestall the development of an assymetrical situation which would be beneficial to the Soviet Union." To counter this situation, Schlesinger announced the U.S. was "re-targeting" Soviet missile bases and placing less emphasis on Soviet population centers.

The "limited nuclear warfare" concept came to the fore in May 1975 when the Pentagon released a paper containing a statement by Schlesinger that the U.S. was prepared to use such weapons in any general war in Western Europe. He believed a limited nuclear attack on a key Soviet installation could show U.S. determination and force the Soviets to negotiate short of all-out war. Opponents of limited nuclear warfare in Congress argued that such conceptions made nuclear warfare all the more likely. In June 1975 the Stockholm-based Institute of Peace Research charged Schlesinger with promoting the long-term deployment of "mini-nukes" to replace conventional nuclear weapons. In July, Schlesinger defended a possible "first strike" with limited nuclear weapons.

Schlesinger's views on such matters won him a reputation as a hard-liner and a general foe of detente with the Soviet Union. After visiting Japan in August 1975 for top-level talks, he described that nation as an "indispensable partner in the Pacific" but "too much of a passive partner." He urged Japan to intensify its rearmament efforts. In early October he toured the NATO capitals of Western Europe, again warning against defense cuts.

On Nov. 3, 1975, in a massive shake-up at the top of the Ford Administration, Schlesinger was dismissed from his position as Secretary of Defense, William Colby was fired from his CIA directorship, and Henry Kissinger, while remaining Secretary of State, relinquished his post as head of the National Security Council. Schlesinger's firing in particular was interpreted as a conciliatory gesture to the Soviet Union. *The Washington Post* commented: "Nowhere else in the world is the departure of James Schlesinger likely to be more closely watched—or as warmly received—as in the Kremlin. To the Soviets, Schlesinger was a powerful and persuasive enemy of detente." The Chinese government, in a rare commentary on U.S. domestic politics, attacked Schlesinger's firing as a capitulation to the Soviets.

In the weeks after Schlesinger's firing, President Gerald Ford conceded, after initial denials of Administration infighting, that there had been "growing tension" within the government, and Henry Kissinger admitted "differences" with Schlesinger on key questions. On Nov. 23 Schlesinger appeared on "Meet the Press" and attributed his dismissal to, among other things, his opposition to limits on defense spending.

Schlesinger momentarily retired from public life. In the fall of 1976 he was visiting the People's Republic of China on the invitation of Mao Tse-tung at the time of Mao's death. When the Carter Administration took office in January 1977, Schlesinger returned to the executive branch as Carter's Secretary of Energy. Schlesinger helped draft Carter's 1977 energy program, but he drew considerable criticism, particularly in Congress, where many called for his resignation. He was eventually fired by Carter in a major cabinet shake-up in July 1979.

[LRG]

For further information:
Elmo Zumwalt, *On Watch* (New York, 1976).

STETTINIUS, EDWARD R. JR.
b. Oct. 22, 1900; Chicago, Ill.
d. Oct. 31, 1949; Greenwich, Conn.
Secretary of State, December 1944-June 1945; Ambassador to the United Nations, June 1945-June 1946.

The son of a partner of the giant J.P. Morgan banking firm, Edward Stettinius attended the University of Virginia but failed to graduate. Rather than devoting his attention to studies, he was active in Christian social service projects including the Young Men's Christian Association.

Stettinius began his professional career with General Motors and then transferred to U.S. Steel. He was named one of the corporation's vice presidents in 1931 and became chairman in 1938. In 1939, Franklin D. Roosevelt appointed Stettinius chairman of the War Resources Board. He subsequently served as director of several other agencies and became undersecretary of state in 1943. In 1944 Roosevelt appointed Stettinius Secretary of State upon the resignation of Cordell Hull. Stettinius, however, had little foreign policy background and had a minor impact on the administration's policies.

When Harry Truman became President Stettinius handed in his resignation. Truman did not personally know him and therefore did not have the confidence in him that Roosevelt did. More important, Truman realized that to have Stettinius in a post, which was next in line for the presidency, would not be politically sound because the Secretary had never held elective office. The President therefore decided to offer the job to James Brynes [q.v.], who had been a leading contender for the 1944 vice presidential nomination. However, the President postponed the acceptance of Stettinius's resignation until after the United Nations Conference in San Francisco.

The Secretary's last official responsibility was the planning of the San Francisco Conference. The delegation chosen by Roosevelt included Sens. Tom Connally (D, Tex.) and Arthur Vandenberg (R, Mich.) [q.v.], Reps. Sol Bloom (D, N.Y.) and Charles Eaton (R, N.J.), former governor Harold Stassen and Virginia G. Gildersleeve, Dean of Barnard College. Roosevelt selected Stettinius to be the delegation chairman. The Secretary found it difficult to work with such prominent personalities. None were willing to accept his leadership or to permit him to speak to the press for the delegation. The group even failed to agree on a daily statement for the media.

Stettinius remained dominated by his delegates even in policy debates. On April 27 the Czechoslovokian government moved to admit the Soviet puppet Lublin government of Poland as a member. Upon the demand of Vandenberg Stettinius took to the floor to oppose the motion. Stettinius's major clash with the Russians came on the role of the Security Council. The Soviet Union insisted that the permanent members of the Council should be able to veto even the discussion of a dispute. Stettinius answered that the U.S. would not join the world body if this occurred. With the issue deadlocked at the San Francisco Conference, Truman sent Harry Hopkins on a special mission to Moscow, where he obtained a reversal of this position from Stalin.

On June 27, the day after the Conference closed, Truman accepted Stettinius's resignation. The President appointed him the first ambassador to the United Nations. Stettinius attended the preparatory conference in London in early 1946, where he again had problems controlling his delegation, which included such major Republicans as John Foster Dulles [q.v.] and Senator Vandenberg. In June of the same year, Stettinius resigned following reports that he had disagreed with James Brynes over policy. Until his death in November 1949, Stettinius suffered from a heart ailment that curtailed his activities.

[JB]

STEVENSON, ADLAI E(WING)
b. Feb. 5, 1900; Los Angeles, Calif.
d. July 14, 1965; London, England.
Democratic presidential candidate, 1952, 1956.

Stevenson was the grandson of Adlai Stevenson, vice president in Grover Cleveland's second term, and the son of Lewis Stevenson, who was active in Illinois Democratic politics. The younger Adlai Stevenson attended the Choate School in Wallingford, Conn., and graduated from Princeton University in 1922. He worked for his family's newspaper in Bloomington, Ill., and studied law at Northwestern University, receiving a J.D. degree in 1926. The following year Stevenson entered a Chicago law firm.

In 1933 Stevenson became special counsel to the Agricultural Adjustment Administration and the following year transferred to the Federal Alcohol Control Administration as assistant general counsel. In 1935 he returned to private law practice in Chicago. Six years later Stevenson went back to Washington as special assistant to Secretary of the Navy Frank Knox. In 1945 he became special assistant to Secretary of State Edward Stettinius. Later in the year he was U.S. minister and representative to the Preparedness Commission for the United Nations. He was senior adviser to the American delegation to the first U.N. General Assembly session, which opened in London in January 1946. Stevenson was alternate delegate at subsequent sessions in 1946 and 1947.

In 1948 Stevenson won the Democratic nomination for governor of Illinois with the backing of Eleanor Roosevelt and Supreme Court Justice William O. Douglas. He then ran as a reform candidate against what he charged was the scandal-ridden administration of incumbent Republican Gov. Dwight

H. Green. Stevenson defeated Green by 572,000 votes, the largest plurality in Illinois history.

From the time of his election as governor, Stevenson was mentioned as a possible 1952 Democratic presidential candidate, and despite his refusal to encourage a national movement, he was nominated on the third ballot. In his acceptance speech Stevenson appealed for an issue-oriented campaign based on thought rather than emotion. His comment, "Let's talk sense to the American people," became for many the trademark of his campaign. Liberal intellectuals in particular came to admire the thoughtful, analytical and urbanely witty character of his speeches, his general avoidance of personal attacks and innuendo and his minimization of traditional campaign ballyhoo.

To many others Stevenson's intellectual style smacked of uncertainty, indecisiveness and lack of a fighting spirit. President Truman, for one, complained that Stevenson's campaign was not aggressive. Stevenson was overheard early in the Convention saying to the Illinois delegation, "I do not dream myself fit for the job [of President] . . . ," and this comment reinforced the impression of uncertainty.

Following his defeat, Stevenson began a six-month tour of the Far East, Middle East and Europe. Upon his return he wrote a series of articles for *Look* magazine. He stated that in the Cold War "anti-Communist preaching wins few hearts." The United States, he said, had to promote economic development in backward countries and live up to its ideals by rejecting McCarthyism and opposing Western colonialism.

As its latest presidential candidate, Stevenson was the unofficial national spokesman of the Democratic Party, and in that capacity he remained in the public eye. At the Democratic National Committee's Southern Conference in March 1954, he denounced McCarthyism, stating that "it is wicked and it is subversive for public officials to try deliberately to replace reason with passion; to substitute hatred for honest difference. . . ." During the same speech he attacked the "massive retaliation" policy recently announced by Secretary of State

John Foster Dulles [q.v.], which relied on the use of strategic nuclear weapons as the U.S. primary defense against Soviet attack and expansion. Stevenson warned that the Soviet Union also had massive retaliatory power and that implementation of the plan "would certainly mean World War III and atomic counter-retaliation." In 1955 he opposed the Administration-sponsored Formosa Resolution on the grounds that it committed the Senate to support almost any action of the President to protect Nationalist China against Communist Chinese attack, including defense of what he believed were the strategically worthless islands of Quemoy and Matsu. In an April 11 radio address, Stevenson warned that the U.S. might lose allies if it went to war over those islands.

During the 1956 campaign, Stevenson again attacked Eisenhower's foreign policy for being too conservative. Addressing the American Legion Convention on Sept. 5, Stevenson stated that the draft could be ended in the "foreseeable future" because the modern Armed Forces needed technically skilled specialized personnel serving for long periods rather than partly trained men enlisted for brief terms. Eisenhower denounced the suggestion as "incredible folly" that led "down the road of surrender," and Republicans ridiculed Stevenson for claiming to know more about military matters than the President, a former military man.

On Oct. 15, during a nationwide television appearance, Stevenson suggested that the United States unilaterally halt further testing of H-bombs in the hope that the Soviet Union would reciprocate. (He had made a similar proposal the preceding April.) Stevenson argued that such a cessation could be a first step towards nuclear disarmament or at least towards a halt to the poisoning of the atmosphere with radioactive fallout. He contended that any subsequent Soviet H-bomb explosions could be detected and that the U.S. could then resume its tests. The Administration believed that testing could not be monitored without on-site inspection in the countries participating in a moratorium, and it therefore opposed any unilateral halt. Stevenson's

suggestion became a political debacle when Soviet Premier Nikolai A. Bulganin, in an Oct. 21 letter to President Eisenhower, backed the Democratic candidate's proposal and called for a test suspension without inspection. Partly because of his controversial foreign policy views, Stevenson was soundly defeated in the 1956 campaign.

In the fall of 1957 the Administration decided to invite Stevenson to help draw up an American program for the North Atlantic Treaty Organization (NATO) and participate in the forthcoming NATO conference in Paris. Stevenson decided not to attend the conference but agreed to work on the program. He stressed the importance of programs to improve living conditions in backward countries and stated in one of his memoranda that "if the Atlantic Community had multilateral economic and trade development plans it would mean a lot more to many people than its purely military anti-Communism does now." However, his views had little influence on the American position at the conference, which stressed military might in deterring the spread of Communism.

During the summer of 1958 Stevenson visited the Soviet Union and met with Soviet Premier Nikita S. Khrushchev. Stevenson concluded that the current leadership of the USSR was more sensitive to public opinion than Stalin and was more pragmatic than ideological. Therefore, he believed, the Kremlin would seriously weigh the desire of the people in the Soviet Union and throughout the world for peace.

Despite his continued popularity in the Democratic Party, Stevenson was easily defeated by John Kennedy at the 1960 Democratic Convention. After the November election, Stevenson expected to be appointed Secretary of State, but instead he received the post of ambassador to the United Nations. In April 1961 Stevenson was not informed about the American role in the Cuban Bay of Pigs invasion, and he denied American involvement before the Security Council. He was enraged upon learning the truth.

The Bay of Pigs episode had far-reaching repercussions on Stevenson's position. Although his personal integrity at the U.N.

was not questioned, his power within the Administration's policymaking councils was limited still further. As a result of the bad advice given Kennedy on the invasion by many of his counselors, the President centralized policy-making functions in the hands of a few trusted White House advisers. Stevenson, therefore, found himself in the humiliating position of having his speeches censored by men with less foreign affairs experience than himself and being forced to support policies he had had no voice in making.

To placate the unhappy Ambassador, Kennedy included Stevenson in policy-making discussions during the Cuban missile crisis of 1962. Stevenson strongly opposed a "surgical" air strike to eliminate the missiles and recommended that Cuba be demilitarized and its integrity guaranteed by the United Nations.

A report of Stevenson's views during the crisis, written by newspaper columnist Charles Bartlett in collaboration with Stewart Alsop [q.v.] damaged relations between Kennedy and the Ambassador still further. Quoting an unnamed official, Bartlett reported that "Adlai wanted a Munich," a complete American capitulation to the Soviets on the issue of offensive missiles. Bartlett's close personal friendship with Kennedy gave the article a special significance, and the report caused a major furor. Both Kennedy and Stevenson vigorously denied the story. Kennedy, however, was slow in coming to Stevenson's defense.

After Kennedy's assassination President Lyndon B. Johnson asked Stevenson to remain at the U.N. Stevenson agreed, and during the next two years he defended American policy in Vietnam and the Dominican Republic before the increasingly unfriendly world body. In failing health, Stevenson suffered a fatal heart attack on a London street in July 1965.

[NNL]

For further information:
Kenneth S. Davis, *The Politics of Honor* (New York, 1967).

SYMINGTON, (WILLIAM) STUART

b. June 26, 1901; Amherst, Mass.
Secretary of the Air Force, August 1947-March 1950; Chairman, National Security Resources Board, April 1950-January 1952; U.S. Senator, 1953-76.

Symington was born in Amherst, Mass., where his father taught romance languages at Amherst College. Still a teenager, he joined the Army in the last year of World War I. Symington attended Yale University from 1919 to 1923. Because of a deficiency in a math requirement, he did not receive his degree until 1946, after he had become a member of the Truman Administration. Following college Symington entered his uncle's coupler business. He soon found fault with the company's product and was discharged. In 1925 he bought an almost bankrupt clay products firm which, by the time he sold it in 1927, had become a success. Symington repeated this process for several other firms during the 1920s and 1930s. He eventually established a reputation as a clever businessman who was able to turn a dying firm into a profitable enterprise.

From 1938 to 1945 Symington was president of the Emerson Electric Manufacturing Co. in St. Louis, where he became known as a businessman who was able to deal successfully and amicably with organized labor. He initiated a profit-sharing plan at Emerson with the result that the plant maintained a high production record during a time of labor-management disputes. Symington's work at Emerson brought him into contact with government officials and, as a result, he was appointed an observer for the Office of Production Management.

Upon the recommendation of John Snyder, Symington was appointed Surplus Properties Board chairman July 1945. In 1947 he became Secretary of the Air Force and called for large defense budgets and a strong Air Force. He felt that the atomic bomb was the most powerful weapon in the world and that the only vehicle capable of delivering it, at least until missile technology was improved, was the airplane. This view was typical of those pro-Air Force officials in government, military and industry who proposed that the key to the future security of the U.S. rested on American capability to carry out a massive atomic assault on the Soviet Union. This strategy, in turn, depended on a strong Air Force. Symington, therefore, vigorously urged increased spending for Air Force development and expansion. As part of this campaign, he worked behind the scenes to establish an independent presidential commission to investigate air power in the postwar period. In January 1948 the President's Commission on Air Policy released its report. The document, written by Thomas K. Finletter , entitled "Survival in the Air Age," called for an immediate increase in Air Force funding and warned the nation to be ready by 1953 to defend itself against possible atomic attack. The report added weight to Symington's insistence on a larger Air Force.

President Truman's announcement in September 1949 of an atomic explosion in the Soviet Union reinforced Symington's claims that the U.S. should rely on atomic power delivered by strategic bombers. He declared that within four years the U.S. needed an Air Force that was instantly ready for war and that the existing 48-wing force should be expanded to a 70-wing group.

In March 1950 Symington resigned his position as Air Force Secretary in protest against Defense Secretary Louis Johnson's slashing of the Air Force budget. Symington said that Air Force combat effectiveness had declined because of reductions in numbers and that prospects for defending the U.S. were bleak because the USSR and its allies had "the world's largest ground army, air force and undersea fleet." In rebuttal to those who demanded a balanced budget, Symington warned that Soviet military power "grows relatively greater as against the strength of the

U.S." In his semi-annual report submitted in April, Symington stated that the USSR's possession of the atomic bomb made it imperative for the U.S. to have a "truly long-range offensive air arm."

After winning the Democratic primary in Missouri in August 1952, Symington waged a successful campaign for senator in November, beating the Republican wave brought on by Eisenhower's campaign for the presidency. In the Senate Symington continued to support high defence spending. By May 1953 he was already charging that the Eisenhower Administration's defense budget cuts were endangering the nation and that the Soviet Union's strength in air power and submarines exceeded that of the U.S.

In April 1956 Symington headed a special subcommittee of the Senate Armed Forces Committee which held hearings on the state of American air power. In a Senate speech in May, he stated, "It is now clear that the U.S. . . . may have lost control of the air" and called for an accounting of U.S. air strength. During the three month hearings the panel heard testimony from a number of military leaders, including Air Force Gen. Curtis LeMay predicting that the U.S. would be behind the Soviets in air power within the decade unless spending was increased. Administration witnesses, however, defended the President's limited budget and maintained that U.S. defenses would continue to be superior to those of the USSR. Following testimony by Secretary of Defense Charles Wilson , Symington charged that the Defense Department was considering going against the wishes of Congress by refusing to increase production. He also maintained that someone in the Department was misleading the American people in describing comparative U.S. and USSR defense strengths.

The subcommittee majority report, issued in January 1957, concluded that U.S. vulnerability to sudden attack had "increased greatly" and that the Soviet Union exceeded America in combat aircraft and would soon close the "quality gap." It stated that the Administration was vacillating on policies regarding preparation for limited and general war and had a "tendency to either ignore or underestimate Soviet military progress." It also said that the Eisenhower Administration had placed financial considerations ahead of defense requirements.

In 1959 Symington charged that a "missile gap" existed between the U.S. and the USSR. He predicted that the Soviet Union would soon have a three-to-one lead over the U.S. in operational intercontinental ballistic missiles. He maintained it would enable the Russians to "wipe out our entire manned and unmanned retaliatory force" with one blow.

Although he had initially supported the war in Vietnam, Symington came out against U.S. involvement in that country in 1967. His change in position was influenced both by his experience on the Senate Foreign Relations Committee, to which he had been assigned in 1961, and by his sympathy for the Air Force and its personnel. Symington maintained that his tenure on the Foreign Relations Committee and his work with Senators J. William Fulbright (D, Ark) [q.v.] and Mike Mansfield (D, Mont.) had taught him to think in terms of America's global commitments and total foreign policy requirements. Viewing Vietnam in this light Symington became convinced that the war was not vital for U.S. security and that it was endangering the American economy. As a result of several trips to Vietnam, he had also learned of the growing discontent among American pilots who felt constricted by the Administration's target limits and believed that the government was willing to sacrifice American lives to prevent North Vietnamese civilian casualities. Symington maintained that if pilots were going to be forced to fight a limited war, it would be better to pull out of Vietnam than to sacrifice their lives. In October 1967 he therefore urged a unilateral ceasefire aimed at initiating peace negotiations. His position on both the Foreign Relations Committee and the Armed Services Committee made him a powerful advocate of de-escalation and withdrawal in Congress.

Throughout his career Symington had voted in favor of most foreign aid bills, but after 1967 he opposed those measures because of his belief that the U.S. was economically and militarily overcommitted throughout the world. He also voted against new weapons development projects because of the frequency with which they were changed or canceled.

In 1969 Symington headed a subcommittee investigating overseas commitments in an effort to reassess U.S. foreign policy in the wake of the Vietnam war. The subcommittee found that commitments and secret agreements had been made throughout the 1960s to such countries as Ethiopia, Laos, Thailand, South Korea and Spain and that the U.S. had 429 major military bases around the world. An agreement permitting U.S. use of bases in Spain in return for grants, loans and improvements caused particular controversy.

Symington pointed out that many major military commitments of the 1960s and 1970s resulted from executive agreements made without the knowledge or consent of Congress, and pressed for a reassertion of congressional authority in foreign policy during the 1970s. For years a supporter of foreign aid, he opposed many aid measures during the Nixon years in his belief that the U.S. was economically and militarily overcommitted throughout the world. Symington stated: "There has to be a viable economy with a strong dollar. And there has to be faith in the system and confidence of the people in their government. Without the second and third, military strength is not security."

Unlike many other doves Symington did not completely turn against the "military establishment." Yet he opposed building new military bases, bombers and an expanded anti-ballistic missile (ABM) system because he believed alternative systems would be more efficient. His opposition to the ABM hurt him politically. In his 1970 reelection campaign Symington won a narrow 37,000-vote victory over his opponent, state Attorney General John C. Danforth, who had received large political contributions from

McDonnell Douglas, a builder of missile components.

Symington spoke out against the extension of the Vietnam war into Cambodia and Laos, supporting the Cooper-Church and McGovern-Hatfield Amendments. In March 1975 Symington with Sens. Humphrey ; McGovern [q.v.] and Clark opposed military aid to the faltering Cambodia government of Lon Nol while supporting additional food and medical help.

Symington also favored measures to ban the importation of Rhodesian chrome ore, withdraw 76,000 U.S. troops stationed abroad and resume U.S. military aid to Turkey, which was cut off in 1974. In 1973 Symington, as acting chairman of the Armed Services Committee, conducted hearings into the possible involvement of the CIA in the Watergate scandal. According to testimony high Administration officials sought to involve the CIA in the Watergate cover-up as well as the burglary of the office of Daniel Ellsberg's psychiatrist.

In 1976 after 24 years in the Senate, Symington chose not to seek re-election.

[JAN]

For further information:
Flora Lewis, "The Education of a Senator," *Atlantic Monthly*, (December 1971).

TAFT, ROBERT A(LPHONSO)
b. Sept. 8, 1889; Cincinnati, Ohio.
d. July 31, 1953; New York, N.Y.
Republican Senator, Ohip, 1939-53;
Senate Majority Leader, 1953.

The grandson of Ulysses Grant's Attorney General and son of the 27th President and 10th Chief Justice of the United States, Robert A. Taft graduated first in his class both at Yale in 1910 and Harvard law school in 1913. During World War I he was an assistant counsel to U.S. Food Administrator Herbert Hoover. In the 1920s and early 1930s, he served in the Ohio legislature as a state representative, house speaker and state senator. In 1938 he won the first of three campaigns for the U.S. Senate. A master of detail and an expert on parliamentary procedure, Taft all but led the Republican minority virtually from the beginning of his Senate career.

Taft quickly emerged as the most articulate champion of the GOP's Midwestern-conservative-isolationist wing and proved to be a major critic of the Truman Administration's postwar foreign program. Nevertheless because of a continuation of wartime bipartisanship policy, he never commanded sufficient support to do more than raise questions and voice objections. Taft opposed the establishment of the International Monetary Fund, doubting its effectiveness in establishing stable exchange rates on a multinational basis. He opposed the World Bank even more strenuously, objecting to the concept of official investment abroad. Such investments, Taft suggested, would lead foreigners to think of Americans as "absentee landlords."

Taft voted for the U.N. Charter in 1945, but only after noting that the Security Council vetoes would make the U.N. effective solely in those matters about which the big powers agreed. He would have preferred establishing a strong international legal order, with a strong international court, rather than an organization based upon a balance of power. Taft also took exception to the apparent absence of a congressional role in determining how to cast American votes at the U.N.

During the spring of 1945 Taft voiced his fears that U.S. military and official economic presence abroad would lead to imperialism. He returned to this theme regularly in the next several years. It became among the most consistant objections he raised to the expanding American presence overseas. Taft opposed the 1947 Greek-Turkish aid bill, designed to prevent a Communist takeover in the area. He questioned the strategic importance of the area and pointed out that intervention so near the Russian border might force Soviet retaliation. Nevertheless, when Truman presented his plea for aid in terms of a fight against Communism, Taft voted for the measure. He believed that to deny the funds under such circumstances would be a sign of American weakness.

Taft raised the same questions about the Marshall Plan in late 1947 and 1948. Again he ultimately voted for the proposal because he thought the circumstances demanded it. But he attempted unsuccessfully to cut funding for the year from $597 million to $400 million. The House tried to cut it further. However Taft, who was seeking the presidential nomination, announced, after consulting with the GOP Policy Committee, that the Senate's appropriation represented a "moral commitment." He warned that the Senate would remain in session until that commitment was met. The House backed down.

Taft refused to support the ratification of the North Atlantic Treaty in 1949. He questioned whether America's willingness to supply arms to Europe would act as more of a deterrent to the Soviets than would the atomic bomb. It would, he insisted, give the Russians the impression that the U.S. was preparing for eventual aggressive action. Taft foresaw even graver dangers. "We have quietly adopted a tendency," he said, "to interfere in the affairs of other nations, to assume that we are a kind of demigod and Santa Claus to solve the problems of the world . . . It is easy to slip into an attitude of imperialism where war becomes an instrument of public policy rather than its last resort." Taft voted against the treaty and futilely fought subsequent requests for arms for the alliance.

Taft opposed Truman's containment policy not only because it suggested imperialism but also because it expanded the President's power to commit the U.S. to a position in the world without congressional authorization. During the debate on the North Atlantic Treaty, he warned that the pact would give the President the power to enter into a European war without consulting Congress for the 20-year term of the agreement. Taft also worried about the economic consequences of so active a policy. He suggested that it would distort the federal budget, leading to excessive deficits and drawing money away from domestic needs as the government strained to finance the bloated defense establishment.

Although Taft opposed U.S. intervention in Europe, he was ambivalent about American involvement in the Far East. He never really developed a coherent policy on the U.S. role in Asia. In 1948 he said, "I believe very strongly that the Far East is ultimately even more important to our future peace than is Europe." He supported sending military equipment to Chiang Kai-shek and criticized the Truman Administration for not doing more to prevent the "fall" of China to the Communists in 1949. After the North Koreans invaded South Korea in June 1950, he charged that the Administration's omission of Korea in its statements defining the American defense perimeter had encouraged the attack. He supported Truman's commitment of ground troops to the conflict and joined Gen. Douglas MacArthur [q.v.] in recommending that the Nationalist Chinese be permitted to invade mainland China.

Yet while backing the President he also made statements critical of the Administration. A month after endorsing Truman's action in Korea, he told reporters, "I would have stayed out," and that if he were the President, "he would get out and fall back to a defensible position in Japan and Formosa." While supporting MacArthur, Taft opposed using either American troops or the atomic bomb in China.

Taft's confusion was a result of his concentration on domestic affairs. More important, he was torn between his desire to stop Communism where it appeared most threatening and his opposition to overseas involvement. Taft's views may also have been influenced by partisan considerations, since he made three unsuccessful attempts to win the Republican presidential nomination in 1944, 1948 and 1952. His failures were generally attributed to his lackluster campaign style, his conservative domestic positions and his isolationist foreign policy.

Taft became majority leader when the Eisenhower landslide brought in a Republican Congress. He did an effective job of uniting his party behind the new

Administration. He and Eisenhower became extremely close, and Taft, in the first few months of the Eisenhower Administration, enjoyed more influence than ever before. By late spring 1953 Taft was seriously ill with inoperable cancer. He retired as majority leader in June, selecting as his successor Sen. William F. Knowland (R, Calif.) [q.v.]. He died on July 31, 1953 in New York City.

[CSJ]

For further information:
James T. Patterson, *Mr. Republican* (Boston, 1972).
William S. White, *The Taft Story* (New York, 1954).

TAYLOR, MAXWELL D(AVENPORT)
b. Aug. 26, 1901; Keytesville, Mo.
Military Representative of the President, July 1961-October 1962; Chairman of the Joint Chiefs of Staff, October 1962-June 1964.

Taylor graduated with the fourth highest average in the West Point class of 1922. Soon after Pearl Harbor, Taylor helped organize the 82nd Airborne Division, later commanding its artillery in the Sicilian and Italian campaigns. He was in command of the 101st Airborne by D-Day and parachuted with the division into Normandy, becoming the first American general to fight on French soil during the war. Following the war Taylor was superintendent of West Point for three years and then served in command and staff positions in Europe, the Far East and in Washington before being named Army Chief of Staff in 1955. As the Army's principal spokesman on defense strategy, Taylor vigorously opposed the Eisenhower Administration's reliance on massive nuclear retaliation, arguing that there was a continuing need for strong ground forces capable of fighting a conventional war. Taylor forcefully took his case to the public in his book *The Uncertain Trumpet*, published in 1959 after he retired from the Army.

John Kennedy was impressed by *The Uncertain Trumpet* and used its arguments to support his own attacks on the Eisenhower Administration's defense policies during the 1960 presidential campaign. When the exile invasion of Cuba sponsored by the Central Intelligence Agency was crushed at the Bay of Pigs, Kennedy asked Taylor to lead an investigation of the CIA's role in the fiasco and to evaluate America's capability for conducting unconventional warfare. The central conclusion of the Taylor report was that the Defense Department, rather than the CIA, should be responsible for major paramilitary operations.

On June 26 Kennedy named Taylor to a newly created White House post as military representative of the President. The post was an interim appointment until there was an opportunity to name Taylor chairman of the Joint Chiefs of Staff. Kennedy was anxious to have a source of independent military advice from a professional detached from the inter-service rivalries of the Pentagon. In his new position, Taylor undertook a study for the President of psychological warfare and led a special committee on counterinsurgency.

Taylor's most important assignment was to lead a special mission to South Vietnam in the wake of major Communist victories in the autumn of 1961 to assess the military situation and recommend how the U.S. should respond. Although a general, Taylor was put in charge of the mission as a concession to those within the Administration who feared direct U.S. military involvement might be advocated by the mission's other leading figure, White House aide Walt W. Rostow [q.v.]. (Taylor was thought to be wary of committing U.S. troops to a land war in Asia.) The mission left Washington Oct. 15, arriving in Saigon Oct. 18. Taylor conferred with the South Vietnamese President Ngo Dinh Diem, South Vietnamese generals and U.S. military advisers and inspected South Vietnamese units in the field before leaving Oct. 25 for talks with Thai leaders in Bangkok. Taylor flew on to Manila Oct. 30, where he wrote his report for the President.

Although it was kept secret at the time, on his return to Washington Nov. 3 Taylor recommended—to the surprise of President Kennedy—sending some 8,000 U.S. combat troops to Vietnam. Taylor told Kennedy the troops were necessary to reassure Diem of the American commitment and to provide the South Vietnamese with a reserve force for emergencies. He acknowledged that it would be difficult to resist pressure for reinforcements once U.S. troops committed American prestige to the war and conceded the danger of backing into a major war, but he concluded U.S. ground troops were necessary to deter the Communists from escalating the conflict. Secretary of Defense Robert McNamara [q.v.] backed Taylor's recommendation. Resistance from the State Department, however, was strong. A compromise devised by McNamara emerged on Nov. 11: the U.S. would increase military aid, send more military advisers and helicopter pilots, and pressure Diem to carry out political reforms—all measures suggested in the Taylor-Rostow report. As a concession to Taylor's request for combat forces, the Pentagon was directed to prepare a plan for sending in troops on a contingency basis. The Administration's public position was that Taylor had recommended against the use of American combat troops. Nevertheless, the Taylor mission and the decisions made in late 1961, David Halberstam wrote in *The Best and the Brightest*, profoundly "changed and escalated the American commitment to Vietnam."

Taylor continued to advise the President on Laos, Vietnam, Berlin and other foreign policy crises during early 1962, until Kennedy appointed him July 20 to serve as chairman of the Joint Chiefs of Staff to replace Gen. Lyman L. Lemnitzer, who was named commander of NATO forces in Europe. After denying in testimony before the Senate Armed Services Committee that his appointment signaled any American reluctance to use nuclear weapons in the defense of Europe, Taylor was approved unanimously by the Senate Aug. 8. Taylor returned to South Vietnam Sept. 10-13 to review the military situation. Meeting newsmen in Manila Sept. 19, he declared that "the Vietnamese are on the road to victory."

Taylor was a major participant in the crucial White House meetings during the Cuban missile crisis of October 1962, advocating a strong response to eliminate Soviet missiles from the island.

During his term as chairman of the joint chiefs, Taylor loyally followed Administration policies in contrast to the other joint chiefs who were often at odds with President Kennedy's policies. He was the only member of the JCS to join the Administration in opposing the development of the RS-70 manned-bomber program. Taylor's support proved essential when the Administration sought Senate ratification of the nuclear test ban treaty with the Soviet Union. His testimony before the Preparedness Subcommittee of the Senate Armed Services Committee and the Senate Foreign Relations Committee on Aug. 14 and 15, 1963 that the treaty would not endanger U.S. security and his denial that the Pentagon had been dragooned into supporting the test ban effectively rebutted the arguments of the treaty's most vociferous opponents.

Reports that the Diem government's repression of the Buddhists was hampering the war effort prompted Kennedy to send Taylor and Defense Secretary McNamara on another mission to Vietnam in September 1963. On the surface, their joint report to the President Oct. 2 continued to express optimism about the military effort and predicted a victory over the Communists by 1965. McNamara, however, reportedly had begun to question Taylor's sanguine confidence that the political situation had not affected the war effort. As a result of Diem's inept handling of the Buddhist crisis, the Administration—with Taylor's concurrence—acquiesced in the military coup that overthrew the Diem regime at the beginning of November.

In June 1964 President Johnson selected Taylor to replace Henry Cabot Lodge [q.v.] as ambassador to South Vietnam. Previously unconcerned about the political situation there, Taylor concluded, shortly after arriving in Saigon, that the repressiveness of the South Vietnamese government was a serious impediment to the successful prosecution of the war. He pressed Maj. Gen. Nguyen Khanh, who had replaced Diem as national leader following a November 1963 military coup, to arrange for the creation of a civilian-drawn constitutional charter. A provisional, civilian High National Council was established in September 1964, but in December it was overthrown by dissident military officers, led by, among others, Air Commodore Nguyen Cao Ky and Gen. Nguyen Van Thieu. Shortly afterwards Taylor called a meeting of the officers and said, "I told you all clearly . . . we Americans were tired of coups. Apparently I wasted my words . . . .Now you have made a real mess." Despite Taylor's exhortations the officers refused to reestablish civilian rule.

Taylor supported the sustained American bombing of North Vietnam that began in March 1965. But when the bombing failed to alter North Vietnam's policies, he tried to resist the ensuing pressure from the U.S. military for the sending of large numbers of American combat troops to South Vietnam. In late March Taylor returned to Washington for a series of major strategy conferences. The Joint Chiefs of Staff and General William Westmoreland favored the deployment of at least two American divisions on search-and-destroy missions in the South Vietnamese interior. Taylor argued for the dispatch of a much smaller number of troops to guard enclaves around U.S. bases. He maintained that the arrival of American combat forces would encourage the South Vietnamese Army to slacken its efforts, arouse anti-Americanism and lead to ever-increasing U.S. military involvement.

Taylor's point of view was accepted by the Administration in early April. But at another high-level strategy conference held in Honolulu on April 19-20 an additional 40,000 American troops were committed to the war effort, although the enclave strategy was not altered. In June Westmoreland argued that the deteriorating military situation in South Vietnam necessitated the introduction of combat troops. In a dispatch to Washington Taylor agreed that circumstances were grave. David Halberstam, in *The Best and the Brightest*, stated that the Ambassador's concurrence with Westmoreland's pessimistic assessment of the direction of the war "removed the last restraint" against the use of American soldiers as combat troops.

In July 1965 Taylor was replaced as ambassador to South Vietnam by the returning Lodge. Later in the year President Johnson appointed him a special presidential consultant, but in that post Taylor no longer had a major influence on policymaking decisions.

Taylor consistently took a hawkish position on the Vietnam war during the remaining years of the Johnson Administration. In March 1968, when Administration sentiment turned against further escalation of American involvement, Taylor, as a member of the Senior Advisory Group on Vietnam, unsuccessfully supported Westmoreland's request for over 200,000 additional troops.

[MLL]

TELLER, EDWARD
b. Jan. 15, 1908, Budapest, Hungary.
Associate Director, Lawrence Livermore Laboratory, Atomic Energy Commission, 1954-

After completing his doctorate in physical chemistry at the University of Leipzig in 1930, Teller studied with Niels Bohr, the distinguished Danish physicist. He left Germany when the Nazis came to power and became an American citizen in 1941. During World War II Teller worked on the Manhattan Project, which developed the atomic bomb, and from 1949 to 1951 he was an assistant director of the science laboratory at Los Alamos, N.M. During the 1950s he taught physics at the University of California. In 1954 he became an associate director of the Atomic Energy Commission's (AEC) Lawrence Livermore Laboratory in Livermore, Calif.

During the 1950s Teller became a leading scientific spokesman for the maintenance of U.S. atomic weapons superiority. He believed that American supremacy was the only means of countering what he viewed as an aggressive Soviet arms policy. Described by *Newsweek* as "the principal architect of the H-bomb," Teller was a leading advocate of that weapon's development. In the 1954 AEC security hearings, he testified against granting J. Robert Oppenheimer a security clearance, claiming that Oppenheimer's opposition to the H-bomb project had delayed its development.

Teller had opposed the three-year moratorium on atomic testing that ended in September 1961 when the Soviet Union resumed atmospheric explosions, and he favored the renewed U.S. testing, which began later that month. Calling nuclear test ban negotiations "dangerous," he said they "have helped the Soviets" and "have impeded our own testing."

During the August 1963 Senate hearings on the nuclear test ban treaty, Teller was the most influential scientist to testify against ratification. His principal objection was to the ban's prohibition of atmospheric tests, which were necessary for the further development of anti-ballistic missiles (ABMs). Teller feared that the Soviets led in ABM production and that the treaty might enable them to increase that lead. Warning that current detection techniques would be ineffective for policing the agreement, Teller also believed that the treaty would inhibit the military's ability to respond in case of war since it stipulated that atomic weapons could be used only three months after repudiation of the agreement.

[MDB]

TRUMAN, HARRY S
b. May 8, 1884; Lamar, Mo.
d. Dec. 26, 1972; Kansas City, Mo.
President of the United States, April 1945-January 1953.

Truman was born into a family of ardent Democrats. His father worked at various times as a farmer, a livestock trader and a grain speculator and, despite several economic reverses, provided a comfortable life for his family. His mother, a devout Baptist who had a powerful influence on Harry, placed great emphasis on morality and education. When Harry was seven the family moved to Independence, Mo., where he attended public schools. Anxious to pursue a military career, he ap-

plied to West Point but was rejected because of poor eyesight. He then joined the National Guard. Truman lacked the money to pay for a college education and, over the next few years, held a number of jobs including mailroom clerk and bookkeeper before becoming a farmer at the age of 22. When World War II broke out, he saw action as an artillery officer in France. Following the war he opened a haberdashery with a friend in Kansas City, Mo.; the business failed in the economic downturn of 1921-22.

Truman had been long interested in entering politics. In 1922 he ran for the administrative post of judge of the Jackson Co. Court. He was backed by the powerful Pendergast machine, which controlled Democratic politics in much of Missouri. He won the contest but lost his reelection bid two years later. In 1926 he was elected president of the Court and occupied that position for eight years. In these posts he supervised public building and carried on an extensive road construction program. Although supporting the Pendergast organization, he was never associated with the scandals that eventually led to its downfall.

With the backing of Tom Pendergast, Truman won a seat in the U.S. Senate in 1934. He was a consistent supporter of Franklin D. Roosevelt's domestic and foreign policies. He played a major role in drafting the Civil Aeronautics Act of 1938 and the Railroad Transportation Act of 1940. His allegiance, however, was primarily to the Party rather than to the President's program. He gained a reputation as a pragmatic, middle-of-the-road politician.

Truman first came to national prominence during World War II when, as chairman of a special watchdog committee, he uncovered inefficiency and corruption in the nation's defense program. As a result of the investigation, he became a power in the Senate and was mentioned as a possible vice-presidential candidate in 1944.

The Democratic Party at the time was divided on the question of a running mate for FDR. Party leaders assumed that the next vice president would soon become President and so would determine the direction of the Democratic Administration into the next decade. The left wing favored the renomination of Henry Wallace [q.v.] who was opposed by big business and Southern conservatives. That section of the Party backed South Carolinian James F. Byrnes [q.v.], the Director of War Mobilization, who had gained the informal title "Assistant President" during the war. However, organized labor refused to support him.

With powerful sections of the Party torn between the two candidates, Roosevelt selected Truman as a compromise. Truman's border-state ties appealed to the South and conservatives, while his support of the New Deal won him the backing of labor and northern liberals. His ties to the Pendergast machine made him acceptable to big city bosses. More important, Roosevelt thought that Truman's popularity on Capitol Hill could help him gain ratification of peace treaties and the U.N. Charter, thus avoiding the problems Woodrow Wilson had faced after World War I. Roosevelt did not think the vice presidential candidate would aid his ticket. Instead he was anxious to have a running mate who would not lose him votes. Truman, with a few enemies, had the necessary qualifications.

Elected in November, Truman served only 83 days. During his short tenure he remained on the edge of decision making. Preoccupied with the war, Roosevelt relied primarily on those advisers such as Harry Hopkins, who had been with him throughout his presidency. Truman was not included in discussions, particularly in foreign policy, and spent most of his time presiding over the Senate. He described himself during that period as a "political eunuch."

On April 12, 1945 Roosevelt died of a cerebral hemorrhage and Harry Truman assumed the presidency. Shocked by FDR's death and staggered by the thought of replacing him, Truman asked reporters, "Boys if you ever pray, pray for me now. . . . When they told me yester-day what had happened, I felt like the moon, the stars and all the planets had fallen on me."

Men who had worked closely with Roosevelt worried about Truman's lack of experience and questioned his ability to lead. David E. Lilienthal, chairman of the Tennessee Valley Authority, wrote in his diary: "Consternation at the thought of that Throttlebottom Truman. The country and the world doesn't deserve to be left this way, with Truman at the head of the country at such a time." Those who had worked with him in the Senate had a different opinion. "Truman will not make a great, flashy President like Roosevelt," Speaker of the House Sam Rayburn predicted. "But, by God, he'll make a good President, a sound President. He's got the stuff in him."

Truman's first days in the White House won praise both from the public and government officials. They were impressed with his ability and willingness to accept the demands of his office. An early public opinion poll showed that seven out of 10 voters approved of Truman's actions. Even conservative Republican Henry Luce wrote that he had confidence in Truman. In part this reaction was a result of the traditional "honeymoon" the public gives a new President; in part it was because Truman was asked to make no important decisions or present new programs. Domestic issues were sidelined and the war was proceeding well. Just as important was Truman's style of operating. His informality and his acknowledgment of his limitations made him approachable to the public. His sense of order and direct decision making contrasted sharply with Roosevelt's use of confusion and conflict among advisers to develop policies, and tensions within the presidential staff declined.

As the war in Europe drew quickly to a close, Truman moved to end the conflict in Asia. He was determined to push for the unconditional surrender of Japan and the abolition of the Japanese monarchy. Anxious to end the war quickly, he rejected suggestions that the U.S. blockade the islands to starve out Japan. Shortly after he had become President he was told of the existence of the atomic bomb. The weapon, however, had not been tested, and Truman decided to mount a massive invasion of the Japanese mainland. When tests in July proved the weapon viable, he reluctantly decided to use it to forestall a bloody invasion. He accepted an advisory committee's recommendation that the bomb be dropped on a military-civilian target without warning. Truman rejected pleas by atomic scientists and such high administration officials as Secretary of War Henry Stimson [q.v.] that the Japanese be shown the force of the bomb before it was used. Anxious to avoid continued U.S. casualties, he maintained there was no time to prepare a demonstration.

The President also refused the recommendations of Joseph Grew and Cordell Hull that the U.S. accept the continuation of the monarchy to speed up surrender. During July the Western Allies issued a proclamation calling for the Japanese surrender. They warned that Japan would have to give up its army, its war-making capacity and its occupied territory but promised the continuation of civil liberties and peacetime industries. The communication made no mention of the future of the emperor. The Japanese refused the ultimatum, and in early August, Truman approved the use of the weapon. After the destruction of Hiroshima and Nagasaki, the Japanese sued for peace but refused to surrender until the U.S. had given assurances that the monarchy would be retained. Truman acquiesced and Japan surrendered on Aug. 14.

Truman assumed the presidency during a difficult time in international affairs. The war in Europe was drawing to a close but the victorious alliance threatened to disintegrate over the issue of the Soviet military occupation of Eastern Europe. The new President was completely inexperienced in international relations and anxious to assert himself on questions dividing the Allies. His desire to lead pushed him during his first year in office to make hasty decisions. With no background in foreign affairs, he relied primarily on his advisers for counsel. These men were deeply split on their ap-

proach to Soviet policy. One group, led by Averell Harriman [q.v.] and William Leahy urged a firm policy to force Russian concessions in Eastern Europe while the other, led by Henry Wallace [q.v.], continued to push for cooperation to ensure a peaceful postwar world. Without a basis for determining Soviet motives and uncertain of his own understanding of foreign affairs, Truman followed the advice of first one faction and then the other. His policies, therefore, vacillated.

Truman initially hoped to continue Roosevelt's policy of cooperation with the Soviet Union. He felt himself committed to FDR's efforts and was reluctant to involve the U.S. in a war over Eastern Europe. Just as important, he viewed Soviet leaders as pragmatic politicians, similar to urban bosses, with whom arrangements could be made through personal diplomacy. Yet his determination to assert himself and his abrasive personality signalled to the Soviets a harsher stand and speeded the development of the Cold War.

During the spring and summer of 1945, Truman attempted to take a firm stand toward the Soviet Union while looking for a way to maintain cooperation. He lectured the Soviet foreign minister in undiplomatic language on the need to live up to the Yalta Accords guaranteeing free elections in Eastern Europe. He also slowed down aid to Russia to pressure Stalin on the issue. Yet in an effort to prevent a break, Truman sent Roosevelt's trusted adviser, Harry Hopkins, to Moscow to try to settle outstanding differences. Hopkins was able to get Stalin's agreement to a compromise government in Poland and his assurances of entry into the war against Japan but could not forestall a worsening of relations. At the Potsdam Conference of July and August, Truman demanded and received a compromise on reparations that limited Soviet claims on Western German goods. More significantly the agreement permitted the redevelopment of the German economy, which Truman considered vital for the economic health of Europe. Still the Soviets refused vigorously to reaffirm support for the Yalta Declaration on Eastern Europe.

Despite Soviet intransigence, Truman declined to use American military might to pressure Stalin. He rejected Winston Churchill's suggestion that the U.S. Army push further into Central Europe during the closing days of the war to give the West a better bargaining position with the Russians after the armistice. He also ignored requests from his military advisers that he reverse Roosevelt's decision to ask for Soviet entry into the war against Japan in return for political concessions in Asia. Truman believed that the best way to handle the Soviet Union was "to stick carefully to our agreements and to try our best to make the Russians carry out their agreements."

Congressional pressure and public opinion gradually moved Truman to a more strident position on the Soviet Union by 1946. Revelations of a Communist spy network in Canada and continued Soviet intransigence at international conferences led many to doubt Russian friendship. Powerful senators such as Arthur Vandenberg (R, Mich.) [q.v.] demanded an end to compromise. Vandenberg was particularly angered at the conduct of Secretary of State James Byrnes [q.v.], whom he thought too willing to make concessions to Stalin. The Secretary's conduct at the Moscow Conference of December 1945 proved a turning point. At that meeting he agreed to diplomatic recognition of the Soviet dominated regimes in Bulgaria and Rumania in return for a broadening of the governments. Vandenberg termed it "one more typical American 'give away'." Truman, also angered at the accord, said that Byrnes had "lost his nerve at Moscow."

By the beginning of 1946 the President had come to believe that a less pliant policy toward the Soviet Union was necessary. Frustrated in efforts to work out settlements to outstanding issues, and under extreme pressure from Congress and the public not to give in further to the Soviets, he developed a stance of "patience with firmness." Negotiations with the Soviet Union could continue, but henceforth any concessions would come from the Russians. Truman accepted George Kennan's [q.v.] view that the Soviet Union was an expansionist power, which because of a desire for security and because of a paranoiac mindset was bent on world conquest. To stop its advance, the U.S. would have to "contain" the USSR. This was to be done primarily through the use of American economic power rather than military might.

During 1946 Truman resisted further concessions to the Soviet Union. He insisted that the USSR remove its troops from Iran, which it had agreed to occupy only until the end of the war. Fearful of Russian penetration into the eastern Mediterranean, he dispatched U.S. warships to Greece and Turkey to discourage Soviet infiltration. He minimized attempts to come to terms with Stalin on Germany and backed unification of the American and British occupation zones to provide for the economic rehabilitation of that nation. Truman continued his commitment to international control of atomic energy, but he did so on terms that made it difficult for the Soviets to accept. He supported the Baruch Plan, submitted to the U.N. in the spring of 1946, which called for inspection of all nuclear sites and disclosure of atomic research before the U.S. would give up its nuclear monopoly. In September 1946, when Secretary of Commerce Henry Wallace denounced the Administration's "get tough policy with the Soviets," Truman asked him to resign. Wallace, once out of office, became the leader of liberals' discontent with the Administration and began activities that led to his presidential candidacy in 1948.

Truman and his advisers, primarily Secretary of State George Marshall [q.v.] and Undersecretary of State Dean Acheson [q.v.], established the cornerstones of the containment policy during 1947 and 1948. In the early months of 1947 the President moved to replace the British presence in Greece and Turkey with American aid to prevent a Communist takeover. To win the support of a Congress hostile to U.S. involvement in Europe, Truman couched his aid message in terms of an ideological struggle against Communist expansion. In enunciating what came to be known as the Truman Doctrine, he called for a clear division between democracy and a way of life that "relies upon terror and oppression . . . and the suppression of personal freedoms." Truman stated, "I believe that it must be the policy of the United States to support free peoples who are resisting attempted subjugation by armed minorities or by outside pressures." Three months later Marshall unveiled the European Recovery Program, called the Marshall Plan at Truman's insistence. This proposal called for massive economic aid to war-torn Europe. Although there was a strong humanitarian element in the program, the Administration also thought the ERP would reestablish economic prosperity and thus eliminate a breeding ground for Communists.

Truman did not intend to use American military power to challenge the Soviets. He refused to intervene in the Communist takeover of Czechoslovakia in February 1948. When the Soviet Union blockaded Berlin in June 1948, the President ignored both cries for the U.S. to abandon the city and demands from the military, particularly Gen. Lucius Clay [q.v.], that U.S. troops open supply routes. Instead, he used an airlift to supply the beleaguered city.

Truman also worked for the ratification of the North Atlantic Treaty of 1949, which committed the U.S. for the first time in its history to a mutual defense pact in Europe. To enable the U.S. to cope with its larger military role, he asked Congress to increase the power of the Secretary of Defense and support development of a modern Air Force, capable of delivering nuclear weapons anywhere in the world. Shortly after the Soviets revealed that they had exploded an atomic device, Truman ordered a crash program to develop the hydrogen bomb to maintain U.S. nuclear superiority.

A large portion of Truman's attention in foreign affairs was devoted to China, where Communists and Nationalists were engaged in a bitter civil war. Early in his first Administration Truman had sent George Marshall on a mission to try to negotiate a truce and form a coalition government. Marshall had failed and returned predicting that if Chiang did not reform his corrupt government no amount of American aid could save him. Truman, on his advice, had attempted to phase out aid to that nation to prevent U.S. involvement in a full-scale war. He was, however, forced to acquiesce to demands from right-wing Republicans for a new mission to China and continuation of some form of assistance. By the summer of 1949 it had become clear that Chiang was losing the war. In an attempt to explain American policy and extricate the U.S. from the situation, Truman ordered Secretary of State Dean Acheson to issue a White Paper on China. He blamed the imminent Communist takeover on corruption in the Nationalist regime.

The fall of China precipitated a storm of protest from the right, which accused Truman of having "sold-out" Chiang by concentrating U.S. aid in Europe. Influenced by the anti-Communist hysteria of the time, the China Lobby insisted that the loss was the result of Communist influence in the State Department. After the formal proclamation of the Communist government, Truman was forced to assure China Lobby leaders that he would not recognize the new regime or permit its admission to the U.N. Truman rejected demands from Sen. William Knowland (R, Calif.) [q.v.] that the U.S. fleet protect Formosa from the Communists and announced that he would not provide military aid or advice to the Nationalist Chinese. He would continue only economic aid. However, after the outbreak of the Korean War, he dispatched the Seventh Fleet to the straits between the two nations.

In light of the fall of China and the Soviet detonation of an atomic bomb, Truman in January 1950 ordered a complete reassessment of American defense and nuclear policy. The report, NSC-68, recommended that the U.S. unilaterally accept responsibility for the defense of the world and begin an immediate largescale buildup of America's defense forces. Truman initially rejected its recommendations and refused to have the report made public. He reasoned that without a major crisis he could not get Congress or the public to support large defense appropriations. When the Korean conflict began in June 1950, Truman began implementing the report's recommendations.

Truman's handling of the Korean situation undermined his domestic support. In response to the North Korean invasion of the South, he sent U.S. troops under U.N. auspices to conduct what was termed a police action. Because the U.N. and not the U.S. was offically fighting the war, Truman had not been forced to ask Congress for a declaration of war. The public initially supported Truman's action, believing that a strong show of force was necessary to contain Communism in Asia. Yet, despite his seeming willingness to fight in Korea, Truman was unable to quiet charges that he was "soft on Communism." Republicans pointed to a speech by Dean Acheson, in which he had failed to include Korea in the U.S. defense perimeter, as a major factor in the outbreak of the war. Within a few months of the outbreak, praise gave way to grumbling, and the Korean conflict became "Truman's War." The failure of containment in Asia and the growth of anti-Communist hysteria directed against the Democratic Party cost Truman in the 1950 election. Although the Democrats retained control of Congress, the margin was held by Southern conservatives, ending hopes for the continuation of the Fair Deal.

Truman became even more unpopular after he fired Gen. Douglas MacArthur [q.v.] as supreme commander of U.N. forces in Korea in April 1951. Following the General's open opposition to a limited war and his politicking with Republican leaders in Congress, Truman announced that he could "no longer tolerate his insubordination" and dismissed him. Liberals supported his action as a necessary defense of presidential power, but members of the China Lobby and those who wanted an increased emphasis on Asia in foreign policy, denounced him. Sen. Joseph R. McCarthy (R, Wisc.) called the President a "sonofabitch" who made his decision while drunk on "bourbon and Benedictine."

In his final State of the Union Message in January 1953, Truman warned Stalin against war with the U.S. and urged continued Western resistance to Communist expansion without plunging the world into nuclear conflict. He also cautioned against legislation aimed at domestic Communism that would promote an "enforced conformity."

During the 1950s Truman frequently spoke out in opposition to the Eisenhower Administration's foreign and domestic programs. He remained active in Democratic politics, backing Averell Harriman for the presidential nomination in 1956 and Stuart Symington [q.v.] in 1960. When John F. Kennedy received the nomination that year, Truman campaigned vigorously for him despite his personal dislike of the Kennedy family. He was a strong supporter of the Johnson-Humphrey ticket in 1964 and generally backed the Great Society legislative program. In 1965 President Johnson flew to Independence to sign the law creating medicare at a ceremony honoring Truman, who had proposed national health insurance in 1945. Truman was a consistant supporter of the Administration's Vietnam policy. He died in Kansas City, Mo. in 1972 at the age of 88.

Historians' assessments of Harry Truman varied widely in the years after his Administration. Initially, it was generally felt that he had skillfully led the nation to accept a permanent peace-time role in world affairs. During the Vietnam war years, however, New Left historians charged that Truman had overreacted to Stalin's legitimate desire for secure borders and was therefore largely responsible for the Cold War. But other historians asserted that Truman's firm policies were the correct response.

[EWS]

For further information:

Bert Cochran, *Harry Truman and the Crisis Presidency* (New York, 1973).

Robert J. Donovan, *Conflict and Crisis: The Presidency of Harry S Truman, 1945-1948* (New York, 1977).

John Lewis Gaddis, *The United States and the Origins of the Cold War* (New York, 1972).

Eric F. Goldman, *The Crucial Decade and After: America, 1945-1960* (New York, 1960).

Cabell Phillips, *The Truman Presidency: The History of a Triumphant Succession* (New York, 1966).

VANDENBERG, ARTHUR H(ENDRICK)

b. March 22, 1884; Grand Rapids, Mich.
d. April 18, 1951; Grand Rapids, Mich.
Republican Senator, Mich., 1928-51.

The son of a harness manufacturer, Arthur Vandenberg took odd jobs as a teenager to help support his family when his father's business failed in 1893. After dropping out of law school in 1902, Vandenberg joined the staff of the Grand Rapids *Herald* as a political reporter. In 1907 he became the paper's publisher and editor. He soon emerged to be one of the most prominent citizens of Grand Rapids as well as a leading Michigan Republican. In 1928 Vandenberg was appointed to fill a Senate seat vacated by the death of Woodbridge N. Ferris (D, Mich.).

With the defeat of many incumbent Republicans during the Depression, Vandenberg moved up quickly in seniority. By 1940 he was a leader of the Party in the Senate. He established a conservative record, opposing most New Deal legislation. In the late 1930s he was the key member of the GOP's isolationist wing. After World War II broke out in 1939, Vandenberg opposed measures giving aid to American allies and led the fight against the modification of the Neutrality Act.

Like many isolationists he supported the President's war measures after Pearl Harbor, beginning what Dean Acheson [*q.v.*] later described as "his long day's journey into our times." Vandenberg chaired a committee of leading Republicans that pledged the Party's support of the war effort. He also served on a bipartisan committee formed to help the Administration plan postwar policy. Vandenberg formally renounced isolationism in a speech to the Senate in April 1944. During the last half of the 1940s, he played a major role in the formation of the U.N. and in gaining congressional support for the organization. President Roosevelt appointed him ranking Republican delegate to the San Francisco Conference of 1945, which drafted the U.N. charter. When he assumed the presidency, Harry Truman renewed the appointment. At Vandenberg's insistence the U.S. delegation at San Francisco pushed for the adoption of Article 51 of the U.N. Charter, which permitted member states to enter into regional security pacts for the maintenance of international peace and security. His resolution later served as the justification for U.S. entrance into such alliances as the North Atlantic Treaty Organization and the Rio Pact. Vandenberg then helped secure Senate ratification of the Charter.

Along with Secretary of State James Byrnes [*q.v.*], Vandenberg was the architect of the Truman Administration's policy of "talking tough" to the Russians." As the representative of a state with a large Polish-American constituency, he vigorously denounced Soviet domination of Eastern Europe and backed calls for a firm U.S. stand on Soviet disengagement. His experience in dealing with the Soviets at International Conferences reinforced his fears that the Soviet Union would not comply with the Yalta Accords. By the early months of 1946, he had become convinced that cooperation between the two powers was impossible. Returning from a foreign ministers' conference in Paris, Vandenberg somberly reported that a "Cold War" now existed and warned that the U.S. must adopt new policies to meet the crisis. During the spring of 1946 the Administration, in the face of growing anti-Soviet feeling, adopted an increasingly firm policy towards Russia. It escalated the rhetoric of the Cold War, cut off American economic aid to the USSR and increased the American nuclear arsenal.

Following the Republican victory in the 1946 congressional elections, Vandenberg assumed the chairmanship of the Foreign Relations Committee. He became, as Acheson wrote, "The key to indispensable Republican cooperation in obtaining legislative approval and the support for policies of the greatest magnitude and novelty." Vandenberg was deeply involved in securing congressional approval of the Truman Doctrine. In February Truman invited Vandenberg and several other influential senators to the White House to discuss aid to Greece and Turkey. During the meeting Vandenberg told the President that if he wanted Congress to appropriate money for the programs he would have to "scare the hell out of the country." Truman accepted this advice and, in his landmark Truman Doctrine address of March 14, 1947, placed his request for aid in terms of a moral crusade against Communism. Vandenberg then led the battle for Senate ratification of the aid package. Largely as a result of his efforts the measure passed in April.

Following Secretary of State George C. Marshall's [q.v.] unveiling of the Marshall Plan in June 1947, Truman invited Vandenberg to work closely with the Administration to frame the legislation for the program. The Senator also advised the Administration on the formation of a number of committees to investigate Europe's needs. Vandenberg worked hard to overcome opposition to the Marshall Plan by conservatives anxious to maintain a balanced budget and pro-China senators, who wanted funds given to Chiang-Kai-shek rather than to European governments. Vandenberg described the plan as a program that would "help stop World War III before it starts." In an impassioned speech to the Senate, he said that if the plan failed, "We have done our final best, if it succeeds our children and our

children's children will call us blessed." He obtained enough Republican support to guarantee passage of the program in June 1948.

Vandenberg was a vigorous advocate of U.S. participation in a Western defense alliance. In May 1948 he presented to his committee a working paper calling on the U.S. to grant military aid to international alliances among its allies. The committee unanimously recommended the proposal, and the Senate passed the resolution in June 1948. The Vandenberg resolution, as it was known, proved the basis for American entrance into the North Atlantic Treaty Organization (NATO). Although suffering from cancer, Vandenberg lobbied for passage of the North Atlantic Treaty in 1949, urging its ratification as the best means for discouraging armed aggression. In a speech to his colleagues in July 1949, he delivered so moving an appeal for support for "the terrifying authority for peace" that members of his party and even some Democrats stood up and cheered him. The Senate passed the treaty that month.

During the last years of his life, Vandenberg continued to support what he termed a "un-partisan foreign policy." He advocated cuts in the 1950 foreign aid bill but continued to advocate economic assistance to prevent war. The Senator supported non-recognition of Communist China but broke with other Republican leaders who demanded armed intervention if necessary to protect Taiwan. During the spring of 1950 he urged a complete reconsideration of foreign policy.

Because of his illness Vandenberg was often absent from the Senate in 1950-51. Yet he appeared to vote for funds for the Marshall Plan and for NATO. Vandenberg died in April 1951.

[JB]

WALLACE, HENRY A(GARD)
b. Oct. 7, 1888; Adair County, Iowa
d. Nov. 18, 1965; Danbury, Conn.
Secretary of Commerce, March
1945-September 1946; Presidential

Candidate, Progressive Citizens of America, 1948.

Henry Wallace's father was a noted agriculturalist and professor at the University of Iowa, where he developed new techniques for breeding livestock and growing grain.

Henry Wallace studied agriculture as a college student and later pioneered a number of new techniques in plant genetics. In 1933 Franklin Roosevelt appointed him Secretary of Agriculture and named him his vice-presidential running mate in 1940. Wallace, however, proved to be unpopular with the party professionals, and Roosevelt appointed him Secretary of Commerce four years later.

During his early months in that post, Wallace was primarily interested in developing free trade agreements to promote disposal of surplus industrial and agricultural goods. By ending trade barriers, Wallace maintained, the threat of a postwar depression would vanish. The Soviet Union played a major role in Wallace's thought. He believed that good relations with the USSR were necessary to insure free trade as well as the creation of his dream for a peaceful postwar world. Wallace saw the Soviet Union as a devastated nation that needed American help and would eventually become an important market for U.S. goods. Wallace doubted Stalin's commitment to world revolution and downplayed his repressive domestic polices.

During the Truman Administration Wallace's primary aim became the preservation of Soviet-American cooperation begun by Roosevelt. In 1945 and 1946, as the Administration adopted an increasingly firm policy towards the Soviet Union, Wallace neglected his Commerce Department duties to concentrate on what he deemed to be deteriorating American-Russian relations. He opposed the Administration's decision to suspend aid to the Soviet Union in order to attempt to force the USSR to become more conciliatory in negotiations on Eastern Europe. He felt that the move would sabotage any hope of peaceful relations between the

two powers. The aid cut-off also threatened Wallace's plan for the establishment of a free market by jeopardizing Soviet economic revival and forcing Russia toward self-sufficiency.

The Truman Administration's decision in September 1945 not to share atomic information estranged Wallace still further. At cabinet meetings he argued that the Soviets would obtain atomic secrets anyway. Stalin, he asserted, could only interpret the American reluctance to share weapons knowledge as meaning that the U.S. intended to use nuclear devices against the USSR.

Wallace muted his criticisms until the spring of 1946. In March, at a dinner for Russian relief, he publicly debated Averell Harriman [q.v.] on Soviet policy. Harriman, an early cold warrior, condemned Soviet domination of Eastern Europe. Wallace defended Stalin's desire to make his boundaries secure from capitalist encirclement. The West, he reminded his audience, had tried to destroy the Bolshevik regime after World War I. He asserted that the U.S. had nothing to gain in protesting Soviet hegemony in the area "but on the contrary everything to lose by beating the tom toms against Russia."

Wallace held the British in part responsible for the Administration's anti-Soviet policies. He blamed Winston Churchill for intriguing with Washington to create an Anglo-American alliance that would commit the U.S. to protect what Wallace saw as a morally bankrupt British empire and to oppose the Soviet Union. Churchill's 1946 speech at Fulton, Mo., provided Wallace with additional evidence of what he viewed as an Anglo-American conspiracy against Russia. During that address the former Prime Minister had called for "a fraternal association of the English speaking peoples" against Communism. Wallace later denounced the speech. He told the President that the U.S. should not tie itself to the defense of the British empire, which he predicted was destined to crumble.

On July 23, 1946 Wallace sent Truman a long memo outlining his opposition to Administration foreign policy. The Secretary noted that Stalin had reasonable grounds to fear and distrust the U.S. America's refusal to share atomic knowledge, its development of a large Air Force with bases all over the world and its arming of Latin American states, all had anti-Soviet overtones. Wallace maintained that it was only natural for Stalin to view these developments with fear. The American refusal to recognize the Soviet leader's desire for security on Russia's Western border and need for access to warm water ports, intensified Stalin's distrust of the West. Wallace singled out the American proposal for the international control of nuclear weapons as being particularly anti-Soviet. He pointed out that the Baruch Plan, as it was known, called on Russia to reveal its nuclear research and submit to inspection before the U.S. had turned over its secrets. Wallace again emphasized the Soviet need for extensive economic aid. Summing up, the Secretary suggested that if the U.S. made a number of limited concessions on atomic weapons, granted the loan, and recognized Soviet interests in Eastern Europe, "an atmosphere of mutual trust and confidence" would develop. Truman ignored the letter. Frustrated, Wallace made plans to resign following the November elections.

On Sept. 12, 1946 Wallace delivered a speech in New York's Madison Square Garden to a meeting sponsored by the Independent Citizens Committee of the Arts, Sciences and Professions (ICCASP) and the National Citizens Political Action Committee (NCPAC). The slant of American foreign policy, Wallace told his audience, should neither be for nor against Britain or Russia. The U.S. should promise the world economic assistance for recovery and work for peace based on a strong United Nations and on mutual trust between the "Big Three." Unfortunately, Wallace asserted, American foreign policy had been influenced by "numerous reactionary elements." The "get tough policy" with the Soviet Union that this group advocated, he maintained, would fail: "The tougher we get, the

tougher the Russians get." Wallace called on the U.S. to recognize the Russian sphere of influence in Eastern Europe. In return, he suggested that the Russians acknowledge American interest in Latin America. Wallace also called on the major powers to recognize the "open door" to trade in China and asked the Soviet Union to keep Eastern Europe open to American trade. He believed that acquiescence to this plan could usher in a period of peaceful competition between the capitalist and the Communist world. As time passed, he hoped, the distinctions between the two systems would blur; capitalism would be socialized and Communism would be democratized.

Wallace's speech won a mixed reception. The Communists in the audience booed him for his anti-Soviet remarks and his call for an open door for American capitalism. His demand for acceptance of spheres of influence confused many liberals. On the one hand they supported his desire for good relations with the Soviet Union, but on the other they were unwilling to recognize repressive Communist regimes. They also thought that his recommendations would undermine the United Nations.

Wallace's speech created confusion in the Truman Administration. Secretary of State James Byrnes [q.v.], negotiating in Paris with the Russians, threatened to resign if Wallace kept on advocating policies that undercut his bargaining position. Sen. Arthur Vandenberg (R, Mich.) [q.v.], the leader of Republican internationalists in the Senate, charged that Wallace threatened bipartisan foreign policy. Wallace also embarrassed President Truman. He told his audience that the President had read his speech and endorsed it. When questioned by the press, Truman claimed that he had just endorsed Wallace's right to deliver the address, not the contents of the speech. Wallace responded that Truman had gone over his talk, carefully approving all the sections.

Following protests by Byrnes and Vandenberg, Wallace pledged to refrain from making foreign policy speeches until the

Paris conference had ended. This did not satisfy the two men, who demanded Wallace's ouster. On Sept. 19 Truman asked Wallace to resign.

Out of office Wallace proved a focus for liberals discontent with the Administration. He contined to give speeches denouncing Truman's domestic and foreign policy. He also used his new post as editor of *The New Republic* to attack the Administration and propose policy alternatives. During the spring of 1947 Wallace concentrated on two issues: the Administration's loyalty program and its proposal for aid to Greece and Turkey. Following revelations of security leaks, Truman had issued a directive tightening procedures for insuring loyalty within government. Wallace denounced the order as a gross violation of constitutional rights. He feared the program would not drive Communists out of the government. Instead, he said, it would bar from public service "the man who has ever read a book, had an idea, supported the ideals of Roosevelt, or fought fascism."

Wallace vigorously opposed U.S. economic and military aid to Greece and Turkey to prevent a Communist takeover in the area. He characterized the Greek government as fascist and reminded the American people that Turkey, neutral during World War II, had been close to the Axis powers. Rather than checking Communist advances, Wallace charged, the U.S. would aid Moscow by siding with the forces of reaction. He proposed a rebuilding program for Greece that would be administered by a coalition of Western and Communist governments.

Wallace had originally endorsed the Marshall Plan as a peaceful, non-political program for rebuilding Europe. However, during the fall of 1947, he broke with Truman on the program. He termed it an unwarranted attempt by the U.S. to interfere in the domestic affairs of European nations. The assistance program, he charged, would enhance the power of the rich in those nations. In addition, Wallace maintained, the requirements for receiving aid made it impossible for Commu-

nist nations to join. He asserted that the goal of the plan was not to unify Europe but to increase the distance between East and West.

Wallace's attack on the Marshall Plan ended any possibility of reconciliation with the Truman Administration. It also lost him the support of the more moderate elements of the liberal movement. Such prominent members of the Americans for Democratic Action (ADA) as Eleanor Roosevelt, Wilson Wyatt and Joseph Rauh attacked Wallace for his criticism of the aid program. However, the Progressive Citizens of America (PCA), a coalition of liberals and Communists, supported Wallace's stand.

In 1948 Wallace ran as an independent candidate for President. His campaign, however, was discredited because of the involvement of members of the American Communist Party and Wallace's own assertion that the U.S. was primarily responsible for the Soviet coup in Czechoslovakia. As a result, Wallace failed to carry a single state in the November election.

After the election, the former Vice President retired to his experimental farm in South Salem, N.Y., but continued to criticize the Administration for its reliance on military alliances. However, after 1950 he joined Truman in denouncing Communist aggression in Korea and repression in Eastern Europe. In 1956 and 1960 Wallace supported the Republican presidential nominees. Four years later he endorsed Lyndon Johnson [*q.v.*] for the presidency. Wallace continued to support liberal domestic policies until his death in 1965.

[JB]

For further information:
John Morton Blum, ed., *The Price of Vision: The Diary of Henry Wallace, 1942-1946* (Boston, 1973).
Norman Markowitz, *The Rise and Fall of the People's Century: Henry Wallace and American Liberalism, 1941-1948* (New York, 1973).
Richard J. Walton, *Henry Wallace, Harry Truman, and the Cold War* (New York, 1976).

Appendix

Chronology

1945

APRIL 12—President Franklin D. Roosevelt dies in Warm Springs, Ga. Harry S Truman is sworn in as President of the United States.

APRIL 16—Truman addresses a joint session of Congress, promising a continuation of Roosevelt's policies and a quick end to the war.

APRIL 16—Truman signs a bill extending lend-lease for one year.

APRIL 25—U.S. and Soviet forces meet for the first time at the Elba River. The U.N. Charter Conference opens in San Francisco.

MAY 7—Germany surrenders unconditionally to the Allies in Reims, France.

MAY 8—V-E Day marks the formal end of the war in Europe.

JUNE 5—The Allies establish occupation zones in Germany. Berlin is divided among the Big Four Powers (Gr. Britain, France, U.S. and USSR).

JUNE 12—Truman orders the withdrawal of U.S. troops into the American zone in Germany.

JUNE 21—The Japanese surrender Okinawa after a struggle that took the lives of 100,000 Japanese and 13,000 Americans.

JULY 5—Gen. Douglas MacArthur reports the liberation of the Philippine Islands after 10 months of fighting and 12,000 American dead.

JULY 16—The U.S. explodes the first atomic bomb near Almogordo, N.M.

JULY 17-AUG. 2—Churchill, Stalin and Truman meet at Potsdam, Germany, to discuss postwar policy toward the conquered nations.

JULY 19—The Senate approves U.S. membership in the International Bank for Reconstruction and Development.

JULY 26—Anglo-American conferees at Potsdam issue an ultimatum of unconditional surrender or complete destruction to Japan.

JULY 28—The Senate ratifies the U.N. Charter by a vote of 89 to 2.

AUG. 6—The U.S. drops an atomic bomb on Hiroshima. The Soviet Union declares war on Japan.

AUG. 9—The U.S. drops an atomic bomb on Nagasaki.

AUG. 14—Japan surrenders unconditionally to the Allies.

AUG. 15—Truman proclaims V-J Day.

AUG. 17—Truman orders Gen. Douglas MacArthur to temporarily divide Korea at the 38th parallel. The Soviets occupy the North while U.S. forces move into the South.

AUG. 29—The occupation of Japan begins. Truman names MacArthur supreme commander for the Allied powers in Japan.

AUG. 31—Truman writes to British Prime Minister Clement Attlee requesting that Britain allow an additional 100,000 Jewish refugees to enter Palestine.

SEPT. 2—Japan formally surrenders on board the U.S.S. *Missouri* in Tokyo Bay.

OCT. 22—Truman recommends a universal military training program to Congress.

DEC. 15—Truman dispatches Gen. George C. Marshall as special ambassador to China.

DEC. 19—Truman recommends to Congress that the armed forces be reorganized into a single department.

1946

JAN. 20—Truman issues an executive order establishing the Control Intelligence Group, the forerunner of the Central Intelligence Agency. He appoints Adm. Sidney W. Souers to head the agency.

MARCH 5—In a speech at Westminster College in Fulton, Mo., Winston Churchill warns of an "Iron Curtain" being drawn across Eastern Europe.

JUNE 14—At the U.N. Bernard Baruch submits an American plan for international control of atomic energy.

JULY 4—Truman proclaims the Philippines an independent nation.

JULY 15—Truman signs the $3.75 billion British loan bill.

AUG.1—Truman signs the Atomic Energy Act of 1946, placing control of all phases of atomic energy, including weapons development, in civilian hands.

OCT. 1—The Nuremberg War Crimes Tribunal sentences 12 Nazi war criminals to death and seven others to prison terms.

NOV. 5—In the general elections, Republicans win control of the House by 59 seats and the Senate by six. In addition, the GOP wins two governorships, bringing the total number of Republican governors to 25.

1947

JAN. 29—Truman announces he is abandoning mediation in China between the Nationalists and the Communists and orders 12,000 Marines home.

MARCH 12—In a major address before Congress, the President outlines the Truman Doctrine of containment of the Soviet Union. He asks Congress for $400 million in aid to Greece and Turkey to prevent Communist takeovers in those countries.

MAY 22—Truman signs the $400 million Greek-Turkish aid bill.

JUNE 5—Secretary of State George C. Marshall proposes "the Marshall Plan" of massive economic aid to Europe.

JUNE 5—The Senate ratifies peace treaties with Italy and with the lesser Axis powers.

JULY 25—Truman signs the National Security Act establishing a unified Department of Defense and creating the National Security Council.

JULY 27—Truman appoints James V. Forrestal first Secretary of Defense.

SEPT. 2—The Inter-American Defense Pact, which provides for united defense against aggression, is signed in Rio de Janeiro.

SEPT. 19—Gen. Albert Wedemeyer submits a report on his China trip to Truman, recommending a five-year U.S. military aid program and encouragement of internal reforms in the Nationalist government.

OCT. 9—Truman instructs the State Department to support the U.N. plan to partition Palestine into Jewish and Arab states.

OCT. 14—The U.S. becomes the first nation to break the sound barrier.

OCT. 18—The House Un-American Activities Committee opens an investigation of alleged Communist infiltration in the movie industry.

OCT. 24—Sen. Robert A. Taft formally announces his candidacy for the 1948 Republican presidential nomination.

OCT. 29—The President's Commission on Civil Rights reports its findings in a paper entitled, "To Secure these Rights." Among the report's recommendations are creation of special federal and state investigative units for civil rights cases, elimination of poll taxes and specific laws against bias in housing, education, health and public services.

NOV. 29—The state of Israel is estab-

lished by a joint U.S.- Soviet-backed decision in the U.N.

DEC. 19—Congress votes a $540 million appropriation for interim aid to France, Italy, Austria and China and receives Truman's request for $17 billion for a four-year European Economic Recovery Program.

DEC. 29—Henry A. Wallace announces his candidacy for the presidency on a third party ticket promising peace and abundance.

1948

MARCH 6—The U.S. and its Western European allies reach an agreement on the formation of a federal government for West Germany and its participation in the Marshall Plan.

MAY 14—Truman gives de facto recognition to the new state of Israel.

MAY 19—The House passes the Mundt-Nixon bill requiring the registration of all Communists and providing penalties for attempts to establish a dictatorship in the U.S. No Senate action is taken.

JUNE 11—The Senate overwhelmingly passes the Vandenberg Resolution stating that the U.S. can associate itself in peacetime with nations outside the Western Hemisphere in collective security agreements.

JUNE 24—The Republican National Convention nominates Gov. Thomas E. Dewey of New York for President and Gov. Earl Warren of California for vice president.

JUNE 24—Soviet occupation forces begin a blockade of Berlin.

JUNE 26—Truman orders all planes in the American European Command to supply Berlin's needs until the Soviets lift their blockade.

JULY 15—The Democratic National Convention nominates Truman for President. Alben Barkley is chosen vice presidential candidate. When the Convention adopts a strong civil rights plank, some conservative Southern delegates walk out.

JULY 17—Southern Democrats opposed to the Party's stand on civil rights form the States' Rights Party which nominates Strom Thurmond for President on a platform calling for racial segregation.

JULY 22—The Progressive Party nominates Henry A. Wallace for President on a platform urging a conciliatory policy toward the Soviet Union.

AUG. 3—Admitted former Communist Whittaker Chambers names Alger Hiss as a former member of a Communist cell in Washington.

NOV. 2—Truman unexpectedly defeats Dewey by approximately 2.2 million popular votes and 114 electoral votes. Thurmond receives 39 electoral votes while Wallace receives none. Democrats also win control of both houses of Congress.

1949

MARCH 2—An Air Force B-50 bomber completes its first non-stop flight around the world while re-fueling aloft. It proves the U.S. can drop an atomic bomb anywhere.

APRIL 4—Twelve nations, including the U.S., sign the North Atlantic Treaty.

APRIL 8—Truman orders the U.S. occupation zone in Germany to be merged with those of Great Britain and France.

MAY 12—The Russian blockade of Berlin ends; Truman terminates the U.S. airlift.

AUG. 5—With Truman's approval, the State Department issues a White Paper blaming the fall of China to the Communists on Chiang Kai-shek's corrupt, inefficient government. It states that no further aid will be given the Chiang government.

AUG. 10—Truman signs a bill organizing the military into the Department of Defense and separate departments of the Army, Navy and Air Force.

SEPT. 21—The U.S. and Western powers end military control of Germany.

SEPT. 22—Truman signs the Mutual Defense Assistance Act which provides for military aid to NATO allies in case of aggression.

SEPT. 23—Truman announces that the Soviet Union has exploded a nuclear bomb.

OCT. 1—A Communist regime under Mao Tse-tung is established in China. It is immediately recognized by France and Great Britain and refused recognition by the U.S.

OCT. 14—A federal court in New York convicts 11 leaders of the American Communist Party of violating the Smith Act in advocating the overthrow of the U.S. government.

OCT. 31—Walter Reuther, president of the United Auto Workers, begins a purge of Communist-dominated unions from the CIO.

1950

JAN. 21—Hiss is convicted of perjury in denying that he gave U.S. secrets to Communists.

JAN. 31—Truman orders a crash program for the construction of the hydrogen bomb.

FEB. 7—In a speech at Wheeling, W. Va., Sen. Joseph R. McCarthy charges that there are 209 Communists in the State Department.

JUNE 25—North Korea invades South Korea. The U.N. Security Council, with Russia absent, declares North Korea the aggressor.

JUNE 30—Truman orders U.S. ground forces into Korea and extends the draft to July 1951.

SEPT. 8—Congress passes the Defense Production Act granting the government wide-ranging powers to impose wage and price controls because of the Korean war.

SEPT. 23—Congress passes the Internal Security Act over Truman's veto. The Act provides for registration of members of Communist-action and Communist-front groups, detention of Communists in national emergencies and establishment of the Subversive Activities Control Board.

OCT. 26—Chinese Communist troops intervene in the Korean conflict.

NOV. 1—Puerto Rican nationalists attempt to assassinate Truman.

NOV. 7—Republicans increase their representation in the House and Senate, picking up five and 31 seats respectively. Nevertheless, Democrats retain control of the Senate 49 to 47 and of the House 235 to 199.

DEC. 29—Gen. Douglas MacArthur recommends that U.N. forces attack Communist China.

1951

JAN. 1—Communist Chinese and North Korean troops drive U.N. forces out of Seoul.

MARCH 7—Gen. Douglas MacArthur ridicules Truman's Korean policies in a statement to the press.

APRIL 11—Truman relieves MacArthur of his command in Korea and replaces him with Gen. Matthew B. Ridgway.

APRIL 19—Addressing a joint session of Congress, MacArthur urges an expanded war against the Communists in Asia.

JULY 7—Negotiations for a cease-fire in Korea begin in Kaesong between the U.N., North Korea and Communist China.

AUG. 1—Truman cancels tariff concessions to all nations under Soviet domination.

SEPT. 8—The U.S. and 47 nations, excluding Russia and China, sign a peace treaty with Japan restoring that nation to full sovereignty. The same day Japan and the U.S. sign a security treaty permitting the U.S. to station troops in Japan.

OCT. 19—The U.S. officially ends its state of war with Germany.

1952

MARCH 29—Truman publicly reveals that he will not be a candidate in the 1952 presidential election.

MAY 1—The State Department bans travel to the Soviet Union and its satellites.

JULY 11—The Republican National Convention nominates Gen. Dwight D. Eisenhower for President over Sen. Robert A. Taft by a vote of 595 to 500. The convention then nominates Sen. Richard M. Nixon for vice president.

JULY 25—The Democratic National Convention meeting in Chicago nominates Adlai Stevenson for President on the third ballot. Sen. John Sparkman is nominated for vice president the following day.

AUG. 4—ANZUS (Pacific Council) is created by the mutual security pact between the U.S., Australia and New Zealand.

AUG. 22—At a Denver, Colo., news conference, Eisenhower says that he would not give blanket endorsement to Sen. Joseph R. McCarthy, but he would back any Republican candidate for Congress.

AUG. 25—Eisenhower tells the American Legion Convention in New York that the U.S. should help the people of Communist countries "liberate" themselves. He omits a passage in his prepared text assailing "character assassins" and promoters of "witch hunts," a veiled reference to McCarthy.

OCT. 24—Eisenhower announces that he will go to Korea if elected.

NOV. 1—The U.S. tests the world's first hydrogen (fusion) bomb.

NOV. 4—Eisenhower defeats Stevenson in the presidential election by over six million votes and receives 442 of 531 electoral votes. The Republicans gain control of both houses of Congress by very narrow margins: 221 to 211 in the House and 48 to 47 in the Senate. There is one independent in each house.

DEC. 2-5—Fulfilling his campaign pledge, Eisenhower visits Korea.

1953

JAN. 20—Eisenhower is inaugurated 34th President of the U.S.

FEB. 2—In his State of the Union address, Eisenhower announces that there is no "sense or logic" in the U.S. assuming "defensive responsibilities on behalf of Chinese Communists." He will therefore, withdraw the Seventh Fleet from the Formosa Strait between Taiwan and mainland China. He also announces that he will let wage and price controls end by April 30.

FEB. 4—McCarthy begins a loyalty-security probe of the State Department.

FEB. 20—Dulles submits the Captive Peoples Resolution to Congress. It rejects "any interpretations or applications" of secret World War II agreements "which have been perverted to bring about the subjugation of free peoples" and deplores Soviet "totalitarian imperialism" in Eastern Europe.

FEB. 28—The Senate Permanent Investigations Subcommittee, chaired by McCarthy, opens televised hearings on subversion in the Voice of America.

MARCH 4—Dulles announces his acceptance of the resignation of State Department China expert John Carter Vincent, under attack by McCarthy.

MARCH 5—Marshal Josef Stalin dies.

MARCH 7—Congress shelves the Captive Peoples Resolution following the announcement of Stalin's death.

MARCH 27—Despite strong opposition, the Senate confirms Charles Bohlen as ambassador to the Soviet Union. Conservatives had accused Bohlen of being part of the "Truman-Acheson policy of appeasement" toward the USSR.

APRIL 2—Japan and the U.S. sign a 10-year treaty of friendship, commerce and navigation.

JUNE 17—Workers in East Germany riot to protest factory speedups and food shortages. Russian tanks are brought in to quell the uprising.

JULY 27—The U.S. and North Korea sign an armistice at Panmunjom. The treaty calls for a demilitarized zone along the 38th parallel and the voluntary repatriation of prisoners of war.

JULY 31—Taft dies of cancer.

AUG. 12—The USSR explodes its first hydrogen bomb.

AUG. 19-22—A coup, engineered by the Central Intelligence Agency (CIA), overthrows the leftist government of Premier Mohammad Mossadegh in Iran and installs a pro-Western regime loyal to Shah Pahlevi.

AUG. 31—McCarthy begins an investigation of possible Communist infiltration in the Armed Forces.

DEC. 3—Eisenhower orders Dr. J. Robert Oppenheimer's security clearance suspended pending a review.

DEC. 4-7—President Eisenhower, British Prime Minister Winston Churchill and French Premier Joseph Laniel confer in Bermuda on the exchange of atomic information.

DEC. 8—Eisenhower delivers his "Atoms for Peace" speech at the U.N., proposing the creation of an international atomic energy agency to pool resources for the peaceful development of nuclear energy.

1954

JAN. 12—Secretary of State John Foster Dulles announces a policy of "massive retaliation," the use of strategic nuclear weapons as America's primary line of defense.

JAN. 21—The Navy launches the first nuclear powered submarine the S.S. *Nautilus.*

FEB. 10—Eisenhower tells newsmen that he can conceive of no greater tragedy than for the U.S. to become involved in all-out war in Indochina.

FEB. 18—The Berlin Conference of foreign ministers fails to reach an agreement on the reunification of Germany.

FEB. 26—By a vote of 50-42, the Senate defeats the Bricker amendment, which would have limited the President's treaty-making powers.

MARCH 1—U.S. sets off its second hydrogen bomb at Bikini Atoll in the Pacific Ocean. The force of the explosion inadvertently exposes 379 persons to radiation, including 23 Japanese fishermen seriously burned on a ship 70-90 miles from the blast center.

MARCH 8—The U.S. and Japan sign a mutual defense treaty, providing for the gradual rearmament of Japan.

MARCH 13—The Organization of American States adopts a U.S. sponsored resolution calling for joint action against any Latin American state falling under Communist control.

MARCH 20—French Chief of Staff Gen. Paul Henry Ely flies to Washington seeking direct U.S. military aid for the beleaguered French garrison at Dien Bien Phu in northern Vietnam.

MARCH 24—Eisenhower announces that Southeast Asia is "of the most transcendent importance to the United States and the Free World."

MARCH 29—Dulles calls for united action in Indochina.

APRIL 22-JUNE 17—The Senate Permanent Investigations Subcommittee holds public hearings into conflicting charges made by the Army and McCarthy.

APRIL 26—The Geneva Conference on Korea and Indochina opens with foreign ministers of 19 nations, including Communist China, present.

MAY 4—Dulles withdraws from the Geneva Convention after his plan for a South Asian defense alliance fails.

MAY 7—The French garrison at Dien Bien Phu surrenders after a 55 day seige.

JUNE 9—Army counsel Joseph Welch reproaches McCarthy for "cruelty and recklessness" in trying to "assassinate" the reputation of Frederick Fisher, a member of Welch's Boston law firm.

JUNE 11—Sen. Ralph Flanders introduces a resolution to remove McCarthy from his committee chairmanships until he answers charges stemming from his action in the 1952 election.

JUNE 18-25—A CIA implemented coup takes place in Guatemala, ousting the leftist government of Jacobo Arbenz.

JUNE 29—In a controversial 4-1 decision, the Atomic Energy Commission refuses to reinstate Dr. J. Robert Oppenheimer's security clearance for access to classified information on nuclear technology. The verdict is based on "proof of fundamental defects in his character" and his associations with Communists.

JULY 21—The Geneva Conference on Indochina ends with the signing of the Geneva Accords, partitioning Vietnam at the 17th parallel and providing for unified elections within two years.

SEPT. 3—Communist China begins heavy shelling of the Pescadores islands claimed by Nationalist China.

SEPT. 8—Australia, Great Britain, France, New Zealand, Pakistan, the Philippines, Thailand and the U.S. form the Southeast Asian Treaty Organization (SEATO), pledging joint action in defense of member nations. Nationalist China is excluded from the alliance.

NOV. 5—Dulles announces the dismissal of career diplomat John Paton Davies, Jr., who had been attacked by McCarthy.

DEC. 2—The U.S. and Nationalist China sign a mutual defense treaty, pledging American retaliation if Communist China attacks Formosa.

DEC. 2—The Senate votes, 67-22, to condemn McCarthy for obstructing the elections subcommittee in 1952, abusing Sen. Watkins and the Select Committee to Study Censure and insulting the Senate during the censure proceedings.

DEC. 28—Dulles indicates at a press conference that aggression in Western Europe would be met with tactical atomic weapons.

1955

JAN. 1—U.S. Foreign Operations Administration begins to supply direct financial aid to South Vietnam, Cambodia and Laos.

JAN. 10—Eisenhower asks Congress for new powers to reduce foreign trade barriers, including a three year extension of the Reciprocal Trade Agreements Act.

JAN. 13—Eisenhower asks Congress to inaugurate a military reserve plan, extend the Selective Service System and to raise military pay, allowances and benefits.

JAN. 28—Congress passes the Formosa Resolution, giving Eisenhower discretionary powers to use U.S. forces in the defense of Formosa and the Pescadores Islands. It is the first time Congress has granted a President such war-making powers in peacetime.

FEB. 23—Eisenhower states that the U.S. would stop testing atomic weapons only under a workable disarmament agreement with effective international inspection.

APRIL 21—The U.S. ends its occupation of Germany.

MAY 9—West Germany is admitted to full membership in the North Atlantic Treaty Organization (NATO).

MAY 15—The U.S., Great Britain, France and the USSR sign a peace treaty with Austria, granting it full independence in return for political neutrality.

JUNE 30—In his second U.N. speech, Eisenhower calls for a "new kind of peace," in which the atom will be used for productive purposes.

JULY 18-23—President Dwight D. Eisenhower, Premier Nikolai Bulganin, Prime Minister Winston Churchill and Premier Edgar Faure hold a summit conference at Geneva. The major topic is German unification.

JULY 21—Eisenhower submits his "Open Skies" proposal at the Geneva summit conference. He suggests that the USSR and the U.S. exchange military blueprints and allow mutual air reconnaissance over their military installations.

AUG. 8—The first conference on the peaceful uses of atomic energy opens in Geneva. Seventy-three nations are represented.

OCT. 27—The foreign ministers of the U.S., Great Britain, France and the USSR meet in Geneva to discuss disarmament, German unification and East-West relations.

1956

JAN. 13—Eisenhower names a panel of eight prominent citizens, headed by James Killian, to monitor the activities of the CIA.

JAN. 16—In a *Life* magazine interview, Dulles defends his "brinkmanship" policies, saying that the U.S. has gone "to the verge of war" to maintain peace. He states that "the ability to get to the verge without getting into the war is the necessary art." "We walked to the brink, and we looked it in the face."

OCT. 23—An armed revolt begins in Budapest, Hungary. As demanded by the rebels, the imprisoned Imre Nagy, a moderate Communist, is brought back to head the government.

OCT. 29—War breaks out in the Middle East as Israel invades the Gaza Strip and the Sinai Peninsula, driving toward the Suez Canal.

OCT. 30—A joint British-French ultimatum to Israel and Egypt demands immediate cessation of all fighting and withdrawal of military forces to positions at least 10 miles from the Suez Canal.

OCT. 31—As Anglo-French forces attack Egyptian installations around the Suez Canal Zone, Eisenhower declares himself opposed to the use of force to settle international disputes.

NOV. 2—The U.S. offers $20 million worth of food and medical supplies to Hungary.

NOV. 4—Khrushchev orders Soviet armored units to crush the Hungarian "fascists." Thirty thousand Hungarians and 7,000 Russians die in the ensuing conflict, which ends a year of unrest and dissent in the Soviet satellites.

NOV. 4—In a letter to Bulganin, Eisenhower urges "in the name of humanity and in the cause of peace" that the USSR halt the bloodshed in Hungary.

NOV. 5—The U.N. votes to organize a police force to restore peace in the Middle East.

NOV. 6—Eisenhower wins reelection in a landslide, defeating Stevenson by over nine million votes and capturing 457 out of 531 electoral votes.

NOV. 8—Eisenhower announces that he has directed the Refugee Relief Administration to speed the processing of Hungarian refugees.

DEC. 6—Eisenhower orders an air and sea lift to bring 21,500 Hungarian refugees to the U.S. by Jan. 1, 1957 or shortly thereafter.

DEC. 31—Sociologist C. Wright Mills's book *The Power Elite* is published.

1957

MARCH 7—Congress approves the Eisenhower Doctrine, giving the President the authority to use military force in the Middle East to preserve "the independence and integrity" of Middle Eastern nations and prevent "overt armed aggression from . . . international Communism."

MARCH 24—Eisenhower and British Prime Minister Harold Macmillan issue a joint communique, after four day conference at Bermuda, stating that the U.S. has agreed to supply guided missiles to Great Britain.

MAY 2—Sen. Joseph McCarthy dies of acute liver failure.

MAY 14—The U.S. resumes military aid to Yugoslavia which had been halted because of Tito's reconciliation with the USSR.

JUNE 3-6—The U. S. formally joins the Military Committee of the Baghdad Pact at a meeting of the Council of Ministers in Karachi, Pakistan.

JULY 16—Secretary of Defense Charles Wilson orders the Armed Forces reduced by 100,000 men by the end of 1957.

AUG. 21—Eisenhower announces a U.S. offer to suspend nuclear weapons tests for two years in return for a Soviet agreement to halt production of fissionable material for weapons and to establish an inspection system.

AUG. 25—The Special Radiation Subcommittee of the Joint Atomic Energy Committee reports that the effect of radioactive fallout is negligible but might increase if atomic tests increase.

OCT. 4—The Soviet Union launches the first artificial earth satellite, *Sputnik*, into orbit. Americans fear a loss of world prestige.

OCT. 8—Eisenhower issues a statement expressing concern that the U.S. is no further advanced in production of intercontinental ballistic missiles.

OCT. 19—The Atomic Energy Commission reports that, according to current estimates, harm to Americans from H-bomb testing appears to be within "tolerable limits."

NOV. 7—In response to the Soviet space launching, Eisenhower appoints James Killian, president of the Massachusetts Insitute of Technology, to manage a program of scientific improvement in the U.S. defense program.

NOV. 7—The Gaither Report, leaked to

the press, finds that because of increased Soviet spending, the USSR will achieve missile superiority over the U.S. by 1959. The group recommends increased military spending and the development of a fallout shelter program to meet the challenge.

NOV. 13—In a nationwide address Eisenhower proposes a considerable increase in defense appropriations to meet the threat of scientific advances by the USSR.

NOV. 25—Sen. Lyndon Johnson's Preparedness Subcommittee of the Senate Armed Services Committee begins an inquiry into the history, status and future of the nation's missile and satellite programs.

NOV. 26—Eisenhower suffers a mild stroke.

DEC. 6—America's first attempt to launch a space satellite ends in failure as the Vanguard rocket explodes on its launch pad before a national TV audience.

DEC. 15—Eisenhower rejects an appeal by Indian Prime Minister Jawaharlal Nehru for a halt in nuclear weapons tests.

DEC. 16-19—At the Paris NATO meeting, the U.S. convinces Great Britain, Italy and Turkey to station U.S. intermediate-range missiles on their territory.

DEC. 17—The U.S. successfully fires the Atlas, its first intercontinental ballistic missile.

1958

JAN. 5—The Rockefeller Brothers Fund releases a report, prepared by Henry Kissinger, warning of massive Soviet success in improving technology and approaching military weapons parity with the U.S.

JAN. 7—Eisenhower requests Congress to appropriate an additional $1.4 billion to speed up and expand missile and air defenses.

JAN. 9—Eisenhower's State of the Union message stresses the need for an accelerated defense effort and the reorganization of the Defense Department to curb interservice rivalry.

JAN. 12—In a letter to Bulganin Eisenhower urges that "outer space should used only for peaceful purposes."

JAN. 13—Eisenhower sends his fiscal 1959 budget to Congress. It provides for moderate increases in military spending and cutbacks in other areas.

JAN. 13—Linus Pauling releases a petition signed by 9,235 scientists, including 36 Nobel Prize laureates, calling for an international nuclear test ban.

JAN. 31—An Army rocket team, led by Dr. Wernher von Braun, sends the first U.S. satellite, Explorer I, into orbit.

MARCH 5—Eisenhower vetoes a bill granting funds for the development of a nuclear powered airplane.

MARCH 31—The USSR announces a unilateral suspension of nuclear tests.

MAY 15—Nixon returns from a stormy 18-day tour of eight South American republics. During the tour he was often assailed by anti-American mobs protesting U.S. alleged support of dictators.

JULY 1—Nuclear scientists representing the Western and Soviet blocs meet in Geneva to convene a "conference of experts to study the possibility of detecting violations of possible agreement on suspension of nuclear weapons tests."

JULY 15—Eisenhower orders U.S. Marines to Lebanon in response to an urgent request from President Camille Chamoun for assistance.

AUG. 6—Eisenhower signs a bill reorganizing the Defense Department. The measure strengthens the powers of the Secretary of Defense and creates a directorate of defense research and engineering.

AUG. 12—U.S. Marines begin withdrawing from Lebanon.

AUG. 22—Eisenhower offers to halt U.S. nuclear tests for one year. He also proposes that the nuclear powers meet in Geneva to seek an agreement on suspending nuclear tests and setting up an inspection system.

AUG. 23—Communist China resumes shelling Quemoy and Matsu.

SEPT. 11—On national TV Eisenhower reiterates the U.S.'s commitment to defend Quemoy and Matsu.

OCT. 6—Peking announces a one week suspension of its bombardment of Quemoy.

OCT. 7—NASA initiates Project Mercury, its first program for manned space flight.

NOV. 4—In mid-term elections the Democrats increase their majorities in both houses of Congress. They control the Senate by 30 seats and the House by 128.

NOV. 10—Khrushchev calls on the U.S., Great Britain and France to "give up the remnants of the occupation regime in Berlin" and implies that he will hand over USSR powers in Berlin to the East Germans if the Western allies do not withdraw troops from the city.

NOV. 11-DEC. 18—The U.S. and USSR hold an inconclusive conference on the Prevention of Surprise Attack in Geneva.

NOV. 22—The U.S. reaffirms its intention to "maintain the integrity" of West Berlin.

DEC. —The John Birch Society is founded.

DEC. 14—The U.S., Britain and France formally reject Soviet demands for their withdrawal from West Berlin.

1959

JAN. 1—Fidel Castro's guerrilla forces overthrow the Batista regime in Cuba. The revolution is greeted sympathetically in the U.S.

JAN. 2—The USSR achieves the world's first moon shot as *Lunik I* passes within a few thousand miles of the moon.

JAN. 5—The White House releases a statement by its science advisory committee questioning the reliability of techniques for detecting underground nuclear tests.

FEB. 2—Eisenhower outlines to Congress a 10-year space program to launch a satellite or space probe vehicle each month starting in mid-1959.

MARCH 23—The peacetime draft is extended until July 1, 1963.

APRIL 4—In an address at Gettysburg College, Eisenhower makes his first commitment to maintain South Vietnam as a separate national state.

APRIL 15—Suffering from terminal cancer, Dulles resigns as Secretary of State.

MAY 11—The foreign ministers of the U.S., Great Britain, France and the USSR meet in Geneva to begin talks on the problems of Berlin, German reunification, an all-German peace treaty and European security.

MAY 24—Dulles dies of cancer.

JUNE 27—The U.S. denounces Cuba before the Organization of American States for contributing to Caribbean tensions and for its slanderous attacks upon the U.S.

JULY 24—Nixon and Khrushchev engage in a political debate at a preview of the U.S. exhibition in Moscow. The discussion, held in the kitchen of a so-called typical American home, becomes known as the "kitchen debate."

AUG. 1—In a radio-TV address from Moscow, Nixon tells the Soviet people that they will continue to live in an era of fear, suspicion and tension if Khrushchev tries to promote the Communization of countries outside the USSR.

AUG. 31—The Joint Atomic Energy Committee's Special Subcommittee on Radiation issues a report concluding that further nuclear tests could be hazardous and urging the establishment of a national civil defense system.

SEPT. 15—Soviet Premier Khrushchev arrives in the U.S. on a good-will visit.

SEPT. 25-17—Agreements made during congenial talks between Khrushchev and Eisenhower at Camp David, Md., prepare the way for a summit meeting the following year.

OCT. 12—The U.S. places an embargo on all exports to Cuba, except medical supplies and food.

OCT. 19—The U.S. Development Loan Fund releases a major policy statement announcing that future loans to underdeveloped countries must be spent on U.S. goods.

OCT. 26—Eisenhower announces his firm intention to defend the U.S. naval base at Guantanamo, Cuba.

NOV. 3—Panamanian nationalists riot over U.S. domination of the Panama Canal Zone.

DEC. 1—The U.S., USSR and 10 other nations sign the Antarctic Treaty, establishing a nuclear-free zone around the Antarctic ice mass and setting up inspection and enforcement procedures.

DEC. 3—Eisenhower embarks on an 11 nation good-will tour of Europe, Asia and North Africa.

DEC. 30—The Navy commissions the *S.S. George Washington*, the first nuclear powered submarine designed to fire Polaris missiles.

1960

JAN. 9—Nixon announces his candidacy for the Republican presidential nomination.

JAN. 19—The U.S. and Japan sign the Mutual Security Treaty under which both countries pledge to maintain and develop their capacities to resist armed attacks.

JAN. 26—Formally restating U.S. policy, Eisenhower reaffirms that there will be no reprisals against Cuba or intervention in its internal affairs.

FEB. 22-MARCH 7—Eisenhower undertakes a four nation goodwill tour of Latin America.

MARCH 15—The Ten-Nation Disarmament Conference begins in Geneva.

MARCH 15—Eisenhower meets with West German Chancellor Konrad Adenauer at the White House, assuring him of U.S. support in maintaining the freedom of West Berlin.

MARCH 17—Eisenhower formally approves a CIA plan to train Cuban emigrés for an invasion of the island.

APRIL 3—Daniel Bell's *The End of Ideology: On the Exhaustion of Political Ideas in the Fifties* is published.

APRIL 22—In a television speech Castro charges that the U.S. is plotting to overthrow his government.

MAY 1—Francis Gary Powers, on a U-2 reconnaissance flight for the CIA, is shot down over the USSR by a surface to air missile.

MAY 5—Khrushchev reveals that an American aircraft has been shot down over Soviet air space and angrily declares it an act of "aggressive provocation." Two days later he produces Powers's confession and the U-2 plane.

MAY 7—Eisenhower announces that the U.S. will resume underground nuclear testing as part of research on detecting such blasts.

MAY 7—The State Department admits that the U-2 plane was "probably" endeavouring to obtain intelligence information.

MAY 9—Secretary of State Christian Herter strongly defends the need for the aerial intelligence program to counter the USSR's ability to prepare secretly for a surprise attack.

MAY 11—In his first public comment on the U-2 incident, Eisenhower accepts personal responsibility for the U-2 flights. It is the first time a head of state has ever openly admitted that his country was spying on others.

MAY 16—After three hours the Paris summit meeting collapses when Khrushchev vehemently demands that Eisenhower apologize for the U-2 flights, punish the culprits responsible and ban future flights. He also revokes his invitation to Eisenhower to visit the USSR later in the spring.

MAY 27—Eisenhower announces the termination of U.S. economic aid to Cuba.

JUNE 12—Eisenhower leaves on a two-week good-will tour of the 12 Far Eastern countries.

JUNE 16—Thousands of Japanese riot against the U.S.-Japanese security treaty. Eisenhower cancels his visit to Japan.

JULY 6—In retaliation for the seizure of millions of dollars worth of American property, the U.S. cuts Cuba's sugar import quota by 700,000 tons.

JULY 9—Eisenhower asserts that the U.S. will never permit the establishment of a Communist regime in the Western Hemisphere.

JULY 13—Kennedy wins the Democratic presidential nomination on the first ballot at the Los Angeles convention. The vote is 806 for Kennedy, 409 for his chief rival Lyndon Johnson. Johnson is chosen vice-presidential candidate at the following session.

JULY 25—Nixon easily wins the Republican presidential nomination on the first ballot in Chicago.

AUG. 19—A Soviet military tribunal sentences Powers to 10 years in prison for espionage.

AUG. 20—The U.S. joins other members of the Organization of American States in voting to sever diplomatic relations with the Dominican Republic and to impose economic sanctions and a complete arms embargo on it for its "acts of aggression" in participating in a plot to overthrow the Venezuelan government.

SEPT. 11—The Inter-American Economic Conference adopts the "Act of Bogota," an extensive social and economic aid program for Latin America.

SEPT. 22—Eisenhower addresses the U.N. General Assembly, proposing national self-determination for African colonies and a five-point program of economic and educational assistance to be administered through the U.N.

OCT. 28—The U.S. requests the Organization of American States to investigate reports that Cuba is receiving large shipments of arms from the Soviet bloc.

NOV. 1—Eisenhower announces that the U.S. would take "whatever steps" necessary to maintain the U.S. naval base at Guantanamo, Cuba.

NOV. 8—Kennedy defeats Nixon in the presidential election by 113,057 votes and receives 303 of the 537 electoral votes. The Democrats retain control of both the House and Senate.

NOV. 17—The CIA briefs Kennedy on its involvement in training Cuban exiles in Guatemala to overthrow Castro.

NOV. 18—Eisenhower orders U.S. naval units to patrol Central American waters to prevent Communist-led invasions of either Guatemala or Nicaragua.

DEC. 14—Western European nations, the U.S. and Canada sign an agreement in Paris creating an Organization for Economic Cooperation and Development.

1961

JAN. 3—The U.S. breaks diplomatic relations with Cuba.

Jan. 4—The Organization of American States votes to impose limited economic sanctions against the Dominican Republic.

JAN. 17—In his farewell address Eisenhower warns against the influence of a "military-industrial complex."

JAN. 20—Kennedy is inaugurated 35th President of the U.S.

JAN. 25—In his first presidential news conference, Kennedy supports the idea of a neutral Laos.

JAN. 28—Kennedy approves a Vietnam counter-insurgency plan that calls for government reform and military restructuring as the basis for expanded U.S. assistance.

FEB. 7—Kennedy orders a ban on most trade with Cuba.

FEB. 16—Kennedy warns of the risk of war if Belgium takes unilateral action in the Congo.

MARCH 13—Kennedy proposes that Latin America join the U.S. in an Alliance for Progress, a ten-year $20 billion program of economic and social development.

MARCH 21—Great Britain, the U.S. and the USSR resume their three-power nuclear test ban conference in Geneva.

MARCH 23—In a televised news conference Kennedy alerts the nation to Communist expansion in Laos and warns that a ceasefire must precede the start of negotiations to establish a neutral and independent nation.

MARCH 28—Kennedy announces the initiation of a program to rapidly increase U.S. military strength.

APRIL 12—Soviet cosmonaut Yuri Gagarin becomes the first man to orbit the earth.

APRIL 17—CIA-trained Cuban exiles begin the Bay of Pigs invasion.

APRIL 20—A Cuban government communique reports the defeat and capture of the invasion force.

APRIL 24—Kennedy accepts full responsibility for the Cuban invasion.

MAY 9-15—Vice President Lyndon B. Johnson visits Southeast Asia and recommends a "strong program of action" in Vietnam.

MAY 31-JUNE 6—Kennedy meets with British and French leaders in Europe.

JUNE 3-4—Kennedy and Khrushchev hold an inconclusive summit meeting in Vienna.

JUNE 9—President Ngo Dinh Diem requests U.S. troops for training the South Vietnamese army.

JULY 25—Kennedy calls for $3.25 billion to meet commitments in the wake of the Berlin crisis and asks Congress for the power to increase the size of the armed forces by 217,000.

AUG. 13—East Germany seals its border with West Berlin to halt the flow of refugees to the West. Work begins on the Berlin wall.

AUG. 16—The U.S. and 19 other American countries adopt the Alliance for Progress charter at Punta del Este, Uruguay.

AUG. 18-21—Vice President Johnson visits Berlin to reaffirm the U.S. commitment there.

SEPT.-DEC.—East Germany hampers U.S. access to East Berlin.

SEPT. 1—The Soviet Union resumes atmospheric nuclear tests.

SEPT. 5—Kennedy announces that the U.S. will resume underground nuclear tests.

SEPT. 16—The U.S. backs U.N. military action in Katanga.

SEPT. 25—Kennedy delivers a "Proposal for General and Complete Disarmament in a Peaceful World" in his major foreign policy address to the U.N.

SEPT. 26—Kennedy signs a bill establishing the U.S. Arms Control and Disarmament Agency.

OCT. 1—South Vietnam requests a bilateral defense treaty with the U.S.

OCT. 4—An international group of protestors urging unilateral disarmament and an end to nuclear testing demonstrates in Moscow.

OCT. 27—U.S. and Soviet tanks confront each other at the Berlin border. They withdraw the next day.

NOV. 1—Fifty thousand demonstrators turn out in 60 cities for The Women Strike for Peace.

NOV. 3—After a trip to Vietnam Gen. Maxwell Taylor reports to Kennedy that prompt U.S. military, economic and political action can lead to victory without a U.S. takeover of the war.

NOV. 26—The "Thanksgiving Day Massacre" results in a major high-level reorganization of the State Department. Chester Bowles is replaced by George Ball as undersecretary of state.

DEC. 7—The U.S. begins its transport of U.N. troops to the Congo to end Katanga's secession.

DEC. 15—Kennedy renews the U.S. commitment to preserve the independence of Vietnam and pledges American assistance to its defense effort.

DEC. 15-17—Kennedy makes a triumphant goodwill tour to Puerto Rico, Venezuela and Colombia.

DEC. 20—The *New York Times* reports that 2,000 U.S. uniformed troops and specialists are stationed in Vietnam.

1962

JAN. 2—The U.S. begins a series of diplomatic "probes" of Moscow regarding Berlin.

JAN. 6—The U.S. resumes diplomatic ties with the Dominican Republic after a 14-month suspension.

JAN. 29—The U.S., the USSR and Great Britain nuclear test ban conference at Geneva adjourns after a three-year period. Talks remain deadlocked over a system of international control.

FEB. 3—Kennedy orders an almost complete end to U.S. trade with Cuba.

FEB. 14—Kennedy announces that U.S. troops in Vietnam are instructed to use weapons for defensive purposes.

MARCH 2—Kennedy announces his decision to resume atmospheric nuclear tests.

MARCH 14—The 17-nation U.N. disarmament conference opens in Geneva.

MARCH 18—In a message to Krushchev Kennedy proposes the joint exploration of outer space.

MARCH 22—The U.S. begins its first involvement in the Vietnam Strategic Hamlet (rural pacification) Program.

APRIL 25—The U.S. opens a nuclear test series in the air over the Pacific.

MAY 15—Kennedy sends 5,000 Marines and 50 jet fighters to Thailand in response to Communist expansion in Laos.

JULY 23—Fourteen nations sign the Geneva Accords guaranteeing the neutrality of Laos.

OCT. 14—U.S. intelligence receives the first photographic evidence of Soviet offensive missiles in Cuba.

OCT. 16—Excom, the President's specially chosen bipartisan advisory committee, convenes on the Cuban missile crisis.

OCT. 22—Kennedy announces a "quarantine" of Cuba to force the removal of Soviet missiles.

OCT. 28—Khrushchev agrees to dismantle the Soviet missiles in Cuba and withdraw Russian weapons under U.N. supervision.

NOV. 3-10—The U.S. supplies emergency military aid to India in its border war with Communist China.

NOV. 20—The U.S. lifts its naval blockade of Cuba.

DEC. 21—Kennedy and Prime Minister Harold Macmillian sign the Nassau Pact granting Great Britain Polaris missiles and pledging the commitment of American and British atomic weapons to a multilateral NATO nuclear force.

DEC. 23—The Cuban government begins the release of prisoners captured in the 1961 Bay of Pigs invasion.

DEC. 31—The U.S. cancels the joint U.S.-Great Britain Skybolt missile project.

1963

JAN.—U.N. troops reunify the Congo.

FEB. 24—A Senate panel reports that annual American aid to South Vietnam is $400 million and that 12,000 Americans are stationed there "on dangerous assignment."

MARCH 19—In a San Jose, Costa Rica, meeting Kennedy and six Latin American presidents pledge resistance to Soviet aggression in the Western Hemisphere.

MARCH 21—A commission headed by retired Gen. Lucius Clay recommends reductions in the U.S. foreign aid program.

APRIL 20—A U.S.-supported 80-day general strike begins in British Guiana and leads to the fall of the Jagan government.

APRIL 22—Twenty-two units of the 7th Fleet are sent to the Gulf of Siam as a "precautionary" measure during fighting in Laos.

MAY 11—Kennedy and Prime Minister Lester Pearson announce a joint defense agreement. Canada agrees to accept nuclear warheads for missiles located in its territory.

JUNE 10—Kennedy delivers a major policy address at American University that calls for a reexamination of Cold War attitudes as a necessary prelude to world peace and announces new test ban negotiations in Moscow.

JUNE 26—On a visit to West Berlin Kennedy delivers his "Ich bin ein Berliner" address that promises continued support of that city.

JULY 8—The U.S. bans virtually all financial transactions with Cuba in a move toward economic isolation of that country.

JULY 15—The U.S., Great Britain and the USSR open disarmament talks in Moscow.

JULY 18—The U.S. and Mexico agree on a settlement of the disputed El Chamizal border area between El Paso, Tex., and Ciudad Juarez, Chihuahua.

JULY 18-19—The U.S. suspends relations and aid to Peru following a military coup.

JULY 25—The U.S., the USSR and Great Britain initial a test ban treaty in Moscow that prohibits nuclear testing in the atmosphere, space and underwater.

AUG. 2—The U.S. cuts off all economic assistance to Haiti to show its disapproval of the dictatorial government of Francois Duvalier.

AUG. 21—The South Vietnam government attacks Buddhist pagodas.

AUG. 24—Vietnam Ambassador Henry Cabot Lodge receives a State Department cable stating that the U.S. can no longer tolerate Ngo Dinh Nhu's influence in President Ngo Dinh Diem's regime.

AUG. 30—The Washington-Moscow hot line is made operational.

OCT. 9—Kennedy approves a $250 million wheat sale to the USSR.

SEPT. 24—The Senate, 80-19, ratifies the partial nuclear test ban treaty.

SEPT. 25—Following a successful military coup against President Juan Bosch, the U.S. suspends diplomatic relations and economic aid to the Dominican Republic.

NOV. 1—South Vietnamese generals stage a successful coup. Diem and Nhu are assassinated.

NOV. 16—Through personal intervention with the Soviet authorities, Kennedy obtains the release of Prof. Frederick Barghoorn, who had been imprisoned in Russia on espionage charges.

NOV. 22—Kennedy is assassinated in Dallas, Tex., by Lee Harvey Oswald. Lyndon Johnson is sworn in as the 36th President.

1964

JAN. 9-12—U.S. troops fire on anti-American rioters in the Panama Canal Zone.

JAN. 10—Panama breaks diplomatic ties with the U.S.

JAN. 25—Echo II, the first U.S.-USSR cooperative space venture, is launched.

FEB. 7—Johnson orders the withdrawal of American dependents from South Vietnam.

APRIL 4—The U.S. and Panama resume diplomatic ties and pledge negotiations on the Canal Zone treaty.

AUG. 3—Johnson instructs the Navy to take retaliatory action against North Vietnam for its alleged attack on the U.S. destroyer Maddox in the Gulf of Tonkin.

AUG. 7—Congress passes the Tonkin Gulf Resolution authorizing Johnson to take "all necessary measures" to "repel any armed attack" against U.S. forces in Southeast Asia and approves in advance "all necessary steps, including the use of armed force," that the President might take to aid U.S. allies in the region.

SEPT. 4—The U.S. recognizes a provisional government established in the Dominican Republic with the support of both junta and rebel representatives.

SEPT. 7—The U.S. suspends military aid to India and Pakistan as a result of the two countries' border clash.

NOV. 3—Johnson wins reelection by a record plurality of 15,975,924 votes and captures 486 electoral votes from 44 states. Democrats win 17 governorships and increase their majorities in Congress.

NOV. 25—U.S. planes airlift Belgian paratroopers into Stanleyville to rescue white hostages held by Congolese rebels.

DEC. 24-JAN. 31—The U.S. halts the bombing of North Vietnam in efforts to get Hanoi to the negotiating table.

DEC. 31—U.S. forces in Vietnam total 184,314.

1965

FEB. 7—Communist forces attack the U.S. air base at Pleiku.

MARCH 2—The U.S. begins Operation Rolling Thunder, the sustained bombing of North Vietnam.

MARCH 4—The U.S. Information Agency closes its facilities in Indonesia because of harassment. The Peace Corps withdraws the following month.

MARCH 8-9—The first American combat troops land in Vietnam.

APRIL 26—Secretary of Defense Robert McNamara states that the Vietnam war effort costs the U.S. about $1.5 billion a year.

APRIL 28—U.S. Marines land in the Dominican Republic allegedly to protect American lives during the civil war.

MAY 2—At a news conference Johnson states that Marines were sent to the Dominican Republic to prevent a Communist takeover as well as to protect American lives.

MAY 16—A four-man U.S. fact-finding team arrives in Santo Domingo in an unsuccessful attempt to help form a coalition government.

JUNE 8—The State Department reports that Johnson has authorized the use of U.S. troops in direct combat if the South Vietnamese Army requests assistance.

JUNE 17—B-52s stage the first mass bombing raid in South Vietnam.

1966

JAN. 17—Four nuclear devices are released in a B-52 collision over Spain. All are recovered by April 7.

JAN. 19—Johnson asks Congress for an additional $12.8 billion for the war in Vietnam.

FEB. 4—The Senate Foreign Relations Committee begins televised hearings on American policy in Vietnam.

FEB. 6-8—At the Honolulu Conference Johnson announces renewed emphasis on "The Other War," the attempt to provide the Vietnamese rural population with local security and develop positive economic and social programs to win their active support.

MARCH 1—The Senate rejects an amendment repealing the Tonkin Gulf Resolution.

APRIL 13—B-52 bombers are used for the

first time against targets in North Vietnam.

APRIL 21—Senate Foreign Relations Committee Chairman J. William Fulbright warns that the U.S. is "succumbing to the arrogance of power."

MAY 1—The U.S. shells Communist targets in Cambodia.

MAY 21—Johnson sends additional troops to Thailand to prevent Communist infiltration.

JUNE 3-13—One of the largest battles of the Vietnam war is fought in the Central Highlands province of Kontum.

JUNE 28—Johnson removes the last American troops from the Dominican Republic.

JUNE 29—Johnson orders the bombing of oil installations at Haiphong and Hanoi.

SEPT. 18-24—The U.S. records 970 casualties in Vietnam for the week.

SEPT. 23—The U.S. military command in Vietnam announces that it is using defoliants to destroy Communist cover.

OCT. 26—Johnson visits U.S. troops in Vietnam, which number 400,000.

1967

JAN. 27—The U.S. signs a 63-nation treaty prohibiting the orbiting of nuclear weapons and forbidding territorial claims on celestial bodies.

FEB. 13—The National Student Association admits that it received funds from the Central Intelligence Agency between 1952 and 1966 for projects overseas.

APRIL 4—The military announces the loss of the 500th plane since Vietnam bombing raids began in 1964.

APRIL 15—One hundred thousand in New York City and 20,000 in San Francisco march to protest U.S. policy in Vietnam.

MAY 17—Sixteen senators critical of Administration policy in Vietnam warn Hanoi, in a letter drafted by Sen. Frank Church, that they are opposed to unilateral American withdrawal.

MAY 19—U.S. planes bomb a power plant in Hanoi in the first strike at the heart of North Vietnam's capital.

MAY 28—The Office of Civil Operations and Revolutionary Development Support (CORDS) is formed, placing the Vietnam pacification program under military control.

JUNE 5—War breaks out in the Middle East between Israel and Egypt, Jordan and Syria.

JUNE 7—Johnson praises a U.N. Security Council resolution calling for a cease-fire in the Mideast War.

JUNE 23-25—Johnson and Soviet Premier Alexei Kosygin hold a Summit Conference at Glassboro State College in New Jersey.

JULY 7—U.S. and Communist forces suffer heavy casualties in fighting near Con Thien.

JULY 7—Congress's Joint Economic Committee issues a report stating that the Vietnam war created "havoc" in the U.S. economy during 1966 and predicting that the war will cost $4 to $6 billion more in 1967 than the $20.3 billion requested by Johnson.

SEPT. 29—In a speech at San Antonio, Tex., Johnson modifies the U.S. position on Vietnam negotiations, saying that the U.S. is willing to stop all bombing if it will promptly lead to negotiations.

OCT. 21—An estimated 35,000 persons participate in a march to the Pentagon to protest U.S. policy in Vietnam.

NOV. 22—In one of the bloodiest battles of the Vietnam war, U.S. forces capture Hill 875 near Dak To.

NOV. 23-28—U.S., U.N. and NATO representatives meet with Turkish and Greek leaders in an effort to avert a war over Cyprus. An agreement is reached Dec. 1.

DEC. 20—U.S. forces in South Vietnam reach 474,300.

1968

JAN. 3—Minnesota Sen. Eugene McCarthy announces his candidacy for the Democratic presidential nomination.

JAN. 23—North Korea captures the U.S. spy ship *Pueblo*.

JAN. 30—During the Tet holiday the Communists mount major offensives in three-fourths of the 44 provincial capitals of South Vietnam.

FEB. 1—Richard M. Nixon formally announces his candidacy for the Republican presidential nomination.

FEB. 20—The Senate Foreign Relations Committee begins hearings on the events leading to the passage of the Tonkin Gulf Resolution.

FEB. 27—U.S. military leaders request 206,000 additional troops for Vietnam.

MARCH 11-12—Secretary of State Dean Rusk testifies before the Senate Foreign Relations Committee on American policy in Vietnam.

MARCH 12—In the New Hampshire Democratic primary, Eugene McCarthy wins a surprising 42% of the vote against Johnson's 48%.

MARCH 16—New York Sen. Robert Kennedy announces his candidacy for the Democratic presidential nomination.

MARCH 17—Representatives of the U.S. and the London Gold Pool work out a two-price system for gold.

MARCH 22—Johnson announces that Gen. William Westmoreland will leave his post as commander of U.S. forces in Vietnam to become Army chief of staff. The move signals a turn from the goal of total victory in Vietnam.

MARCH 25-26—The Senior Advisory Group on Vietnam meets to discuss proposed troop increases and recommends against further escalation.

MARCH 31—In a televised speech Johnson announces that he has ordered a halt to the bombing of 90% of North Vietnam. He also announces that he will not run for reelection.

APRIL 4—Martin Luther King is assassinated in Memphis, Tenn. The killing leads to riots in Washington, Chicago and numerous other cities.

APRIL 11—24,000 military reservists are called to active duty.

APRIL 27—Vice President Hubert Humphrey announces that he will seek the Democratic presidential nomination.

MAY 3—Johnson announces that the U.S. and North Vietnam have agreed to begin formal peace talks in Paris.

MAY 12—Vietnam peace talks begin in Paris.

JUNE 5—Sirhan Bishara Sirhan assassinates Robert F. Kennedy in Los Angeles.

JUNE 13—The Senate ratifies the U.S.-USSR consular treaty.

JULY 1—Johnson signs the Nuclear Non-Proliferation Treaty.

AUG. 21—Soviet troops enter Czechoslovakia.

OCT. 31—Johnson announces a halt to all bombing of North Vietnam as prelude to expanded peace talks.

NOV. 5—Richard Nixon wins the presidential race with 43.4% of the popular vote and 302 out of 538 electoral votes.

DEC. 22—North Korea releases the 82 crew members of the *Pueblo*.

DEC. 31—The total number of Americans killed in Vietnam in 1968 reaches 14,592.

1969

JAN. 20—Richard M. Nixon is sworn in as the 37th President of the United States

JAN. 30—North Vietnam and the National Liberation Front reject the U.S. proposal to restore neutrality to the Demilitarized Zone.

FEB. 23–MARCH 2—President Nixon visits five West European nations and consults with their leaders during a tour that he said was intended to create a "new spirit of consultation" and "confidence" between the U.S. and its European allies.

MARCH 14—President Nixon decides to proceed with a revised anti-ballistic missile (ABM) defense plan.

MARCH 26—The Women Strike for Peace pickets Washington in the first large anti-war demonstration since Nixon's inauguration.

MARCH 28—Dwight David Eisenhower dies.

MARCH 29—American combat deaths in Vietnam reach 33,641, exceeding those in the Korean war.

APRIL 15—A U.S. Navy intelligence plane is shot down over North Korea as an intruder in North Korean territorial air space.

MAY 14—President Nixon proposes an eight-point peace plan for Vietnam; it provides for mutual troop withdrawal.

JUNE 8—President Nixon announces the withdrawal of 25,000 troops from Vietnam.

JULY 26–AUG. 3—President Nixon tours eight countries in Asia and Europe, emphasizing his belief that peace in Asia depends on Asians themselves. Highlights of the tour are an unannounced visit to South Vietnam and a stop in Rumania.

SEPT. 18—President Nixon, addressing the U.N. General Assembly, urges U.N. members to aid negotiations for ending the war in Vietnam.

OCT. 1—President Nixon allows draft deferments for graduate students.

OCT. 15—Anti-war demonstrations take place thoughout the U.S. in a massive protest coordinated by the Vietnam Moratorium Committee in Washington; among rallies, speeches and religious services, one of the largest gatherings is a meeting of about 100,000 people in Boston Common.

NOV. 3—President Nixon announces a U.S.-South Vietnam plan to withdraw U.S. troops from Vietnam.

NOV. 15—In escalating anti-war protests sponsored by the New Mobilization Committee to End the War in Vietnam (the New Mobe), more than 250,000 people participate in Washington in the largest such demonstration ever held; the rally follows a three-day March Against Death in which more than 40,000 people took part.

NOV. 17—Preliminary Strategic Arms Limitation Talks (SALT) are opened by U.S. and Soviet negotiators in Helsinki, Finland.

DEC. 1—The first draft lottery since 1942 is held at Selective Service System headquarters.

1970

FEB. 10—The U.S., British and French embassies in Moscow accept a Soviet proposal for four-power talks on Berlin.

FEB. 10—The Army charges Capt. Thomas K. Willingham with unpremeditated murder in connection with the alleged civilian massacre at Songmy (My Lai).

FEB. 10-13—Defense Secretary Melvin Laird visits South Vietnam to study Vietnamization and U.S. troop withdrawals.

FEB. 12-17—U.S. and Soviet delegates discuss the peaceful use of nuclear explosions.

FEB. 18—President Nixon submits a foreign policy outline to Congress.

MARCH 5—The nuclear nonproliferation treaty goes into effect.

MARCH 6—President Nixon appeals to the Soviet Union and Britain to help restore the 1962 Geneva agreements on Laos.

MARCH 6—Pro-Communist Pathet Lao rebels propose a five-point peace plan.

MARCH 14—The *Columbia Eagle,* a U.S. freighter bound for Thailand with Air Force munitions, is siezed by two armed crewmen and diverted to Cambodia. (It may be seen as an anti-war protest by the two crewmen.)

MARCH 16-22—The New Mobilization Committee to End the War in Vietnam (New Mobe) sponsors a national "anti-draft week."

APRIL 2—Massachusetts Gov. Francis W. Sargent signs a bill challenging the legality of the war in Vietnam.

APRIL 4—The largest Washington prowar demonstration since America's involvement in Vietnam is held.

APRIL 8—The *Columbia Eagle* is released by Cambodia.

APRIL 11—Willy Brandt concludes a week-long visit to the United States.

APRIL 16—SALT sessions resume after a recess.

APRIL 17—Assistant Secretary of State Joseph J. Sisco cancels his trip to Jordan after anti-American riots there.

APRIL 20—President Nixon announces plans to withdraw more troops from Vietnam.

APRIL 20-MAY 1—The U.S. and South Vietnam extend fighting to Cambodia.

APRIL 23—President Nixon ends occupational draft deferments and deferments for fathers.

APRIL 30—President Nixon announces the major U.S. troop offensive into Cambodia.

MAY 4—Four students are killed by National Guardsmen at Kent State University in Ohio.

MAY 4—The Soviet Union and China assail Nixon's expansion of the war to Cambodia.

MAY 6—Communist delegates to the Paris peace talks boycott in protest of the U.S. bombing of North Vietnam.

MAY 6 & MAY 9—President Nixon confers with student anti-war protestors.

JUNE 29—U.S. ground troop withdrawal from Cambodia is completed.

JULY 31—Israel joins Egypt and Jordan in accepting the U.S. Middle East peace plan.

AUG. 14—The Vienna phase of the SALT sessions ends.

AUG. 20—President Nixon and Mexican President Gustavo Diaz Ordaz meet and propose a treaty concerning U.S.–Mexican border disputes.

AUG. 30—Vice President Agnew completes a weeklong Asian tour.

SEPT. 15–20—Golda Meir visits the U.S. and talks to President Nixon, Secretary of State William P. Rogers and others.

OCT. 5—President Nixon completes an eight-day trip to Europe.

OCT. 10—North Vietnam denounces Nixon's five-point peace plan (made on Oct. 7).

OCT. 22—President Nixon and Soviet Foreign Minister Andrei A. Gromyko confer in Washington.

OCT. 23—Nixon addresses the United Nations.

NOV. 12—U.S. policy toward Communist China changes; U.S. delegates to the U.N. argue against Communist China's expulsion from the organization.

NOV. 17—The first anniversary of the SALT sessions is marked.

1971

JAN. 7—Defense Secretary Melvin R. Laird visits Thailand to assess the military situation in Indochina.

JAN. 8–11—Defense Secretary Melvin R. Laird visits South Vietnam to assess the military situation in Indochina.

JAN. 12—Rev. Philip F. Berrigan and five others are indicted on charges of conspiring to kidnap Henry Kissinger.

FEB. 11—A treaty prohibiting installation of nuclear weapons on the ocean floor is signed by 63 nations.

FEB. 21—The U.S. and 20 other United Nations members sign an international treaty to end illegal drug sales.

MARCH 29—First Lt. William L. Calley, Jr., is convicted by an Army court-martial of the premeditated murder of at least 22 South Vietnamese civilians in the My Lai "massacre" of March 16, 1968. (Calley is sentenced March 31 to life at hard labor, but the sentence is reduced Aug. 20 to 20 years.)

APRIL 14—President Nixon relaxes a 20-year embargo on trade with Communist China.

APRIL 17—The U.S. table tennis team leaves Communist China after a week-long tour.

APRIL 24—Marchers mass in Washington and San Francisco and hold peaceful rallies urging Congress to end the war in Indochina immediately.

APRIL 30—Rev. Philip Berrigan and seven others are indicted for plotting to kidnap Henry A. Kissinger and blow up heating tunnels in government buildings.

MAY 3–5—Anti-war protests organized by the Peoples Coalition for Peace and Justice are held in Washington.

MAY 9—Secretary of State William P. Rogers returns after his five-nation tour of the Middle East.

JUNE 15—*The New York Times* halts publication of a series of Vietnam war articles drawn from a secret Pentagon study because of a temporary court order. (Publication of the articles began on June 13.)

JUNE 16—The U.S. Conference of Mayors urges President Nixon to withdraw all troops from Vietnam by the end of the year.

JUNE 18 & JUNE 19—*The Washington Post* publishes articles on the involvement of the U.S. in the Vietnam war based on a classified Pentagon study.

JUNE 21—Communist Chinese Premier Chou En-lai says that withdrawal of U.S.

support from Taiwan would facilitate better relations between the U.S. and Communist China.

JUNE 22 & JUNE 23—The *Boston Globe* and the *Chicago Sun-Times* publish articles based on the classified Pentagon study.

JUNE 30—The Supreme Court rules that articles based on classfied Pentagon material may be published by newspapers.

JULY 9—U.S. troops relinquish total responsibility for defense of the area just below the demilitarized zone to South Vietnamese troops.

JULY 16 & 22—The U.S., Great Britain, France and the Soviet Union meet in Berlin to discuss the area's future.

AUG. 2—The U.S. ends 20 years of opposition to Communist China's presence in the United Nations by announcing future support of China's membership.

OCT. 4—Secretary of State William P. Rogers addresses the U.N. General Assembly, asking for the seating of Communist China on the Security Council and speaking against the expulsion of Nationalist China (Taiwan) from the General Assembly.

OCT. 20-25—Henry Kissinger visits Peking to arrange the agenda and itinerary for President Nixon's forthcoming trip to Communist China.

DEC. 13-14—President Nixon and French President Georges Pompidou confer on the devaluation of the dollar.

DEC. 20-21—President Nixon meets with British Prime Minister Edward Heath in Bermuda to discuss world problems.

1972

JAN. 16—Religious leaders from 46 Protestant, Catholic and Jewish denominations, meeting in Kansas City, Mo., to discuss Vietnam, ask the Administration to withdraw all American troops and refuse aid to the Indochinese governments.

JAN. 30—Defense Secretary Melvin R. Laird announces that no men will be called up for military duty until April.

FEB. 21—President Nixon arrives in China.

FEB. 22 & 23—President Nixon meets with Chinese Premier Chou En-lai for policy discussions.

FEB. 27—President Nixon and Premier Chou En-lai release a joint communique showing the results of their talks.

FEB. 28—President Nixon returns from China.

FEB. 28—The Nationalist Chinese Foreign Ministry (of Taiwan) issues a statement denouncing the Sino-U.S. communique.

MARCH 23—The U.S. delegation to the Paris peace talks announces an indefinite suspension of the conference, until North Vietnamese and National Liberation Front representatives enter into "serious discussions" on concrete issues determined beforehand.

APRIL 15-20—Hundreds of anti-war demonstrators are arrested in incidents across the country as the escalation of the bombing in Indochina provokes a new wave of protests.

APRIL 20-24—Henry A. Kissinger, President Nixon's adviser on national security, secretly visits the Soviet Union to confer with Leonid I. Brezhnev, the Soviet Communist Party leader.

APRIL 27—The Paris peace talks resume after a one-month break.

MAY 4—The U.S. and South Vietnam call an indefinite halt to the Paris peace talks after the 149th session.

MAY 26—President Nixon and Soviet General Secretary Brezhnev sign agreements limiting offensive and defensive strategic weapons.

JUNE 9–12—Henry Kissinger makes a private visit to Tokyo, but also meets with Japanese government and political leaders to discuss Asian security and Japan's economic differences with the U.S.

JULY 6–17—U.S. and Soviet space planners meet at the U.S. Manned Spacecraft Center in Houston, Tex.

JULY 7—The U.S. and the USSR sign an agreement detailing the first areas of study in science and technology in which scientists of both nations will cooperate.

JULY 8—President Nixon announces the sale of at least $750 million of American wheat, corn and other grains to the Soviet Union.

JULY 12—Sen. George McGovern wins the Democratic presidential nomination.

JULY 13—The Paris peace talks resume after a 10-week suspension.

SEPT. 26–27—Henry Kissinger holds more private talks with North Vietnamese representatives in Paris.

OCT. 18—The U.S. and the Soviet Union sign a three-year trade pact.

OCT. 19–20—Henry Kissinger and other U.S. officials hold meetings with South Vietnamese President Nguyen Van Thieu in Saigon.

NOV. 7—Richard M. Nixon is reelected President.

NOV. 20 & 21—Henry Kissinger and Le Duc Tho hold more private discussions to work out a final Indochina peace agreement.

DEC. 4—Henry Kissinger and Le Duc Tho resume private Indochina peace talks near Paris after a nine-day recess.

DEC. 4—U.S. and Soviet representatives sign an agreement authorizing each nation to construct a new embassy complex in the other's capital.

DEC. 8—Foreign ministers of the NATO states conclude their regular two-day winter session in Brussels.

DEC. 8—The *Pentagon Papers* trial in Los Angeles of Daniel Ellsberg and Anthony J. Russo is declared a mistrial.

DEC. 13—Paris peace talks recess with no agreement.

DEC. 26—Harry S. Truman dies.

1973

JAN. 8–12—Henry Kissinger and Le Duc Tho hold more secret Indochina peace talks.

JAN. 10—The Watergate trial opens.

JAN. 20—President Nixon is inaugurated for his second term.

JAN. 22—Lyndon B. Johnson dies.

JAN. 23—U.S. and North Vietnam sign a cease-fire accord in Paris.

FEB. 15—The U.S. and Cuba sign a five-year agreement to curb the hijacking of aircraft and ships between the two countries.

FEB. 21—Laos and the Communist Pathet Lao rebels sign a cease-fire agreement aimed at ending the 20-year war in Laos.

FEB. 26—Two of the 15 counts against defendants Daniel Ellsberg and Anthony J. Russo, Jr., are dropped.

MAY 1–2—President Nixon and West German Chancellor Willy Brandt confer in Washington.

MAY 9—Henry Kissinger completes four

days of intensive talks with Soviet leaders at the estate of Leonid I. Brezhnev.

MAY 22—Henry Kissinger and Le Duc Tho end their talks on implementation of the Vietnam truce agreement.

MAY 29—President Nixon refuses to give oral or written testimony to the grand jury or the Senate select committee investigating the Watergate case.

JUNE 13—A new accord aimed at strengthening the Jan. 27 cease-fire agreement in South Vietnam is signed in Paris by the U.S., North Vietnam, South Vietnam and the National Liberation Front.

JUNE 25—Soviet Communist Party General Secretary Leonid Brezhnev ends his visit to the U.S.

JULY 6—A U.S. consulate general is officially opened in Leningrad.

JULY 9—Secretary of State William P. Rogers and Czechoslovak Foreign Minister Bohuslav Chnoupek sign a consular convention in Prague to help normalize trade and travel between the two countries.

SEPT. 22—Henry A. Kissinger is sworn in by U.S. Chief Justice Warren E. Burger as the 56th Secretary of State.

OCT. 10—Spiro T. Agnew resigns as vice president and pleads no contest to one charge of income tax evasion. By plea bargaining, he escapes imprisonment on the tax charge and prosecution on charges of bribery and conspiracy.

OCT. 17—President Nixon holds talks with the foreign ministers of Saudi Arabia, Morocco, Kuwait and Algeria at the White House to end fighting in the Middle East.

DEC. 6—Gerald R. Ford is sworn in as vice president after confirmation by both houses of Congress. President Nixon had chosen him for the post after Vice President Agnew resigned.

1974

JAN. 4—President Nixon refuses to comply with subpoenas for tapes and documents issued him by the Senate Watergate Committee.

JAN. 15—Experts examining the Watergate tape recordings surrendered by President Nixon report that an 18½-minute gap had been caused by at least five separate erasures, rather than a single accidental one as the White House had contended.

FEB. 4–5—Soviet Foreign Minister Andrei A. Gromyko confers with President Nixon and Secretary of State Henry Kissinger in Washington.

FEB. 28—The U.S. and Egypt resume full-scale diplomatic relations, which were severed in 1967.

MARCH 24–28—Henry Kissinger talks with Leonid Brezhnev, Andrei Gromyko and other Soviet officials in Moscow.

APRIL 28–MAY 2—Henry Kissinger confers with officials from the Soviet Union, Algiers, Egypt and Israel in an effort to promote an Israeli-Syrian troop disengagement.

MAY 3–9—Henry Kissinger holds talks with Middle East leaders in continuing efforts to end Israeli-Syrian fighting.

MAY 31—Israeli and Syrian military officials sign a cease-fire agreement in Geneva brought about by Henry Kissinger.

JUNE 8—The U.S. and Saudi Arabia sign an agreement in Washington for economic and military cooperation.

JUNE 12–18—President Nixon visits Egypt, Saudi Arabia, Syria, Israel and Jordan.

JUNE 14—President Nixon and President Anwar Sadat sign an accord in Cairo by which the U.S. will provide Egypt with nuclear technology for peaceful purposes.

JUNE 18–19—NATO meets in Ottawa.

JUNE 26—Government leaders of NATO member nations sign a declaration on Atlantic relations.

JUNE 27–JULY 3—President Nixon and Soviet Communist Party General Secretary Leonid Brezhnev hold summit meetings in Moscow.

AUG. 9—Richard M. Nixon resigns as President. Gerald R. Ford is sworn in.

SEPT. 4—The U.S. and the German Democratic Republic (East Germany) establish formal diplomatic relations.

SEPT. 8—President Ford grants former President Nixon a full pardon.

SEPT. 16—President Ford signs a proclamation offering clemency to Vietnam war era draft evaders and military deserters.

SEPT. 18—The second round of the Strategic Arms Limitation Talks (SALT II) resumes in Geneva after a six-month recess.

NOV. 5–7—Henry Kissinger visits five Middle East capitals to discuss Arab-Israeli conflict.

NOV. 18–22—President Ford becomes the first U.S. chief executive to travel to Japan.

NOV. 19–20—President Ford and Premier Kakuei Tanaka of Japan confer in Japan.

NOV. 23–24—President Ford and Leonid Brezhnev hold talks in Vladivostok to discuss the limitation of nuclear weapons.

1975

JAN. 31—SALT II resumes in Geneva after a three-month recess.

FEB. 10–15—Secretary of State Henry Kissinger visits the Middle East to determine

the possibility of further negotiations.

FEB. 16–17—Henry Kissinger and Soviet Foreign Minister Andrei Gromyko meet in Geneva to discuss the Middle East conflict.

FEB. 24—The U.S. ends its 10-year arms embargo against India and Pakistan.

MARCH 22—Henry Kissinger suspends his latest efforts to achieve a second Israeli-Egyptian troop disengagement agreement.

MARCH 29—The withdrawal of all American troops from South Vietnam and release of the last of the U.S. war prisoners held by the Communists are completed.

APRIL 12—The U.S. closes its embassy in Pnompenh, Cambodia, as Khmer Rouge rebel troops take over.

APRIL 14—The American airlift of homeless children to the U.S. from South Vietnam ends. A total of about 14,000 children had arrived.

MAY 11—About 50,000 people gather in the Sheep Head Meadow in Central Park in New York City to celebrate the end of war in Vietnam and Cambodia.

MAY 14—U.S. air, sea and ground forces battle Cambodian forces to free the 39 crewmen of the *Mayaguez,* an American merchant ship, after its seizure May 12.

MAY 19–20—Henry Kissinger and Soviet Foreign Minister Andrei Gromyko hold talks in Vienna.

MAY 22–23—NATO holds its semiannual talks in Brussels.

MAY 28–29— NATO holds its summit meeting in Brussels, attended by President Ford.

MAY 28–JUNE 3—President Ford makes his first trip as President to Europe.

JUNE 11–12—Israeli Prime Minister Yitzhak Rabin confers with President Ford and Secretary of State Henry Kissinger in Washington on the possibility of reviving peace negotiations with Egypt.

JULY 16—A major purchase of wheat by the Soviet Union from U.S. exporters is announced.

JULY 17—Spacecraft from the U.S. and the Soviet Union link together in space.

JULY 30—Leaders of 35 nations meet in Helsinki, for the largest summit conference in European history, to sign the final document of the Conference on Security and Cooperation in Europe (CSCE).

AUG. 21—Henry Kissinger arrives in Israel to resume shuttle diplomacy toward attaining Middle East peace.

SEPT. 4—Israel and Egypt sign a U.S.-mediated interim agreement.

DEC. 1–5—President Ford visits the People's Republic of China, holding four days of talks with Chinese leaders including Chairman Mao Tse-tung and Deputy Premier Teng Hsiao-ping.

DEC. 8—A veto by the U.S. blocks a United Nations Security Council resolution condemning Israel for its air raid on Palestinian refugee camps in Lebanon Dec. 2.

1976

JAN. 21–23—Henry Kissinger attends meetings with Leonid Brezhnev, Andrei Gromyko and other Soviet officials in Moscow to discuss SALT.

JAN. 26—The U.S. vetoes a United Nations Security Council resolution on the Middle East.

FEB. 16–24—Henry Kissinger visits Venezuela, Peru, Brazil, Colombia, Costa Rica and Guatemala to confer with their presidents on trade and other issues.

FEB. 20—SEATO formally disbands.

MARCH 16—The U.S. State Department halts U.S.–Soviet talks because of actions taken by the Soviet Union in Angola.

MARCH 26—Henry Kissinger and Turkish Foreign Minister Ihsan Sabri Caglayangil sign an accord allowing the reopening of U.S. military installations in Turkey in return for military and economic assistance.

MARCH 30–31—King Hussein of Jordan conducts an official visit to Washington.

JUNE 21—Henry Kissinger addresses the annual ministerial meeting of the Organization for Economic Cooperation and Development (OECD) in Paris.

JUNE 23–24—Henry Kissinger and South African Prime Minister John Vorster hold talks in West Germany.

JULY 14—Jimmy Carter is declared the Democratic presidential nominee. Sen. Walter F. Mondale, his choice of a running mate, is approved.

JULY 17—West German Chancellor Helmut Schmidt concludes a three-day visit to Washington, during which he held talks with President Ford.

SEPT. 4–6—Henry Kissinger meets with South African Prime Minister John Vorster in Zurich, Switzerland, for a second round of talks.

SEPT. 6—The U.S.-led United Nations Command and North Korea agree to partition the Joint Security Area in the Demilitarized Zone.

SEPT. 24—Rhodesian Prime Minister Ian Smith accepts a proposal presented by Henry Kissinger for transfer of power to Rhodesia's black majority.

SEPT. 14—Henry Kissinger arrives in Tanzania to begin a series of talks with African leaders.

NOV. 2—Jimmy Carter is elected President.

NOV. 15—The U.S. vetoes the admission of Vietnam into the United Nations.

DEC. 6–10—NATO holds year-end meetings in Brussels.

Bibliography

TRUMAN ADMINISTRATION

FOREIGN AFFAIRS

Accounts of American foreign policy during the Truman presidency have dealt mainly with the origins and strategies of the Cold War with the Soviet Union. Specific incidents, such as the Iranian crisis of 1945-46, or specific policy arrangements, such as the Marshall Plan, are tied to the question of American relations with the Soviet Union. A good beginning is Thomas G. Paterson, ed., *The Origins of the Cold War*, 2nd ed. (Lexington, Mass., 1974), which includes a sampling of differing interpretations and a good bibliography. The earliest chronicles of Truman's diplomacy tended to defend the basic premises of American policy; see for example, Joseph Marion Jones, *The Fifteen Weeks* (New York, 1955), a favorable view of the Marshall Plan's intent. Herbert Feis, an economist and consultant to the State Department, wrote extensively on major diplomatic matters, occasionally criticizing aspects, but not fundamental ones, of American initiatives; see Feis, *From Trust to Terror* (New York, 1970). In the 1960s a growing body of scholars, led by Gabriel Kolko, *The Politics of War* (New York, 1968), and William Appleman Williams, *The Tragedy of American Foreign Policy*, 2nd ed. (New York, 1972), blamed American diplomats, not Soviet leaders, for the severity of tensions after World War II. Although commonly dubbed "New Left" historians to denote the Marxist or economist determinist perspective of many of them, these analysts do not agree among themselves as to reasons for American belligerency. A few, notably Kolko, contend that confrontation between the leading capitalist and leading Communist powers was inevitable. Others, such as Gar Alperovitz, *Atomic Diplomacy: Hiroshima and Potsdam* (New York, 1965), single out Truman and some of his aides for the coming of the Cold War. Daniel Yergin, *The Shattered Peace* (New York, 1977), faults not only Truman, but adds to the list a figure who had fared well in many accounts, George Kennan. A career diplomat, Kennan had argued for a policy of "containment," as opposed to direct military confrontation or renewed negotiations. See Kennan's anonymous "Mr. X" memorandum, "Sources of Soviet Conduct," *Foreign Affairs* (July 1947), pp. 566–582. See also Truman's *Memoirs*, 2 vols.

Since the mid-1960s the New Left or "revisionist" historians have succeeded in placing those with other points of view, less than hostile to American diplomatists, on the defensive. The works of Adam Ulam, *The Rivals; America and Russia since World War II* (New York, 1971) and John Lewis Gaddis, *The*

United States and the Origins of the Cold War, 1941-1947 (New York, 1972), admit to U.S. errors, but explain American policymakers' responses as ones conditioned by Soviet fears and ill will. Good overviews of this scholarly debate are Charles S. Maier, "Revisionism and Beyond: Considerations on the Origins of the Cold War," *Perspectives in American History* 4 (1970), pp. 313-47, and Warren F. Kimball, "The Cold War Warmed Over," *American Historical Review* 79 (1974), pp. 1118-1136. Interpretations should change with the opening of the papers of the major decision makers deposited in private archives and the declassification of secret documents. Two collections of materials long closed to the public have recently been published: *Executive Sessions of the Senate Foreign Relations Committee* (Historical Series) (Washington, 1976), Vols. 1-2, years 1947-51, and the continuing series, *Foreign Relations of the United States*, published by the U.S. Department of State.

Among the memoirs of American diplomats several works stand out. George F. Kennan, *Memoirs*, 2 vols. (Boston, 1967, 1972), has received praise both for substance and style. Robert Murphy, *Diplomat Among Warriors* (New York, 1964), is the autobiography of another career diplomatist, whose perspective towards the Soviet Union differs from that of Kennan. Philip Jessup, *The Birth of Nations* (New York, 1976), is good on American responses to the rising nationalism of Asian powers and to United Nations policy.

Cold War considerations now appear to have dominated U.S. policy regarding Europe and its devastation from World War II. On the Marshall Plan, see Harry Price, *The Marshall Plan and Its Meaning* (Ithaca, 1955), a standard treatment; Hadley Arkes, *Bureaucracy, the Marshall Plan, and the National Interest* (Princeton, 1973) for its attention to the bureaucracy's role; and Susan M. Hartmann, *The Marshall Plan* (Columbus, 1968). The creation of the North Atlantic Treaty Organization is best recounted in Robert E. Osgood, *NATO: The Entangling Alliance* (Chicago, 1963); and Lawrence S. Kaplan, "The United States and the Origins of NATO," *Review of Politics* 31 (1969), pp. 210-22. A clear statement is John Gimbel, *The Origins of the Marshall Plan* (Stanford, 1976). The forthcoming volume of Forrest Pogue's multi-volume biography of George C. Marshall should add additional information on the plan's creation.

There has been much discussion over the reason for deploying nuclear weapons against Japan. Gar Alperovitz, *Atomic Diplomacy* (New York, 1965), maintained that Truman used the bomb, in part, to impress upon the Soviet Union the new power of the United States. Alperovitz's thesis engendered much debate, ably summarized in Martin Sherwin, "The Atomic Bomb as History: An Essay Review," *Wisconsin Magazine of History* 53 (1969-1970), pp. 128-34. Sherwin's own work on the topic is outstanding; see his *A World Destroyed: The Atomic Bomb and the Grand Alliance* (New York, 1975).

America's China policy has long received close attention. U.S. Department of State, *United States' Relations with China* (Washington, 1949), is the famous White Paper on China and constitutes the official Department opinion on the "fall" of China to the Communist Chinese. Frances R. Valeo, ed., *The China White Paper* (Washington, 1949), is a summary. Herbert Feis, *The China Tangle* (Princeton, 1953) and Tang Tsou, *America's Failure in China, 1941-50* (Chicago, 1963), are critical of American leaders for the loss of China. Two general, thoughtful works on U.S.-Asian relations merit special notice: Warren I. Cohen, *America's Response to China* (New York, 1971), and Robert A. Hart, *The Eccentric Tradition: American Diplomacy in the Far East* (New York, 1976). Ernest R. May, ed., *The Truman Administration and China* (Philadelphia, 1975), is a good collection of materials on China and Truman.

Other Works

Acheson, Dean. *Present at the Creation: My Years in the State Department* (New York, 1969).
——. *Sketches from Life of Men I Have Known* (New York, 1961).
Adler, Les K., and Thomas G. Paterson. "Red Facism: The Merger of Nazi Germany and Soviet Russia in the American Image of Totalitarianism, 1930's-1950's," *American Historical Review* 75 (1970), pp. 1046–1064.
Ambrose, Stephen E. *Rise to Globalism: American Foreign Policy, 1938-1976* (Baltimore, 1976).
Aron, Raymond. *The Imperial Republic: The United States and the World, 1945-1973* (Englewood Cliffs, N.J., 1974).
Aronson, James. *The Press and the Cold War* (Indianapolis, 1970).
Baldwin, David A. *Economic Development and American Foreign Policy, 1943-1962* (Chicago, 1966).
Barnet, Richard J. *Roots of War: the Men and Institutions behind U.S. Foreign Policy* (New York, 1972).
Behrman, Jack N. "Political Facts in U.S. International Financial Cooperation, 1945-1950," *American Political Science Review* 47 (1953), pp. 431-60.
Bernstein, Barton J. "The Quest for Security: American Foreign Policy and International Control of Atomic Energy, 1942-1946," *Journal of American History* 60 (1974), pp. 1003-1044.
——. "Roosevelt, Truman, and the Atomic Bomb," *Political Science Quarterly* 90 (1975), pp. 23-70.
Bhana, Surendra Bhana. *The United States and the Development of the Puerto Rico Status Question, 1936-1968* (Lawrence, Kan., 1975).
Bickerton, Ian. "President Truman's Recognition of Israel," *American Jewish Historical Quarterly* 58 (1968), pp. 173-240.
Bingham, Jonathan B. *Shirt-Sleeve Diplomacy: Point 4 in Action* (New York, 1954).
Bohlen, Charles E. *Witness to History, 1929-1969* (New York, 1969).
Brown, Seyom. *The Faces of Power: Constancy and Change in United States Foreign Policy from Truman to Johnson* (New York, 1968).
Byrnes, James F. *Speaking Frankly* (New York, 1947).
Campbell, Thomas M., and George C. Herring, eds., *The Diaries of Edward R. Stettinius, Jr., 1943-1946* (New York, 1975).
Cohen, Bernard C. *The Political Process and Foreign Policy: The Making of the Japanese Peace Settlement* (Princeton, 1957).
Colbert, Evelyn. *Southeast Asia in International Politics, 1941-1956* (Ithaca, 1977).
Crabb, Cecil V., Jr. *Bipartisan Foreign Policy; Myth or Reality* (Evanston, 1957).
Curry, George. *James F. Brynes* (New York, 1965).
Divine, Robert A., ed. *American Foreign Policy since 1945* (Chicago, 1969).
——. *Foreign Policy and U.S. Presidential Elections*, 2 vols. (New York, 1974).
Donovan, John C. *The Cold Warriors: A Policy-Making Elite* (Lexington, Mass., 1974).
Druks, Herbert. *Harry S. Truman and the Russians, 1945-1953* (New York, 1966).
Dunn, Frederick S. *Peace-Making and the Settlement with Japan* (Princeton, 1963).
Eubank, Keith. *The Summit Conferences, 1919-1960* (Norman, Okla., 1966).
Feis, Herbert. *The Atomic Bomb and the End of World War II* (Princeton, 1970).
——. *The Birth of Israel: The Tousled Diplomatic Bed* (New York, 1969).
——. *Japan Subdued: The Atomic Bomb and the End of the War in the Pacific* (Princeton, 1961).
Ferrell, Robert H. *George C. Marshall* (New York, 1966).
Gardner, Lloyd C. *Architects of Illusion: Men and Ideas in American Foreign Policy, 1941-1949* (Chicago, 1970).
Graebner, Norman. *Cold War Diplomacy: American Foreign Policy, 1945-1960* (Princeton, 1962).

——, ed. *The Cold War: A Conflict of Ideology and Power* (New York, 1976).

——. *An Uncertain Tradition: American Secretaries of State in the Twentieth Century* (New York, 1961).

Halle, Louis J. *The Cold War as History* (New York, 1947).

Harriman, W. Averell. *America and Russia in a Changing World: A Half Century of Personal Observations* (Garden City, 1971).

Horowitz, David. *From Yalta to Vietnam: American Foreign Policy in the Cold War* (New York, 1967).

——, ed. *Containment and Revolution* (Boston, 1967).

Isaacs, Stephen D. *Jews and American Politics* (New York, 1974).

Kennan, George F. *American Diplomacy, 1900-1950* (Chicago, 1950).

——. *Russia and the West under Lenin and Stalin* (Boston, 1961).

Kolko, Gabriel. *The Roots of American Foreign Policy* (New York, 1963).

Kolko, Gabriel, and Joyce Kolko. *The Limits of Power: The World and United States Foreign Policy* (New York, 1972).

LaFeber, Walter. *America, Russia, and the Cold War, 1945-75* 3rd. ed. (New York, 1976).

Lippmann, Walter. *The Cold War* (New York, 1947).

Lukacs, John. *A New History of the Cold War* (Garden City, N.Y., 1966).

McLellan, David S. *Dean Acheson: The State Department Years* (New York, 1976).

Maddox, Robert James. *The New Left and the Origins of the Cold War* (Princeton, 1973).

Mann, Peggy. *Ralph Bunche: UN Peacemaker* (New York, 1975).

Mazuzan, George T. *Warren R. Austin at the U.N., 1946-1953* (Kent, Ohio, 1977).

Osgood, Robert E., et. al. *America and the World: From the Truman Doctrine to Vietnam* (Baltimore, 1970).

Osgood, Robert E. *Ideals and Self-Interest in America's Foreign Relations* (Chicago, 1953).

Quade, Quentin L. "The Truman Administration and the Separation of Powers: The Case of the Marshall Plan," *Review of Politics* 27 (1965), pp. 58-77.

Paterson, Thomas G., ed. *Cold War Critics: Alternatives to American Foreign Policy in the Truman Years* (Chicago, 1971).

Perlmutter, Oscar William. "Acheson vs. Congress," *Review of Politics* 22 (1960), pp. 5-44.

——. "The 'Neo-Realism' of Dean Acheson," *Review of Politics* 26 (1964), pp. 100-23.

Powers, Richard J. "Containment: From Greece to Vietnam—and Back?" *Western Political Quarterly* 22 (1969), pp. 846-61.

Radosh, Ronald. *American Labor and United States Foreign Policy* (New York, 1969).

——. *Prophets on the Right; Profiles of Conservative Critics of American Globalism* (New York, 1975).

Richardson, J.L. "Cold War Revisionism: A Critique," *World Politics* 24 (1972), pp. 579-612.

"Russia—Defeat and Occupation," *Collier's* (October 1951).

Sander, Alfred. "Truman and the National Security Council: 1945-1947," *Journal of American History* 59 (1972), pp. 369-88.

Smith, Gaddis. *Dean Acheson.* (New York, 1972).

Smith, Walter Bedell. *My Three Years In Moscow* (Philadelphia, 1950).

Snetsinger, John. *Truman, the Jewish Vote and the Creation of Israel* (Stanford, 1974).

Theoharis, Athan. *The Yalta Myths: An Issue in U.S. Politics, 1945-1955* (Columbia, Mo., 1970).

Walker, Richard L. R. *Edward Stettinius, Jr.* (New York, 1965).

Whelen, Joseph G. "George Kennan and His Influence on American Foreign Policy," *Virginia Quarterly Review* 35 (1959), pp. 196-220.

Wittner, Lawrence S. *Rebels Against War: The American Peace Movement, 1941-1960* (New York, 1969).

Yavenditti, Michael J. "The American People and the Use of the Atomic Bombs on Japan: the 1940s," *Historian* 36 (1974), pp. 224-47.

The Origins of the Cold War

Bernstein, Barton J. "The Early Cold War," *Progressive* 34 (August 1970), pp. 39-42.

Davis, Lynn Etheridge. *The Cold War Begins: Soviet American Conflict over Eastern Europe* (Princeton, 1974).

Feis, Herbert. *Between War and Peace: The Potsdam Conference* (Princeton, 1960).

Fleming, D.F. *The Cold War and Its Origins, 1917-1960*, 2 vols. (Garden City, 1961).

Gardner, Lloyd C., et. al. *The Origins of the Cold War* (Waltham, Mass., 1970).

Harriman, W. Averell, and Elie Abel. *Special Envoy to Churchill and Stalin, 1941-1946* (New York, 1975).

Herring, George C., Jr. *Aid to Russia: Strategy, Diplomacy, and the Origins of the Cold War* (New York, 1973).

Hess, Gary R. "The Iranian Crisis of 1945-46 and the Cold War," *Political Science Quarterly* 89 (1974), pp. 117-46.

McNeill, William H. *America, Britain and Russia: Their Cooperation and Their Conflict* (New York, 1970).

Paterson, Thomas G. *Soviet-American Confrontation: Postwar Reconstruction and the Origins of the Cold War* (Baltimore, 1974).

Rose, Lisle A. *After Yalta: America and the Origins of the Cold War* (New York, 1973).

———. *The Coming of the American Age, 1945-1946: The United States and the End of World War II* (Kent, Ohio, 1973).

Schlesinger, Arthur M., Jr. "Origins of the Cold War," *Foreign Affairs* 46 (1967), pp. 22-52.

Williams, William Appleman. *American-Russian Relations 1781-1947* (New York, 1952).

Wooley, Wesley T., Jr. "The Quest for Permanent Peace—American Supranationalism, 1945-1947," *Historian* 35 (1972), pp. 18-31.

American and Europe 1945-52

Clay, Lucius D. *Decision in Germany* (Garden City, 1950).

Davis, Franklin M., Jr. *Come as a Conqueror; The United States Army's Occupation of Germany 1945-1949* (New York, 1967).

Davison, Walter Phillips. *The Berlin Blockade: A Study in Cold War Politics* (Princeton, 1958).

Gimbel, John. *The American Occupation of Germany: Politics and the Military, 1945-1949* (Stanford, 1968).

Kertesz, Stephen D., ed. *The Fate of East Central Europe* (South Bend, 1956).

Koenig, Louis W. "Foreign Aid to Spain and Yugoslavia: Harry Truman Does His Duty," In *The Uses of Power*, Alan F. Westin, ed. (New York, 1962), pp. 74-116.

Kuklick, Bruce. *American Policy and the Division of Germany: The Clash with Russia over Reparations* (Ithaca, 1972).

MacNeill, William H. *Greece: American Aid in Action, 1947-1956* (New York, 1956).

Mosely, Philip E. "Hopes and Failures: American Policy toward East Central Europe, 1941-1947," *Review of Politics* 17 (1955), pp. 461-85.

Smith, Jean, *The Defense of Berlin* (Baltimore, 1963).

Smith, Jean Edward, ed. *The Papers of General Lucius D. Clay: Germany, 1945-1949* (Bloomington, Ind., 1974).

Xydis, Stephen G. "America, Britain, and the USSR in the Greek Arena, 1944-1947," *Political Science Quarterly* 78 (1963), pp. 581-96.

China

Beal, John Robinson. *Marshall in China* (Garden City, N.Y., 1970).

Buhite, Russell D. *Patrick J. Hurley and American Foreign Policy* (Ithaca, 1973).

Chern, Kenneth S. "Politics of American China Policy," *Political Science Quarterly* 91 (1976-1977), pp. 631-47.

Dulles, Foster Rhea. *American Policy toward Communist China 1949-1969* (New York, 1972).

Fairbank, John King. *The United States and China.* (Cambridge, Mass., 1971).

Fetzer, James. "Senator Vandenberg and the American Commitment to China, 1945-1950," *Historian* 36 (1974), pp. 283-303.

Purifoy, Lewis McCarroll. *Harry Truman's China Policy: McCarthyism and the Diplomacy of Hysteria, 1947-1951* (New York, 1976).

Rose, Lisle A. *Roots of Tragedy: The United States and the Struggle for Asia, 1945-1953* (Westport, Conn., 1976).

DEFENSE

America's defense organization faced many dilemmas at the end of World War II, nearly all of which have received attention. Publications on James Forrestal, Secretary of the Navy (1944-47), and the first Secretary of Defense (1947-49), are Walter Millis, ed., *The Forrestal Diaries* (New York, 1951), and Arnold A. Rogow, *James Forrestal* (New York, 1963). On the unification of the Navy and War departments, see Demetrios Caraley, *The Politics of Military Unification* (New York, 1966). Russell F. Weigley, *The American Way of War* (New York, 1973), contains several chapters and an excellent bibliography on post-World War II military strategy. See also, Samuel P. Huntington, *The Soldier and the State: The Theory and Politics of Civil-Military Relations* (Cambridge, Mass., 1957). The decision to develop the hydrogen bomb is scrutinized in Warner R. Schilling, "The H-Bomb Decision," *Political Science Quarterly* 81 (1961), pp. 24–46, and Herbert F. York, *The Advisors: Oppenheimer, Teller, and the Superbomb* (San Francisco, 1976), the latter study written by a nuclear scientist.

More work is needed on the origins and conduct of the Korean conflict, 1950-53. Concerning the outbreak of war, see Alfred Crofts, "The Start of the Korean War, Reconsidered," *Rocky Mountain Social Science Journal* 7 (1970), pp. 109-17, and the relevent sections of Walter LaFeber, *America, Russia, and the Cold War* (New York, 1976). For general, introductory purposes, consult Allen Guttmann, ed., *Korea: Cold War and Limited War*, 2nd ed. (Lexington, Mass., 1972). S.L.A. Marshall, *The Military History of the Korean War* (New York, 1963) is a convenient summary. President Truman's dismissal of Gen. Douglas MacArthur as commander of U.N. forces in Korea has received much attention, though not recently. Most writers side with the President; see Richard Rovere and Arthur M. Schlesinger, Jr., *The MacArthur Controversy and American Foreign Policy* (New York, 1965), and John W. Spanier, *The Truman-MacArthur Controversy and the Korean War* (Cambridge, Mass., 1959). D. Clayton James, MacArthur's official biographer, should soon provide us with an extensive defense.

Other Works

Dalfiume, Richard. *Desegregation of the Armed Forces: Fighting on Two Fronts, 1939–1953* (Columbia, Mo., 1969).

Davis, Vincent. *Postwar Defense Policy and the U.S. Navy, 1943–1946* (Chapel Hill, 1966).

Hammond, Paul Y. *Organizing for Defense: The American Military Establishment in the Twentieth Century* (Princeton, 1961).

Hewes, James E., Jr. *From Root to McNa-*

mara: *Army Organization and Administration, 1900–1963* (Washington, 1975).

Kolodziej, Edward A. *The Uncommon Defense and Congress, 1945–1963* (Columbus, Ohio, 1966).

Lee, R. Alton. "The Army 'Mutiny' of 1946," *Journal of American History* 53 (1966), 555–71.

LeMay, Curtis E. *Mission with LeMay* (New York, 1965).

Piccard, Paul C. "Scientists and Public Policy: Los Alamos, August-November, 1945," *Western Political Quarterly* 17 (1965), pp. 251–62.

Wellman, Paul I. *Stuart Symington* (Garden City, 1960).

Korea

Berger, Carl. *The Korea Knot: A Military-Political History* (Philadelphia, 1964).

Caridi, Ronald J. *The Korean War and American Politics* (Philadelphia, 1969).

Clark, Mark W. *From the Danube to the Yalu* (New York, 1954).

Collins, J. Lawton. *War in Peacetime: The History and Lessons of Korea* (Boston, 1969).

Detzer, David. *Thunder of the Captains:*

The Short Summer in 1950 (New York, 1977).

Goodrich, Leland M. *Korea: A Study of U.S. Policy in the United Nations* (New York, 1956).

Halperin, Morton H. "The Limiting Process in the Korean War," *Political Science Quarterly* 78 (1963), pp. 13-39.

Higgins, Trumbull. *Korea and the Fall of MacArthur: A Precis in Limited War* (New York, 1960).

Lofgren, Charles A. "Mr. Truman's War: A Debate and Its Aftermath," *Review of Politics* 31 (1969), pp. 223-41.

MacArthur, Douglas. *Reminiscences* (New York, 1964).

Mueller, John E. "Trends in Popular Support for the Wars in Korea and Vietnam," *American Political Science Review* 65 (1971), pp. 358-75.

Norman, John. "MacArthur's Blockade Proposals against Red China," *Pacific Historical Review* 26 (1957), pp. 161-74.

Ridgway, Matthew B. *The Korean War: How We Met the Challenge* (Garden City, N.Y., 1967).

———. *Soldier: The Memoirs of Matthew B. Ridgway* (New York, 1956).

Stone, I. F. *The Hidden History of the Korean War* (New York, 1952).

EISENHOWER ADMINISTRATION

FOREIGN AFFAIRS

The largest portion of the literature dealing with the Eisenhower Administration focuses on the development and execution of foreign policy. The works on this subject can be divided very broadly into three categories: traditional, those that accept the Cold War policies of the Administration; realist, those that criticize Eisenhower's stand as too ideologically oriented and ignorant of these realities of big power politics; and revisionist, those that view the U.S. as a historically expansionist power and maintain that many of the crises of the period could have been avoided by more moderate action on the part of the Administration. For a traditionalist view of the period see, Paul Seabury, *The Rise and Decline of the Cold War* (New York, 1967) and Desmond Donnelly, *Struggle for the World: The Cold War, 1917-1965* (New York, 1965). Realist interpretations include *John*

Spanier, American Foreign Policy Since World War II (New York, 1971), Seyom Brown, *The Faces of Power: Constancy and Change in United States Foreign Policy from Truman to Johnson* (New York, 1968) and Louis J. Halle, *The Cold War as History* (New York, 1967). Revisionists have yet to give Eisenhower the attention they have devoted to the Truman Administration. Major studies in this school include William Appleman Williams, *The Tragedy of American Diplomacy* (New York, 1962), Walter LaFeber, *America, Russia and the Cold War, 1945-66* (New York, 1967) and Stephen E. Ambrose, *Rise to Globalism: American Foreign Policy, 1938-1970* (Baltimore, 1971).

The figure of John Foster Dulles dominated foreign policy during the period. For an early articulation of his views see his *Life* Magazine article, "A Policy of Boldness," (May 19, 1952) and "Policy for Security and Peace," *Foreign Affairs*, XXXII (1954). The Secretary of State unveiled his concept of "brinkmanship" in James Shepley, "How Dulles Averted War," *Life* (Jan. 16, 1956). Townsend Hoopes award winning biography of Dulles, *The Devil and John Foster Dulles* (Boston, 1973) is critical of his moralism and unilateralism, which Hoopes thinks often exacerbated diplomatic crises. Hoopes contrasts Eisenhower's realism with Dulles's impulsive crusading zeal. The President emerges as the Administration's dominant foreign policy figure, restraining the Secretary of State. One of Dulles's leading critics from the academic world, Hans Morgenthau, wrote an essay in Norman Graebner, ed., *An Uncertain Tradition* (New York, 1961) that focuses on how the Secretary's fear of the Republican Right, and particularly Sen. Joseph McCarthy, shaped his diplomacy. For more sympathetic accounts of Dulles see Richard Goold-Adams, *The Time of Power: A Reappraisal of John Foster Dulles* (London, 1962), John Robinson Beal, *John Foster Dulles: A Biography* (New York, 1957) and Louis Gerson, *John Foster Dulles* (May, 1957). Dulles's successor, Christian A. Herter, is discussed in George B. Noble, *Christian A. Herter* (New York, 1970).

A large number of Administration critics have published important memoirs. See, in particular, George F. Kennan, *Memoirs* (Boston, 1972) dealing with Cold War policy and Chester Bowles, *Promises to Keep* (New York, 1971) focusing on relations with underdeveloped nations. Compare and contrast the columns of the *New York Times's* two foremost columnists, James Reston and Arthur Krock for their appraisals of the Administration's diplomacy. Both have published anthologies of their best articles: James Reston, *Sketches in the Sand* (New York, 1967) and Arthur Krock, *In the Nation, 1932 to 1966* (New York, 1966). Walter Johnson, ed., *The Papers of Adlai Stevenson* (Boston, 1974-76) includes an excellent collection of speeches and articles critical of the Administration in volumes four through six.

There are numerous regional studies of American foreign policy during the Eisenhower era. For U.S. policy toward Europe see, Anatole Rapoport, *The Big Two: Soviet-American Perceptions of Foreign Policy* (New York, 1971) and Bennett Kovrig, *The Myth of Liberation: East-Central Europe in U.S. Diplomacy and Politics since 1941* (Baltimore, 1973). For studies of the North Atlantic Treaty Organization see Robert E. Osgood, *NATO: The Entangling Alliance* (Chicago, 1962) and Klaus Knorr, ed., *NATO and American Security* (Princeton, 1959). Contemporary writers advocating early relaxation of tension in Europe include, C. L. Sulzberger, *The Big Thaw* (New York, 1956), George Kennan, "Overdue Changes in Our American Foreign Policy," *Harper's Magazine* (August, 1956) and "Peaceful Coexistence: A Western View," *Foreign Affairs* (January 1960), and his most important, *Russia, The Atom, and the West* (New York, 1957). For an important justification of a hardline stand in Europe see Dean Acheson's interview in *U.S. News and World Report* (Jan. 17, 1958).

Valuable studies of the Berlin crisis include Jean E. Smith, *The Defense of Berlin* (Baltimore, 1963), Jack M. Schick, *The Berlin Crisis, 1958-1962* (Philadelphia, 1971) and Robert M. Slusser, *The Berlin Crisis of 1961* (Baltimore, 1973). For Eisenhower's diplomacy in the Middle East see John C. Campbell, *Defense of the Middle East* (New York, 1960), a good survey of the entire areas. Herman Finer, *Dulles over Suez* (Chicago, 1964) is critical of how the Secretary of State handled the crisis, while Carey B. Joynt, "John Foster Dulles and the Suez Crisis" in Gerald N. Grob, ed., *Statesmen and Statecraft of the Modern West* (Barre, Mass., 1967) defends the Secretary of State's performance.

Robert N. Burr, *Our Troubled Hemisphere: Perspectives in United States-Latin American Relations* (Washington, 1967) is an excellent overview of Latin American diplomacy during the Eisenhower Administration. Theodore Draper, *Castro's Revolution* (New York, 1962) attacks the Castro takeover while William Appleman Williams, *The U.S., Cuba and Castro* (New York, 1962) is more sympathetic to the new government.

There is an extensive literature on U.S. policy in the Far East, particularly in Vietnam. Foster Rhea Dulles, *American Foreign Policy Toward Communist China, 1949-1969* (New York, 1972) includes chapters documenting the deterioration of relations between the two powers. For a discussion of early U.S. intervention in Vietnam see particularly Bernard B. Fall, *The Two Viet-Nams* (New York, 1963) and George M. Kahin and John W. Lewis, *The United States in Vietnam* (New York, 1969). For a detailed study of the events behind the 1954 Geneva Accords see Melvin Gurtov, *The First Vietnam Crisis: Chinese Communist Strategy and United States Involvement, 1953-1954* (New York, 1967), Philip Devillers and Jean Lacoutre, *End of a War: Indo-China, 1954* (New York, 1969) and Robert F. Randle, *Geneva: 1954* (Princeton, 1969). Compare these works with the documents available in the *Pentagon Papers* (Boston, 1971).

The question of disarmament has been deeply analyzed. See particularly, Bernard G. Bechhoefer, *Postwar Negotiations for Arms Control* (Washington, 1961), a comprehensive treatment of the American disarmament program. Critics of the American stand during the period include Richard J. Barnet, *Who Wants Disarmament?* (Boston, 1960), Edgar M. Bottome, *The Balance of Terror: A Guide to the Arms Race* (Boston, 1971) and Joseph P. Murray, *From Yalta to Disarmament: Cold War Debate* (New York, 1961).

Other Works

Acheson, Dean, *Power and Diplomacy* (Cambridge, Mass., 1958).

Adler, Selig, *The Isolationist Impulse: Its Twentieth Century Reaction* (New York, 1957).

Baldwin, David, *Economic Development and American Foreign Policy, 1943-1962* (Chicago, 1966).

Berding, Andrew H., *Dulles on Diplomacy* (Princeton, 1965).

Bowles, Chester, *Ideas, People and Peace* (New York, 1958).

———, *The New Dimensions of Peace* (New York, 1950).

Cohen, Bernard C., *The Press and Foreign Policy* (Princeton, 1963).

Commanger, Henry Steel, "The Perilous Folly of Senator Bricker," *The Reporter* (October 13, 1953).

Dean, Arthur A., "The Bricker Amendment and Authority Over Foreign Affairs," *Foreign Affairs* (October, 1953).

Divine, Robert A., *Since 1945: Politics and Diplomacy in Recent American History* (New York, 1975).

Donelan, Michael, *The Ideas of American Foreign Policy* (London, 1963).

Drummond, Roscoe and Gaston Coblentz,

Duel at the Brink: John Foster Dulles' Command of American Power (Garden City, 1960).

Dulles, Eleanor Lansing, *John Foster Dulles: The Last Year* (New York, 1963).

Elliot, William Y.; et al., *The Political Economy of American Foreign Policy* (New York, 1955).

Feis, Herbert, *Foreign Aid and Foreign Policy* (New York, 1961).

Finletter, Thomas K., *Foreign Policy: The Next Phase* (New York, 1958).

———, *Power and Policy* (New York, 1954).

Graebner, Norman A., *The New Isolationism: A Study in Politics and Foreign Policy since 1950* (New York, 1956).

Gukin, Michael, *John Foster Dulles: A Statesman and His Times* (New York, 1972).

Hatch, Alden, *The Lodges of Massachusetts* (New York, 1973).

Henderson, John W., *The United States Information Agency* (New York, 1969).

Herz, John H., *International Politics in the Atomic Age* (New York, 1959).

Hoffman, Stanley, ed., *Contemporary Theory in International Relations* (Englewood Cliffs, 1960).

Hughes, Emmet J., *America the Vincible* (Garden City, 1959).

Johnson, Haynes and Bernard M. Gwertzman, *Fulbright: The Dissenter* (New York, 1968).

Jurika, Stephen, ed., *From Pearl Harbor to Vietnam: The Memoirs of Admiral Arthur Radford* (Stamford, 1980).

Kaplan, Morton, *System and Process in International Politics* (New York, 1957).

———, *Nuclear Weapons and Foreign Policy* (New York, 1957).

Kissinger, Henry A., *The Necessity for Choice: Prospects of American Foreign Policy* (New York, 1960).

Kolko, Gabriel, *Roots of American Foreign Policy* (Boston, 1969).

Kolko, Joyce and Gabriel Kolko, *The Limits of Power: The World and U.S. Foreign Policy 1945-1954* (New York, 1972).

Magdoff, Harry, *The Age of Imperialism* (New York, 1969).

May, Ernest R., "Eisenhower and After" in May, ed., *The Ultimate Decision: The President as Commander-in-Chief* (New York, 1960).

Medaris, John B., *Countdown for Decision* (New York, 1960).

Miller, William, *Henry Cabot Lodge* (New York, 1967).

Osgood, Robert E., *Ideals and Self-Interest in America's Foreign Relations: The Great Transformation of the 20th Century* (Chicago, 1953).

Osgood, Robert E., et al., *America and the World: From the Truman Doctrine to Vietnam* (Baltimore, 1970).

Padelford, Norman J. and George A. Lincoln, *The Dynamics of International Politics* (New York, 1962).

Pye, Lucian W., "Soviet and American Styles in Foreign Aid," *Orbis* IV (Summer, 1960).

Radosh, Ronald, *American Labor and United States Foreign Policy* (New York, 1970).

Rosenau, James N., ed., *International Politics and Foreign Policy* (New York, 1961).

Rostow, Walt W., *The Diffusion of Power: An Essay in Recent History* (New York, 1972).

———, *The United States in the World Arena: An Essay in Recent History* (New York, 1960).

Slessor, John, *Strategy for the West* (New York, 1954).

Smith, Merriman, *A President's Odyssey* (New York, 1961).

Sorensen, Thomas C., *The Word War* (New York, 1968).

Steel, Richard, *Pax Americana* (New York, 1967).

Thomas, Ann Van Wynen and A. J. Thomas Jr., *Non-intervention: The Law and Its Import in the Americas* (Dallas, 1966).

Vagts, Alfred, *A History of Militarism: Civilian and Military* (New York, 1959).

Wittner, Lawrence S., *Rebels Against War: The American Peace Movement 1941-1960* (New York, 1969).

Asia

Bachrack, Stanley, D. *The Committee of*

One Million: "China Lobby" Politics 1953-1971 (New York, 1976).

Barnet, Richard J., *Roots of War* (New York, 1972). Origins of Vietnam War.

Bator, Victor, *Vietnam: A Diplomatic Tragedy: The Origins of the United States Involvement* (Dobbs Ferry, 1965).

Cameron, Allan W., *Vietnam Crisis: A Documentary History* (Ithaca, 1971).

Clubb, Oliver E., "Formosa and the Offshore Islands in American Policy 1950-1955," *Political Science Quarterly* (December, 1959).

Cooper, Chester L., *The Los Crusade: America in Vietnam* (New York, 1970).

Dunn, Frederick S., *Peacemaking and the Settlement with Japan* (Princeton, 1963).

Halberstam, David, *The Best and the Brightest* (New York, 1972).

———, *The Making of a Quagmire* (New York, 1964).

Honey, P. J., ed., *North Vietnam Today: Profile of a Communist Satellite* (New York, 1962).

Jones, Howard P., *Indonesia: The Possible Dream* (New York, 1971).

Kalb, Marvin and Elie Abel, *Roots of Involvement: The U.S. in Asia, 1784-1971* (New York, 1971).

Lansdale, Edward G., *In the Midst of Wars: An American's Mission to Southeast Asia* (New York, 1972).

Poole, Peter A., *The U.S. and Indochina from FDR to Nixon* (Hinsdale, Ill., 1973).

Rankin, Karl Lott, *China Assignment* (Seattle, 1964).

Reischauer, Edwin O., "The Broken Dialogue with Japan," *Foreign Affairs* (October, 1960).

Ridgway, Matthew B., *The Korean War* (New York, 1967).

Schlesinger, Arthur M. Jr., *The Bitter Heritage: Vietnam and American Democracy, 1941-1968* (Boston, 1968).

Shaplen, Robert, *The Lost Revolution: Twenty Years of Neglected Opportunities in Vietnam and of American Failures to Foster Democracy There* (New York, 1965).

Steele, A. T., *The American People and China* (New York, 1966).

Stevenson, Charles A., *The End of Nowhere, American Policy Toward Laos Since 1954* (Boston, 1972).

Europe and the Cold War

Acheson, Dean, "The Illusion of Disengagement," *Foreign Affairs*, XXXVI (April, 1958).

Crankshaw, Edward, *Khrushchev: A Career* (New York, 1966).

Duchacek, Ivo, "Czechoslovakia," in Stephen D. Kertesz, ed., *The Fate of East Central Europe* (Notre Dame, 1956).

Dulles, Eleanor L., *The Wall: A Tragedy in Three Acts* (Columbia, S.C., 1972).

Fontaine, André, *History of the Cold War* (New York, 1970).

Gelber, Lionel, *America in Britain's Place: The Leadership of the West and Anglo-American Unity* (New York, 1961).

Graebner, Norman, *Cold War Diplomacy* (New York, 1962).

———, ed., *The Cold War: A Conflict of Ideology and Power* (New York, 1976).

Hammond, Paul Y., *Cold War and Detente* (New York, 1975).

Harriman, W. Averell, *America and Russia in a Changing World: A Half Century of Personal Observations* (Garden City, 1971).

Horowitz, David, ed., *Containment and Revolution* (Boston, 1967).

Houghton, Nealie Doyle, ed., *Struggle Against History: U.S. Foreign Policy in the Age of Revolution* (New York, 1968).

Kaplan, Lawrence S. "The U.S. and the Atlantic Community: The First Generation," in John Braeman and David Brody, eds., *Twentieth Century American Foreign Policy* (Columbus, 1971).

Kennan, George F., *Realities of American Foreign Policy* (Princeton, 1954).

Lukacs, John, *A New History of the Cold War* (Garden City, 1966).

Neustadt, Richard E., *Alliance Politics* (New York, 1970).

Planek, Charles R., *The Changing Status of German Reunification in Western Diplomacy, 1955-1966* (Baltimore, 1967).

Plishcke, Elmer, "Eisenhower's 'Corres-

218

pondence Diplomacy' with the Kremlin:
Case Study in Summit Diplomatics,"
Journal of Politics (February 1968).

Schwartz, Harry, *The Red Phoenix: Russia
Since World War II* (New York, 1961).

Tatu, Michel, *Power in the Kremlin: From
Krushchev to Kosygin* (New York, 1969).

Theoharis, Athan, G., *The Yalta Myths*
(Columbia, Mo., 1970).

Ulam, Adam B., *Expansion and Coexistence: The History of Soviet Foreign Policy, 1917-1967* (New York, 1968).

———, *The Rivals: America and Russia
since World War II* (New York, 1971).

Vigneras, Marcel, *Rearming the French*
(Washington, 1957).

Latin America

Berle, Adolf A., Jr., *Latin America: Diplomacy and Reality* (New York, 1962).

Bonsal, Philip W., *Cuba, Castro and the
United States* (Pittsburgh, 1971).

Dozer, Donald M., *We Good Neighbors?
Three Decades of Inter-American Relations, 1930-1960* (Gainesville, Fla., 1959).

Eisenhower, Milton, *The Wine is Bitter*
(Garden City, 1963).

Gillin, John and K. H. Silvert, "Am-
biguities in Guatemala," *Foreign Affairs*,
XXXIV (April, 1956).

Lewis, Gordon K., *Puerto Rico: Freedom
and Power in the Caribbean* (New York,
1963).

McClellan, Grant S., ed., *U.S. Policy in
Latin America* (New York, 1963).

Mecham, J. Lloyd, *The United States and
Inter-American Security, 1889-1960* (Austin, 1961).

Mezerik, A. G., *Cuba and the United
States* (New York, 1963).

Pike, Frederick B., "Guatemala, the United
States, and Communism in the
Americas," *Review of Politics*, XVII (Ap-
ril, 1955).

Ronning, C. Neale, *Law and Politics in
Inter-American Diplomacy* (New York,
1963).

Taylor, Philip B., Jr., "The Guatemala Affair: A Critique of United States Foreign
Policy," *American Political Science Review*, L (September, 1956).

Middle East and Africa

Bowles, Chester, *Africa's Challenge to the
Americans* (Berkeley, 1957).

Dougherty, James E., "The Aswan Decision in Perspective," *Political Science
Quarterly* (March, 1959).

Eden, Anthony, *The Suez Crisis of 1956*
(Boston, 1966).

Emerson, Rupert, "American Policy in Africa," *Foreign Affairs* (January 1962).

Engler, Robert, *The Politics of Oil*
(Chicago, 1961).

Fitzsimmons, M. A., "The Suez Crisis and
the Containment Policy," *Review of Politics* (October, 1957).

Hammond, Paul Y. and Sidney S. Alexander, *Political Dynamics in the Middle
East* (New York, 1972).

Nutting, Anthony, *No End of the Lesson*
(London, 1967). Middle East.

Polk, William R., *The United States and
the Arab World* (Cambridge, Mass.,
1969).

Robertson, Terrence, *Crisis: The Inside
Story of the Suez Conspiracy* (London,
1964).

Roosevelt, Kermit, *Counter Coup: The Struggle for the Control of Iran* (New
York, 1980).

Smolansky, O.M., "Moscow and the Suez
Crisis, 1956: A Reappraisal," *Political
Science Quarterly* (December, 1965).

Weissman, Stephen R., *American Foreign
Policy in the Congo: 1960-1964* (Ithaca,
1974).

Disarmament

Brennan, Donald G., ed., *Arms Control,
Disarmament and National Security*
(New York, 1961).

Bull, Hedley, *The Control of the Arms
Race* (New York, 1961).

Dean, Arthur H., *Test Ban and Disarmament: The Path of Negotiation* (New
York, 1966).

Gettleman, Marvin, *A Summary of Disarmament Documents, 1945-1962* (San
Francisco, n.d.).

Levine, Robert A., *The Arms Debate*
(Cambridge, Mass., 1963).

Nogee, Joseph L., *Soviet Policy Toward International Control of Atomic Energy* (Notre Dame, 1961).

Roberts, Chalmers M., *The Nuclear Years: The Arms Race and Arms Control, 1945-1970* (New York, 1970).

Schelling, Thomas C. and Morton H. Halperin, *Strategy and Arms Control* (New Haven, 1961).

Spanier, John W. and Joseph L. Nogee, *The Politics of Disarmament: A Study in Soviet-American Gamesmanship* (New York, 1962).

The Central Intelligence Agency

Agee, Philip, *Inside the Company: CIA Diary* (New York, 1975).

Berman, Jerry J., and Morton H. Halperin, eds., *The Abuses of the Intelligence Agencies* (Washington, 1975).

Dulles, Allen W., *The Craft of Intelligence* (New York, 1963).

Marchetti, Victor, and John D. Marks, *The CIA and the Cult of Intelligence* (New York, 1974).

Powers, Francis Gary and Curt Gentry, *Operation Overflight* (New York, 1970).

Ransom, Harry H., *Central Intelligence and National Security* (Cambridge, Mass., 1958).

U.S. Commission on CIA Activities within the United States, *Report to the President by the Commission on CIA Activities within the United States* (Washington, 1975).

U.S. Senate, Select Committee on Intelligence Activities, *Alleged Assassination Plots Involving Foreign Leaders* (Washington, 1975).

———, *Intelligence Activities and the Rights of Americans* (Washington, 1976).

Wise, David, and Thomas B. Ross, *The Invisible Government* (New York, 1964).

DEFENSE

Eisenhower's adoption of a "New Look" policy, with its emphasis on strategic nuclear weapons and economy in defense spending, was considered a dramatic departure in defense at the time. For a description of the program see Warner Schilling, Paul Y. Hammond and Glenn Snyder, *Strategy, Politics and Defense Budget* (New York, 1962). Samuel P. Huntington, *The Common Defense: Strategic Programs in National Politics* (New York, 1961) is the best overall assessment of the defense program. Richard Aliano, *American Defense Policy from Eisenhower to Kennedy, 1957-1961* (Athens, Ohio, 1975) focuses closely on the policy debate during Eisenhower's second Administration.

The policy produced a great debate within the Pentagon, where a large number of prominent military officers criticized the Administration. Matthew D. Ridgway, *Soldier* (New York, 1956) and Maxwell Taylor, *Swords into Plowshares* (New York, 1972) emphasize the need for a more varied defense capable of fighting conventional as well as nuclear war. James Gavin, *War and Peace in the Space Age* (New York, 1958) echoes this demand and contains a plea for the development of missiles. Curtis LeMay with MacKinlay Kantor, *Mission with LeMay: My Story* (New York, 1965) traces the life of the chief advocate of reliance on strategic bombers. Military officials were not the only people calling for a change in Administration policy. Under Henry Kissinger's direction, the Council on Foreign Relations produced a popular and extremely influential study, *Nuclear Weapons and Foreign Policy* (Garden City, 1958), calling for a more diversified defense policy and increased development of missiles.

During the last years of the decade, a debate raged over whether a "missile gap" existed between the U.S. and the Soviet Union. The controversy was prompted by the successful launching of the Soviet satellite *Sputnik* and the leaking of the Gaither Report to the press in the fall of 1957. For material on the Gaither Report see Morton H. Halperin, "The Gaither Committee and the Policy Process," *World Politics* (April, 1961). Edgar M. Bottome, *The Missile Gap: A Study of the Formation of Political and Military Policy* (Rutherford, 1971) and Roy E. Licklider, "The Missile Gap Controversy," *Political Science Quarterly* XVIII both discuss the controversy which became an issue in the 1960 presidential campaign. For a discussion of intragovernment maneuvering that slowed down missile development see Edmund Beard, *Developing the ICBM: A Study in Bureaucratic Politics* (New York, 1976).

During the Eisenhower Administration the space program grew out of the Defense Department's missile program. For studies of the early space program see Robert L. Rosholt, *An Administrative History of NASA, 1958-1963* (Washington, 1966) and Loyd S. Swenson, Jr., James M. Grumwood and Charles C. Alexander, *This New Ocean: A History of Project Mercury* (Washington, 1966).

In his farewell address, President Eisenhower warned of the growth of the "miliatry-industrial complex . . . the conjunction of an immense military establishment and a large arms industry." The dangers of the association became the theme of a large body of literature. See especially Fred J. Cook, *The Warfare State* (New York, 1962), Richard J. Barnet, *The Economy of Death* (New York, 1969), and Sidney Lens, *The Military-Industrial Complex* (Philadelphia, 1970). Seymour Melman, a Columbia University professor of engineering, became one of the most conspicuous critics of the association. See his *Pentagon Capitalism: The Political Economy of War* (New York, 1970) and the earlier *Our Depleted Society* (New York, 1965).

Other Works

Aron, Raymond, *The Great Debate: Theories of Nuclear Strategy* (Garden City, 1965).

Baldwin, Hanson W., *The Great Arms Race: A Comparison in U.S. and Soviet Power Today* (New York, 1958).

Barclay, C. N., *The New Warfare* (New York, 1954).

Borklund, C. W., *The Department of Defense* (New York, 1968).

———, *Men of the Pentagon: From Forrestal to McNamara* (New York, 1966).

Brodie, Bernard, *Strategy in the Missile Age* (Princeton, 1959).

Caraley, Demetrios, *The Politics of Military Unification* (New York, 1966).

Coffin, Tristram, *The Armed Society: Militarism in Modern America* (Baltimore, 1964).

Dietchman, Seymour, *Limited War and American Defense Policy* (Cambridge, Mass., 1964).

Dinerstein, H. S., *War and the Soviet Union: Nuclear Weapons and the Revolution in Soviet Military and Political Thinking* (New York, 1962).

Duscha, Julius, *Arms, Money and Politics* (New York, 1964).

Fryklund, Richard, *One Hundred Million Lives: Maximum Survival in a Nuclear War* (New York, 1962).

Gilpin, Robert, *American Scientists and Nuclear Weapons Policy* (Princeton, 1962).

Glines, Carroll, V., Jr., *The Compact History of the United States Air Force* (New York, 1973).

Goldwin, Robert A., ed., *America Armed: Essays in U.S. Military Policy* (Chicago, 1963).

Hahn, Walter F. and John C. Neff, eds., *American Strategy for the Nuclear Age* (New York, 1960).

Halperin, Morton H., *Limited War in the Nuclear Age* (New York, 1960).

Hammond, Paul Y., *Organizing for the Defense: The American Military Establishment in the Twentieth Century* (Princeton, 1961).

Hersh, Seymour M., *Chemical and Biologi-*

cal Warfare: America's Hidden Arsenal (Garden City, 1969).

Huntington, Samuel, Changing Patterns of Military Politics (New York, 1962).

———, The Soldier and the State: The Theory and Politics of Civil-Military Relations (New York, 1957).

Huszar, George B. de, ed., National Strategy in an Age of Revolutions: Addresses and Panel Discussions of the Fourth National Military-Industrial Conference (New York, 1959).

Kahn, Herman, On Thermonuclear War (Princeton, 1960).

Kaufmann, William W., ed., Military Policy and National Security (Princeton, 1956).

———, The Requirements of Deterrence, Memorandum No. 7 (Princeton, 1954).

Knorr, Klaus and Thornton Read, Limited Strategic War (New York, 1962).

Kolodziej, Edward A., The Uncommon Defense and Congress, 1945-1963 (Columbus, 1966).

Lansdale, Edward G., In the Midst of Wars: An American's Mission to Southeast Asia (New York, 1972).

Miksche, F. O., The Failure of Atomic Strategy and a New Proposal for the De-fense of the West (New York, 1958).

Mills, Walter, Arms and Men: A Study in American Military History (New York, 1956).

Morgenstern, Oskar, The Question of National Defense (New York, 1959).

Osgood, Robert E., Limited War: The Challenge to American Security (Chicago, 1957).

Parry, Albert, Russia's Rockets and Missiles (Garden City, 1960).

Schwartz, Urs, American Strategy: A New Perspective (Garden City, 1966).

Schwiebert, Ernest G., A History of Air Force Ballistic Missiles (New York, 1965).

Smith, Bruce L. R., The Rand Corporation: Case Study of A Nonprofit Advisory Agency (Cambridge, Mass., 1966).

Snyder, Glenn H., Deterrence and Defense: Toward a Strategy of National Security (Princeton, 1961).

Turner, Gordon G. and Richard D. Challenger, eds., National Security in the Nuclear Age: Basic Facts and Theories (New York, 1960).

Twining, Nathan F., Neither Liberty nor Safety: A Hard Look at U.S. Military Policy and Strategy (New York, 1966).

KENNEDY ADMINISTRATION

FOREIGN AFFAIRS

Among the vast number of works written on Kennedy's foreign policy, three are particularly useful overviews of the period. Richard Walton, Cold War and Counterrevolution: The Foreign Policy of John F. Kennedy (New York, 1972) is critical of the Administration, seeing its policies as a continuation of Cold War attitudes. Roger Hilsman, To Move a Nation: The Politics of Foreign Policy in the Administration of John F. Kennedy (Garden City, 1967) is an excellent favorable account that concentrates primarily on those topics of which Hilsman, as undersecretary of state, had personal knowledge—Southeast Asia, the Congo and Cuba. Walt W. Rostow, The Diffusion of Power: An Essay in Recent History (New York, 1972) is a favorable analysis of both the Kennedy and Johnson Administrations that has come under sharp attack by revisionist historians. Arthur Schlesinger, Jr., A Thousand Days (Boston, 1965) also contains valuable information on foreign affairs.

Several major crises highlighted the Kennedy years. For a discussion of the Soviet-American confrontation over Berlin see Jack M. Schick, The Berlin Crisis, 1958-1962 (Philadelphia, 1971). The Administration's abortive 1961 Bay of Pigs invasion is discussed by Haynes Johnson, *The Bay of Pigs: The Leaders Story* (New York, 1964) and Karl E. Mayer and Tad Szulc, *The Cuban Invasion: The Chance of a Disaster* (New York, 1962). Graham Allison, *The Essence of Decision: Explaining the Cuban Missile Crisis* (Boston, 1971) examines the process of policy formulation during the Cuban missile crisis in October 1962. Also valuable is Robert F. Kennedy, *Thirteen Days: A Memoir of the Missile Crisis* (New York, 1969), a personal account by one of the President's closest advisers.

Kennedy's attempts to negotiate a test ban treaty with the Soviet Union are discussed by Arthur Dean, U.S. representative to the test ban talks, in *Test Ban and Disarmament: The Path of Negotiation* (New York, 1966). Also valuable as a study of the political events leading to the signing and ratification of the treaty is Mary Milling Lepper, *Foreign Policy Formulation: A Case Study of the Nuclear Test Ban Treaty of 1963* (Columbus, 1971). For a useful chronology of events surrounding the negotiations see Lester Sobel, *Disarmament and Nuclear Tests, 1960-1963* (New York, 1964).

U.S. attempts to deal with problems in the Congo during the early 1960s are examined in detail by Stephen Weissman, *American Policy in the Congo, 1960-1964* (Ithaca, 1974). American relations with Latin America focused on the Alliance for Progress, which is analyzed in Jerome Levinson and Juan de Oris, *The Alliance That Lost Its Way: A Critical Report on the Alliance for Progress* (Chicago, 1970).

U.S. problems with its allies are examined carefully by Henry A. Kissinger, *The Troubled Partnership: A Reappraisal of the Atlantic Alliance* (New York, 1965) and by Richard Neustadt, *Alliance Politics* (New York, 1970). An excellent description and analysis of U.S. relations with its closest ally, Great Britain, is David Nunnerly, *President Kennedy and Britain* (New York, 1972).

A large body of literature traces the growing U.S. commitment in Vietnam. Most useful is David Halberstam, *The Best and the Brightest* (New York, 1972), an opinionated study that focuses on the role of American leaders in the struggle. *The Pentagon Papers* are invaluable in tracing U.S. involvement in Southeast Asia but are often difficult to use because of their poor organization. For a readable account based on *The Pentagon Papers* see Ralph Stavins, et al, *Washington Plans an Aggressive War* (New York, 1971), which attacks American leadership during this period. An excellent chronology of the events in Southeast Asia is John Galloway, *The Kennedys and Vietnam* (New York, 1971).

General

Attwood, William, *The Reds and the Blacks* (New York, 1967). Guinea.

Barnet, Richard J., *Intervention and Revolution* (New York, 1968).

Bohlen, Charles E., *The Transformation of American Foreign Policy* (New York, 1969).

Bowles, Chester, *Promises to Keep* (New York, 1971).

Brown, Seyom, *The Faces of Power: Consistency and Change in United States Foreign Policy from Truman to Johnson* (New York, 1968).

Bundy, McGeorge, "The Presidency and the Peace," *Foreign Affairs* (April, 1964).

Carey, Robert O., *The Peace Corps* (New York, 1970).

Cochen, Bert, *Adlai Stevenson* (New York, 1969).

Davis, Kenneth Sydney, *The Politics of Honor* (New York, 1967). Adlai Stevenson.

Destler, I. M., *Presidents, Bureaucrats, and Foreign Policy: The Politics of Organizational Reform* (Princeton, 1972).

Draper, Theodore, *Abuse of Power* (New York, 1967).

Emerson, Rupert, *Africa and United States*

Policy (Englewood Cliffs, 1967).

Fairlie, Henry, "A Cheer for American Imperialism," *The New York Times Magazine*, (July 11, 1965).

Feis, Herbert, *Foreign Aid and Foreign Policy* (New York, 1964).

———, *The Arrogance of Power* (New York, 1967).

———, *Old Myths and New Realities* (New York, 1964).

Fulbright, J. William, *Prospects for the West* (Cambridge, Mass., 1963).

Galbraith, John Kenneth, *Ambassador's Journal: A Personal Account of the Kennedy Years* (Boston, 1969).

Halle, Louis J., *The Cold War as History* (New York, 1967).

Hance, William A., ed., *Southern Africa and the United States* (New York, 1968).

Hartley, Anthony, "John Kennedy's Foreign Policy," *Foreign Policy* (Fall, 1971).

Hatch, Alden, *The Lodges of Massachusetts* (New York, 1973).

Hodgson, Godfrey, "The Establishment," *Foreign Policy* (Spring, 1973).

Horowitz, David, *The Free World Colossus* (New York, 1965).

Johnson, Haynes and Bernard M. Gwertzman, *Fulbright: The Dissenter* (New York, 1968).

Johnson, Richard A., *The Administration of United States Foreign Policy* (Austin, 1971).

Kateb, George, "Kennedy as Statesman," *Commentary* (June, 1966).

Kennan, George F., *Memoirs: 1960-1963* (Boston, 1972).

Kolko, Gabriel, *Roots of American Foreign Policy* (Boston, 1969).

Leuchtenburg, William, "President Kennedy and the End of the Postwar World," *The American Review* (Winter 1963).

Miller, William, *Henry Cabot Lodge* (New York, 1967).

Radosh, Ronald, *American Labor and United States Foreign Policy* (New York, 1970).

Rostow, Walt W., *View From the Seventh Floor* (New York, 1964).

Shriver, Sargent, *Point of the Lance* (New York, 1964).

Terchek, Ronald J., *The Making of the Test Ban Treaty* (The Hague, 1970).

Walton, Richard J., *The Remnants of Power: The Tragic Last Years of Adlai Stevenson* (New York, 1968).

Williams, G. Mennen, *Africa for the Africans* (Grand Rapids, 1969).

Windmiller, Marshall, *The Peace Corps and Pax Americana* (Washington, 1970).

Asia

Barnet, Richard J., *Roots of War* (New York, 1972). Origins of Vietnam War.

Bator, Victor, *Vietnam: A Diplomatic Tragedy: The Origins of the United States Involvement* (Dobbs Ferry, 1965).

Chomsky, Noam, *American Power and the New Mandarins* (New York, 1967). Vietnam.

Critchfield, Richard, *The Long Charade: Political Subversions in the Vietnam War* (New York, 1968).

Dommen, Arthur J., *Conflict in Laos* (New York, 1971).

Fall, Bernard B., and Roger Smith, eds., *Anatomy of a Crisis: The Laotian Crisis of 1960-1961* (Garden City, 1969).

Fitzgerald, Frances, *Fire in the Lake: The Vietnamese and the Americans in Vietnam* (Boston, 1972).

Gettleman, Marvin E. and Susan, and Kaplan, Lawrence and Carol, *Conflict in Indochina* (New York, 1970).

Goldstein, Martin, *American Policy Toward Laos* (Rutherford, 1973).

Halberstam, David, *The Making of a Quagmire* (New York, 1964).

Hurley, Robert Michael, "President John F. Kennedy and Vietnam, 1961-1963," unpublished doctoral dissertation, University of Hawaii, 1970.

Kahin, George M., and John W. Lewis, *The United States in Vietnam* (New York, 1967).

Lacouture, Jean, *Vietnam: Between Two Truces* (New York, 1966).

Lansdale, Edward G., *In the Midst of Wars: An American's Mission to Southeast Asia* (New York, 1972).

Shaplen, Robert, *The Lost Revolution: The U.S. in Vietnam, 1946-1966* (New York, 1966).

Steele, A. T., *The American People and China* (New York, 1966).

Stevenson, Charles A., *The End of Nowhere, American Policy Toward Laos Since 1954* (Boston, 1972).

Toye, Hugh, *Laos: Buffer State or Battle Ground* (New York, 1968).

Europe and the Cold War

Burns, Eedson L. M., *A Seat at the Table* (Toronto, 1972). Nuclear test ban discussions.

Dean, Arthur, *Test Ban and Disarmament: The Path of Negotiation* (New York, 1966).

Harriman, W. Averell, *America and Russia in a Changing World* (Garden City, 1971).

Jacobson, Harold D., *Diplomats, Scientists and Politicians* (Ann Arbor, 1966). Nuclear policy.

LaFeber, Walter, *America, Russia, and The Cold War, 1945-1971* (New York, 1967).

Moulton, Harland B., *From Superiority to Parity: The United States and the Strategic Arms Race, 1961-1971* (Westport, 1972).

Newhouse, John, *De Gaulle and the Anglo-Saxons* (New York, 1970).

Planck, Charles R., *The Changing Status of German Reunification in Western Diplomacy, 1955-1966* (Baltimore, 1967).

Slusser, Robert M., *The Berlin Crisis of 1961* (Baltimore, 1973).

Tatu, Michel, *Power in the Kremlin: From Krushchev to Kosygin* (New York, 1969).

Whiteside, Henry O., "Kennedy and the Kremlin: Soviet-American Relations, 1961-1963," unpublished doctoral dissertation, Stanford University, 1969.

Latin America

Abel, Elie, *The Missile Crisis* (New York, 1966).

Allison, Graham, *Essence of Decision: Explaining the Cuban Missile Crisis* (Boston, 1971).

Berle, Adolf A., Jr., *Latin America: Diplomacy and Reality* (New York, 1962).

Bonsal, Philip W., *Cuba, Castro and the United States* (Pittsburgh, 1971).

Burr, Robert N., *Our Troubled Hemisphere: Perspectives on United States-Latin American Relations* (Washington, 1967).

Chayes, Abram, *The Cuban Missile Crisis: International Crises and the Rule of Law* (New York, 1973).

Crane, Robert, "The Cuban Missile Crisis: A Strategic Analysis of American and Soviet Policy," *Orbis* (Winter, 1963).

Dewart, Leslie, "The Cuban Missile Crisis Revisited," *Studies on the Left* (Spring, 1965).

Fall, Bernard B., *Anatomy of a Crisis* (Garden City, 1969).

George, Alexander, "The Cuban Missile Crisis, 1962," in Alexander George, et al, *The Limits of Coercive Democracy* (Boston, 1971).

Larson, David L., ed., *The "Cuban Crisis" of 1962* (Boston, 1963).

Levinson, Jerome, and Juan de Onis, *The Alliance that Lost its Way: A Critical Report on the Alliance for Progress* (Chicago, 1970).

Lewis, Gordon K., *Puerto Rico: Freedom and Power in the Caribbean* (New York, 1963).

Lowenthal, Abraham P., "Alliance Rhetoric Versus Latin America Reality," *Foreign Affairs* (April, 1970).

Martin, John Bartlow, *Overtaken by Events: The Dominican Crisis from the Fall of Trujillo to the Civil War* (Garden City, 1966).

Mezerik, A. G., *Cuba and the United States* (New York, 1963).

McClellan, Grant S., ed., *U.S. Policy in Latin America* (New York, 1963).

Morrison, DeLesseps S., *Latin American Mission: An Adventure in Hemisphere Diplomacy* (New York, 1965).

Rogers, William D., *The Twilight Struggle: The Alliance for Progress and the Politics of Development in Latin America* (New York, 1967).

Thomas, Hugh, *Cuba: The Pursuit of Freedom* (New York, 1971).

Walton, Richard J., *The United States and Latin America* (New York, 1972).

Wells, Henry, *The Modernization of Puerto Rico: A Political Study of Changing Values and Institutions* (Cambridge, Mass., 1969).

Williams, William Appleman, *The United States, Cuba, and Castro* (New York, 1962).

The Central Intelligence Agency

Agee, Philip, *Inside the Company: CIA Diary* (New York, 1975).

Berman, Jerry J., and Morton H. Halperin, eds., *The Abuses of the Intelligence Agencies* (Washington, 1975).

Dulles, Allen W., *The Craft of Intelligence* (New York, 1963).

Marchetti, Victor, and John D. Marks, *The CIA and the Cult of Intelligence* (New York, 1974).

U.S. Commission on CIA Activities within the United States, *Report to the President by the Commission on CIA Activities within the United States* (Washington, 1975).

U.S. Senate, Select Committee on Intelligence Activities, *Alleged Assassination Plots Involving Foreign Leaders* (Washington, 1975).

———, *Intelligence Activities and the Rights of Americans* (Washington, 1976).

Wise, David, and Thomas B. Ross, *The Invisible Government* (New York, 1964).

DEFENSE

During the Kennedy years the Pentagon was dominated by the presence of Robert S. McNamara. The definitive work on McNamara is yet to be written, but Henry Trewhitt, *McNamara: His Ordeal in the Pentagon* (New York, 1971) is a useful and readable study. Of more limited interest are William F. Kaufmann, *The McNamara Strategy* (New York, 1964) and James F. Roherty, *Decisions of Robert S. McNamara* (New York, 1964). In *Congress and the Nation: 1945-1964* (Washington, 1965), the staff of the *Congressional Quarterly* has compiled a good detailed summary of McNamara's policies under Kennedy.

A number of useful works are devoted to specific controversies involving the Defense Department. The best study of the TFX controversy is Robert J. Art, *The TFX Decision: McNamara and the Military* (Boston, 1968). The "missile gap" was an important campaign issue in 1960 and is dealt with in Edgar Bottome, *The Missile Gap: A Study of the Formation of Military and Political Policy* (Rutherford, 1971). For reasons of economy and efficiency, McNamara ordered the Army, Navy and Air Force to cooperate in the research, development and procurement of new weapons. This policy created tensions within the Pentagon and is the subject of a study by Demetrios Caraley, *The Politics of Military Unification: A Study of Conflict and the Policy Process* (New York, 1966). Martha Derthick, in *The National Guard in Politics* (Cambridge, Mass., 1971), explains why McNamara was unable to merge the National Guard with the Reserves.

In his 1961 farewell address President Dwight D. Eisenhower warned against the growth of the "military-industrial complex . . . the conjunction of an immense military establishment and a large arms industry." The dangers of the "military-industrial complex" became the theme of a vast literature critical of the Pentagon. A good starting point in this area is Marcus G. Raskin, "The Kennedy Hawks Assume Power from the Eisenhower Vultures," in Leonard S. Rodberg and Derek Shearer, eds., *The Pentagon Watchers: Students Report on the National Security* (New York, 1970). Seymour Melman, a Columbia University engineering professor, became a conspicuous critic of defense spending. His study, *Our Depleted Society* (New York, 1965), was an important contribution to the literature. Other indictments of the Pentagon include Tristram Coffin, *The Armed Society: Militarism in Modern America* (Baltimore, 1964); Seymour Hersh, *Chemical and Biological Warfare* (Garden City, 1969); and Clark R. Mollenhoff, *The Pentagon* (New York, 1967).

Other Works

Borklund, C. W., *The Department of Defense* (New York, 1968).

———, *Men of the Pentagon: From Forrestal to McNamara* (New York, 1966).

Davis, Vincent, *The Admirals Lobby* (Chapel Hill, 1967).

Fitzgerald, Frances, *Fire in the Lake* (Boston, 1972).

Gilpin, Robert, *American Scientists and Nuclear Weapons Policy* (Princeton, 1962).

Glines, Carroll, V., Jr., *The Compact History of the United States Air Force* (New York, 1973).

Hammond, Paul Y., *Organizing for Defense: The American Military Establishment in the Twentieth Century* (Princeton, 1961).

Huntington, Samuel P., *The Common Defense: Strategic Programs in National Politics* (New York, 1961).

Landsdale, Edward G., *In the Midst of Wars: An American's Mission to Southeast Asia* (New York, 1972).

LeMay, Curtis E., with MacKinlay Kantor, *Mission with LeMay: My Story* (New York, 1965).

Lowe, George E., *The Age of Deterrence* (Boston, 1964).

Lyons, Gene, *Schools for Strategy: Education and Research in National Security Affairs* (New York, 1965).

McCahill, William P., *The Marine Corps Reserve: A History* (Washington, 1966).

Moulton, Harland B., *From Superiority to Parity: The United States and the Strategic Arms Race, 1961-71* (Westport, 1973).

Schwarz, Urs, *American Strategy: A New Perspective* (Garden City, 1966).

Schwiebert, Ernest G., *A History of Air Force Ballistic Missiles* (New York, 1965).

Smith, Bruce L. R., *The Rand Corporation: Case Study of A Nonprofit Advisory Agency* (Cambridge, Mass., 1966).

Taylor, Maxwell G., *Swords and Plowshares* (New York, 1972).

Twining, Nathan F., *Neither Liberty nor Safety: A Hard Look at U.S. Military Policy and Strategy* (New York, 1966).

Weigley, Russell F., *History of the United States Army* (New York, 1967).

Yarmolinsky, Adam, *The Military Establishment: Its Impact on American Society* (New York, 1971).

JOHNSON ADMINISTRATION

FOREIGN AFFAIRS

Among the vast number of works that deal with Johnson's foreign policy, Walt W. Rostow, *The Diffusion of Power: An Essay in Recent History* (New York, 1972) gives an excellent overview of the period. The study, written by one of the more controversial members of the White House staff, is a favorable analysis of Johnson's policy that has come under attack by revisionist historians. Lyndon Johnson's memoir, *The Vantage Point* (New York, 1971) is a bland but extremely valuable account of the inner workings of policy formation. For an analysis of foreign policy during Johnson's first years in the White House see Philip Geyelin, *Lyndon B. Johnson and the World* (New York, 1966).

The Vietnam war dominated foreign policy decision-making during the Johnson Administration. The most valuable study of the conflict is *The Pentagon Papers*, commissioned by the Department of Defense. The *Papers*, which trace American involvement in Southeast Asia from the 1950s through the 1960s, are comprehensive but are often difficult to use because of their poor organization and use of Defense Department jargon. For a readable account of the war based on *The Papers* see Ralph Stavins et al., *Washington Plans an Aggressive War* (New York, 1971), which is highly critical of American leadership. A more balanced interpretation of the *Papers* is presented by Les Gelb and Richard Betts in *The Irony of Vietnam* (Washington, 1979). Also critical of policymakers, particularly those who were holdovers from the Kennedy staff, is David Halberstam, *The Best and the Brightest* (New York, 1972), which focuses on the influence that Cold War attitudes and overconfidence had on the leaders' perceptions of the conflict. John Galloway, *The Gulf of Tonkin Resolution* (Rutherford, N.J., 1970) is an excellent study of the events that surrounded the passage of the 1964 Tonkin Gulf Resolution, which gave Johnson almost unlimited power to escalate the war without congressional approval. Townsend Hoopes, *The Limits of Intervention* (New York, 1969) is a first rate description of events leading to Johnson's decision to de-escalate the war in March 1968. Also important is "Viet Nam Reappraisal," *Foreign Affairs* XLVII (July, 1969) by Clark M. Clifford, a close friend and adviser of the President who was extremely influential in persuading Johnson to change his policy. For an excellent chronology of the war see Lester Sobel, ed., *South Vietnam: U.S.-Communist Confrontation in Southeast Asia* (New York, 1966-1974), Vols. I-IV.

Johnson's second important foreign crisis was his decision to send troops to the Dominican Republic in April 1965. The best account of the day-to-day events of this period is *Dominican Diary* (New York, 1965) by Tad Szulc, who was an on-the-scene correspondent in Santo Domingo. Jerome Slater, *Intervention and Negotiation: The United States and the Dominican Intervention* (New York, 1970) is essential reading as is *Overtaken by Events: The Dominican Crisis from the Fall of Trujillo to the Civil War* (New York, 1966) by John Barlow Martin, ambassador to the Dominican Republic at that time.

General

Allison, Graham, Ernest May and Adam Yarmolinsky, "Limits to Intervention," *Foreign Affairs* (January, 1970).

Barnet, Richard J., *Intervention and Revolution* (New York, 1968).

Bohlen, Charles E., *The Transformation of American Foreign Policy* (New York, 1969).

Brown, Seyom, *The Faces of Power: Consistency and Change in United States Foreign Policy from Truman to Johnson* (New York, 1968).

Copeland, Miles, *The Game of Nations:* *The Amorality of Power Politics* (New York, 1969).

Davis, Kenneth Sydney, *The Politics of Honor* (New York, 1967). Adlai Stevenson.

Draper, Theodore, *Abuse of Power* (New York, 1967).

Fulbright, J. William, *The Arrogance of Power* (New York, 1967).

Galbraith, John Kenneth, "The Plain Lessons of a Bad Decade," *Foreign Policy* (Winter, 1970-1971).

Hodgson, Godfrey, "The Establishment," *Foreign Policy* (Spring, 1973).

Horowitz, David, *Free World Colossus: A*

Critique of American Foreign Policy in the Cold War (New York, 1971).

Johnson, Haynes, and Bernard M. Gwertzman, *Fulbright: The Dissenter* (Garden City, 1968).

Johnson, Richard A., *The Administration of United States Foreign Policy* (Austin, 1971).

Kolko, Gabriel, *Roots of American Foreign Policy* (Boston, 1969).

Radosh, Ronald, *American Labor and United States Foreign Policy* (New York, 1970).

Sellen, Robert W., "Old Assumptions Versus New Realities: Lyndon Johnson and Foreign Policy," *International Journal* (Spring, 1973).

Spanier, John W., *American Foreign Policy Since World War II* (New York, 1971).

Steel, Ronald, *Pax Americana* (New York, 1967).

Walton, Richard J., *The Remnants of Power: The Tragic Last Years of Adlai Stevenson* (New York, 1968).

Europe and the Cold War

Burns, Eedson L. M., *A Seat at the Table* (Toronto, 1972). Nuclear test ban discussions.

Harriman, W. Averell, *America and Russia in a Changing World* (Garden City, 1971).

Katris, John A., *Eyewitness in Greece: The Colonels Come to Power* (St. Louis, 1971).

LaFeber, Walter, *America, Russia, and the Cold War, 1945-1971* (New York, 1971).

Moulton, Harland B., *From Superiority to Parity: The United States and the Strategic Arms Race, 1961-1971* (Westport, 1972).

Neustadt, Richard E., *Alliance Politics* (New York, 1970).

Newhouse, John, *De Gaulle and the Anglo-Saxons* (New York, 1970).

Planck, Charles R., *The Changing Status of German Reunification in Western Diplomacy, 1955-1966* (Baltimore, 1967).

Tatu, Michel, *Power in the Kremlin: From Khrushchev to Kosygin* (New York, 1969).

Terchek, Ronald J., *The Making of the Test Ban Treaty* (The Hague, 1970).

Turner, Arthur Campbell, *The Unique Partnership: Britain and the United States* (New York, 1971).

Latin America

Burr, Robert N., *Our Troubled Hemisphere: Perspectives on United States-Latin American Relations* (Washington, 1967).

Craig, Richard B., *The Bracero Program: Interest Groups and Foreign Policy* (Austin, 1971).

Draper, Theodore, "The Dominican Intervention Reconsidered," *Political Science Quarterly*, LXXXVI (March, 1971).

————, *The Dominican Revolt: A Case Study in American Policy* (New York, 1968).

Kurzman, Dan, *Revolt of the Damned* (New York, 1965). The Dominican Republic.

Levinson, Jerome, and Juan de Onis, *The Alliance that Lost its Way: A Critical Report on the Alliance for Progress* (Chicago, 1970).

Lowenthal, Abraham F., "Alliance Rhetoric Versus Latin America Reality," *Foreign Affairs* (April, 1970).

————, *The Dominican Intervention* (Cambridge, Mass., 1972).

Rogers, William D., *The Twilight Struggle: The Alliance for Progress and the Politics of Development in Latin America* (New York, 1967).

Wagner, Harrison R., *United States Policy Toward Latin America: A Study in Domestic and International Politics* (Stanford, 1970).

Walton, Richard J., *Beyond Diplomacy: A Background Book on American Military Intervention* (New York, 1970). Contains a chapter on the 1965 Dominican crisis.

————, *The United States and Latin America* (New York, 1972).

Wells, Henry, *The Modernization of Puerto Rico: A Political Study of Changing Values and Institutions* (Cambridge, Mass., 1969).

Africa, Asia and the Middle East

Arsenault, Raymond, "White on Chrome:

Southern Congressmen and Rhodesia 1962-1971," *Issue*, II (Winter, 1972).

Attwood, William, *The Reds and the Blacks* (New York, 1967). Guinea.

Dulles, Foster Rhea, *American Policy Toward Communist China, 1949-1969* (New York, 1972).

Emerson, Rupert, *Africa and United States Policy* (Englewood Cliffs, 1967).

Hance, William A., ed., *Southern Africa and the United States* (New York, 1968).

Heikal, Mohamed Hassanein, *The Cairo Documents* (New York, 1973).

Polk, William R., *The United States and the Arab World* (Cambridge, Mass., 1969).

Reischauer, Edwin O., *The United States and Japan* (Cambridge, Mass., 1965).

Silverberg, Robert, *If I Forget Thee O Jerusalem: American Jews and the State of Israel* (New York, 1970).

Williams, G. Mennen, *Africa for the Africans* (Grand Rapids, 1969).

Young, Kenneth T., *Negotiating with the Chinese Communists: The United States Experience, 1953-1967* (New York, 1968).

Southeast Asia

Adams, N., and A. McCoy, *Laos: War and Revolution* (New York, 1970).

Austin, Anthony, *The President's War* (Philadelphia, 1971).

Ball, George W., "Top Secret: The Prophecy the President Rejected," *Atlantic Monthly* (July, 1972).

Barnet, Richard J., *Roots of War* (New York, 1972).

Bator, Victor, *Vietnam, A Diplomatic Tragedy: The Origins of the United States Involvement* (Dobbs Ferry, 1965).

Black, Eugene R., *Alternative in Southeast Asia* (New York, 1969).

Bodard, Lucien, *The Quicksand War* (Boston, 1967).

Brandon, Henry, *Anatomy of Error: The Inside Story of the Asian War on the Potomac, 1954-1969* (Boston, 1969).

Central Office of Information, London, *Vietnam, Laos and Cambodia: Chronology of Events 1945-1968* (London, 1968).

Chandler, David P., "Cambodia's Strategy of Survival," *Current History*, LVIII (December, 1969).

Chomsky, Noam, *American Power and the New Mandarins* (New York, 1967).

———, *At War with Asia* (New York, 1970).

Cooper, Chester L., *The Lost Crusade: America in Vietnam* (New York, 1970).

Critchfield, Richard, *The Long Charade: Political Subversion in the Vietnam War* (New York, 1968).

Darling, Frank C., *Thailand and the United States* (Washington, 1965).

Dommen, Arthur J., *Conflict in Laos* (New York, 1971).

Draper, Theodore, *Abuse of Power* (New York, 1967).

Fall, Bernard B., *Viet-Nam Witness 1953-1966* (New York, 1966).

Fitzgerald, Frances, *Fire in the Lake: The Vietnamese and the Americans in Vietnam* (Boston, 1972).

Gettleman, Marvin E. and Susan, and Kaplan, Lawrence and Carol, *Conflict in Indochina* (New York, 1970).

Goldstein, Martin, *American Policy Toward Laos* (Rutherford, 1973).

Graff, Henry F., *The Tuesday Cabinet: Deliberation and Decision on Peace and War under Lyndon Johnson* (Englewood Cliffs, 1970).

Hatch, Alden, *The Lodges of Massachusetts* (New York, 1973).

Hickey, Gerald C., *Accommodation and Coalition in South Vietnam* (Santa Monica, 1970).

Kahin, George M., and John W. Lewis, *The United States in Vietnam* (New York, 1967).

Kail, F. M., *What Washington Said: Administration Rhetoric and the Vietnam War, 1949-1969* (New York, 1973).

Kalb, Marvin, and Elie Abel, *Roots of Involvement: The U.S. in Asia 1884-1971* (New York, 1971).

Kirk, Donald, *Wider War: The Struggle for Cambodia, Thailand and Laos* (New York, 1971).

Komer, Robert W., "The Other War in Vietnam—A Progress Report," *Department of State Bulletin* (Oct. 10, 1966).

Kraslow, David, and Stuart H. Loory, *The Secret Search for Peace in Vietnam* (New York, 1968).

Lacouture, Jean, *Vietnam: Between Two Truces* (New York, 1966).

Lansdale, Edward G., *In the Midst of Wars: An American's Mission to Southeast Asia* (New York, 1972).

Leifer, Michael, *Cambodia: The Search for Security* (New York, 1967).

Lodge, Henry Cabot, *The Storm Has Many Eyes* (New York, 1973).

Lomax, Louis E., *Thailand: The War That Is, the War That Will Be* (New York, 1967).

McAlister, John T., Jr., *Vietnam: The Origins of Revolution* (New York, 1969).

Mecklin, John, *Mission in Torment: An Intimate Account of the U.S. Role in Vietnam* (Garden City, 1965).

Miller, William, *Henry Cabot Lodge* (New York, 1967).

Moore, John Norton, *Law and the Indochina War* (Princeton, 1972).

Neuchterlein, Donald E., *Thailand and the Struggle for Southeast Asia* (Ithaca, 1965).

Nighswonger, William A., *Rural Pacification in Vietnam* (New York, 1966).

Pike, Douglas, *War, Peace and the Viet Cong* (Cambridge, Mass., 1969).

Porter, Gareth, *A Peace Denied: The United States, Vietnam, and the Paris Agreement* (Bloomington, 1975).

Schlesinger, Arthur M., Jr., *The Bitter Heritage: Vietnam and American Democracy, 1941-1966* (Boston, 1967).

Shaplen, Robert, *The Lost Revolution: The U.S. in Vietnam, 1946-1966* (New York, 1966).

——, *The Road from War: Vietnam 1965-1970* (New York, 1970).

——, *Time out of Hand: Revolution and Reaction in Southeast Asia* (New York, 1969).

Shurman, Franz, Peter Dale Scott and Reginald Zelnik, *The Politics of Escalation in Vietnam* (New York, 1966).

Starobin, Joseph R., *Eyewitness in Indochina* (New York, 1968).

Stevenson, Charles A., *The End of Nowhere: American Policy Toward Laos Since 1954* (Boston, 1972).

Taylor, Maxwell, *Swords and Plowshares* (New York, 1972).

Taylor, Telford, *Nuremberg and Vietnam: An American Tragedy* (New York, 1971).

Toye, Hugh, *Laos: Buffer State or Battle Ground* (New York, 1968).

U.S. Senate, Committee on Foreign Relations, *The Vietnam Hearings 1966* (New York, 1966).

Wilson, David A., *The United States and the Future of Thailand* (New York, 1970).

Windchy, Eugene, *Tonkin Gulf* (Garden City, 1971).

Wit, Daniel, *Thailand: Another Vietnam?* (New York, 1968).

DEFENSE

During the Johnson Administration the Pentagon was primarily concerned with the conduct of the Vietnam war. The best source for the study of the conflict is *The Pentagon Papers*, a comprehensive history of the growing American commitment commissioned by Secretary of Defense Robert S. McNamara. For an excellent, highly critical account of policymaking based on *The Pentagon Papers* see Ralph Stavins, et al, *Washington Plans An Aggressive War* (New York, 1971). In a similar vein, see David Halberstam, *The Best and the Brightest* (New York, 1972). Halberstam, a correspondent in Vietnam during the early war years, describes how decision makers' Cold War attitudes contributed to escalation of the conflict. For a study tracing McNamara's evolution from "hawk" to "dove" see Henry Trewhitt, *McNamara: His Ordeal in the Pentagon* (New York, 1971). John Galloway, *The Gulf of Tonkin Resolution* (Rutherford, 1970) analyzes events surrounding the passage of the Resolution that gave Johnson advance approval of any military actions he might take in Vietnam. Townsend Hoopes, *The Limits of Intervention* (New York, 1969) details events leading to the March 1968 decision not to escalate American involvement further. Lester Sobel, ed., *South Vietnam: U.S. Confrontation in Southeast Asia* (New York, 1966-74), Vols I-IV contains an excellent chronology of the war.

Other Works

Borklund, C. W., *The Department of Defense* (New York, 1968).

————, *Men of the Pentagon: From Forrestal to McNamara* (New York, 1966).

Davis, Vincent, *The Admirals Lobby* (Chapel Hill, 1967).

Enthoven, Alain C., and K. Wayne Smith, *How Much Is Enough?* (New York, 1971).

Glines, Carroll V., Jr., *The Compact History of the United States Air Force* (New York, 1973).

McNamara, Robert S., *The Essence of Security* (New York, 1968).

Moulton, Harland B., *From Superiority to Parity: The United States and the Strategic Arms Race, 1961-71* (Westport, 1973).

Schwarz, Urs, *American Strategy: A New Perspective* (Garden City, 1966).

Schwiebert, Ernest G., *A History of Air Force Ballistic Missiles* (New York, 1965).

Smith, Bruce L. R., *The Rand Corporation: Case Study of A Nonprofit Advisory Agency* (Cambridge, Mass., 1966).

Twining, Nathan F., *Neither Liberty nor Safety: A Hard Look at U.S. Military Policy and Strategy* (New York, 1966).

Weigley, Russell F., *History of the United States Army* (New York, 1967).

Yarmolinsky, Adam, *The Military Establishment: Its Impact on American Society* (New York, 1971).

Southeast Asia

Austin, Anthony, *The President's War* (Philadelphia, 1971).

Boyle, Richard, *The Flower of the Dragon: The Breakdown of the U.S. Army in Vietnam* (San Francisco, 1972).

Brandon, Henry, *Anatomy of Error: The Inside Story of the Asian War on the Potomac, 1954-1969* (Boston, 1969).

Broughton, Jack, *Thud Ridge* (Philadelphia, 1969).

Cooper, Chester L., *The Lost Crusade: America in Vietnam* (New York, 1970).

Draper, Theodore, *Abuse of Power* (New York, 1967).

Fall, Bernard B., *Hell in a Very Small Place: The Siege of Dien Bien Phu* (Philadelphia, 1967).

Fitzgerald, Frances, *Fire in the Lake: The Vietnamese and the Americans in Vietnam* (Boston, 1972).

Graff, Henry F., *The Tuesday Cabinet: Deliberation and Decision on Peace and War under Lyndon Johnson* (Englewood Cliffs, 1970).

Hooper, Edwin Bickford, *Mobility, Support, Endurance: A Story of Naval Operational Logistics in the Vietnam War 1965-1968* (Washington, 1972).

Kahin, George M., and John W. Lewis, *The United States in Vietnam* (New York, 1967).

Kail, F. M., *What Washington Said: Administration Rhetoric and the Vietnam War, 1949-1969* (New York, 1973).

Kalb, Marvin, and Elie Abel, *Roots of Involvement: The U.S. in Asia 1784-1971* (New York, 1971).

Lansdale, Edward G., *In the Midst of Wars: An American's Mission to Southeast Asia* (New York, 1972).

Littauer, Raphael, and Norman Uphoff, eds., *The Air War in Indochina* (Boston, 1972).

Marshall, S. L. A., *Ambush* (New York, 1969).

————, *Battles in the Monsoon: Campaigning in the Central Highlands of Vietnam, Summer 1966* (New York, 1967).

——, *The Fields of Bamboo* (New York, 1971).

Mulligan, Hugh A., *No Place to Die: The Agony of Viet Nam* (New York, 1967).

Oberdorfer, Don, *Tet!* (Garden City, 1971).

Taylor, Maxwell G., *Swords and Plowshares* (New York, 1972).

Westmoreland, William C., *Report on the War in Vietnam* (Washington, 1969).

——, *A Soldier Reports* (New York, 1976).

Windchy, Eugene, *Tonkin Gulf* (Garden City, 1971).

NIXON/FORD ADMINISTRATION

FOREIGN AFFAIRS

In the forefront of the Nixon/Ford Administraion were several global issues. Tad Szulc's *The Illusion of Peace: Foreign Policy in The Nixon Years* (New York, 1978) provides an excellent overview of the Richard Nixon-Henry Kissinger stewardship of U.S. foreign policy. A more critical analysis of the period can be found in George F. Kennan's *The Cloud of Danger* (Boston, 1977). Kennan charged that the U.S. had overcommitted itself and recommended a paring down, so as to more easily cope with important issues. In contrast, Henry Brandon in *The Retreat of American Power* (Garden City, 1973) praises the Nixon-Kissinger team for overseeing the rapid withdrawal of the United States from world domination. Secretary of State Henry Kissinger has been the subject of many writers. Marvin and Bernard Kalk, *Kissinger* (Boston, 1974) presents a favorable account of Kissinger's diplomatic efforts through 1973. A sympathetic intellectual evaluation of Kissinger's foreign policy philosophy can be found in John G. Stoessinger, *Henry Kissinger: The Anguish of Power* (New York, 1976). In his *Diplomacy For a Crowded World* (Boston, 1976), George Ball criticizes Kissinger's unilateral diplomacy, asserting that it was successful for gaining domestic political support but not in establishing lasting structures of world peace and American security.

An abundant amount of foreign policy literature focused on Asia. An excellent starting point is Peter Poole's *The United States and Indochina: From FDR To Nixon* (Hinsdale, Ill., 1973). Former Central Intelligence Agency official Robert G. Sutter describes the Chinese efforts to improve U.S. relations in his *China Watch: Toward Sino-American Reconciliation* (Baltimore, 1978). Sutter concludes that "realists" in both Peking and Washington finally won out in 1972, when both nations recognized the need to balance power. Of growing concern during the Nixon-Ford years were problems in the Middle East. Robert W. Stookey's *America and the Arab States: An Uneasy Encounter* (New York, 1975) stresses that U.S. economic health and security are linked directly to the volatile Arab states. The Arab-Israeli issue is placed into the larger context of Middle East policy by Bernard Reich in *Quest For Peace: United States-Israeli Relations and the Arab-Israeli Conflict* (New Brunswick, 1977).

General Works

Andrews, Craig Neal, *Foreign Policy and the New American Military* (Beverly Hills, 1974).

Aron, Raymond, *The Imperial Republic:* *The United States and the World, 1945–1973* (Englewood Cliffs, 1974).

Azyliowicz, Bard E. O'Neill, ed., *The Energy Crisis and U.S. Foreign Policy* (New York, 1975).

Barber, Stephen, *America In Retreat* (New

York, 1970).

Blaufarb, Douglas S., *The Counterinsurgency Era: U.S. Doctrine and Performance, 1950 to the Present* (New York, 1977).

Buckley, William Frank, *Inveighing We Will Go* (New York, 1972).

Buncher, Judith F., ed., *Human Rights And American Diplomacy, 1975-1977* (New York, 1977).

Combs, Jerald A., comp., *Nationalist, Realist and Radical: Three Views of American Diplomacy* (New York, 1972).

Coolidge, Archibald Cary, *The United States as a World Power* (New York, 1971).

Coufoudakis, Van, "U.S. Foreign Policy and the Cyprus Question: An Interpretation," *Millennium* (Winter, 1976-77).

Edwards, David V., *Creating a New World Politics: From Conflict to Cooperation* (New York, 1973).

Falk, Richard A., *What's Wrong with Henry Kissinger's Foreign Policy* (Princeton, 1974).

Falk, Stanley L., ed., *The World in Ferment: Problem Areas for the United States* (Washington, 1970).

Falkowski, Lawrence S., *Presidents, Secretaries of State and Crises in U.S. Foreign Relations: A Model and Predictive Analysis* (Boulder, 1978).

Gilpin, Robert, *U.S. Power and the Multinational Corporation: The Political Economy of Foreign Direct Investment* (New York, 1975).

Graubard, Stephen, *Kissinger* (New York, 1973).

Gujiral, M.L., *U.S. Global Involvement: A Study of American Expansionism* (New Delhi, 1975).

Halloran, Richard, *Conflict and Compromise: The Dynamics of American Foreign Policy* (New York, 1973).

Hickman, Martin B., comp., *Problems of American Foreign Policy* (Beverly Hills, 1975).

Hoxie, Ralph Gordon, *Command Decision and the Presidency: A Study in National Security Policy and Organization* (New York, 1977).

Jones, Alan M., ed., *U.S. Foreign Policy in a Changing World: The Nixon Administration, 1969-1973* (New York, 1973).

Kaplan, Morton A., *Dissent and the State in Peace and War; An Essay on the Grounds of Public Morality* (New York, 1970).

Kintner, William Roscoe, and Richard B. Foster, eds., *National Strategy in a Decade of Change: An Emerging U.S. Policy* (Lexington, 1973).

Krasner, Stephen D., *Defending the National Interest: Raw Materials, Investments and U.S. Foreign Policy* (Princeton, 1978).

Landau, David, *Kissinger: The Uses of Power* (Boston, 1972).

Lehman, John F., *The Executive, Congress and Foreign Policy: Studies of the Nixon Administration* (New York, 1974).

Lesh, Donald R., ed., *A Nation Observed: Perspectives on America's World Role* (Washington, 1974).

Nixon, Richard, *United States Foreign Policy for the 1970's. A Report by President Richard Nixon to the Congress, February 25, 1971* (New York, 1971).

Osgood, Robert E., *Retreat from Empire? The First Nixon Administration* (Baltimore, 1973).

Owen, Henry, and Charles L. Schultze, *Setting National Priorities* (Washington, 1976).

Parenti, Michael, *The Anti-Communist Impulse* (New York, 1970).

Paul, Roland A., *American Military Commitments Abroad* (New Brunswick, 1973).

Perusse, Roland I., ed., *Contemporary Issues in Inter-American Relations* (San Juan, 1972).

Pusey, Merlo John, *The U.S.A. Astride The Globe* (Boston, 1971).

Roberts, Chalmers M., "Foreign Policy Under a Paralyzed Presidency," *Foreign Affairs* (July, 1974).

Rostow, Eugene V., *Peace in the Balance: The Future of American Foreign Policy* (New York, 1972).

Scheer, Robert, *America After Nixon; The Age of the Multinationals* (New York, 1974).

Schlafly, Phyllis, and Chester Ward, *Kissinger On The Couch* (New York, 1974).

234

Schneider, William, "Public Opinion: The Beginning of Ideology," *Foreign Policy* (Winter, 1974–75).

Schurmann, Herbert Franz, *The Role of Ideas in American Foreign Policy; A Conference Report* (Hanover, N.H., 1971).

Sorensen, Theodore C., "Watergate and American Foreign Policy," *World Today* (December, 1974).

Stegenga, James A., ed., *Toward A Wiser Colossus; Reviewing and Recasting United States Foreign Policy* (Lafayette, 1972).

Stern, Laurence, *The Wrong Horse: The Politics of Intervention and the Failure of American Diplomacy* (New York, 1977).

The Middle East

Alroy, Gil C., *The Kissinger Experience: American Policy in the Middle East* (New York, 1975).

Arakie, Margaret, *The Broken Sword of Justice: America, Israel and the Palestine Tragedy* (London, 1973).

Churba, Joseph, *The Politics of Defeat: America's Decline in the Middle East* (New York, 1977).

Drinan, Robert F., *Honor the Promise: America's Commitment to Israel* (Garden City, 1977).

Golan, Matti, *The Secret Conversations of Henry Kissinger: Step-By-Step Diplomacy in the Middle East* (New York, 1976).

Hakleh, Emile A., *Arab-American Relations in the Persian Gulf* (Washington, 1975).

Harris, George S., *Troubled Alliance; Turkish-American Problems in Historical Perspective, 1945–1971 (Washington, 1972)*.

Klebanoff, Shoshana, *Middle East Oil and U.S. Foreign Policy, With Special Reference to the U.S. Energy Crisis* (New York, 1974).

Mangold, Peter, *Superpower Intervention in the Middle East* (New York, 1978).

Pranger, Robert J., *American Policy for Peace in the Middle East, 1969–1971: Problems of Principle, Maneuver and Time* (Washington, 1971).

Quandt, William B., *Decade of Decisions: American Policy Toward the Arab-Israeli Conflict, 1967–1976* (Berkeley, 1977).

Rostow, Eugene V., ed., *The Middle East: Critical Choices for the United States* (Boulder, 1976).

Safran, Nadav, *Israel, The Embattled Ally* (Cambridge, Mass., 1978).

Sheehan, Edward, *The Arabs, Israelis and Kissinger: A Secret History Of American Diplomacy In The Middle East* (New York, 1976).

"Step by Step in the Middle East," *Journal of Palestine Studies* (Spring/Summer, 1976).

Tucker, Robert W., "Israel and the United States: From Dependence to Nuclear Weapons?" *Commentary* (May, 1975).

Ullman, Richard H., "After Rabat: Middle East Risks and American Roles," *Foreign Affairs* (December, 1975).

Asia

Barnett, A. Doak, *China and the Major Powers in East Asia* (Washington, 1977).

——, *A New U.S. Policy Toward China* (Washington, 1971).

Brodine, Virginia, comp., *Open Secret: The Kissinger-Nixon Doctrine in Asia* (New York, 1972).

Bueler, William M., *U.S. China Policy and the Problem of Taiwan* (Boulder, 1971).

Chay, John, ed., *The Problems and Prospects of American-East Asian Relations* (Boulder, 1977).

Clough, Ralph N., *East Asia and U.S. Security* (Washington, 1975).

——, *Island China* (Cambridge, Mass., 1978).

Cohen, Jerome Alan, et al., *Taiwan and American Policy; The Dilemma in U.S.-China Relations* (New York, 1971).

Destler, I.M., *Managing an Alliance: The Politics of U.S.-Japanese Relations* (Washington, 1976).

Fairbanks, John K., *The United States and China* (Cambridge, Mass., 1971).

Fifield, Russell Hunt, *Americans in Southeast Asia: The Roots of Commitment* (New York, 1973).

Gelb, Leslie H., and Richard K. Betts, *The*

Irony of Vietnam: The System Worked (Washington, 1979).

Goldstein, Martin E., *American Policy Toward Laos* (Rutherford, 1973).

Haendel, Dan, *The Process of Priority Formulation: U.S. Foreign Policy in the Indo-Pakistani War of 1971* (Boulder, 1977).

Harrison, Selig S., *The Widening Gulf: Asian Nationalism and American Policy* (New York, 1978).

Hinton, Harold C., *Three and a Half Powers: The New Balance In Asia* (Bloomington, Ind., 1975).

Hohenberg, John, *New Era in the Pacific: An Adventure in Public Diplomacy* (New York, 1972).

Hon, Eugene, *Nixon's Trip—The Road to China's Russian War* (San Francisco, 1972).

Johnson, Stuart E., *The Military Equation in Northeast Asia* (Washington, 1979).

Kalb, Marvin L., *Roots of Involvement: The U.S. in Asia, 1784–1971* (New York, 1971).

Kintner, William Roscoe, *The Impact of President Nixon's Visit to Peking on International Politics* (Philadelphia, 1972).

Kirk, Donald, *Wider War: The Struggle for Cambodia, Thailand and Laos* (New York, 1972).

Kubek, Anthony, *The Red China Papers: What Americans Deserve to Know About U.S.-China Relations* (New Rochelle, 1975).

Kunhi Krishnan, T.V., *The Unfriendly Friends, India and America* (Thompson, Conn., 1974).

MacFarquhar, Roderick, comp., *Sino-American Relations 1949–1971* (New York, 1972).

May, Ernest R., and James C. Thompson, Jr., *American-East Asian Relations: A Survey* (Cambridge, Mass., 1972).

Meyers, William, and M. Vincent Hayes, eds., *China Policy; New Priorities and Alternatives* (New York, 1972).

Moorsteen, Richard Harris, and Morton Abramovitz, *Remaking China Policy: U.S.-China Relations and Governmental Decision-making* (Cambridge, Mass., 1971).

Ravenel, Earl, ed., *Peace with China? U.S. Decisions for Asia* (New York, 1971).

Rosovsky, Henry, ed., *Discord in the Pacific: Challenges to the Japanese-American Alliance* (Washington, 1972).

Scalapinao, Robert A., *American-Japanese Relations in a Changing Era* (New York, 1972).

——, *Asia and the Road Ahead: Issues for the Major Powers* (Berkeley, 1975).

Selden, Mark, *Remaking Asia; Essays on the American Uses of Power* (New York, 1973).

Shawcross, William, *Sideshow: Kissinger, Nixon and the Destruction of Cambodia* (New York, 1979).

Sih, Paul K., ed., *Asia and Contemporary World Problems: A Symposium* (New York, 1972).

Sihanouk Varman, Norodom, *My War with the CIA: The Memoirs of Prince Norodom Sihanouk* (New York, 1973).

Simon, Sheldon W., *Asian Neutralism and U.S. Policy* (Washington, 1975).

Sullivan, Marianna P., *France's Vietnam Policy: A Study in French-American Relations* (Westport, Conn., 1978).

Van der Linden, Frank, *Nixon's Quest for Peace* (Washington, 1972).

Yung-hwan, Jo, ed., *U.S. Foreign Policy in Asia: An Appraisal* (Santa Barbara, 1978).

The Western Hemisphere

Black, Jan Knippers, *United States Penetration of Brazil* (Philadelphia, 1977).

Fox, Annette B., et al., *Canada and the United States: Transnational and Transgovernmental Relations* (New York, 1976).

Kaufman, Edy, *The Superpowers and Their Spheres of Influence: The United States and the Soviet Union in Eastern Europe and Latin America* (New York, 1977).

MacEoin, Gary, *No Peaceful Way: Chile's Struggle for Dignity* (New York, 1974).

Martin, John Bartlow, *U.S. Policy in the Caribbean* (Boulder, 1978).

Petras, James F., *The United States and*

Chile: Imperialism and the Overthrow of the Allende Government (New York, 1975).

Uribe Arce, Armando, *The Black Book of American Intervention in Chile* (Boston, 1975).

Europe and the Soviet Union

Barnet, Richard J., *The Giants: Russia and America* (New York, 1977).

Beam, Jacob, *Multiple Exposure: An American Ambassador's Unique Perspective on East-West Issues* (New York, 1978).

Bell, Coral, *The Diplomacy of Detente: The Kissinger Era* (New York, 1977).

Calleo, David, P., *The Atlantic Fantasy: The U.S., Nato and Europe* (Baltimore, 1970).

Catlin, George Edward Gordon, Sir, *Kissinger's Atlantic Charter* (Gerrards Cross, Britain, 1974).

Donovan, John, ed., *U.S. and Soviet Policy in the Middle East* (New York, 1972).

Griffith, William E., *Peking, Moscow and Beyond: The Sino-Soviet-American Triangle* (Washington, 1973).

Kaiser, Karl, *Europe and the United States: The Future of the Relationship* (Washington, 1973).

Mally, Gerhard, *Interdependence: The European-American Connection in the Global Context* (Lexington, 1976).

Mazlish, Bruce, *Kissinger: The European Mind in American Policy* (New York, 1976).

Newhouse, John, *DeGaulle and the Anglo-Saxons* (New York, 1970).

Pfaltzgraff, Robert L., Jr., "The United States and Europe; Partners in a Multipolar World?" *Orbis* (Spring, 1973).

Pittman, John, "Detente-Main Stake in the Struggle," *World Marxist Review* (October, 1974).

Sakharov, Andrei Dimitrievich, *My Country and the World* (New York, 1975).

Sheldon, Della W., ed., *Dimensions of Detente* (New York, 1978).

Sobel, Lester A., ed., *Kissinger and Detente* (New York, 1975).

Stessinger, John George, *Nation in Darkness—China, Russia and America* (New York, 1975).

Strauss, David, *Menace in the West: The Rise of French Anti-Americanism in Modern Times* (Westport, 1978).

Africa

Arkhurst, Frederick S., ed., *U.S. Policy Toward Africa* (New York, 1975).

Packenham, Robert A., *Liberal America and the Third World: Political Development Ideas in Foreign Aid and Social Science* (Princeton, 1973).

U.S. National Security Council, Interdepartmental Group for Africa, *The Kissinger Study of Southern Africa: National Security Study Memorandum 39 (Secret)* (Westport, 1976).

DEFENSE

The problem of resolving defense needs with detente was the major focus of policy formulation in the Nixon/Ford years. Detente meant an easing of tensions between Moscow and Washington, but critics were fearful that the United States was giving away too much and that the Soviets would gain an advantage. A monograph, directed to the general public, that discusses the issue in global terms is Drew Middleton's *Retreat From Victory* (New York, 1973). A pessimistic theme is pursued by Rudolph J. Rummel in *Peace Endangered: The Reality of Detente* (Beverly Hills, 1976). The questions of adjusting defense options to foreign policy is assessed by Morton H. Halperin, *Defense Strategies for the Seventies* (Boston, 1971).

Alarmed by the magnitude of global weapons expenditure, Henry Kissinger calls for clearly defined doctrines and a new international order to deal with the problem in the second edition of his *Nuclear Weapons and Foreign Policy* (New York, 1969). Adding credence to Kissinger's claim is *World Military Expenditures and Arms Control Transfers 1967-1976* (Washington, 1978), issued by the United States Arms Control and Disarmament Agency. The volume is an invaluable source of statistical data, revealing the amount of money spent by each nation on its military establishment. An excellent analysis of American and Soviet capabilities is Edward Luttwack's *The U.S.-U.S.S.R. Nuclear Weapons Balance* (Beverly Hills, 1974). Despite rhetoric to the contrary, the Senate had little influence on the Strategic Arms Limitation Talks (SALT), according to Alan Platt, *The U.S. Senate and Strategic Arms Policy 1969-1977* (Boulder, Colo., 1978).

The frustration of Vietnam contributed, in part, to the end of the draft and the creation of an all-volunteer army. Two excellent studies of the topic are: Jerald C. Bachman, et al., *The All Volunteer Force: A Study of Ideology in the Military* (Ann Arbor, 1977); and Harry A. Marion, *A Case Against a Volunteer Army* (New York, 1971).

Other Works

Andrews, Craig N., *Foreign Policy and the New American Military* (Beverly Hills, 1974).

Beard, Edmund, *Developing the ICBM: A Study in Bureaucratic Politics* (New York, 1976).

Betts, Richard K., *Soldiers, Statesmen and Cold War Crises* (Cambridge, Mass., 1977).

Bezboruah, Monorajan, *U.S. Strategy in the Indian Ocean: The International Response* (New York, 1977).

Binkin, Martin, *Support Costs in the Defense Budget: The Submerged One-Third* (Washington, 1972).

Blechman, Barry M., et al., *The Soviet Military Buildup and U.S. Defense Spending* (Washington, 1977).

Bletz, Donald F., *The Role of the Military Professional in U.S. Foreign Policy* (New York, 1972).

Bottome, Edgar M., *The Missile Gap* (Rutherford, 1971).

Boyle, Richard, *The Flower of the Dragon: The Breakdown of the U.S. Army in Vietnam* (San Francisco, 1972).

Carson, Williams R., *Consequences of Failure (New York, 1974).*

Chase, John D., "U.S. Merchant Marine—For Commerce and Defense," *U.S. Naval Institute Proceedings* (May, 1976).

Clemens, Walter C., *The Superpowers and Arms Control: From Cold War to Inter-dependence* (Lexington, 1973).

Clough, Ralph N., et al., *The United States, China and Arms Control* (Washington, 1975).

Coffey, Joseph I., *Strategic Power and National Security* (Pittsburgh, 1971).

Congressional Quarterly Staff, *U.S. Defense Policy: A Study of Conflict and the Policy Process* (Boston, 1977).

Cox, Arthur M., *The Dynamics of Detente: How to End the Arms Race* (New York, 1976).

Dvorin, Eugene P., ed., *The Senate's War Powers: Debate on Cambodia from the Congressional Record* (Chicago, 1971).

Endicott, John E., and Roy W. Stafford, *American Defense Policy* (Baltimore, 1977).

Farley, Philip, *Arms Across the Sea* (Washington, 1978).

Fitzgerald, Frances, *Fire in the Lake: The Vietnamese and the Americans in Vietnam* (Boston, 1972).

Fox, T. Ronald, *Arming America: How the U.S. Buys Weapons* (Cambridge, Mass., 1974).

Gerhardt, James M., *The Draft and Public Policy* (Columbus, 1971).

Goode, Stephen, *The National Defense System* (New York, 1972).

Goodpaster, Andrew J., *For the Common Defense* (Lexington, 1977).

Greenbacker, John E., "Where Do We Go From Here?" *U.S. Naval Institute Proceedings* (June, 1976).

Greenwood, John, et al., *American Defense*

238

Policy Since 1945: A Preliminary Bibliography (Lawrence, Va., 1973).

Habib, Philip C., "Department of State] Urges Congressional Approval of Agreement with Turkey in Defense Cooperation," *Department of State Bulletin* (October, 1976).

Holst, T. T., and W. Schneider, eds., *Why ABM? Policy Issues in the Missile Defense Controversy* (Elmsford, N.Y., 1965).

Johnson, David T., and Barry R. Schneider, *Current Issues in U.S. Defense Policy* (New York, 1976).

Kaplan, Morton A., ed., *Isolation or Interdependence? Today's Choices for Tomorrow's World* (New York, 1975).

Keeley, John B., *The All-Volunteer Force and American Society* (Charlottesville, Va., 1978).

Lambeth, Benjamin, *Selective Nuclear Options in American and Soviet Strategic Policy* (Santa Monica, 1976).

Lansdale, Edward G., *In the Midst of Wars: An American's Mission to Southeast Asia* (New York, 1972).

Lens, Sidney, *The Day Before Doomsday* (New York, 1977).

Liska, George, *Quest for Equilibrium: America and the Balance of Power on Land and Sea* (Baltimore, 1977).

Littauer, Raphael, and Norman Uphoff, eds., *The Air War in Indochina* (Boston, 1972).

Long, Franklin A., et al., *Arms, Defense Policy and Arms Control* (New York, 1976).

Luttwak, Edward N., "The Defense Budget and Israel:" *Commentary* (February, 1975).

Marmion, Harry A., *A Case Against a Volunteer Army* (New York, 1971).

Martin, Lawrence, ed., *The Management of Defense* (New York, 1976).

Myrdal, Alva, *The Game of Disarmament: How the United States and Russia Run the Arms Race* (New York, 1977).

Nathan, James A., and James K. Oliver, "Public Opinion and U.S. Security Policy," *Armed Forces and Society* (January, 1975).

Owen, David, *The Politics of Defense* (New York, 1972).

Palmer, Bruce, Jr., and Tarr Curtis, "A Careful Look at Defense Manpower," *Military Review* (September, 1976).

Philips, David Morris, "Foreign Investment in the United States: the Defense Industry," *Boston University Law Review* (November, 1976).

Quanbeck, Alton H., and Barry M. Blechman, *Strategic Forces: Issues for the Mid-Seventies* (Washington, 1973).

Reeves, Thomas, and Karl Hess, *The End of the Draft* (New York, 1970).

Russett, Bruce M., *What Price Vigilance: The Burden of National Defense* (New Haven, 1970).

Schlesinger, James R., "A Testing Time for America," *Atlantic Community Quarterly* (Spring, 1976).

Smith, Clyde A., "Constraints of Naval Geography on Soviet Naval Power," *Naval War College Review* (February, 1974).

"U.S. Defense Policy and the B-1 Bomber Controversy: Pros and Cons," *Congressional Digest* (December, 1976).

Useem, Michael, *Conscription, Protest and Social Conflict* (New York, 1973).

Weidenbaum, Murray L., *The Economics of Peacetime Defense* (New York, 1974).

Index

167, 172–173; SALT 49, 88, 91, 96–97; Jackson on 69; Johnson sends troops to Dominican Republic 57; J. Schlesinger on 152; Kennan on 80; Kennedy on 82–83; Kissinger on 88, 96–97; Lovett on 106; Marshall on 113–114; McCarthy on 117; McCloy on 120; McGovern on 123; Nitze and defense policy study 130–132; North Atlantic Treaty 3, 106, 114, 160, 168, 171; See also NORTH Atlantic Treaty Organization; nuclear-threat deterrance policy 35, 37–41, 137–139; OAS formation 114; Ridgway on 139–140; Rio Pact 114; SEATO 54; Symington on 157–158; Taylor on 162; U.S.-Soviet defense strengths 45, 88, 157–158; U-2 flight incident & Cuban missile crisis link 121
DEWEY, Gov. Thomas—35
DIEM, Ngo Dinh—9, 22, 28–29, 32, 60–61, 64–65, 101–102, 148, 162
DIFFUSION of Power 1957–1972 The (book)—146
DILLON, Douglas—74
DIPLOMACY For A Crowded World, In (book)—10
DOMINICAN Republic—15, 57, 72
DULLES, Allen W(elsh)—Profile 31–34; 66
DULLES, John Foster—Profile 34–42; 6, 79, 100; as Secretary of State 34–42; China policy 37, 40–41, 99; Germany and Berlin dispute 37–38, 41; Korean war armistice 37; Mideast policy 37–38, 40–41; nuclear-threat deterrance policy 35, 37–41, 137–138; on postwar Eastern Europe 6, 100; Soviet policy 35–41, 43, 137–138; Vietnam war 29, 39–40, 138

E

EAGLETON, Sen. Thomas F. (D, Mo.)—59
EGYPT—37, 40–41, 44, 49, 92–93, 143, 148
EISENHOWER, Dwight D(avid)—Profile 42–46; 12–13, 28; Chinese policy 6–7, 40, 43–45, 71, 76–77, 99, 138; covert CIA activities 32–33, 66; Cuban policy 45–46, 68; Korean war 43; Latin American aid 45–46; Mideast policy 44–45, 82; NATO policy 46; nuclear defense policy 44–45, 139, 161; postwar European redevelopment 43; Soviet policy and disarmament 43–46, 68, 79, 137–138; Vietnam war 44, 138–139
ELY, Paul Henry—138
ESPIONAGE—45–46, 68, 212; See also CENTRAL Intelligence Agency
EUROPE—See FOREIGN Aid; MARSHALL Plan; TRUMAN Doctrine; country names

EUROPEAN Coal & Steel Community—119
EUROPEAN Defense Community (EDC)—37–38, 43
EUROPEAN Economic Community (EEC)—68
EUROPEAN Recovery Program (ERP)—See MARSHALL Plan

F

FAIRBANK, John K(ing)—Profile 47
FEDERAL Bureau of Investigation (FBI)—22
FINLETTER, Thomas K.—157
FISHER, Adrian—52
FOOD & Agriculture Organization—1
FOOD for Peace program—82, 123, 143–144, 150
FORD, Gerald R(udolph)—Profile 47–50; 96, 152; CIA operations probe 49; defense policy 49; Mideast 48–50; Soviet policy 48–49; Vietnam war 48–50
FOREIGN Affairs (magazine)—25–26, 81
FOREIGN Aid—2, 50–51, 54, 70, 114; Africa 96; congressional position on 70, 97, 105–106, 111–114, 160, 171; Eisenhower 43, 45–46; European Recovery Program (Marshall Plan)—See MARSHALL Plan; Food for Peace program 82, 123, 143–144, 150; Germany 3–4, 22–23, 70, 118–119; See also GERMAN Policy (postwar); Great Britain 1–2; Greece and Turkey 25, 100, 111, 159, •167–168, 171, 174; ban on Greek military aid 97; India 16; Israel 92; Kennedy 11, 46, 82, 150; Latin America 11, 45–46, 82, 143–144, 150; Lovett 105–106; Taiwan 75–76; Truman 2–3, 25; Vietnam military aid curbed 21, 49
FORMOSA—4–7; see also CHIANG Kai-Shek, CHINESE Policy
FORMOSA Resolution (1955)—44
FORMOSA Straits—39–41, 43–45
FORRESTAL, James V(incent)—Profile 50–1
FORRESTAL, Michael—102
FOSTER, William C(hapman)—Profile 51–53
FRANCE—44, 144
FREI, Eduardo—67
FULBRIGHT, J(ames) William—Profile 53–59; 72, 113; Cuban missile crisis 55–56; defense policy 54; opposes postwar U.N. policy 53; Indochina 54; Mideast 5–; Soviet Union 54–56, 58; Vietnam war 56–58, 149

G

GAVIN, James M.—57, 139–140
GEORGE, Sen. Walter F. (D, Ga.)—13